PENGUIN  C

T0249144

IN DEFENCE OF TH

MARCUS TULLIUS CICERO (106–43 BCE), Roman orator and
statesman, was born at Arpinum of a wealthy local family. He
was taken to Rome for his education with the idea of a public
career and, by the year 70, he had established himself as the leading barrister in Rome. In the meantime, his political career was
well under way and he was elected praetor for the year 66. His
ambitious nature enabled him to obtain those honours which
would normally only have been conferred upon members of the
Roman aristocracy. One of the most permanent features of his
political life was his attachment to Pompey. As a politician he
compromised for the good of the Republic; as a statesman, his
ideals were more honourable and unselfish than those of his
contemporaries. Cicero was the greatest of the Roman orators,
possessing a wide range of technique and an exceptional command
of the Latin tongue. He followed the common practice of publish-
ing his speeches, but he also produced a large number of works
on the theory and practice of rhetoric, on religion, and on moral
and political philosophy. He played a leading part in the develop-
ment of the Latin hexameter. Perhaps the most interesting of all
his works is the collection of 900 remarkably informative letters,
published posthumously. These not only contain a first-hand
account of social and political life in the upper classes at Rome,
but also reflect the changing personal feelings of an emotional
and sensitive man.

SIOBHÁN MCELDUFF is assistant professor of Latin Language
and Literature in the Department of Classical, Near Eastern and
Religious Studies at the University of British Columbia. A native
of Ireland, she is a graduate of Trinity College, Dublin, the University of Victoria (BC) and the University of Southern California.
Her research is on the history and theory of translation in Rome
and, in particular, the role of Cicero in that history; she has published several articles on this topic and is currently working on a
monograph on the subject. She also works on the history of classical reception among the working class in the 18th and 19th
centuries, with particular reference to Ireland.

MARCUS TULLIUS CICERO

In Defence of the Republic

Translated with an Introduction and Notes by
SIOBHÁN McELDUFF

PENGUIN BOOKS

PENGUIN CLASSICS

Published by the Penguin Group
Penguin Books Ltd, 80 Strand, London WC2R ORL, England
Penguin Group (USA) Inc., 375 Hudson Street, New York, New York 10014, USA
Penguin Group (Canada), 90 Eglinton Avenue East, Suite 700, Toronto, Ontario,
Canada M4P 2Y3 (a division of Pearson Penguin Canada Inc.)
Penguin Ireland, 25 St Stephen's Green, Dublin 2, Ireland (a division of Penguin Books Ltd)
Penguin Group (Australia), 250 Camberwell Road, Camberwell, Victoria 3124, Australia
(a division of Pearson Australia Group Pty Ltd)
Penguin Books India Pvt Ltd, 11 Community Centre, Panchsheel Park, New Delhi – 110 017, India
Penguin Group (NZ), 67 Apollo Drive, Rosedale, Auckland 0632, New Zealand
(a division of Pearson New Zealand Ltd)
Penguin Books (South Africa) (Pty) Ltd, 24 Sturdee Avenue, Rosebank, Johannesburg 2196, South Africa

Penguin Books Ltd, Registered Offices: 80 Strand, London WC2R ORL, England

www.penguin.com

First published in Penguin Classics 2011
024

Translation and editorial material © Siobhán McElduff, 2011
All rights reserved

The moral right of the author and translator has been asserted

Set in 10.25/12.25pt PostScript Adobe Sabon
Typeset by Jouve (UK), Milton Keynes
Printed in Great Britain by Clays Ltd, Elcograf S.p.A

ISBN: 978-0-140-45553-3

www.greenpenguin.co.uk

Contents

In Defence of the Republic

Chronology

106 Cicero born (3 January).

91–87 Social War.

89 Cicero serves in the army of Pompey the Great's father.

88 Start of First Mithridatic War. Sulla's first march on Rome. Marius flees Rome.

86 Death of Marius.
Philosophical and Rhetorical Works: *On Invention* (date uncertain).

83–81 Second Mithridatic War.

83 Sulla's second march on Rome. Proscriptions of Marius' supporters.

81–79 Sulla's dictatorship.

81 Cicero's first extant speech (*In Defence of Quinctius*).

80 Cicero delivers *In Defence of Roscius of Ameria*. Marries Terentia (*c.* 80).

79–77 Cicero travels to the east and studies rhetoric in Athens and Rhodes.

78 Death of Sulla.

c. 76 Cicero delivers *In Defence of Roscius the Actor*.

75 Cicero's quaestorship in Sicily.

74–63 Third Mithridatic War.

73–71 Verres governor of Sicily.

70 Delivers *Against Verres*. First consulship of Pompey and Crassus. Tribunes' power of veto restored. Senate loses exclusive control of juries.

69 Cicero plebeian aedile. Delivers *In Defence of Marcus Fonteius*.

67 *Lex Gabinia* gives Pompey the command in the war against
    the pirates.

66 Cicero's praetorship. Delivers *For the Manilian Law*. Pom-
    pey given command in the Third Mithridatic War.

65 Birth of Cicero's son Marcus.

63 Cicero's consulship. Catilinarian conspiracy. Cicero deliv-
    ers *On the Agrarian Law II* (January). *Catilinarians* delivered
    and Catilinarian conspirators executed (December). Tullia
    marries for the first time (*c.* 63).

62 Pompey returns to Italy and disbands his army. Clodius
    desecrates the rites of Bona Dea (December). Cicero delivers
    In Defence of Archias.

61 Clodius acquitted in the Bona Dea affair.

60 First Triumvirate (Caesar, Crassus and Pompey) formed.

59 First consulship of Caesar. Julia, Caesar's daughter, marries
    Pompey. Clodius adopted by Fonteius and becomes a ple-
    beian (March). Cicero unsuccessfully defends Gaius Antonius
    (his co-consul in 63) on an unknown charge.

58 Clodius tribune of the plebs. Cicero leaves Rome to go into
    exile (20 March). Caesar takes up his five-year command of
    the province of Gaul.

57 Centuriate assembly passes bill for Cicero's recall (4 August).
    Cicero returns from exile (4 September). Delivers *On his house*
    (29 September).

56 Cicero delivers *In Defence of Sestius*. Triumvirs renew their
    pact. Cicero successfully defends Marcus Caelius on a charge
    of public violence brought by Clodius.

55 Second consulship of Crassus and Pompey.
    Philosophical and rhetorical works: *On the Orator*.

54 Julia dies in childbirth.

53 Crassus killed by the Parthians at the battle of Carrhae.
    Cicero elected to the College of Augurs.

52 Milo kills Clodius (January). Pompey appointed sole con-
    sul. Cicero delivers *In Defence of Milo* (April).

51–50 Cicero governor of Cilicia.

51 Philosophical and rhetorical works: *On the Republic* and
    On the Laws (date uncertain).

50 Caesar asks the Senate to be allowed to stand for the consulship *in absentia* but is refused. Cicero returns to Italy
(November).

49 Cicero arrives in Rome (4 January). Caesar crosses the
Rubicon; start of the civil war between Caesar and Pompey
(10 January); Cicero joins Pompey's forces (June).

48 Pompey defeated at Pharsalus (August) and murdered in
Egypt (September). Cicero returns to Italy and remains in
Brundisium until September 47, when Caesar grants him an
unconditional pardon.

46 Defeat of Republican forces in Africa. Cato the Younger
commits suicide (February). Cicero divorces Terentia and
marries his ward, Publilia.
Philosophical and rhetorical works: *Brutus, Orator, Stoic
Paradoxes*.

45 Tullia dies (February). Cicero divorces Publilia.
Philosophical and rhetorical works: *Academica, On Ends,
Tusculan Disputations, On the Nature of the Gods*.

44 Caesar named dictator for life. Assassinated (15 March).
Philippics 1–4 (August).
Philosophical and rhetorical works: *On Old Age, On Divin-
ation, On Fate, Topics, On Friendship, On Duties*.

43 Battle of Mutina; Antony defeated but both consuls are
killed (April). Formation of the Second Triumvirate. Cicero
murdered (7 December).

General Introduction

Cicero's life

Arpinum was, on the whole, a not terribly remarkable provincial town about 80 miles from Rome. But the year 106 was to see two momentous events in its history, the most momentous since its free residents received Roman citizenship in 188. On 1 January one of its native sons, the great general Gaius Marius, began his first consulship; two days later, a woman named Helvia gave birth to Marcus Tullius Cicero after an easy labour. His father, a member of the local nobility, might have dreamt of his new-born son reaching the dizzying heights of the consulship, but it is unlikely that even the most ambitious father would dream of his son becoming so famous an orator that the name of Cicero would be seen by later Romans as 'not just the name of a man, but of eloquence'.[1]

Cicero's place of birth and the status of his family were always to prove attractive targets for his opponents.[2] While some later sources claimed that the Ciceros descended from Volscian royalty, others said that his father was a fuller – a processor of cloth – a rather smelly business in the ancient world (it involved human urine and lots of it), and that Cicero had been raised in his shop.[3] In truth, his background was probably neither so grand nor so low. The Ciceros were not just a family of local significance but were connected to important Roman families by blood and friendship and even to Gaius Marius himself (albeit distantly). In later years Cicero would proudly tell the story of the consul of 115, Marcus Aemilius Scaurus, visiting Arpinum and approving so much of his grandfather's opposition to the introduction of the secret ballot there that he wished that he had come to Rome to pursue a political career on the national stage.[4] However, despite the fact that we know more about Cicero than any other ancient individual, we know very little about his mother and not a great deal more of his father. It appears that his father was more of a scholar than a politician and suffered from ill-health, but still had high ambitions for both his sons (Quintus, Cicero's younger brother, was born *c.* 102), bringing them to Rome in the 90s to improve their chances of having the career Scaurus had wished for their grandfather.

The newly arrived Cicero spent a very short time with the great orator Lucius Licinius Crassus[5] (although Crassus was conservative in his opinions he had supported the attempts by Marcus Livius Drusus[6] to extend Roman citizenship to more Italian allies); he died in 91, having contracted pneumonia after speaking passionately against the consul Lucius Marcius Philippus. Another early mentor was the famous orator, Marcus Antonius (the grandfather of Mark Antony); he died in 87 at the hands of Marius' supporters. The triumvirate of early mentors was rounded out by the augur Mucius Scaevola, who also died in 87. Cicero would later immortalize the trio in his dialogue *On the Orator*.

Cicero and Quintus were unfortunate enough to arrive in a Rome that was being ripped apart by opposing forces and on the verge of civil war. Roman politics was a massively complicated and competitive system (some might say snake-pit) of obligations, families and rank individualism, and one attempts to define its various factions only at great risk. However, the basic division of Roman politics in the Late Republic was between the *populares* (translated throughout this text as 'men of the people') and the *optimates* ('the finest citizens'). The *populares* are sometimes described as a left-wing or democratic faction and the *optimates* as the conservative or reactionary party; there is a great deal of truth in this, but it is deceptive as well. The *populares* were not a political party but a collection of individuals who turned to the people to push through legislation, sometimes in the people's interests, but frequently to serve their own needs; we should always remember that one of the most famous *populares*, Julius Caesar, had himself made dictator for life (an office that was only intended to be held for six months), a move that hardly seems democratic no matter how you spin it. The *optimates* believed in the authority of the Senate above all. The leaders of both factions frequently controlled street gangs and many did not care for anything much beyond consolidating their own power. Despite the fact that Marius was a *popularis* hero, Cicero's father seems to have steered well clear of him and his supporters and Cicero was to be a devoted *optimate* all his life, although claiming from time to time to be *popularis* as well (see *On the Agrarian Law of Rullus*, chapters 7, 15).

Cicero enters the public stage

From 90 to 89 Cicero served under Gnaeus Pompeius Strabo (the father of Pompey the Great) in the Social War, the war between Rome and her Italian allies or *socii*.[7] The following year was also spent in the army, under the future dictator Lucius Cornelius Sulla. Cicero, however, was never an enthusiastic soldier and after this period of service he went happily back to his studies, producing his first work on oratory, *On Invention* (he would probably have been horrified to know that this was to become one of his most read works in the Middle Ages). The Social War was only the start of a series of wars that would rage through Italy over this century: a vicious civil war between the generals Gaius Marius and Sulla was brewing. If Marius was a *popularis* hero, Sulla might be seen as the ultimate member of the *optimates* – though, like many *optimates*, he was willing to run roughshod over the Roman constitution when it suited him.[8] This struggle was marked by its utter viciousness on both sides. Sulla's ultimate victory in 82 led to the proscriptions – lists of enemies of the state, whom it became legal and profitable to hunt down. In the end, these lists contained ninety senators (including fifteen ex-consuls) and 2,600 equestrians, all murdered and their estates confiscated and auctioned off. Sulla was also made dictator – illegally assuming the power for more than the six months allowed. His reforms resulted in an expanded

Senate (to 600), juries becoming exclusively drawn from senators and the hamstringing of the often turbulent office of the tribune of the plebs. The tribuneship became a dead end career move since its holders were now forbidden from holding any higher political office; it also lost its powerful right of veto (which was to be restored by Pompey in 70).

The Sullan dictatorship is the setting for Cicero's first extant speech, a defence of Publius Quinctius in a rather unimportant private case which he argued in 81.[9] Cicero was only the second choice, as the previous advocate, Marcus Junius, was called away on official business; Cicero was unfortunate enough to face as the prosecutor Quintus Hortensius, Rome's leading orator. In the next year he took on a more prominent case, that of the accused parricide Sextus Roscius of Ameria.[10] Roscius had the double misfortune of having a very large estate and a very dead father; in an era of fortune-hunters this caught the eye of Chrysogonus, Sulla's freedman and minion. He accused Roscius of parricide and snapped up his estate worth 6 million sesterces for the paltry sum of 2,000 sesterces. Broke and an enemy of a powerful man, Roscius could find no one else to defend him until Cicero agreed to take up his case. Cicero took the highly risky tactic of pointing the finger at the powerful Chrysogonus, although he carefully avoided implicating the dictator. His choice paid off and his success made him an up and coming advocate.

It was shortly after this (probably in 79) that he left Rome to travel east with his brother Quintus, for health reasons as well as to improve his oratory, touring and studying in Athens and Rhodes.[11] During this period he found time to marry his formidable first wife Terentia, a very wealthy woman in her own right. It was probably her money that made it possible for Cicero to launch his political career and run for quaestor in 76 (his term of office was in 75). He was elected at the age of thirty, the youngest age permitted by law, and could look forward to entering the Senate after his year in office. His time as quaestor was spent in the town of Lilybaeum in Sicily, aiding the governor Sextus Peducaeus (then in his second year of office); Sicily was one of Rome's richest provinces and Cicero could, like many others, have taken advantage of this opportunity to enrich himself, but he resisted the temptation. As he travelled home after a successful year in office he dreamt of being celebrated on his return to Rome; that dream was not to last long. When he arrived in the resort town of Puteoli, he met someone who asked him for the news from Rome. Cicero replied by saying he had no news as he was coming from his province – this was the cue for the praise to begin. 'Oh yes,' was the answer, 'from Africa.' Cicero corrected him, 'No, Sicily.' At this point a helpful third party said, 'Oh yes, you were quaestor in Syracuse'[12] – the other end of the island. Cicero gave up and decided to play tourist and stop hoping that he would hear his name echoed to the skies. But he never forgot that to be out of Rome and away from the Forum and the Senate was to be forgotten.

It was Cicero's time in Sicily that led to the first speech included in this volume, the successful prosecution of Verres, the rapacious governor of Sicily from 73 to 71. In winning this case, Cicero triumphed over Verres *and* Quintus Hortensius, then the reigning king of Rome's orators. This year (70) was also to see Cicero's election to the office of aedile (the first rank of the public offices that started one on the *cursus honorum*, the series of offices that led one hopefully to the consulship), at the youngest minimum age (thirty-seven). More political success ensued: in 67 he was elected for praetor (also at the youngest possible age of thirty-nine). In 64 he was elected to the giddy heights of the consulship: he had ennobled his family by winning the highest magistracy in Rome. In between these momentous events, Cicero was also to welcome a beloved daughter (Tullia) and son (Marcus) into the world.[13]

As the events of Cicero's year as consul are covered in the Introductions to *On the Agrarian Law of Rullus* and the *Catilinarians*, now is not the place to talk about them. Suffice it to say here that Cicero uncovered and crushed a conspiracy by a disaffected nobleman called Catiline, an act he saw as the crowning achievement of his career. As even a cursory reading of his speeches shows, he was never to stop talking about this event (one Roman author commented that he 'praised his consulship not without reason, but without end'[14]). However, the controversial execution of several of the conspirators on dubious legal grounds and without a trial explains some of the need for his self-praise: it was a defensive move against his enemies. Additionally, we have to remember that as a 'new man' Cicero never quite fitted in with the traditional aristocracy and could not fall back on the lustre of his ancestors to recommend him: all he (and his family) had was Cicero and his achievements. Yet neither of these can quite explain *all* his self-praise.

Cicero's fall and exile

Cicero's hopes of playing an important role in politics in the years after his consulship were stymied by a new order, one where three men were to come to control Rome. After Pompey the Great's triumphant return in 62 from successful campaigns in the east against the pirates and Mithridates, King of Pontus, Cicero cultivated him assiduously, expecting great returns for having spoken in favour of his command:[15] he was to be sorely disappointed. Thwarted by a Senate that blocked his efforts to gain land for his soldiers, Pompey turned to Julius Caesar and Marcus Licinius Crassus. In 60 these formed a power block, now known as the First Triumvirate (Cicero was invited to join but refused, despite the troubles he was facing over his actions during the Catilinarian conspiracy). In 59 Caesar held his first consulship and passed an agrarian law providing the land Pompey wanted, despite the Senate's hostility and vetoes by the tribunes (Pompey provided Caesar with an armed force that made this possible). Caesar's colleague Bibulus retreated to his house and declared he was watching the sky for auspices – which would mean that any action of Caesar's was illegal. Caesar simply ignored him.

Under this new power-structure, Cicero's enemies began to move. Chief among these was a former friend, Publius Clodius Pulcher, who had been among those armed to protect Cicero during the Catilinarian conspiracy. However, relations grew decidedly frosty after the Bona Dea affair of 62. Clodius had dressed as a woman in order to infiltrate the female only rites in honour of Bona Dea (the 'Good Goddess') which were then being held in the house of Julius Caesar and presided over by

his wife and mother. Clodius was quickly discovered; in the
scandal that ensued, Caesar divorced his wife with the famous
words 'Caesar's wife must be above suspicion' and Clodius was
tried for sacrilege. During the trial a rather reluctant Cicero
was called to break his alibi (Clodius claimed he had been far
from Rome on the day; Cicero had seen him in the city). After
some of the most incredible bribery ever practised in a Roman
court (this is saying something given the amount of bribery that
frequently took place), Clodius was acquitted. He never forgot
the offence – nor some of Cicero's witticisms at his expense.[16]
Despite the contretemps at Caesar's house, Clodius still managed to forge an alliance with the triumvirate and cast off his
patrician status by having himself adopted by a plebeian (see
On his House, chapters 34–8); this allowed him to run for tribune of the plebs.

    In 58 the newly elected tribune Clodius passed a bill which
stated that anyone who had executed a Roman citizen without
a trial should be exiled from Rome; Cicero fled Rome before
Clodius even named him, an act he was later to regret bitterly.
A second bill specifically named Cicero and extended his exile
to 400–500 miles from Rome – a phenomenal distance that
would mean he had to spend the rest of his life on the fringes of
the Roman world. As it turned out, he spent a wretched exile in
Thessalonica bewailing every second of it, blaming false friends
for recommending he flee Rome and blaming himself for destroying his family's honour and lives and for all they had to suffer in
his absence.[17] We would probably sympathetically describe him
as experiencing a nervous breakdown; the Romans – a nation
that believed in self-control and stoicism – would have been far
less generous. Besides, whatever emotional and psychological
turmoil Cicero experienced he had also suffered a tremendous
loss of face, especially by fleeing rather than fighting things out
to the bitter end with Clodius.

Cicero's return

His restoration in 57 did not give him the chance he hoped for
to once more play an important role in Roman politics, as he

was beholden to Pompey and the triumvirate for his return. Cicero found himself politically side-lined and obliged to do whatever the triumvirs wanted – and what they wanted was to be able to use his influence and the finely tempered weapon of his oratory. Cicero found himself forced to defend men he despised – such as Gabinius, one of the consuls of 58 he blamed for his exile. (It was probably some small consolation that he lost that case.) Perhaps as bad as the political impotence he experienced was watching the Republic dominated by three men and the Senate emasculated. As a result, Cicero turned increasingly to writing literature on oratory and philosophy. It was during this period that he composed the treatises *On the Republic* and *On the Orator*, which sought to define the well-rounded public speaker as a cultural ideal. Both of these were fictional dialogues (as were many of his later writings) with parts allocated to Romans of Cicero's own or slightly earlier eras. Even if Cicero could no longer play a pivotal role in politics, by writing these he sought to foster a consensus around key principles of republican governance in response to the turbulence of the times.

Even the collapse of the triumvirate after the death of Crassus in 53 and the death of Pompey's wife, Julia, Caesar's daughter, did not bring the freedom or political stability Cicero craved. The year 53–52 also saw an endless sequence of riots that ground Rome's electoral machinery to a halt; perhaps the only thing that cheered Cicero up in these long years was the death of Clodius at the hands of Milo in 52 (*In Defence of Milo* is a revised version of his defence speech for Milo). In 51 Cicero was bundled off to Cilicia as an unwilling governor. For a man who hated to be out of Rome, governing Cilicia was a miserable experience, especially as he had to wage a military campaign; Cicero was never a very keen soldier, even if in this instance he met with some significant military success. To make matters worse, during his time away from Rome Terentia and Tullia organized a marriage between Tullia[18] and the charming but reprobate Caesarian Dolabella (it was not to be a happy marriage).

The end of the Republic

Cicero arrived back in Rome in January 49, only days before a new civil war was about to break loose between Caesar and Pompey. On 10 January 49 Caesar left behind his province and illegally crossed the Rubicon with his forces. Although he was keen for a compromise that would keep the Republic from being ripped apart by civil war, Cicero threw his lot in with Pompey – and the losing side. With Caesar's victory over Pompey and the Republic's forces at the battle of Pharsalus on 9 August 48, the end of the Republic was in sight, even if the death throes would last a long time. In 46 and 45 Caesar dealt further crushing blows to any hope of a military (or any real) opposition by defeating Republican forces in Africa and Spain. Militarily (and later legally, when he was made dictator for life in 44), Caesar was the only power in Rome. If it had been humiliating to live under the triumvirate, it was even harder to live under the rule of one man, even a man such as Caesar. Cicero responded by again retreating to literature, writing more works on philosophy and oratory (including *Brutus* and *Orator*). As traumatizing as anything else he experienced in those years was the death of his beloved daughter, Tullia, in February 45. Cicero went almost insane with grief; although he read every text he could find on grief, nothing could console him for the loss of one whom he considered a second self. He even divorced his new young wife Publilia (he had divorced Terentia in 46) for not mourning Tullia's death enough.

What must have given him comfort was the remarkably short duration of Caesar's dictatorship for life: on the Ides of March (the 15th) 44 a group of Caesar's closest friends murdered him. Their reasons were various: his assumption of the position of dictator for life, his planned absence to go and fight the Parthians in the east, the appointment of the consuls for the next three years and, for some, a sincere desire to restore the Republic. Cicero was not among their number though he was ecstatic about the assassination. For a brief period it seemed as if the Republic would be restored as long as some arrangement could be made between Mark Antony and the assassins (see Introduction to the *Philippics*). But in the end no compromise was possible. Perhaps this was Cicero's finest moment: faced with a triumphant Antony and a city that Caesar's assassins were forced to leave, he found his tongue once more and delivered speech after speech against Antony, all now collectively known as the *Philippics*. The last speech of Cicero to be circulated was the *Fourteenth Philippic*, delivered on 21 April 43 – the same day that the last army to take its orders from the Senate met with Antony at Mutina. Although victorious, both consuls died as a result of the battle and a toothless Senate no longer possessed a military force. Cicero was to publish no more speeches, although he turned to other forms of communication in order to advance his ideals and leave a republican (and Ciceronian) legacy for future generations of Romans. His philosophical works, such as *On Friendship*, *On Old Age* and *On Duties*, blended Roman history, his own personal experience and Greek philosophy to create a new and influential language of ethical and philosophical discourse.

Even as Cicero worked on these there came the Second Triumvirate of Antony, Octavian and Lepidus – and more proscriptions. Smarting from Cicero's invective, Antony placed Cicero on the list along with his son, brother and nephew (only Cicero's son was to survive the bloodbath). We are told that among those sent to murder Cicero was a man he had once defended on a charge of parricide (whether the story is true or not we cannot tell); when the assassins met up with him on 7 December 43, Cicero was being carried in a litter by his desperate slaves. He ordered them to set the litter down and, looking calmly at his murderers, he stretched out his neck for the blow. His head and hands were taken to Rome and placed on the speakers' platform in the Forum; those who saw them wept, thinking that there they saw the soul of Antony laid bare. Such was to be Cicero's last grisly appearance in Rome. In later years Octavian, now the emperor Augustus, was to catch one of his grandsons trying to hide a volume of Cicero he was reading; he

picked the volume up and read a portion, then handed it back
with the words 'an eloquent man, my boy, eloquent and a lover
of his country'.[19]

Whatever one thinks of Cicero – and he can sometimes be a
hard man to like, with his vanity, self-importance, occasional
cowardice and willingness to compromise his principles – he
was perhaps the last man in an era of warlords to believe in the
idea of the Republic, a very lonely position to hold. He was
also one of the few in the Late Republic who never thought of
turning to an army to force his will upon the state. If that was
a mistake, it was an honourable one.

The world of Cicero's oratory

Cicero 'did not speak just in order to speak';[20] oratory enabled
him to advance, to become an integral part of a social network
that valued connections and favours. Lacking ancestors who
had held any political office in Rome – let alone the consulship –
Cicero relied on his oratory to forge connections. This should
alert us to the incredible importance of oratory to the Romans;
public speaking formed an arena where elites clashed and the
ambitious – like Cicero – could use rhetoric to climb the political ladder. Despite the increasing use of armies to settle disputes
between individuals, oratory still held tremendous importance.
To understand Cicero's speeches one must first understand the
arenas for their performance – for that is what they were. What
we think of as Roman rhetoric, that is the printed words on the
page, is only a shadow of what it was. It was not just Cicero's
words that moved but his performance; in fact, Cicero was
often held back until other members of the defence team had
spoken, as his ability to move a jury to tears was unparalleled
(he often found himself carried away by the emotion of the
moment as well). He was a performer (though he would have
loathed that term)[21] as well as a speaker; words, movement,
gesture and voice all combined to make him a formidable
opponent wherever he spoke. Here are the three major arenas
for his rhetoric:

1. The Senate (*Catilinarian I, Philippic I*)

The Senate was the chief legislative body of Rome and had immense (almost total) power over foreign and domestic policy, but it was actually the various assemblies that were called upon to pass laws. It was made up of wealthy individuals; membership was for life, unless one was convicted of a criminal offence, removed for immoral behaviour or fell below the property qualification. However, membership was not inherited: to become a member of the Senate one first had to hold the quaestorship, a position for which one had to be at least thirty, thus the Senate was never going to be a body of the young and restless. Under Sulla the membership went from 300 to 600; 200 was a bare quorum, while 400 was a packed Senate. Despite the various civil wars and proscriptions, the membership of the Senate was fairly stable until Caesar, at least in terms of the families that produced many of its members. Although there were rules of precedence and regulations, it was often a rowdy place and a speaker had to be willing to deal with interruptions[22] and hostile crowds gathering (or gathered by various politicians) outside. You could say a great deal in the Senate that would have a present-day politician banned from any modern legislative body; the level of abuse tolerated was remarkable. The only concerns that might hold you back were worries about the power of your target (*Philippic II* could have been delivered in the Senate – it was only Cicero's sense of self-preservation that prevented him) or fear that they might then rise to their feet and deliver an equally powerful stream of abuse about you.

2. The Courts (*Against Verres, In Defence of Archias, the Poet, In Defence of Sestius, In Defence of Milo*)

It may seem remarkable for such a sophisticated and wealthy state, but Rome lacked both a police force and a public prosecutor. All prosecutions in Rome, therefore, were taken on the initiative of private citizens. Such a system naturally meant that those lower on the social scale or outsiders had to first find someone who would take their case or defend them; for those who were not Roman citizens (such as the Sicilians in the trial of Verres), finding a Roman citizen to plead your case was essential. However, it was not just the low and the weak who might turn to an orator like Cicero; those tied to him by a complex network of favours and obligations would expect him to come to their aid. In fact, acting in defence of someone was considered an exemplary way to discharge responsibilities and bind others to you (or to pay off a debt); prosecutors were supposed to have a good and personal reason to prosecute rather than be on a moral crusade.

Trials were not conducted in the calm and quiet of a modern courtroom; in fact, there was *no* courtroom. Most trials took place in the Forum, rain or shine. A speaker thus had to deal not just with a jury and the presiding praetor but the weather and the noise from any crowd that might gather; these crowds could be extremely noisy and a good speaker might use that to his advantage. There were at least seven *quaestiones publicae*, courts that tried public offences and which were normally presided over by a praetor. He did not act like a modern judge but was mainly there to ensure there were no irregularities of procedure or mass bribery; he did *not* explain points of law or guide the jury. Defendants were not normally kept in custody but were allowed to stay at home until convicted; they often chose to speak in their defence but could also rely on their team to speak for them.

Under Sulla juries were made up of senators; in 70 the *lex Aurelia* changed this to a mix of senators, equestrians and a third class called the *tribuni aerarii*. The average size of a jury was 75, though the numbers could climb stratospherically for extremely important trials. The prosecution made its case first, then the defence; only after they had presented the overall outline of their cases were witnesses called and cross-examined. (The exception is the extortion court where Verres was tried.) Although Cicero would have a good idea of the evidence he was facing, as this had to be lodged before the trial (allowing sometimes for the intimidation of witnesses), when he spoke for the defence he might not know all the witnesses the prosecution would call, but had to cover himself in case there were surprises. Jurors voted by secret ballot with little balls or tablets with A (for acquittal) or C (for condemnation), scratching out whichever letter they did not want to vote. Some jurors might mark the plaque with NL for *non liquet* – not proven; a prosecutor had to persuade an absolute majority to vote for condemnation to get a conviction.

Much that the defence and the prosecution said in a Roman court often seems irrelevant to the modern reader and for that reason it has often been argued that Roman trials had little to do with the guilt or innocence of the individual but more to do with character. That is not precisely true, although character did play a huge role in a Roman courtroom; there was an expectation that guilt or innocence should be proven, although one could also argue that a crime had been committed for a good reason or that a decent citizen was worth protecting from a vindictive or power-hungry citizen.[23]

Cicero's last case before the courts was *In Defence of Milo* in 52. (He also pleaded two forensic speeches in front of Caesar as sole judge, the *On Behalf of Ligarius* and *On Behalf of King Deiotarus*.)

3. The Assemblies (*For the Manilian Law*, *Catilinarian II*, *On the Agrarian Law II*)

Despite the fact that Rome was an oligarchy, the people held considerable power; although in elections the votes of the wealthier tribes counted for more than those of the urban poor, the poor were still worthy of being wooed – and bribed. What made the assemblies important was not just their votes, but the prestige that their acclaim gave an orator. The shouts of the crowd – for all that there was no way that the entire population of Rome could crowd into the Forum – granted considerable status.

However, large crowds did not just gather for elections; any magistrate could call and address an assembly, which would consist of those who were able and willing to come to the Forum to hear him. These were distinct from formal voting assemblies where the people would elect magistrates, pass laws and occasionally gave verdicts on senators charged with certain offences. These crowds could involve huge numbers – as high as 15,000–20,000;[24] given that Cicero would have to address these numbers without the benefits of amplification or a tele-prompter, one can see the challenge he (and other orators) faced in trying to get their message across and the physical demands of being an orator in Rome. It must have been an unnerving experience to climb the speaker's platform in the Forum and know that all those thousands were standing wait-ing for you to speak.

The circulation of Cicero's speeches

It is hard to know precisely what relationship the speeches we possess have to the ones Cicero delivered. We only know of one time where Cicero read out a speech from a written text and that was for a particular reason – the speech was addressed to the Senate after his return from exile and he had not addressed a crowd for a year, hence nerves and the importance of the speech resulted in this unusual step. However, while Cicero might write out important sections of his speeches – the open-ing and closing sections (called the *exordium* and *peroratio*) – and draft the outline of the rest, he improvised much of what he said in court, to the Senate and before the people. This means that our texts of the speeches are, on the whole, reconstructed from his memory, polished and perhaps altered considerably (such as *In Defence of Milo*). Sometimes later circumstances – for example, the fallout from Cicero's actions during the Catilinarian conspiracy – might require changes (the *Catilinar-ians* were carefully edited with the rest of his consular speeches and circulated in 60).

However, some might take notes of his speeches as he deliv-ered them and these might circulate without Cicero's consent. *In Defence of Milo* is a good example of this; there was a copy of the actual speech Cicero delivered which was extant until the 50s CE at least. It is unlikely that Cicero sanctioned this and, in fact, he may have put the version we now possess into circulation as an attempt to get his side across.

The translations

One approaches translating an author as brilliant as Cicero with a great deal of fear. His genius for language overwhelms you at almost every sentence; I firmly believe that no one ever made Latin prose work as brilliantly as he did. The language sang for him in new and marvellous ways. Faced with such brilliance one is always aware of the limits of one's own ability (and the inflexibility of the English language). To start with the obvious point: Latin is not English. Latin is an inflected language, which means that the function of a word in a sentence is not indicated by word order but by the ending of a word; as a result, Latin can withhold certain critical words necessary to interpret the meaning of a sentence until the very end. To do so in English is frequently impossible. Where possible I have tried to reflect the impact of a final word or the structure of a sentence, but more often than not to make a sentence comprehensible in English one must rearrange the delicate pattern of Cicero's prose. Cicero's prose is also noted for its use of prose rhythm, with certain sentence and phrase endings (called *clausulae*) preferred for their ability to round off an idea or a sentence with a certain pleasing sound. Again, this is something that English has more problems with because of the inflexibility of its sentence structure.

But the problems of translating Cicero are not just in the language but in the loss of a world-view. Certain accusations that clearly carried great weight in Rome have lost much of their weight. Take this small phrase from *In Defence of Milo*, chapter 30: *oppressa virtute audacia est*, which I translate as 'a wild assault was crushed by the actions of a *man*'. The literal translation would be closer to 'recklessness was crushed by manliness'. Perhaps this is fair enough as a translation but it does not show the power of Cicero's words. *Audacia*, or a reckless way of behaving without regard for others, tradition or laws, is a much more serious social offence to Romans than charging someone with recklessness alone might be for us (in certain circumstances we can admire recklessness). *Virtus* is the proper way of behaving for a Roman male, hence 'manliness' – a word that few people would use today with a straight face – as one of its possible translations. In a few words Cicero deftly makes Milo the quintessential Roman man in all that he does, whereas Clodius is described as acting wildly without regard for others or proper Roman behaviour. *Virtus* and *audacia*, like many other Latin words, are a package deal rather than a single English concept, and to continually translate them in the same way is to miss the complexity of the Latin word. Thus sometimes I have translated *virtus* as 'character', sometimes as 'courage' and sometimes as 'heroism'. Likewise, *audacia* is sometimes translated as 'arrogance' rather than 'recklessness'.

Another issue lies with words that mark serious Roman social issues which we, on the whole, do not experience. Take the threat represented by *latrones* (singular *latro*), a word I have usually translated as 'outlaws'. Outlaws or bandits were a serious problem in the Republic and a genuine challenge for the state, and in Cicero they are also used as a frightening and inverted mirror of civil society.[25] However, if we were to accuse someone of being a bandit or outlaw, our audience is perhaps as likely to think of romantic images of Robin Hood as anything else. An accusation of living a life of *latrocinium*, that is, of living the life of a *latro*, had the impact in Rome that to accuse someone of being a terrorist has in current political speech. In spite of this, I have resisted translating it as such except for two places where I have translated it as 'terrorism' (*Catilinarian I*, chapter 27, and *On his House*, chapter 107); despite the anachronism of the word in these chapters, nothing else seemed to get across the force of Cicero's accusation.

Cicero's rhetoric was a very potent weapon. It also took different forms depending on whether he was addressing the Senate, the courts or an assembly of the people. At times it can be incredibly complex, forcing the listener to pay close attention in order to understand his meaning, while on other occasions it is very simple and invites audience participation. A good example of the latter can be found in chapter 22 of Cicero's *Second Speech on the Agrarian Law of Rullus*, in which he asks a series of questions where the only answer is '*Rullus*'.

One can easily imagine the effect of an audience of thousands screaming out Rullus' name.

If Cicero did not eschew simplicity, neither was he afraid of complexity; he was quite willing to use an elegant and mannered style that an audience today would never tolerate. However, while Cicero's oratory can sometimes be difficult, it was never impossible for a Roman to understand. A translation that baffles the reader does not, I feel, serve Cicero well, even if it appears more faithful to the Latin. As such, I have tried to retain the complexity of Cicero's language and sentences, while ensuring they are intelligible to a modern audience not as steeped in elaborate rhetoric as Cicero's was. I have also broken up his larger periodic structures as English simply cannot manage paragraph-long sentences in the way Latin can. Additionally, where Cicero is abusive (and he was a master of abuse) I have tried to render that abuse in ways that make sense to a modern audience: if Cicero did not pull his punches, neither should the translation. Lastly, Cicero can sometimes be highly repetitive in his speeches, a necessary tactic in dealing with large crowds, as was exaggeration. It was the only way to ensure that his message would get across. I have left both repetition and exaggeration in place, even if this means that his speeches seem over the top or somewhat redundant in places; I encourage the reader, however, to imagine how such portions would be effective as Cicero stood before his original audience.

NOTES

1. Quintilian, *Institutes of Oratory* 10.1.112.
2. Catiline accused him of being only a foreign resident of Rome (Sallust, *Catiline* 31) and a rival prosecutor once called him a foreign king (*In Defence of Sulla* 22).
3. Plutarch, *Life of Cicero* 1.
4. *On the Laws* 3.16.36.
5. Consul in 95, censor 92.
6. Cicero would later buy his house on the Palatine (see *On his House*).
7. Fought between 91 and 87, the Social War revolved around

Rome's reluctance to expand her citizenship (and hence the benefits her citizens received from her expanding empire) to her Italian allies.

8. Although he was a devoted *optimate*, Cicero loathed Sulla but always spoke highly of Marius, even writing an epic poem on his life.

9. It was not his first case, simply the first speech he published. Cicero was to go on to publish many, many more speeches: all told we have fifty-eight complete or nearly complete speeches from Cicero, dating from 81 to 43. We have fragments of sixteen more and know of five that were published but are not extant; there were at least eighty-three more that seem never to have been published (though they may have circulated in copies taken down in court or in the Senate). Of the surviving speeches, thirty are forensic (law-court) speeches; thirteen are deliberative speeches and there are fourteen *Philippics*.

10. This was the first murder case to be tried in Sulla's new court for murder cases, the *quaestio de sicariis et veneficiis*.

11. Plutarch tells us that he also found it convenient to escape Sulla's anger (*Cicero* 3).

12. The anecdote was told in 54, *In Defence of Gnaeus Plancius* (64–6).

13. We cannot be sure of the date of Tullia's birth but Marcus was born in 65.

14. Seneca the Younger, *On the Shortness of Life* 5.1.

15. See *For the Manilian Law*.

16. When Clodius complained to Cicero that Clodia, his sister, would not give him a foot of space in the theatre for his clients, although she had plenty to spare, being the wife of the consul, Cicero told him not to worry as she'd lift the other foot for him – a crude allusion to the rumour that Clodius and his sister were sleeping together.

17. His letters to Terentia are drenched with guilt and self-pity; see, for example, *Letters to his Friends* 14.2 and 14.4. And his family certainly suffered a great deal in his exile – Terentia was dragged across the Forum at one point.

18. It was already her third; frequent marriages and divorces were not uncommon among the Roman elite.

19. Plutarch, *Cicero* 49.

20. Catherine Steel, *Reading Cicero: Genre and Performance in Latin Republican Rome* (London: Duckworth, 2005), p. 23.

21. Cicero himself studied with the great actor Roscius, though he

was careful to mark the orator's performance as distinct from that of the actor. There were serious social reasons for this: acting in Rome was a low-status profession, one not practised by respectable people, while oratory was the art of people with high status. It was critically important for an orator to act without appearing to act.

22. See *Letters to Atticus* 1.16.10 for a good example of how Cicero dealt with such debates – he was a master of wit, so it was a brave person who decided to cross swords with him.

23. For Roman jury expectations, see Andrew Riggsby, 'Did the Romans Believe in their Verdicts?', *Rhetorica* 15 (1997), pp. 235–51.

24. For more on the role of the crowd, see Fergus Millar, *The Crowd in Rome in the Late Republic* (Ann Arbor, MI: University of Michigan Press, 1998).

25. Those interested in this topic should read Thomas Habinek, 'Cicero and the Bandits', in *The Politics of Latin Literature: Writing, Identity, and Empire in Ancient Rome* (Princeton, NJ: Princeton University Press, 1998), pp. 69–87.

Further Reading

The problem with talking about books on Cicero, as Cicero once said of Pompey, is not finding a place to start but one to stop. The following is only a selection of the many excellent works on Cicero and the Late Republic; I have tried to include material that is easily accessible as well as more specialized works. But the first place to start is with Cicero's own voluminous writings, all of which are available in translations with facing Latin texts in the Loeb Classical Library. For someone who wants a glimpse of Cicero's day-to-day concerns, the letters are particularly recommended. There is also an entertaining but not always reliable ancient biography by Plutarch, which is available in Penguin Classics, along with several other lives of important Romans of this period in a collection called *Fall of the Roman Republic*. Before I move onto the more scholarly material I should mention Robert Harris' two gripping novels on Cicero, *Imperium* and *Lustrum* (the latter published in the US as *Conspirata*). Both are well worth reading for anyone who wants Cicero to spring to life.

Anything marked with an asterisk below is a work that is particularly accessible to the reader with no specialist knowledge in Roman history, politics or society.

Biographies of Cicero and his family

* Anthony Everitt, *Cicero: The Life and Times of Rome's Greatest Politician* (New York: Random House, 2001).
Manfred Fuhrmann, *Cicero and the Roman Republic*, trans. W. E. Yuill (Oxford: Blackwell, 1992).

Thomas Mitchell, *Cicero: The Ascending Years* (New Haven, CT: Yale University Press, 1979).

Thomas Mitchell, *Cicero: The Senior Statesman* (New Haven, CT: Yale University Press, 1991).

* Elizabeth Rawson, *Cicero: A Portrait* (Ithaca, NY: Cornell University Press, 1983).

David Stockton, *Cicero: A Political Biography* (Oxford: Oxford University Press, 1971).

* Susan Treggiari, 'Home and Forum: Cicero between Public and Private', *Transactions of the American Philological Association* 128 (1998), pp. 1–23.

* Susan Treggiari, *Terentia, Tullia and Publilia: The Women of Cicero's Family* (London: Routledge, 2007).

General studies of rhetoric

William Dominik (ed.), *Roman Eloquence: Rhetoric in Society and Literature* (London: Routledge, 1997).

William Dominik and Jon Hall (eds.), *A Companion to Roman Rhetoric* (Malden, MA: Blackwell, 2007).

* Thomas Habinek, *Ancient Rhetoric and Oratory* (Malden, MA: Blackwell, 2005).

George Kennedy, *The Art of Rhetoric in the Roman World, 300 BC–AD 300* (Princeton, NJ: Princeton University Press, 1972).

Studies of the Late Republic and other politicians

Peter Brunt, *Social Conflicts in the Roman Republic* (London: Chatto and Windus, 1971).

Peter Brunt, *The Fall of the Roman Republic and Other Related Essays* (Oxford: Oxford University Press, 1988).

* Philip Freeman, *Julius Caesar* (New York: Simon and Schuster, 2008).

* Adrian Goldsworthy, *Julius Caesar: Life of a Colossus* (New Haven, CT: Yale University Press, 2008).

Erich Gruen, *The Last Generation of the Roman Republic* (Berkeley: University of California Press, 1974).

* Tom Holland, *Rubicon: The Triumph and Tragedy of the Roman Republic* (London: Little, Brown, 2003).

Fergus Millar, *The Crowd in Rome in the Late Republic* (Ann Arbor, MI: University of Michigan Press, 1998).

Robert Morstein-Marx, *Mass Oratory and Political Power in the Late Roman Republic* (Cambridge: Cambridge University Press, 2004).

Elizabeth Rawson, *Intellectual Life in the Late Roman Republic* (Baltimore, MD: Johns Hopkins University Press, 1985).

Robin Seager, *Pompey: A Political Biography* (Oxford: Blackwell, 1979).

* Ronald Syme, *The Roman Revolution* (Oxford: Oxford University Press, 2002).

W. Jeffrey Tatum, *The Patrician Tribune: Publius Clodius Pulcher* (Chapel Hill: University of North Carolina Press, 1999).

Lily Ross Taylor, *Party Politics in the Age of Caesar* (Berkeley: University of California Press, 1949).

Lily Ross Taylor, *Roman Voting Assemblies* (Ann Arbor, MI: University of Michigan Press, 1966).

Roman law and trials (many of these rely heavily on Cicero, our major source for this period)

Michael Alexander, *Trials in the Late Roman Republic, 149 BC to 50 BC* (Toronto: University of Toronto Press, 1990).

Michael Alexander, *The Case for the Prosecution in the Ciceronian Era* (Ann Arbor, MI: University of Michigan Press, 2002).

Richard Bauman, *Crime and Punishment in Ancient Rome* (London: Routledge, 1996).

Abel H. Greenidge, *The Legal Procedure of Cicero's Time* (New York: A. M. Kelley, 1971).

Andrew Riggsby, 'Did the Romans Believe in their Verdicts?', *Rhetorica* 15 (1997), pp. 235–51.

Andrew Riggsby, *Crime and Community in Ciceronian Rome* (Austin: University of Texas Press, 1999).

Studies of Ciceronian rhetoric and speeches

Michael von Albrecht, *Cicero's Style: A Synopsis* (Leiden: Brill, 2003).

Andrew Bell, 'Cicero and the Spectacle of Power', *Journal of Roman Studies* 87 (1997), pp. 1–22.

Joan Booth (ed.), *Cicero on the Attack: Invective and Subversion in the Speeches and Beyond* (Swansea: Classical Press of Wales, 2007).

Shane Butler, *The Hand of Cicero* (London: Routledge, 2002).

Antony Corbeill, *Controlling Laughter: Political Humour in the Late Roman Republic* (Princeton, NJ: Princeton University Press, 1996).

Andrew Lintott, *Cicero as Evidence: A Historian's Companion* (Oxford: Oxford University Press, 2008).

James May, *Trials of Character: The Eloquence of Ciceronian Ethos* (Chapel Hill: University of North Carolina Press, 1988).

James May, *Brill's Companion to Cicero: Oratory and Rhetoric* (Leiden: Brill, 2002).

Jonathon Powell and Jeremy Patterson (eds.), *Cicero the Advocate* (Oxford: Oxford University Press, 2004).

Jonathon Price, 'The Failure of Cicero's *First Catilinarian*', *Studies in Latin Literature and Roman History* 9 (1998), pp. 106–28.

* Catherine Steel, *Reading Cicero* (London: Duckworth, 2005).

Ann Vasaly, *Representations: Images of the World in Ciceronian Oratory* (Berkeley: University of California Press, 1993).

Note on the Text

In any volume such as this, painful choices have to be made about what should be included and what omitted. In making my selection, I have tried to pick those speeches that allow the reader a sense of Cicero's career as a whole, warts and all, even if this means including some that do not show him at his finest. I have also tried to include those that give the reader a sense of the wider problems besetting the Republic – such as provincial maladministration and the need for land reform.

For this reason I begin with *Against Verres*, a speech against the execrable governor of Sicily. Provincial extortion was a massive problem (and, sadly, one not resolved by any act or speech of Cicero) and Cicero was taking a risk in standing up to powerful men by prosecuting Verres. I include, also, speeches where Cicero argues for extraordinary commands that could be seen as harmful for the Republic (*For the Manilian Law*); speeches against agrarian laws – and their overly powerful boards (*On the Agrarian Law of Rullus*); speeches against disaffected nobles seeking to overthrow the state (*Catilinarians I and II*); and speeches in defence of poets and the role of poetry in a civilized society (*In Defence of Archias, the Poet*). Of speeches after Cicero's exile, I have included excerpts from *On his House*, to show the price Cicero paid for his actions during the Catilinarian conspiracy, and excerpts from *In Defence of Sestius*, on his vision of an ideal agreement of the orders and the various classes of society. I conclude with two speeches, the *First* and *Second Philippics*, that are often seen as Cicero's finest hour, as he risked his life to face down Antony.

Against Verres I

Delivered 5 August 70 in the extortion court

Even by the remarkably low standards set by his peers, Verres, the execrable governor of Sicily from 73 to 71, stood out in all the wrong ways. His greed (he apparently managed to strip Sicily of the massive sum of 40 million sesterces) was staggering and was made possible by his immunity from prosecution while he held the governorship. While in office, Roman governors had absolute power and no one within the province could dispute that power or their actions, and control from Rome was non-existent. Unsurprisingly, corruption under such a system was rife. Running for office was expensive and those who managed to attain a rich province normally planned to make back their money from its unfortunate residents. The sole hope for provincials was to wait until the governor's term of office was finished and turn to the quaestio de pecuniis repetundis, *the extortion court in Rome, and hope to claw back some of their losses. However, winning a case here was difficult because the juries were drawn from the ranks of the Senate – the friends and colleagues of the accused[1] and men who themselves might one day also be prosecuted in this court for extortion. Despite their wealth, jurors were not averse to being bribed for their votes, and someone who had reaped rich rewards from his province would not be slow to spread some of that wealth around if it meant an acquittal. To complicate matters, there was ethnic prejudice: the complainants were non-Roman outsiders attempting to drive a* Roman *senator into exile.*

As if this did not make prosecution difficult enough, since there was no public prosecutor provincials had to find a Roman citizen to take on the role, not always an easy task as prosecutors

*often found themselves unpopular. The Sicilians were lucky
enough to persuade Cicero to take on the task despite his normal reluctance to play the role of prosecutor. Cicero's previous
connections with Sicily partially explain why he took such a
risk. These began in 75 when he was quaestor, aiding the governor of Sicily in the day-to-day administration of the island;
Cicero was stationed in Lilybaeum (modern Marsala), a town
in the western part of the island. He was rightfully proud of his
ethical behaviour during his term and counted many Sicilians
among his friends. This, coupled with his rising reputation as
an orator, made him a natural person for the Sicilians to approach
to undertake what was likely to be a risky prosecution. Trouble
started for Cicero before he even began the case when a rival
prosecutor, Quintus Caecilius Niger, a former quaestor of
Verres, tried to wrest control from him. (In Rome, when two
individuals claimed the right to prosecute someone in a case of
this nature, their claims were assessed before any trial took
place; those facing prosecution could take advantage of this
process (called a divinatio) to put in place a prosecutor of their
choosing who would deliberately make a mess of their case.)
Cicero deftly saw off this challenge and took charge of the case
against Verres.[2]*

*Verres and his team's next move was to attempt to have the
trial postponed until the following year, when his leading
defence speaker, Quintus Hortensius, would be consul.[3] The
defence took advantage of Cicero's need to gather evidence for
this case: when Cicero asked for 110 days to achieve this,
another prosecutor stepped forward and said that he needed
108 days to gather evidence in Greece for a different extortion
trial. That would mean that this case would be tried before
Verres' and Verres' trial would be postponed until the next
year. Cicero's response was to gather evidence in fifty days, a
remarkable achievement given the amount of evidence and
number of witnesses he produced. Cicero's solution to a difficult prosecution was to overwhelm the defence with the mass
of evidence he had gathered, spending very little time on his
opening speech. Although it is probably true that many extortion trials did use a number of witnesses to hammer home*

their case (see chapter 55 below), the number that Cicero called was unique. After this speech alone he called twenty-six Roman citizens, sixteen non-Romans, thirteen embassies (two from Italy, eleven from Sicily) – and he had plenty more in reserve for the second action. These witnesses occupied three days after his speech, probably giving about thirty hours of testimony.

Beyond the need to drive home Verres' guilt so clearly that not even the most corrupt jury could vote to acquit him, Cicero was working under severe time constraints. The trial began at the eighth hour (which meant most of the day had passed); there were only ten days until Pompey's games when the trial would have to be broken off, to resume on 2 September. After this the ludi Romani (Roman Games) would be held from 5 to 19 September, further postponing the trial. Presumably, Verres thought that his defence would take the stage after the 19th. But following Cicero's host of witnesses there was to be no defence – in fact, Verres was so badly affected that he asked for and received a postponement for a day due to illness. Perhaps, realizing his case was lost, Hortensius rarely interrupted witnesses by cross-questioning.[4] Verres abandoned the case, taking his ill-gotten gains and fleeing to Massilia, modern Marseilles. Those who do not want to think of a man as dreadful as Verres living out the rest of his life in comfort will be pleased to know that in 43 Mark Antony proscribed and killed him for his property.

Was Verres guilty? Undoubtedly. Was he the absolute monster that Cicero portrays him as over the course of this speech and his other (undelivered) speeches against Verres? Probably not: it is hard to believe that anyone could be so horrific and stupid an individual. However, Cicero's exaggerations should not lead us to assume that Verres was a charming man who just happened to be unfortunate enough to get Cicero as a prosecutor and a jury scared of losing the court to the equestrians. The evidence that Cicero accumulated speaks of three years of wholesale looting of Sicily and dreadful ill-treatment of her citizens; the fact that there were other equally dreadful governors should not blind us to Verres' many terrible deeds. We

*should also remember that Cicero won his case against a jury
predisposed to vote in favour of one of their own and to dis-
believe or disregard accusations from provincials.*

*But Cicero did not solely rely on the evidence, although com-
pared to his other speeches this one may seem relatively
unsophisticated, with its bare narrative of Cicero's aims and
efforts in securing evidence; it is a deft and carefully plotted
piece of rhetoric. Throughout, Cicero plays on both the fears
and vanity of the jury and displays considerable skill in presenting Verres as an outsider in terms of values to the senatorial
elite, essentially convincing them that they should cut Verres
loose to save themselves. (It was a strategy he was to repeat
against other enemies such as Catiline.)*

1. Jurors, it seems that at this crisis of our Republic it is not a
human but a divine plan that has handed you the very thing
you should hope for: a unique opportunity to dismiss the hatred of our class[5] and the infamous reputation of our courts.
These days one can hear everywhere – and not just among the
Roman people but even among foreign tribes – the comment
that our current courts will never convict a rich man no matter
how guilty he may be. This opinion damages the Republic and
endangers you. 2. Right at this very crisis of our class and our
courts, when there are men standing by who attempt to enflame
the hatred of the Senate with their speeches at assemblies and
with their laws, a defendant, Gaius Verres, has been charged.
And although everyone already considers him condemned
because of his career and his deeds, he is as good as acquitted
(to quote his own boast) because of his enormous wealth.
Jurors, cheered on by a hopeful Roman people, I undertook to
act in this case, not to increase the hatred of our class but to
help you fight against the infamous reputation that affects us
all. I am prosecuting a man whose case will enable you to win
back the now vanished good opinion of the courts, to return to
the good graces of the Roman people and to make amends with
foreign nations; I am prosecuting a man who was an embezzler

of the treasury, the tormenter of Asia and Pamphylia, the looter of Rome's legal system and the curse and cancer of Sicily.[6]

3. If your verdict is honest and matches your solemn oath as jurors, you will retain the authority which should be yours; but if the wealth of that . . . *person* shatters all regard for your oath and for truth, I shall gain this: it will be clear that the defendant had jurors and the prosecutor a defendant – but the Republic did not get an honest verdict. Although Gaius Verres set many traps for me on land and sea (some I escaped by keeping my eyes open and others I parried through the energetic service of my friends), I shall confess to you that I never felt then that I was running so many dangerous risks nor was as terribly afraid as I am now, right here in this court. 4. Though they trouble me greatly, I am not so disturbed by the expectations raised by my prosecution and the gathering of this huge crowd as I am by *his* evil plots, the plots he lays for me, for all of you, for our praetor Manius Glabrio,[7] the Roman people, our allies, foreign tribes, our class and even the good name of the Senate – all at one and the same time. For he never stops repeating that only men who have furtively stolen enough just for themselves should be afraid but *he* openly made off with enough to satisfy a great number of people and adds, for good measure, that nothing is so sacred it cannot be corrupted, nothing so well guarded money cannot capture it.

5. If he were as secretive in his actions as he is reckless in his efforts, perhaps he would have deceived me sometime or somehow. But it turns out quite nicely that his exceptional recklessness was combined with incredible stupidity; he made his plans and hopeful efforts to corrupt this court as transparent as his thieving. Once only, he says, he was scared: when I first formally indicted him.[8] When he was freshly (although it was no fresh unpopularity and infamy, but one of old and long standing, that he felt the heat of) arrived from his province, he hit an inconvenient time to corrupt the court. 6. So when I asked for a brief time to go to Sicily to make inquiries, *he* found someone who would ask for a two-day-shorter period to make inquiries in Achaia – but the aim was not for the investigator to achieve the same result with his diligence and hard work that my labour

and sleepless nights helped me attain. That Achaean 'investigator' never even made it to Brundisium![9] *I* covered all of Sicily in fifty days and as a result I became so familiar with the evidence and injuries of all the peoples and individuals involved that it was clear to everyone that *he* sought his investigator *not* to prosecute someone, but to take up my time slot.

Here is what that absolutely brazen-faced lunatic is thinking. 7. He understands that I am so prepared and equipped with evidence for this trial that I shall nail him with his thefts and crimes, not just in your hearing but in everyone's sight. He sees that many senators are witnesses to his reckless behaviour, he sees many of the equestrian class crowding around; in addition, there are Roman citizens and allies here whom he has greatly injured. He sees also that many important embassies, authorized by their peoples from the communities friendliest to us, have assembled here. 8. Although this is the case, his opinion of all decent men is so low and he considers the senatorial courts so ruined and corrupt that he repeats endlessly in *public* that there was a good reason he was greedy for money, since his own experience is that only money gives one such great protection. He adds that he bought time itself for his own trial – not an easy thing – so he would be able to buy the rest more easily afterwards and sail out of the path of the oncoming storm even though he was not able to evade the blast of the criminal charge.

9. If he placed his hopes – well, I cannot say in his case – in some honourable defence or someone's eloquence or influence, he would certainly not be corralling and netting all this quarry. He would not look down despisingly on the senatorial class and pick at his whim a senator who would find himself a defendant and would come to trial while Verres was preparing what he needed for his defence.[10] 10. I can easily see what his hopes and plans are in this situation. I am not, however, able to comprehend what he honestly believes can happen with this praetor and this jury. But I understand one thing – and the Roman people agreed with me when the original jury was challenged[11] – that his hopes of safety consisted of relying entirely on his money to protect him, thinking that if that defence was lost nothing else could help.

There is no talent so immense nor oratorical skill so fluent that it could defend his career on any front, a career which everyone knows stands long-convicted and condemned by his many vices and crimes. 11. I shall pass over the stains and disgraces of his youth. What else did his quaestorship, the first step in a public career, consist of except his *own quaestor* robbing Gnaeus Carbo of public funds? Except fleecing and betraying a consul? Except deserting an army, abandoning a province and violating the close relationship forged by the lot and its oath?[12] His time as a lieutenant[13] was a disaster for all Asia and Pamphylia, provinces where he plundered many homes, more cities and *all* the shrines. Then he revived his old ways and repeated his quaestorship, to Dolabella's great harm; Verres, his deputy and acting quaestor and Verres' wrongdoing brought him hatred. And then he did not just desert Dolabella but deliberately attacked and betrayed him! 12. His time as city praetor saw holy temples and public works ransacked; at the same time, in his administration of justice, he awarded and arbitrarily gave away the possessions of decent men in defiance of all precedent. To cap it all, he erected many massive monuments to his personal vices in the province of Sicily, a place he harassed for three years and destroyed so much of that even now we cannot hope to restore it to its former condition: even many years under honourable governors could only partially achieve that.

13. When he was governor, the Sicilians did not have their own laws, our Senate's decrees or even the rights all people naturally possess. Everyone in Sicily now has only whatever escaped the notice of this ravenous, sex-mad man or proved more than even he could swallow. No case was judged for three years unless at his agreement; no one's father or even grandfather left him an inheritance in terms so watertight that Verres did not arbitrarily award it to someone else. New, perverse rules squeezed countless sums of money from the resources of those who farmed public land;[14] our most faithful allies were treated like enemies; Roman citizens were crucified like slaves. The guiltiest individuals used their money to get him to set them free, while, without hearing their cases, he condemned

and exiled very honourable and unimpeachable men who were not even at their own trials. He threw open highly protected harbours and great and secure cities to pirates and raiders; he starved to death the sailors and soldiers of the Sicilians – our allies and friends; to the great disgrace of the Roman people, he lost and destroyed our best and fittest fleets.[15] 14. While governor, he took away the Sicilians' most ancient treasures, some the gifts of wealthy kings to beautify their cities, some gifts from our triumphant commanders or items they had restored to Sicilian communities[16] – he stripped *everything*. He did not only do this with public statues and works of art, but even plundered all the most sacred, consecrated and venerated shrines. He left the Sicilians not one statue of a god he thought showed even a little craft or ancient workmanship.

To be honest, I am held back by a sense of shame from bringing up his appalling lust for sexual outrages and crimes as I do not wish, by mentioning them, to increase the distress of those who were not able to keep their children and wives untouched by his kinks. 15. Do I hear someone protest that he committed these offences so secretly people do not know about them? I think there is not a man alive who has heard his name and who cannot relate his unholy actions – I should be more afraid that people might consider I skipped over many of his crimes rather than invented some. In fact, I do not think this crowd came here to hear about his crimes but to rehear those it already knows.

Since this is the situation, that insane loser now tries another line of attack with me; his aim is not to block me with another's eloquence or rely on someone's influence, clout or power. He pretends to place his trust in those, but as he does nothing secretly I see what he is doing: he waves around the empty titles of nobility, that is, the names of arrogant men, who, instead of impeding my case because they are nobles, help it because they are notorious. 16. He pretends to trust in their protection, although he has been hard at work for a long time scheming something else. Jurors, I shall now briefly lay out for you his current hopes and schemes, but first I beg you to hear how he has arranged his case from the start. When first he returned from his province, he drew up a contract for extensive and expensive bribery of this court. He stuck to this plan right up to the end – until the jurors were rejected. He abandoned it completely after the rejections and the jury panel was drawn up because the good fortune of the Roman people confounded his hopes in the drawing of the lot, while my carefulness in rejecting jurors did the same for his shamelessness.

17. The case was turning out well. The list of your names, you, the members of this court, were in everyone's hands. There seemed no chance of any mark, colour or underhand symbol being smeared on a tablet;[17] suddenly Verres went from high spirits and joy to being so low and downcast that it seemed that he was not just already condemned in the minds of the Roman people but in his own. Then suddenly, a few days after the consular elections,[18] he revived his old plans, but with more money, using the same men to prepare the same plots against your reputations and all our fortunes. Small signs and evidence first made me aware of this, but once I became suspicious, I soon had a precise knowledge of all their top-secret plans.

18. As a huge crowd of people was accompanying the newly elected consul Hortensius home from the Campus Martius, Gaius Curio just happened to encounter the crowd – and I would have it understood that there is no insult intended in bringing up Curio's name. But to be sure, I am telling you of comments he would hardly have talked about so openly and in the middle of such an immense crowd if he had not wanted them repeated. Besides, I shall use such extreme caution when I speak that everyone will understand the respect I have for our friendship and his position. 19. He sees Verres in the crowd right by the arch of Fabius,[19] calls out his name and congratulates him loudly without saying anything to Hortensius, the man who had just been elected consul, or to his relatives and friends who were also present. He stops and embraces him and orders him to not worry. 'I announce', he says, 'that today's election acquits you.' Many honourable men heard this and informed me at once – in fact, as soon as anybody caught sight of me, they told me. To some it seemed outrageous, to others silly; it seemed silly to those who thought the case depended on the

witnesses, the conduct of the case, the power of the court – not the election of the consuls. It seemed outrageous to those who looked deeper, and saw that his congratulations implied the court had been corrupted. 20. The most honourable thought and said to each other and to me that 'now it was out in the open that there clearly were no courts'. The man who thought himself already convicted yesterday is now acquitted after his defending counsel was elected consul! What of it? Will that ensure that all Sicily, all the Sicilians, all our businessmen in Sicily and all the public and private documents now at Rome achieve nothing? Nothing – since the consul-elect is unwilling! What? The jurors will not listen to his crimes, or to the witnesses or public opinion in Rome? No! The power and preference of one man supersedes all!

I shall speak truthfully, jurors, as the situation deeply disturbed me. The better people were, the more they said, '*He* will escape you, but *we* shall not have control of the courts for much longer. And after Verres' acquittal who could object to the transference of the courts?' 21. Everyone was worried; Verres' sudden joy did not shake them as much as the novel congratulations of an extremely important man did. I wanted to lie about how it troubled me; I wanted to hide the sorrow in my mind with my expression and cover it with my silence. And, lo and behold, right at that time when the praetors-elect were casting their lots and the oversight of the extortion court fell to Marcus Metellus' lot,[20] I was told that Verres was congratulated and he sent his slaves home to announce the news to his wife. 22. Clearly, this did not please me; however, I did not yet understand quite how much I should fear the way that lot fell. Then, the trustworthy men who investigated everything for me informed me that a certain senator transferred baskets filled to the brim with Sicilian cash to a Roman equestrian, but the senator held on to something like ten baskets – all earmarked to be used during my election. That night he summoned bribery agents from every tribe; one of them, who considered himself under particular obligation to me, came to me that very same night and gave an account of what he had said to them, how he had reminded them of how generously he had treated them when he ran for praetor and in the most recent elections for the consuls and praetors, and how he promised them on the spot as much money as they wanted if they ensured I was not elected as aedile. At this point, some of them said they did not dare to do this, or that it was not possible – but they found one man by the name of Quintus Verres, from the Romilian tribe, a brave friend from the same family, an agent from best bribery school and a pupil and friend of Gaius Verres' father; he said that he could promise to manage it if he was paid 500,000 sesterces. Then some others said that they would go in on it with him. As this was the situation, my informant very kindly gave me advance warning to take great care.

24. I was beset by several serious problems in one short period. The elections were upon us and there I was campaigning against a huge amount of money. The trial was approaching and those Sicilian money baskets also were a threat there. I was hindered from acting unreservedly on anything related to the trial out of fear of the impact on the elections; because of the trial, I could not devote myself entirely to my candidacy. There was no sense in threatening the bribery agents, since I saw they were aware that this trial would preoccupy and tie me up. 25. And at that very moment, I hear that Hortensius has summoned the Sicilians to his home; in that situation the Sicilians certainly acted with independence and did not turn up when they understood why he was sending for them. Meanwhile, the voting for me began; *he* considered himself its ringmaster as he had with the rest of the elections. That masterful man ran around the tribes, along with his bewitching and popular son, calling on and meeting with his father's friends – the bribery agents. When this came to their attention, the Roman people unreservedly made sure that the cash of a man whose wealth had not been able to drag me from the path of integrity would not drag me down at the elections.

26. After those elections I was no longer burdened by worries about my candidacy and had a much freer mind; I thought about and did nothing unless it related to this trial. And then, jurors, I discovered the plans they had organized and set in motion to create some way to put off the trial so it would take

place when Marcus Metellus was praetor. That would give them the following advantages: first, Marcus Metellus was very friendly to their case; second, Hortensius would be consul – and not just Hortensius but Quintus Metellus! Listen to what a good friend he was: he gave him such a show of his goodwill that it looked as if he had repaid Verres for buying votes for him. 27. Did you think I would be silent on such an important matter? Or when the Republic and my reputation were in such danger that I would value anything more than my duty and my position? The other consul-elect sent for the Sicilians; some of them came since Lucius Metellus had been praetor in Sicily. This is what he said to them: he was consul; one brother had Sicily as his province while another would be in charge of the extortion court; many precautions had been taken so that no harm could befall Verres.

28. I beg you to tell me, Metellus, what is perversion of justice if not this? If not frightening witnesses, and, in particular, the Sicilians, men scared and crushed by the weight of your influence, by fear of a consul *and* the power of two praetors? What would you do for an innocent man or a relative when you abandon your duty and position for a man completely ruined and unconnected to you? Your behaviour makes what he says over and over about you seem true to those who do not know you. 29. For people asserted that Verres used to say that you had become consul not 'by fate'[21] – as the rest of your family had – but through his efforts. So there will be two consuls and a president of a court because of his 'goodwill'. 'Not only will we escape', he said, 'having Marcus Glabrio, a man far too conscientious in presiding over the court and too acquiescent to the people's judgement, but we shall gain another advantage. Marcus Caeso is a juror; he will be aedile, along with the prosecutor, and is a man respected and well known in the courts. It will be no use at all to have him on a jury that we shall try to corrupt. When he was a member of the jury in Gaius Junius' court,[22] he did not just take the shameful actions on that occasion seriously, but publicized them. After the first of January we shall not have him ás a juror. 30. Nor will we have Quintus Manlius and Quintus Cornificius, two very strict and incor-

ruptible jurors, because they will be tribunes of the plebs.[23] Publius Sulpicius, an unrelenting and incorruptible juror, has to begin his magistracy[24] on the fifth of December. Nor will we have Marcus Crepereius, of that well-known, rigorous equestrian family and upbringing; or Lucius Cassius[25] of a family known for its extreme severity on all topics and particularly on giving verdicts; or Gnaeus Tremellius, a diligent man who has great respect for his oath; these three, men of the old school, have been elected as military tribunes. They will not be in the jury pool after the first of January. We shall even appoint by lot the person to fill the vacancy left by Marcus Metellus, since he will be presiding over this trial! So, after the first of January, as the praetor and almost the entire court will have been changed, we shall baffle at our whim the prosecutor's terrible threats and the great hopes resting on this trial.'

31. Today is the fifth of August; you began to assemble at one o'clock.[26] They will not even count this day! There are ten days before the votive games[27] which Gnaeus Pompey will hold; these will take away fifteen days and then the Roman Games will follow immediately. So almost forty days will have intervened and it is then that they think they will make their response to my case; by making speeches and giving excuses, they will easily spin the time out until the Victory Games.[28] The Plebeian Games[29] follow hard upon these; after those there will be either no or very few days on which a trial can be held. Thus, after the prosecution is stale and cold, Marcus Metellus as praetor would preside over the trial as if it were a new one. If I *had* lacked confidence in his word, I would not have kept him as a juror. 32. But as it is, however, I would prefer that this case take place while he is a juror, not praetor, and trust him more with a voting tablet when he is sworn in than with those of others when he is not.[30]

Jurors, I now ask your opinion on what you think my next action should be. For I know that even without speaking a word you will give me the advice I must follow. If I use all the time I am lawfully entitled to,[31] I shall reap the rewards of my labour, hard work and diligence: such a prosecution would make it clear that no one within living memory came to court more prepared, more perceptive or with a better-arranged case. But in the middle of the praise showered on my hard work there is a risk that the defendant will slip from our grasp. What, then, can be done? That, I think, is quite clear and obvious. 33. The praise I would have reaped from an uninterrupted speech I shall keep for another time; as it is, I shall prosecute this man using records, witnesses, private and public documents and other evidence. This struggle will be between me and you, Hortensius. To speak candidly: if I thought that here we were going to fight it out in oratory and refuting criminal charges, I would expend my energy on my prosecution speech and elaborating on the charges, but since you have decided to fight me not as *your* natural impulse would demand but unscrupulously as the demands of *his* case do, I must outmanoeuvre your strategy. 34. Your plan is to begin your response after two sets of games; mine is to complete the first stage[32] of the trial before the first one is held. Your scheme will be judged cunning – my manoeuvre necessary.

To return to what I had begun to say – that this struggle will be between you and me – here is the situation. I undertook this case at the request of the Sicilians, thinking it brought me considerable honour and glory that people who had experienced my incorruptibility and diligence were willing to put to the test my integrity and pertinacity. Then after I embarked on it, I set myself a greater task, one which would show the Roman people my goodwill towards the Republic. 35. For it did not seem a worthy test of my hard work and effort to bring a man to court who had already been condemned in everyone's eyes, unless your unbearable dominance and chauvinism – something you have employed over recent years in a number of trials – would be used even to defend the case of this desperate man. But now, since your oppression and reign over the law-courts give you such delight, and there are men around whose lust and infamy do not shame or tire them out and – as if it were their job – seem to scramble to make the Roman people hate and resent them – I declare I have undertaken a great and personally very risky cause, but one for which I must use all the strength and diligence my youth[33] gives me. 36. Since the shamelessness and outrageous actions of a cabal are dragging down our whole class (not to mention how the infamy of our courts is threatening us), I declare that I am a prosecutor hostile to such men, a dogged and determined adversary worthy of their hatred. I claim that as mine. *I demand that as mine.* I shall do this as magistrate. I shall do this from the platform the Roman people wished me to stand on from the first of January, and with them at my side I shall act against evil and for the Republic. I promise the Roman people this will be the most magnificent spectacle I give as an aedile.[34] I warn. I promise. I give them notice. Those who habitually deposit, accept, handle or promise bribes, those who hold the money or act as go-betweens for corrupting courts or promise their muscle or shamelessness, should not commit or even *think* about that unholy crime in *this* court.

37. In January Hortensius will be a consul with full military and civil authority, but I shall be an aedile – little more than a private citizen. Yet the case I am promising to argue is so important, so welcome and pleasing to the Roman people, that in comparison to me the consul himself will appear (if such a thing can be!) even less than a private citizen. This is not just talk: I shall lay out with definitive evidence all the wicked and criminal verdicts given over the ten years[35] since the Senate gained control of the courts. 38. I shall tell the Roman people why during the fifty years[36] the equestrians were in control of this court there was no trial where there was even the slightest suspicion of votes being sold for money. And *why*, after the Senate gained control of the courts and the Roman people lost their power over all of you, after his conviction Quintus Calidius[37] said that a jury could not in all decency convict an ex-praetor for less than 3 million sesterces. The Senate's control is why during Quintus Hortensius' term as praetor, after the senator Publius Septimius was convicted, he was fined for extortion and because he had sold his vote when a juror. 39. The same was true of the senators Gaius Herennius and Gaius Popilius, both convicted for embezzling public funds; it was made very clear in the case of Marcus Atilius' conviction for treason. All these men had sold their votes. When Verres, as

city praetor, was in charge of the lots, there were senators who voted against a defendant although they did not have a clue about his case. There was even a senator who took money from the defendant to swing the jury *and* from the prosecutor to condemn the defendant![38] 40. What possible protest can match this blemish, this disgrace, this catastrophe for our entire class: *while the senatorial class provided our community's jurors*, the juries' votes were marked with different colours.[39] You have my promise that I shall deal with all of this diligently and severely.

Finally, what do you think will be my state of mind if I discover an abuse of the law has been committed in *this* court for some similar reason? Especially when I can prove beyond doubt that Verres frequently repeated in the presence of many witnesses that he had a powerful friend who gave him the confidence to loot his province, and he was not just seeking money for himself but, given how he had allotted the three years of his time as governor in Sicily, would think he had done quite well for himself if he could deposit the profit from one year to his bank account – for he would give the proceeds of one year to his patrons and defence team and keep all the profit from his most profitable year for his jury. 41. I knew the Roman people were thoroughly shaken by such comments; which is why I recently mentioned to Marcus Glabrio, when I was challenging the jurors, that I thought the result of all this would be that foreign nations would send embassies to the Roman people to ask them to abolish our extortion laws and courts. For if there were no courts, then every individual would steal only what he felt was enough for himself and his children; now, because of the state of our courts, each one steals what will be enough for himself, his patrons, his supporters, the praetor *and* the jurors. This need is bottomless; they can only give enough to satisfy the avarice of the greediest, not to pay for the legal victories of the guiltiest.

42. These are our famous courts! This is the glorious reputation of our class! The allies of the Roman people do not wish there to be extortion courts, courts our ancestors established to protect our allies! Would Verres ever have held any faint hope of acquittal if he did not also fully share that evil opinion of

you? Since he thinks that you are like him in crimes, perjury and greed, you should hate him more than the Roman people do – if such a thing is possible. 43. By the immortal gods, jurors, you need to think and act here. Like a prophet I warn you, I know this well: the gods gave you this chance to free our entire class from hatred, envy, infamy, disgrace. People believe there is no rigour in our courts, no scruples and *that there are now no courts at all*. The Roman people sneer at and despise us; our heavy and constant infamy consumes us. 44. This was why the Roman people asked us so eagerly to restore the power of the tribunes;[40] it might have seemed as if it were speaking out for that but it was really demanding honest courts. When Gnaeus Pompey, a remarkably brave and distinguished man, was bringing a motion in the Senate to restore the tribunes' veto, that very wise and great man Quintus Catulus saw this; when he was asked his opinion, he said this with all his great authority: 'Senators have presided over the courts wickedly and shamefully, but if they had shown willingness in their verdicts to live up to the Roman people's expectations, they would not be so eager for the return of the tribunes' veto.'

45. Finally, as Pompey held his first public meeting outside the city[41] as consul-elect and showed he would restore the tribunes' power of veto, as it was so much looked for, right at that point in his speech a rumble and a thankful murmur ran through the assembly. But then, when he said at the same assembly that the provinces had been devastated and tormented, the courts were foul and criminal and he wanted to look at that issue and resolve it, *then* the Roman people showed their approval, not with a rumble but with an almighty noise. 46. There are now men positioned on watch-towers; they observe how each and every one of us conducts himself, upholds his oath and preserves the laws. For they see that even after the restoration of the tribunes' power, only one senator – one with very little money – was convicted. While they are not unhappy about that conviction, they certainly do not think it is something they should spend a lot of effort in praising. To be honest, there is not much to praise about a case where no one is able to or even tries to corrupt you. 47. This is a court in which you

will judge the defendant and the Roman people will judge *you*.
Here, with this man, it will be seen if it is possible that a senatorial jury can condemn someone extremely guilty – and extremely
rich. Here is a defendant whose case is made up of nothing
except a large amount of money and an even larger amount of
immorality; if you acquit him, the only suspicion that can hang
over you is the worst one. It will not look as if he cancelled out
his many great vices by influence, by blood-relationships, by
any proper action or even by the fact that his vices were not
beyond the norm.

48. To close this speech, jurors, this is how I shall conduct
the case: I shall offer evidence so glaring, so well witnessed and
so enormously blatant that no one can press you as a personal
favour to acquit him. I have a clear path and plan of action, one
which has enabled me to investigate and gain an exact knowledge of their stratagems. My conduct of this case will open not
just the ears but the eyes of the Roman people to all their tricks.
49. After so many years you – yes, *you* – can now remove and
destroy the disgraceful reputation and infamy our class has
laboured under. Everyone agrees that since the present courts
were established there has never been a jury so brilliant or so
well thought of. If anything amiss occurs here, no one will
decide that other, more suitable jurors should be looked for
among our class, but that they should be sought from an entirely
different one. 50. It is for this reason I look first to the immortal
gods; I think they hope for the same as I do: that no one finds
in this court any disloyal person, except for someone who has
long had a reputation as such. If it turns out that there are many
of this sort here, I assure you, the jurors *and* the Roman people,
that I would lay down my life before I laid down the energy and
perseverance needed to pursue their shameless behaviour. 51. I
promise that with hard work and through dangers and hostili-
ties I shall vigilantly pursue any dereliction of duty.

Glabrio, you can ensure one does not occur by using your
authority, wisdom and diligence. Stand up for the courts, stand
up for strictness, honesty, integrity and respect for oaths; stand
up for the Senate so that when the court has shown its worth,
the Roman people can praise and thank it. Think about who

you are, the position you hold, what you ought to give to the
Roman people and what you owe to your ancestors. Call to
your mind the law your father passed,[42] which gave the Roman
people the best and most rigorous extortion courts. 52. Great
precedents surround you and prevent you from forgetting the
praise due to your family; they remind you day and night that
your father was very brave, your grandfather[43] very wise and
your father-in-law highly respected. If you have the force and
energy of your father to stand up to shameless men, the intelligence of your grandfather Scaevola to foresee the plots prepared
against your reputation and the rest of the jury, if you have
the firmness of your father-in-law Scaurus,[44] no one will be able
to move you from an honest and correct verdict. The Roman
people will understand that, with so honourable and honest a
praetor and with so choice a jury, the amount of a guilty
defendant's wealth will make him seem guiltier rather than provide him with an escape route.

53. I am resolved not to make the blunder of allowing the
praetor and jury in this case to be changed. I shall not allow
this case to be so prolonged that the consuls can send their lictors to summon the same Sicilians who did not budge when the
consul-elect sent his slaves to summon them in a group – certainly
a novel move.[45] I shall not allow that wretched men – who
before were allies and friends of the Roman people, but are
now their slaves and suppliants – are stripped at a consul's
command, not just of their legal rights and all their fortunes
but even the chance to bewail their lost rights.

54. Clearly I shall not allow the defence to respond forty
days after my closing speech when the lapse of time will ensure
my speech for the prosecution is forgotten, nor allow the case
to be ruled on when this crowd from all over Italy will have left
Rome, a crowd drawn from everywhere and here now because
of the elections, games and the census. The praise your verdict
will bring and the risk you take of giving offence is yours, the
labour and worry, mine. I think the knowledge of what is at
stake and the memory of who said what should belong to
everyone. 55. What I shall do is nothing new – it has been
done before by men who are now the leading citizens of our

community[46] – that is, I shall immediately bring on my witnesses. But, jurors, what is new is how I shall organize the witnesses to cover the whole case, and when I have supported their testimony with questions, arguments and speeches, then I shall show how the witnesses align with specific charges. There will be no difference between the usual form of prosecution and my new one – except that usually the witnesses are produced after all the arguments have been made. Here they will be produced along with each charge and the other side will also have the opportunity for questions, arguments and speeches. If there is anyone who misses uninterrupted speeches and accusations, he will hear it in the second stage of the trial; he should understand that my action comes from necessity and I act this way to outmanoeuvre their cunning.

This will be the first part of the prosecution: 56. We allege that Gaius Verres committed many lecherous and cruel actions both against Roman citizens and allies, many unholy ones against gods and men and extorted 40 million sesterces from Sicily. I shall prove this so clearly, with witnesses, public and private records and proofs, that you will decide that even if I had the time and free days at my command there was still no need for a long speech.

I have spoken.

For the Manilian Law

Delivered in 66 to the people from
the Rostra[1] in the Forum

This speech, also known as On the Command of Pompey, *delivered when Cicero was praetor, was his first political speech. He had delivered many in the courts before, many in the Senate and many while campaigning for office, but none from the Rostra. His topic: handing the command of the war in Asia with Mithridates, king of Pontus, to Gnaeus Pompey.*

Rome first gained a permanent foothold in Asia when Attalus III of Pergamum left her his kingdom in 133; in 129 the Romans formally organized the territory into the province of Asia. It was an immense source of revenue for the state, for Roman tax collectors and various rapacious governors. As might be imagined, none of this endeared them much to the locals. Hence the appeal of Mithridates IV Eupator, the king of Pontus, who provided the Romans with one of their greatest challenges. He succeeded to the throne of Pontus around 119 at fourteen years of age and fought three wars with Rome: the somewhat unimaginatively but conveniently named First Mithridatic War (88–84), Second Mithridatic War (83–81) and the Third Mithridatic War (74–63), of which the last was being fought at the time of this speech.

There is not space here to give more than a brief sketch of the genesis of the wars between Rome and Pontus, though some information will aid in understanding what was at stake. Mithridates expanded out of Pontus and conquered Colchis and the Crimean peninsula, where various smaller Greek states seem to have seen him as a welcome protector against the threat of the Romans on the one side and the Scythians on the other. In 91 Sulla, then governor of Cilicia, expelled Mithridates' choice for the king of Cappadocia and placed Ariobarzanes on the throne. As soon as Sulla left Asia, Tigranes (Mithridates' son-in-law and ally) drove Ariobarzanes from the throne at Mithridates' instigation. At the death of Nicomedes II the king of Bithynia, his successor, Nicomedes III, was also driven from his throne, to be replaced by Mithridates' choice.

At this time, Rome was occupied by the Social War and her resources were seriously engaged elsewhere; however, when the Senate sent the ex-consul Manius Aquilius as an ambassador to restore both kings to their thrones, Mithridates gave way. But Aquilius did not stop there; eager to make money, he encouraged Nicomedes to invade Pontus. (The Romans had forces in the region under the command of Lucius Cassius, the then governor of Asia.) Mithridates complained to the Romans, who responded by warning him not to use force to expel Nicomedes; he in turn promptly reoccupied Cappadocia.

While war was declared in 89, it was in the spring of 88 that the First Mithridatic War truly began. Given the extent of Roman misrule and greed in Asia, it is not surprising that Mithridates was initially welcomed by many Greek states. Although lenient with some Romans who fell into his hands, he was vicious with others, including Aquilius (for his death, see chapter 11 with note 14). He also ordered his commanders in various towns to kill all the Romans and Italians, free or slaves, they could find; around 80,000 people were slaughtered.

In 87 Sulla was dispatched to deal with the situation; he agreed to terms with Mithridates which left the king with Pontus but laid a huge indemnity of 20,000 talents on the entire province; this was to leave it in debt for many years. However, Sulla's agreement was never ratified, and Lucius Murena, who had been left in charge of two legions, took the opportunity to attack Mithridates, and thus began the Second Mithridatic War. Murena entered Pontus but was defeated in 82 at the River Halys; this did not stop him from claiming the title of imperator, victorious general, and eventually holding a triumph. Peace was renewed in 81 but again never ratified. In 75 Mithridates declared war once more, making an alliance with Sertorius, a rebel Roman general in Spain. The consul Lucius

Lucullus was sent to Asia with command of five legions, the other consul, Marcus Aurelius Cotta, was sent to Bithynia, while the praetor Marcus Antonius was sent to secure control of the sea. Cotta met with failure and was shut up in Chalcedon; Lucullus had considerably more success. He entered Pontus in 73 and defeated Mithridates' army in 72 at Cabira on the River Lycus. However, Mithridates fled to Tigranes and when Lucullus demanded his surrender, the Romans came into conflict with Tigranes' considerable power and military resources. While Lucullus had some great military successes in Armenia, there were also some setbacks: his army mutinied in 68 and in 67 a force, under his lieutenant Gaius Triarius, was almost totally wiped out. Subsequently, his opponents in Rome began to move against him; the result was the lex Manilia, *proposed by Gaius Manilius, tribune of the plebs for 66.*

As this speech deals extensively with Pompey's military career, I shall not discuss it here beyond a comment on his command in 67 against the pirates (piracy was a considerable problem in the Mediterranean during this period); in that year, Aulus Gabinius, a tribune of the plebs, had proposed that a single general be given command of this war. His proposal granted this general enormous power, giving him imperium *for three years over the entire Mediterranean and all the provinces for 50 miles inland. Although Gabinius did not mention the general, it was clear that the people would chose Pompey; the Senate reacted violently and Gabinius was lucky to escape without being lynched. Pompey's campaign against the pirates was phenomenally successful, clearing the Mediterranean in about three months. In 66, Gaius Manilius proposed that the command of the war against Mithridates should be transferred to Pompey. Under his proposal, Pompey would retain all the powers he had under the* lex Gabinia *and receive authority, not just over the Roman provinces in the area (Asia, Bithynia and Cilicia) but across all Asia as far as Armenia. Such an immense amount of power being invested in one man was bound to attract violent reactions from the* optimates, *especially as it required the current consuls to resign before the end of their year of office. Quintus Lutatius Catulus and Quintus Hortensius*

spoke strongly against it, while, among others, Cicero and
Gaius Julius Caesar spoke for it; all the tribes voted in favour.

To support this measure, Cicero went against the wishes of
the faction he was closest to in the Senate. The question of
why remains. Certainly, Pompey was extremely powerful and
Cicero was very ambitious; Pompey's aid in a campaign for the
consulship would be worth a great deal. His support of the
measure also made him popular with the people, who clearly
were in favour of Pompey's command. He would also help the
equestrians, whose interests Cicero had always backed; they
hated Lucullus, supported Pompey and it was their interests
which were at stake in Asia.

The speech divides into three main sections. The first (chap-
ters 1–19) deals with the necessity for the war (hardly something
anyone needed to be convinced of). The second part (chapters
20–26) discusses the sheer size and danger of the war (again,
probably not something anyone needed to be convinced of).
The last (chapter 27 onwards) deals with the choice of the
commander and is a panegyric for Pompey, both as a com-
mander and a human being of extraordinary decency. While
one doubts that any mortal person could ever approach the
heights that Cicero's praises raise Pompey to, they are still a
fascinating sketch of the qualities that the Romans wanted to
believe a commander and governor could and should possess.

1. Citizens, although the sight of you crowding an assembly
has always given me immense pleasure, and I consider this
place[2] the most important one from which to plead, and as
granting deep honour to a speech, I have kept myself from
treading this path to glory – one always open to prominent
men – not by inclination but because of the principles by which
I have governed my life since I came of age. As I did not dare to
approach this influential place before today because of my
youth (I had resolved that nothing should be presented here
except the finished and polished product of my talent and hard
work), I thought all my time should be devoted to my friends

in their times of need. 2. So, while this place was never without men to champion your cause, I expended my energy honourably and irreproachably in dealing with the dangers to private individuals – for which you have voted me the greatest rewards. Citizens, when the postponement of the elections meant the votes of all the assembled centuries placed me at the top of the polls *three times*, I quickly understood your verdict on me and your advice to other candidates.[3] Now, since I possess the great authority you bestowed on me when you elected me, and as much ability in the law-courts as an energetic man can gain from his daily practice there, I shall certainly use whatever authority I possess among those who gave it to me. Surely, if my oratory can enable me to achieve anything, I shall demonstrate this to those who voted to reward that ability rather than to anyone else. 3. What is more, I see I should above all be properly delighted that, unaccustomed as I am in how to speak from the Rostra, the topic is one on which no one could be at a loss for words. For I must speak about the exceptional, the unique, abilities of Gnaeus Pompey – and with *him* it is harder to find a place to stop than to begin! In fact, I have to look not for a place to start but a place to end.

4. So, to begin with the origin of this whole situation: two very powerful kings, Mithridates and Tigranes, are waging a critical and dangerous war against your subjects and allies. Both – Mithridates by being left incompletely subdued and Tigranes through provocation[4] – consider that they now have the opportunity to seize our province of Asia. Every day Roman equestrians, worthy men, whose considerable capital is at stake, invested as it is in collecting your taxes, receive letters from Asia; because of my close connection with their class,[5] these men have informed me of what is at stake for the Republic and the danger to their own capital. 5. In your province of Bithynia,[6] many villages have been burned to the ground and the kingdom of Ariobarzanes,[7] which borders your subject territories, is entirely in the enemy's hands; Lucius Lucullus, in spite of his great achievements, is withdrawing from the fight. His successor[8] is not well enough prepared to conduct a war of this size; all allies and citizens urgently demand one person

alone to command the war, the single – the only – man our
enemies fear. 6. You see the situation: now consider what needs
to be done.

I think my first task is to discuss what type of war this is,
then its importance and, finally, the right commander to select.
It is the type of war that should particularly awaken your courage and kindle in you a desire for victory. The glorious reputation
your ancestors handed down to the Roman people and a reputation for greatness in all your deeds and for supremacy in
warfare are not the only things at stake here. The safety of our
allies and friends is at stake, a safety for which many of your
ancestors waged hard wars. Rome's greatest and most dependable revenues are at stake. If you lose these revenues, you will
no longer have the luxuries of peace and the resources for war.
The properties of many citizens are at stake, citizens whose
interests you must consider for their own sake – and for the
Republic's. 7. Since, beyond any other race, you have always
sought fame and been greedy for glory, you must wipe out the
stain incurred in the first war with Mithridates,[9] a stain which
has seeped in and has been too long a black mark on the name
of the Roman people. He – the man who, throughout Asia and
a multitude of states, on one day, with one message, one stroke
of the pen, singled out Roman citizens to be murdered and
butchered – has not only *not* paid the penalty appropriate for
his crime[10] but is still king twenty-three years later! He is not a
king content with lurking in the shadows of Pontus and Cappadocia, but one who comes out of his ancestral kingdom and
struts about your subject lands in broad daylight.

8. Our commanders have fought with this king in a way that
ensured they brought home victory's trappings – not victory.
Lucius Sulla and Lucius Murena – two very brave men, and
great commanders – celebrated triumphs over Mithridates, but
this was as far as their victories went: although they defeated
and conquered him, he still continued to rule. Still, we must
praise them for what they achieved and pardon them for what
they left undone, as the political situation called Sulla back to
Italy, where he recalled Murena.[11] 9. Mithridates, however,
devoted the entire interval between wars not to forgetting the

old war but preparing himself for the new one. After building and fitting out a great fleet and raising a massive army from wherever he could, he made a show of attacking his neighbours on the Bosphorus and sent messengers with dispatches as far as Spain to the generals we were then fighting there, so that faced with war on land and sea, with two enemy armies acting in concert and in two very different and distant locations, you would have to fight for supremacy torn by a war on two fronts.[12] 10. The inspired strategy and unique courage of Gnaeus Pompey defeated the danger from Sertorius and Spain, a front with by far the greater support and strength. On the other front, Lucius Lucullus, an exceptional man, conducted his campaign in such a way that his initial remarkable and great achievements did not seem due to his good luck but to his character, and the recent disasters with which his campaign ended appeared not to be his fault but down to bad luck. I shall speak more about Lucullus later, and I shall speak about him in such a way, citizens, that my oration will not look as if it is depriving him of his true praise or giving him false praise.

11. As for the honour and reputation of your empire – the opening topic of my speech – reflect on how you should think about this. Your ancestors often went to war after minor mistreatment of our merchants and shipowners. So, tell me, how should you feel after one message caused the death of all those thousands of Romans in one fell stroke? Our elders decided to wipe out Corinth, that shining city of Greece, because it had addressed Roman ambassadors rather disrespectfully.[13] Will you allow a king, who killed an ambassador[14] – *an ex-consul*, indeed! – after piling chains on him, whipping him and torturing him in every way he could, to go unpunished? Your ancestors would not allow any infringement of the freedom of Roman citizens; will *you* shrug off the taking of their lives? They avenged ambassadors violated by words alone; will you do nothing about the murder of one after he was tortured in every possible way? 12. Beware, in case it turns out that, just as it was their greatest achievement to pass on to you a great reputation, it becomes your greatest shame to be unable to defend and preserve their gift. Then again, tell me how should you

bear the terrible threat to the safety of your allies? King Ariobarzanes, an ally and friend to the Roman people, was driven
out of his kingdom.[15] Two kings threaten all Asia – and not just
your enemies but your friends and allies; communities all over
Asia and Greece must look for help because of the size of the
threat. They demand one particular commander from you, a
demand they know they cannot make without considerable
danger as you have already sent them someone else.[16]

13. They see and feel as you do: there is one man who possesses all the essential qualities and is close to the action[17] – and
that makes them feel his absence all the more. They feel his
arrival – indeed, *his name* – has checked and slowed the enemy's
attacks even though he is only there to fight a naval war with
the pirates. Since they are not allowed to speak out loud, in
silence they ask you to judge them worthy to have their safety
entrusted to a man such as him – just as you have done with
your allies in other provinces. Or even more worthy, because
we have empowered and sent into their province men with such
characters that even if they defend an allied city from the enemy,
they march into it much as a victorious enemy does a captured
city. They had already heard of Pompey, but now that they see
in the flesh his great self-control, mercy and human decency,
they think that the people with whom he stays the longest are
the happiest on earth.

14. If, even though they were personally uninjured, our
ancestors waged war with Antiochus, Philip, the Aetolians and
the Carthaginians, on behalf of their allies, how eager should
you be, men provoked by injuries, to defend the safety of your
allies *and* your empire, especially when what is at stake is your
greatest source of revenue? Citizens, revenues from other provinces barely enable us to protect them; Asia is so rich and fertile
that she easily excels all other countries in the productiveness
of her fields, in the variety of her crops, the size of her pastures
and the sheer volume of her exports. So if you wish to keep
both your military advantage and peacetime comforts, not only
must you protect this province from catastrophe, but from *fear*
of catastrophe. 15. In other cases it is when catastrophe strikes
that a loss is incurred; but with taxes, it is not just the onset of

trouble but the fear of it that brings catastrophe. Even when there is no invasion, people give up their cattle farming, abandon agriculture and cease trade on the seas when the enemy's forces are close by. Then one cannot retain any tax revenue from customs duties, tithes or grazing fees, and an entire year's income is often lost because of a single rumour of danger and one moment of fear of war. 16. Tell me, what do you think are the thoughts of those who pay taxes to us or who manage or collect them when two kings with huge armies are on their doorstep?[18] When one cavalry raid can in hours destroy a whole year's revenue? When tax collectors consider that province a high-risk zone for their large slave staff as they gather the taxes from the pastures, arable land, the ports and custom houses? Do you think that you will profit from their work if you do not protect those who produce that profit – and not just, as I said before, protect them from catastrophe but also from the fear of it?

17. I said when I began discussing the nature of this war that I would finish by talking about how it is affecting the property of many Romans. This is not something you should ignore; your good sense demands that you carefully take it into account. For the tax collectors – an extremely honourable and distinguished group – have transferred their business interests and capital to Asia; their business and fortunes ought by their nature to be your concern. If we have always thought that taxes form the backbone of the state, we shall certainly be right to say that the class that collects them supports all other classes. 18. Additionally, you should think of the enterprising and hard-working men from other classes, some of whom are doing business in person in Asia; in their absence you should look after their interests. And there are still further groups who have a great deal of money invested there. Your sense of human decency should lead you to protect so many fellow-citizens from ruin, and your intelligence should make you realize that the ruin of so many citizens cannot be separated from the Republic's. In the first place, it matters very little if we recover our tax base after a victory but the tax collectors lose their investment; their ruin will ensure they do not have the capacity to bid on the contracts, and fear will make sure that others have no desire to bid.

19. Secondly, we should remember the lesson the same province and the very same Mithridates taught us at the beginning
of the Asiatic war, especially as we learnt it the hard way. We
know that after many people lost great fortunes in Asia, the
suspension of repayments caused credit to collapse in Rome. It
is not possible for so many to lose property and fortunes in one
community without dragging many others down with them.
Protect the Republic from this and trust me (although you can
see it for yourselves): the system of credit and finance which
operates in the Forum, and in Rome, is completely inseparable
from the money at risk in Asia. This cannot be lost without
taking with it Rome's banking system.[19] This is why you should
not allow yourselves to hesitate in throwing your weight and
all your energy into this war, a war to defend your reputation,
the safety of your allies, a huge portion of your revenue and the
fortunes of many fellow-citizens – all connected with the good
of the Republic.

20. Since I have spoken about the nature of the war, I shall
now speak a little about its sheer size. For it could be said that,
although the war is inevitable, its extent is not something to be
particularly afraid of. On this point I need to take particular
care in case you feel the very thing you should take precautions
against is beneath your attention. So it is clear that I give Lucius
Lucullus the praise which a brave man, a wise person and a
great commander deserves: I tell you that when he arrived in
Asia, Mithridates' army was large, well equipped with everything it needed, and Mithridates himself was besieging and
vigorously attacking Cyzicus,[20] the most splendid and loyal city
in Asia. Lucius Lucullus raised this extremely dangerous siege
by heroism, perseverance and strategy. 21. He defeated and
sank a large, well-equipped fleet which was speeding towards
Italy, propelled by passionate hatred and commanded by Ser-
torian officers. He also wiped out many other forces in battles,
opening up Pontus to our legions, a place the Romans had previously found closed at every access point. By simply turning
up and advancing he took Sinope and Amisus[21] where Mithridates had palaces, both of which were packed with supplies; he
added many other cities in Pontus and Cappadocia. The king,

stripped of his ancestral kingdom, went begging to other kings and nations. And Lucullus achieved all this without burdening our allies or drawing on our taxes.[22] Enough praise, I think – generous enough that you see that those who now sneer at this law did not give equal praise to Lucius Lucullus when they spoke from this platform.

22. Given what I have just said, I imagine someone will ask the reasonable question of how the remainder of the war can amount to anything significant. I shall answer. Firstly, Mithridates fled from his kingdom just as they say the notorious Medea did when she fled from Pontus;[23] we are told she scattered her own brother's limbs behind her all along the route of her father's pursuit, so that pausing to collect them, and his paternal grief, would slow him down. Like her, the fleeing Mithridates left behind him in Pontus all his enormous cache of gold and silver[24] and all manner of beautiful objects piled up in his kingdom (some of this he had inherited, some he had looted from all over Asia during his first war). While our men were rather too careful in collecting this, the king himself slipped from their hands. Happiness slowed our men's pursuit just as grief did Aeetes'.

23. Tigranes, the king of Armenia, took Mithridates in as he fled in fear, braced him as he worried about his fortunes, gave him backbone and new life. After Lucius Lucullus and his army arrived in Tigranes' kingdom, still more nations were whipped up against our commander. Nations the Roman people had never thought of going to war with, or even disturbing, were filled with fear; a deep-seated and violent belief spread through the barbarian nations that the army had been brought to these shores to loot a very wealthy and revered shrine.[25] And thus a new, terrifying fear goaded on many large tribes. To add to the problems, our army was affected by its overwhelming remoteness and a longing for family, even though it had captured a city in Tigranes' kingdom and enjoyed success in the field. 24. I shall say no more on this matter here.[26] The outcome was that our soldiers wanted an early retreat from these regions rather than pushing deeper. Mithridates, with the assistance of refugees from his own kingdom and a great number of additional forces provided by many kings and tribes, had already rallied

his own troops. We know it is usually the case that when kings' fortunes are crushed, they attract resources from many powerful people in sympathy; this is especially the situation with other kings and those who have kings as their rulers, as they see a royal name as something great and sacred.

25. So it was that in defeat Mithridates was able to accomplish results he would never have dared to hope for in the days of his prosperity. And after he recovered his kingdom, he was not content to arrive back home (an outcome beyond his wildest hopes) after being driven from it, but even attacked our victorious and glorious army. Citizens, allow me to pass over our defeat – as poets who write about Roman history do – a defeat so terrible that our commander heard about it from reports from natives instead of a messenger from the battle.[27] 26. Lucius Lucullus, right at the hour of his misfortune and military disaster, might still have been able to remedy the situation to some degree; but then, believing a limit should be set on a long command, in accordance with our traditions, you, the people, commanded him to release from duty those soldiers who had completed their service and transfer others to Manius Glabrio. I know there is much I am not mentioning here: visualize all that for yourselves, reflect on how great this war has become, a war in which many powerful kings are allying to fight, aggravated tribes are starting up again, a war which fresh nations are taking up and one that your new commander will undertake after the defeat of a veteran army.

27. I think I have talked long enough about why this war is inevitable by its very nature and dangerous because of its size. It would appear that I only need speak about picking the general for the war and appointing him to lead such an important campaign. Citizens, I only wish you had such a tremendous supply of brave and incorruptible men that you would find it difficult to select a particular person to take charge of this war! But now, since Pompey is the only man to have overcome by his heroism not just the current generation but also the legacy of the previous one, what can cast a shadow of doubt in anyone's mind?

28. It is my belief that a supreme commander must have these four qualities: knowledge of military affairs, heroism, a

commanding presence and good fortune. Who has ever been –
or could help being – more knowledgeable about war than
Pompey? He was tutored from his childhood and schooldays
by training in a great war and in the school of war by fighting
in his father's army against our bitterest enemy.[28] From the last
days of his childhood he was a soldier in the army of a great
general. He was himself a general of a great army while still an
adolescent; he has fought more often with the enemy than anyone else has squabbled with his rivals; he has waged more wars
than others have read about; he has held more commands than
others have dreamed of. From the end of his boyhood he was
schooled in the art of war, not by abstract theory but by holding his own commands, not by military disasters but by
successes, not by the number of campaigns fought but by victories he won. In short, is there any type of warfare in which the
Republic's misfortune has not trained him? Civil, Gallic, Spanish wars (the last waged against a hostile alliance of Roman
citizens and very war-like tribes), slave and naval wars – this
man alone has not just fought dissimilar wars, with different
enemies, but been successful in them *all*. This clearly shows
that there is no matter involving military experience which is
beyond his knowledge.

29. What speech could do justice to the abilities of Gnaeus
Pompey? What can I say which is worthy of him, new to you
or that everyone has not already heard? And a general must not
just possess the talents which everyone considers necessary,
that is, hard work in dealing with problems, courage in the face
of danger, acting with purpose, swiftness in finishing a campaign and wisdom in planning ahead. Although, it is certain,
we have never seen nor heard of a general who possesses all
these qualities more than Pompey. 30. My witness is Italy,
which Lucius Sulla himself – a great conqueror – confessed that
Pompey's heroic assistance freed. My witness is Sicily, the
island he rescued, not with the terror of war but with strategic
speed, even though many threats surrounded it. My witness is
Africa,[29] which, although it had been overrun with hordes of
the enemy, ran red with their blood. My witness is Gaul,
through which he opened a path to Spain for our legions by

exterminating the Gallic tribes. My witness is Spain, which saw
him repeatedly beat – and crush – many enemies.[30] And again
and again Italy is my witness, which was in the grip of a horrible and dangerous slave war; it sought his aid although he
was absent. That war dwindled away and evaporated at the
anticipation of his arrival and was entirely destroyed and buried when he arrived.[31] 31. Finally, these days every region is my
witness, as is every foreign nation and tribe, every sea, every
shore, every bay and every harbour.

In recent years,[32] what place throughout our seas had such
secure defences that it was completely safe? What place was so
remote that it escaped the notice of pirates? What traveller did
not risk death since he had to choose between sailing in winter
or when the sea was awash with pirates? Who would have
thought that many commanders in a single year or one commander over the course of many years could have ended such a
massive war – a longstanding and widespread disgrace? 32.
During these years, did you have a single province free from
pirate raids? Were any of your tax revenues safe? Did you
defend any of our allies? Did your navy protect anyone? How
many islands do you think people deserted? How many allied
cities did fear empty – or pirates capture? Why talk of distant
lands! There was once a time when it was the particular pride
of the Roman people to fight wars far from home and to defend
not our own roofs but the fortunes of our allies at the outer
defences of the empire. Do I have to tell you that in these past
years the sea was closed to our allies when our own army could
not even depart from Brundisium[33] except in the depths of winter? Why should I complain about the capture of ambassadors
from foreign tribes on their way to Rome when we had to ran-
som our own ones! Do I have to tell you that the sea was not
safe for merchants when twelve lictors[34] fell into the hands of
the pirates? 33. Or that the noble cities of Cnidus or Colophon
or Samos and innumerable others were captured, when you
know that your own ports – ports from which you draw the
breath of life – fell into the hands of pirates? Are you honestly
unaware that the port of Caieta was looted in full view of a
praetor when it was crowded with ships? Or that the children

of the very man who had waged war with pirates in the past were abducted from Misenum by pirates?[35] Why should I complain about the misfortune – that disgraceful blot on the Republic – at Ostia when, almost within your sight, pirates captured and sunk a fleet placed under the command of a Roman consul? By the immortal gods! How could the superhuman abilities of one remarkable man bring, in such a short time, such a ray of hope to the Republic that you, men who only recently saw an enemy fleet along the banks of the Tiber, hear now that there is no pirate ship within the banks of the Mediterranean.[36]

34. Although you all know the speed with which this was accomplished, *I* should still mention it here. Was anyone ever so gripped by passion for business or pursuit of profit that they travelled to as many places or finished so many journeys with the speed that the storm clouds of war swept across the sea when Pompey was our general? Although it was not the sailing season, he landed in Sicily, reconnoitred in Africa and from there sailed to Sardinia, securing the three granaries of the Republic with very strong defences on land and sea. 35. Then, after he had returned to Italy, he strengthened the two provinces of Spain and Transalpine Gaul with garrisons and ships, sent more ships to the coast of the Illyrian Sea, Achaia and all Greece and provided the Adriatic and Italian waters with great defences on land and sea. And it was he himself who, within forty-nine days – counting from the day he left Brundisium – added all of Cilicia to the empire of the Roman people.[37] No matter where they were, all the pirates were either captured or killed or surrendered to the authority and power of Pompey alone. To add to this, after the Cretans sent ambassadors all the way to Pamphylia to plead with him, he did not dash all their hopes of surrendering on terms, but demanded hostages.[38] At the end of winter, Pompey made his preparations for this great and interminable war, which had spread far and wide and distressed every nation and tribe; he began it at the start of spring; he ended it in the middle of summer.

36. Such is his inspired and remarkable ability for command. And what about the other qualities I mentioned a little while ago, of which he has a surfeit? For in a supreme and

perfect commander, one ought not only to seek an ability to wage war, as there are many other exceptional skills which are the aides and comrades of this ability. First, commanders must be extremely incorruptible and self-controlled in every situation. They must be true to their word, brilliant, accessible and decent people. Let us briefly consider how many of these qualities Gnaeus Pompey has. Citizens, although he possesses them to the highest degree, you can see and understand them better when you compare him with others rather than examining him on his own. 37. Can we count a man as a commander if the position of centurion has been and continues to be auctioned off in his army? Can we imagine that a man has great and honourable intentions for the Republic when he has distributed among various magistrates money he drew from the treasury to conduct a war because he wanted to hang onto his province, or, because of greed, left it in Rome to turn a profit? Citizens, I see from your response that you know of men who have done such things; but I name no names and thus no one can become angry with me – unless he wants first to admit his guilt.

Who here does not know that our commanders' greed results in our armies bringing with them enormous destruction? 38. Remember how in recent years our commanders marched in Italy through the fields and towns of Roman citizens,[39] and then it will be only too easy for you to imagine their behaviour among foreign tribes. In the past few years, what do you think has happened more often: that our soldiers have destroyed more hostile *cities* with their weapons or more *allies* by wintering in their communities? A commander cannot restrain an army if he cannot control himself; he will not be severe when he sits in judgement on others if he does not want others to judge him severely. 39. Given this, are we surprised that Pompey stands out so much, when people say that as his legions marched into Asia wherever they went the hands and marching feet of his immense army caused no harm to any non-combatant? And in addition, there are daily reports and letters on how our soldiers act in their winter-quarters: not only is no one forced to spend on their upkeep, but no one is allowed to do so even if they want to! Remember, our ancestors wanted to find a refuge *from* winter, not *for* greed, under their allies' roofs.

40. Now, consider how self-controlled he is in everything else. What do you think was the source of his incredibly rapid advance? It was not the exceptional strength of his rowers, some never-before-heard-of navigational skill or a new wind that brought him so quickly into a remote region. Rather, the temptations which usually delay other people did not slow him down: he was not seduced by greed to plunder, by desire to pleasure, by beautiful surroundings to delight himself, by the fame of a city to learn more about it, nor to rest because of his labours. He did not even think it worth his time to view the statues, paintings and other art treasures of Greece – treasures other men think they should steal. 41. The result is that now everyone from these regions sees Gnaeus Pompey not as a man sent from Rome, but as one fallen from heaven. They are finally starting to believe there were once Romans with this level of self-restraint, something foreign tribes were beginning to think an unbelievable and false legend. Now your empire starts to shed its bright light over those nations. Now they understand there was a reason why their ancestors preferred to serve the Roman people than to rule others, as we then had magistrates with this level of self-control. Private individuals can approach him so easily and their complaints about injuries from others are listened to so willingly that, although his standing outstrips that of princes, he is as accessible as a commoner.

42. Citizens, you have learnt from this platform how brilliant his strategy is, how powerful and flowing his speech – a skill which naturally commands respect. How highly do you think our allies value his word when our enemies, no matter who they are, judge it to be completely unbreakable? Such is his human decency that it is hard to know whether our enemies fear his courage more when fighting him than cherish his mercy after they are conquered. Is there anyone who doubts that he should be in charge of this war, when it appears he was born by divine strategy to end all wars in our time? 43. And since a commanding presence is of great importance also in conducting wars and in the art

of war, there is certainly no doubt that the illustrious person I have just referred to will also be a great commander. Who is unaware that how our enemies and allies evaluate our commanders strongly affects the conduct of wars? We know that in such crises people are swayed to feel contempt, hate or love as much by a preconceived notion and rumour as by solid reasoning.

As I was saying, whose name has ever been more world-famous? Whose achievements comparable? Have you ever given anyone else such great and remarkable signs of your approval – a gift that gives the greatest prestige? 44. Or do you honestly believe that there is no region so deserted that it has not heard of that day when the Roman people as one, cramming into the Forum and packing the temples which give a glimpse of this platform, demanded that Gnaeus Pompey be given sole command of a world war? I shall not say more, nor prove by using other men as examples how important a commanding presence is in war; instead, let us take our example of all that is outstanding from Gnaeus Pompey himself. On the very day you appointed him commander of your war with the pirates, the mere mention of his name and his reputation caused a sudden plunge in the high price of corn (although it had been very scarce), to a level it would be hard to reach during a long peace and after a period of great agricultural production.

45. Citizens, after the terrible defeat in Pontus, which I unwillingly reminded you of a short while ago, when our allies were panic-stricken, our enemies' resources and courage were growing and the province did not have decent garrisons, had not the good fortune of the Roman people miraculously met the crisis with the arrival of Gnaeus Pompey, you would have lost Asia. His arrival checked Mithridates, then aglow with his unaccustomed victory, and slowed down Tigranes who was threatening Asia with a massive army. Can anyone doubt what he *will* accomplish with his courage when he has already achieved so much through his reputation? Or how easily he will save our allies and revenues when he is in command of an army, since the mere whisper of his name has already defended them? 46. Has the extent of the man's reputation among the enemies of Rome not been made clear by the fact that, in such a short time,

people from so many distant and disparate regions have surrendered only to him? Or by the fact that although we had an army
and commander on their island, ambassadors from the common
assembly of Crete went to Gnaeus Pompey, even though he was
nearly at the ends of the earth, and said that all the Cretan states
wished to surrender to him?[40] Furthermore, didn't even the
notorious Mithridates send an ambassador to Pompey[41] when
he was in Spain? (For Pompey has always considered the man an
ambassador, although people who were particularly annoyed
that Pompey received that honour preferred to call him a spy
rather than an ambassador.) Citizens, you can now evaluate
how strongly you think his presence will affect those kings and
foreign tribes, increased as it is by his many great achievements
and your sanction.

47. It just remains for me to say a few cautious words on
good luck. No one can boast of his own luck, but we can
remember and commemorate it in others, as is right when men
speak of what is in the lap of the gods. This is my judgement:
command and armies were frequently entrusted to Maximus,
Marcellus, Scipio,[42] Marius and other great commanders, not
just because of their abilities but because of their good fortune.
We can be sure that some exceptional men have received the
favour of the gods to help them on their path to eminence, fame
and great achievements. But when I talk about Pompey's luck, I
shall employ such restraint when I speak that I shall not say that
good fortune is his to command, but show that I remember the
past and look forward to the future; thus my speech will not
appear displeasing or ungrateful to the immortal gods. 48. So I
shall not speak about his great good luck in his achievements at
home, at war, on land and sea, how, not only have his fellow-
citizens acquiesced to, our allies complied with and our enemies
obeyed, his wishes, but even the winds and the weather! In a
very few words: there has never been a man shameless enough
that he secretly hoped the immortal gods would grant him as
many great favours as they have given to Gnaeus Pompey. Citizens! You should desire – as I know you do – that this good
fortune will be forever his, for the sake of our common good,
our empire and for the man himself.

49. Why? Because this war is so unavoidable that it cannot be ignored and so great that it must be conducted with the utmost care. When you can place in command a general who possesses such an exceptional knowledge of war, unique abilities, a brilliant presence and outstanding good fortune, do you really hesitate to use a blessing the immortal gods have presented to you on a platter to protect and make the Republic greater? 50. If Gnaeus Pompey were now living as a private citizen in Rome, we should still select him and send him to fight this great war. However, as a fortunate circumstance has been added to all these other great advantages and he is conveniently on the spot, has an army and is immediately able to take charge of the one now under another's command, *what are we waiting for?* Why are we not following the leadership of the immortal gods and handing over this war with the king to a man who has aided the Republic each time we have entrusted an important issue to him?

51. Ah, but you will say that Quintus Catulus – a very illustrious man, the Republic's great friend and someone who has received the highest honours you can give – and Quintus Hortensius[43] – who has been granted the highest distinctions of office, fortune, character and talent – disagree. I admit that their opinion has held considerable weight with you on other occasions and that should continue to be the case. But in this situation – ignoring the fact that you will find the opinions of extremely brave and prominent men directly contradict theirs – we can set aside 'opinion' and find out the truth from the facts themselves, a task which is made easier because my opponents also concede that everything I have said so far is true, they agree that this great war is inevitable and that Pompey alone possesses all the greatest qualifications. 52. So what does Hortensius say?

'If one person alone must have supreme command, then Pompey is the most worthy. Still, it should not be conferred entirely on one man.'

That line of argument is outdated and events refute it even more than words. Quintus Hortensius, you were the very person who gave a long and powerful speech in the Senate, with all your extensive eloquence and unique oratorical ability, against that brave man Aulus Gabinius when he promulgated a bill to appoint a single commander to fight against the pirates. You then spoke further against his law from this very platform.[44] 53. What? By the immortal gods, if your opinion had carried more weight with the Roman people than their own safety and interests, would we today have this glorious empire which rules the world? Did it look like an empire to you when Roman ambassadors, quaestors and praetors were being captured? When we were prevented from communicating publicly and privately with every province? When we found all seas closed to us and could transact no private or public business overseas?

54. Was there ever a state in the past – I shall not speak of the Athenian one which we are told once controlled a maritime empire of considerable size, or the Carthaginian empire which became very powerful because of its fleet and maritime resources, or Rhodes whose naval skill and fame is remembered even today – was there ever a state so weak or island so tiny that it could not defend its own ports, fields and some part of the coast and surrounding region? But, by Hercules, for several years before the *lex Gabinia*, the legendary Roman people, who up to our own times held a reputation for invincibility in naval war, had not only to go without the greatest part of the benefit but the reputation of empire as well. 55. We, the men whose ancestors defeated the kings Antiochus and Perseus[45] and the Carthaginians in every naval battle (and the Carthaginians were a race highly trained and well equipped for maritime warfare), were no match for the pirates in any encounter. We, who previously kept Italy safe *and* were able to use the reputation of our empire to guarantee the safety of all our allies, no matter how distant – remember this was when the island of Delos, although located far away from us in the Aegean Sea and a place everyone visited with merchandise and cargo, feared nothing though it was small, crammed with riches and had no walls – we did not just have to avoid our provinces, Italy's shores and our own ports, but even the Appian Way! And yet, although our ancestors left us this speaker's platform decorated with naval trophies and spoils taken from conquered fleets, Roman magistrates were not ashamed to climb it.

56. Quintus Hortensius! The Roman people ruled that you and those who agreed with you spoke with good intentions; even so, in a matter of public welfare, they preferred to listen to their own troubles rather than your guidance. Thus it was that one law, one man and one year freed us from our misery and disgrace and ensured that at last we looked like the rulers of land and sea, of all nations and tribes. 57. This is why I think it is even more unworthy that there have been objections to – well, I do not know whether to say to Gabinius or Pompey or (something closer to the truth) to both – Aulus Gabinius becoming Pompey's lieutenant, although he is very eager to take up that position.[46] Was it because the person who asked for a particular lieutenant for such a major war was not fit to obtain his request, even though others brought out *their* chosen lieutenants to pillage our allies and loot the provinces? Or because the man whose law put the safety and honour of the Roman people and all nations on a firm footing should not be allowed to share the fame of the commander and army appointed on his advice and at his personal risk?

58. Or are we so conscientious in the case of Gabinius alone, who should have special rights in this war waged under his law, under the commander and army he himself appointed through your votes, even though Gaius Falcidius, Quintus Metellus, Quintus Caelius Latiniensis and Gnaeus Lentulus[47] – men I name with all respect – could become lieutenants the year after they served their terms as tribunes of the plebs. I hope the consuls will bring his appointment before the Senate;[48] if they hesitate or are reluctant, I publicly declare that I shall do so! Nor will someone's hostile motion stop me from turning to you and defending your law and the honour you granted. Nothing will stop me except a veto – and there I think the men who now threaten to use one will reflect a few times on how far to push things. Citizens, in my opinion Aulus Gabinius alone shares in Gnaeus Pompey's achievements in the war with the pirates because he made sure you voted for Pompey as sole commander to wage that war, and Pompey brought the war to a successful conclusion after it was entrusted to him.

59. It only remains for me to talk about Quintus Catulus'

influential statements. When he asked you on whom you would pin your hopes had you placed them all on Pompey and something happened to him, you rewarded Catulus' character and position with a considerable tribute when almost in one voice you said that you would pin them on him. For he is the type of man who cannot but direct any problem wisely (no matter how great or difficult it is), conduct it honestly and conclude it manfully. But I violently disagree with him on this subject: the more uncertain and brief human life is, the more the Republic ought to benefit from a great man's life and ability while the gods allow.

60. 'But there should be no innovation which is against the precedents and the traditions of our ancestors.'

I shall not use this platform to speak of how our ancestors obeyed precedent in peace but pragmatism in war. They always adapted new strategies for new emergencies. I shall not speak of how one commander ended two critical wars, that is the Punic and Spanish Wars, and how Scipio, the one and same man, destroyed two extremely powerful cities which were the greatest threats our empire faced.[49] I shall not bring up how, not long ago, you and your fathers thought that the hopes of this empire should be placed in Gaius Marius alone, the man who conducted the war with Jugurtha, the Cimbri and Teutoni.[50] 61. As for Gnaeus Pompey's case – in which Quintus Catulus asserts there should be no innovations – recall how many innovations Quintus Catulus has assented to for Pompey! What is more of an innovation than a young man with no public standing raising an army in our hour of need? *He raised one.* Or commanding one? *He commanded one.* Waging a war brilliantly as a general? *He waged one.* What could be more of an innovation than a very young man, who was considerably younger than the age one can enter the Senate, receiving a military command, being entrusted with Sicily and Africa[51] and conducting a war in the latter? He was uniquely incorruptible, dignified and heroic in those provinces; he concluded a great war in Africa and returned with a triumphant army. Who ever heard of a mere equestrian having a Roman triumph?[52] The

Roman people not only turned out to watch him, but thought it was something they should see and celebrate with absolute enthusiasm.

62. What was more unusual than a Roman equestrian being sent with consular powers to wage a very great and terrible war when there were two highly distinguished and brave consuls? *We sent him.* And then, when some in the Senate said that we should not choose to send a man who had held no public office, rather than a consul, people say that Lucius Philippus commented that he was not sending him instead of *a* consul but instead of *two* consuls.[53] They pinned such immense hopes of a successful war on Pompey that they entrusted the duties of two consuls to one young man's military ability. What could be as unique as the senatorial decree which exempted Pompey from legal restrictions so that he could become consul before the age he could legally hold any other magistracy?[54] What could be as remarkable as a senatorial decree authorizing a Roman equestrian to hold a second triumph? We have never seen as many innovations within living memory as those introduced for him.

63. And it was the guidance of Quintus Catulus and other extremely honourable men of his rank which set in motion these numerous and striking innovations. That is why they should take care in case it seems a deep and unendurable injustice that *you* take their advice about Gnaeus Pompey's merit, but *they* reject your advice and judgement on the same man, especially as the Roman people can, with perfect right, defend their choice against all critics, as it was in the teeth of their opposition that you chose Pompey, alone, from all your options, to take charge of the war against the pirates. 64. If you had done that impetuously and without proper care for the Republic, it would be right for them to try to overrule your enthusiasm with their guidance. But if it was you who realized then what would be best for the Republic, and you alone brought back honour to our empire, and safety to the whole world in the face of their opposition, they should confess that they and our other leaders must obey the authority of the entire Roman people. This war in Asia against kings not only requires the famed military ability Pompey has to a unique degree, but also his many

other great abilities. It is difficult for any Roman commander to be so busy with his duties in Asia, Cilicia, Syria and in the interior of Asia that he thinks of nothing except the enemy and glory. And then, even if certain commanders are somewhat restrained by their sense of shame or self-control, it is still the case that the sheer number of rapacious commanders ensures no one believes it.

65. Citizens, it is difficult to express just how much foreign nations hate us because of the appetites and injustices of the men we have sent as commanders to them. Do you think there was a shrine in those countries that our magistrates respected, a community they considered inviolable or a home that could be closed or secured against them? In reality, because of their passion for loot, they seek out wealthy and affluent cities so that they can invent some pretext for war against them. 66. I would happily debate with these highly distinguished men, Quintus Catulus and Hortensius, face-to-face on this topic – they know of the harm done to our allies, they see their catastrophes, hear their complaints. Which of these do you think is true: that you send an army against enemies on *behalf* of your allies or *against* allies and friends under the pretence that they are enemies? What Asian community could contain the pride and egotism, not just of a commander or his lieutenant, but even one military tribune?[55] That is why even if you have a candidate who appears capable of overcoming royal armies in pitched battle, unless he can keep his eyes, hands and thoughts from our allies' money and wives and children, from the treasures of their shrines and towns and from royal gold and riches, he is not a fit person to send to this Asian war against the kings. 67. Do you think that they have not targeted every wealthy community? Or that they consider any wealthy community not a legitimate target? Citizens, it was not just his military reputation that made the coastal regions ask for Gnaeus Pompey's appointment – it was his self-restraint. They saw that, with a few exceptions, their governors were growing wealthy from public funds and were not achieving anything with fleets that existed only on paper, except to make us look as if we were adding to our disgrace by incurring more losses.

The men who think that we should not entrust everything to one man are (naturally!) ignorant of the greed with which men set out for the provinces, the expenditures they have incurred and the deals they have made – as if we were unaware that it is not just his character that makes Gnaeus Pompey 'Great', but the vices of others!

68. Therefore, do not hesitate to entrust everything to this one man, who is the only person found all these long years whom the allies welcome into their cities, along with his army. But if you think, citizens, my cause requires some authoritative voices, you have that of Publius Servilius,[56] a man thoroughly experienced in war and in all manner of important issues, whose achievements on every military front are so great that no one should carry more weight with you when you deliberate on war. There is also the voice of Gaius Curio,[57] a man marked by the honours you have granted and his own great achievements, who is endowed with brilliance and foresight; there is that of Gnaeus Lentulus,[58] in whom you have seen excellent counsel and great dignity, a return for the high positions you have voted him; there is that of Gaius Cassius,[59] a true man who possesses honour and unique firmness. Reflect, all of you, on whether the authority of such men enables us to respond to the arguments of those who oppose this law.

69. Gaius Manilius, it is all this that makes me heartily support and applaud your law, your motives and your proposal; I encourage you, with the authority of the Roman people behind you, to stick to it and not tremble at threats of violence from anyone. Firstly, I consider you have enough courage and determination; secondly, when we see gathered once more a great mass of people who roar out their support for placing the same man as last year in command,[60] why should we doubt your proposal or ability to pass it? For my part, I promise and place at your disposal and at that of the Roman people whatever energy, advice, effort and talent I possess, whatever power the gift of the Roman people has granted me as praetor, and I promise to use my influence, faithfulness and firmness of character to achieve our purpose.

70. I ask all the gods to witness this – and especially those

who stand guard over this holy place and who see deeply into the minds of all who enter public life: I am not acting here at anyone's request to curry favour with Gnaeus Pompey by supporting this cause, in the hope of using someone's status to find protection from dangers or support in gaining public office. As far as lies in the power of a mere mortal, I shall easily deflect any danger, for my incorruptible nature will shield me. It is not one person or a speech from this platform that will grant me public office, but my constant hard work – if such is your desire. 71. Citizens, that is why, whatever I have undertaken in this cause, I assert that I have undertaken it entirely for the Republic's sake. Rather than it appearing as if I sought someone's gratitude, I know I have even incurred a great deal of enmity – some hidden, some open – enmity I could have avoided but which has its uses for you. But, I, *I* have decided that having been given this office and been honoured by your great gifts, I should place your desires, the position of the Republic and the safety of the provinces and our allies above my own advantage and self-interest.

Second Speech on the Agrarian Law of Rullus (extracts)

Delivered on 1 or 2 January 63 to
the people from the Rostra in the Forum

It is unfortunate that we know nothing of the sponsor of this bill, Publius Rullus, one of the tribunes of the plebs for 63, beyond what Cicero himself tells us – and he is hardly a disinterested party. That is, if one discounts the comment by Pliny the Elder that Rullus' father was the first man in Rome to serve an entire boar at a banquet (Natural History 8.210). At the very least this would suggest some degree of wealth, entire boars not being cheap. However, apart from this, we must rely on Cicero for all of our knowledge of the contents of the bill, its aims and for Rullus himself.

Regardless of the subject matter, the occasion of this speech had to be a thrilling one for Cicero. As consul, it was his first speech to the people; the man from Arpinum had finally arrived and could ascend the Rostra as the person who had ennobled his family. However, what must have made this a particularly thrilling occasion was that Cicero would speak on an agrarian law, a highly controversial topic and one of huge interest to the urban plebs. Agrarian laws – laws distributing or redistributing land owned by the Roman state – had a long and controversial history in Roman politics. The Roman state owned a great deal of land throughout Italy and the rest of the empire since it was its practice to confiscate portions of the land of those it had conquered. This land became state property, ager publicus; it could either be given to colonies of Roman citizens or rented to individuals. (These tenants had considerable security of tenure and were allowed to do what they wished with the land.) As

Rome expanded in the second century, so did the amount of land that belonged to the state and the number of slaves available to farm such land. The rise of large slave-farmed tracts of land, called latifundia, displaced rural dwellers, who flowed to Rome, swelling the ranks of the urban poor.

Previous attempts to deal with the problems had not ended well for their proposers. Just touching on the most famous example, that of the Gracchi brothers, will give a sense of the dangers in proposing an agrarian law. Tiberius and Gaius Gracchus were members of an old and noble Roman family and held the position of tribune of the plebs in 133 and 123/2 respectively. They attempted to limit the amount of public land individuals could hold and proposed new colonies of the urban poor, sometimes outside Italy. Those who held large portions of land reacted with extreme hostility, and for their troubles both brothers were more or less lynched by the Senate. Rullus had to know that he risked a great deal by following in their footsteps and it is reasonable to believe that he did not do so without some significant backing; Julius Caesar and Marcus Licinius Crassus have both been suggested as possible backers. Both had a great deal to gain from becoming members of Rullus' proposed board, which would oversee his agrarian commission.

Rullus' bill could not be termed short. It had at least forty clauses which mandated the following: a board of ten men (the decemviri) with praetorian power for five years was to be created and elected by seventeen of the thirty-five Roman tribes; candidates had to declare their candidacy in person; it would sell land whose sale had been sanctioned by a senatorial decree of 81; this would pay for some of the land the board planned to distribute to colonists in Italy; it could impose taxes on public land outside Italy and confiscate war booty of gold and silver which had not been paid to the treasury or used on monuments (Pompey was exempted from this requirement); and it could sell land outside Italy that had become the property of the Roman people after 88. It is clear that no matter how beneficial this law might be, it would concentrate an enormous amount of power in the hands of the members of the board – hence the interest of men like Caesar and Crassus.

Cicero had to tread carefully in discrediting the bill as it had considerable inherent appeal for the urban plebs. He begins by attacking the populares, *the 'men of the people', for not being truly devoted to their interests and betraying the traditions of the Gracchi. He devotes a considerable amount of time representing himself as a true consul of the people – a claim that tends to make scholars frown, as Cicero was very far from belonging to the* populares. *But in one sense he is truthful: as a man without ancestors, one often despised by the nobles, he owed a great deal to the people. It is self-serving rhetoric, of course, but it should also be noted that his opponents were as self-serving. Cicero's overall argument is clear: this is not a measure that benefits the people as its aim is for its framers to have tyrannical powers (chapter 15), powers that Cicero will carefully unveil. (The theme of their 'royal' power to act at whim is repeated in chapters not translated: 34, 45, 47.) He also relies on the people's sense of pride in the extent of Rome's empire, an empire, he argues, that this bill will break up by selling off large portions of land outside Italy. He is also careful to honour the people repeatedly. In a bold move at the close of the speech, Cicero, a man without ancestors, presents himself as the true representative of the Roman ancestors, the* maiores. *Whatever one thinks of Cicero's arguments, it is clear that the Roman people found them convincing: the assembly defeated Rullus' bill.*

1. Citizens, our ancestors began the custom of the men you have elected using their first public address to combine thanks for your kindness with praise of their ancestors – a gift which enables them to live up to the models[1] their families gave them. Their speeches sometimes enable you to discover that some are worthy of their ancestors, but more manage to look so hugely indebted to them that their descendants will still be paying that debt off. I, citizens, do not have the ability to speak to you about my ancestors; this is not because they were not the same as I, who share their blood and was brought up in the same school as they were, but because they never received the people's

praise and stayed out of the spotlight your honours give. 2. I worry that it will look arrogant to speak of myself before you, ungrateful to stay silent. It is extremely difficult for me personally to remind you of the efforts by which I achieved this position and yet I cannot stay quiet about the great gifts you have given to me. Because of this, I shall use a certain moderation in how I speak; I shall say a little – and only as will be necessary – to mention the honour you have granted me, why you judged me worthy of this exceptional and great honour, and why I think you, the people who made that decision, will continue to believe me so.

3. You chose me to be the first new man to become consul in a long time – almost the first within living memory.[2] You wanted to break through the defences the nobility had set up around this position, which they kept fortified every way they could, and, with me as your standard-bearer, tear them down for future generations. You did not just elect me consul, something in and of itself a great honour, but elected me in a way that few nobles from our community have managed and no new man before me. Certainly, if you will be kind enough to cast your minds over all the previous new men, you will see that those who were elected consuls at their first attempt were elected only after long, hard work and because of some lucky chance, running for the position many years after they were praetor and when they were considerably older than the legal minimum age.[3] Those who ran for consul at the minimum age suffered defeats before their eventual election; I am the only new man within memory who ran for consulship as soon as he was legally entitled to and became consul on his first try. As a result, it does not seem that I stole the office you gave me by exploiting an opening provided by another candidate's campaign, or dragged it out of you by begging over and over, but won it through merit.

4. Citizens, as I just mentioned, it brings great honour to me to be the first new man elected in many years, in my first run and at the earliest age. But nothing could be a greater mark of distinction than the fact that during the assembly that elected me, you did not hand in your tablets secretly – which protects your free vote – but raised your voices as one to show your

enthusiastic goodwill towards me. I was declared consul not with the last votes, but at the first moment you gathered, not by the individual voices of the heralds, but by the voice of the Roman people raised in a unanimous shout. 5. Citizens, I consider your marked and unique gift a very great reward for my courage *and* as a joy that will bring me even more responsibility and worry. My mind is occupied by many weighty problems which do not let me rest day or night. The first is that of being a consul. This is a great and difficult task for anyone, but it is particularly true for me, a man whom no one will pardon for any errors made, and who will barely (and begrudgingly) be praised for his achievements. There will be no reliable advice if I have doubts, nor will the nobility give me any dependable assistance if I am in trouble.

6. If I were the only person being dragged into danger, I would bear it calmly, but it appears to me that there are men around who will blame all of you for preferring me to the nobility, not just when I make what they think are intentional slips but also for what they think are accidental ones. But it is my belief that I should patiently endure all this rather than not carry out my duties as consul so well that everything I do or recommend as an elected official reflects back praise on you for electing and recommending me. In addition to the great hard work and difficulty of performing my duties as consul, I have decided that I should not act like previous consuls in the rules and principles I obey. Some of them have fled from the sight of you and particularly from approaching this platform, while others have not been exactly eager to seek it out. I shall not just take the easy route of saying here that I am a consul of the people; I already called myself that in the Senate on the first of January – not exactly the place to make such comments. 7. Given that I know that it was not the will of powerful men or the influence of a cabal that elected me consul in preference to high nobles, but the vote of the entire Roman people, what else could I do *except* be a man of the people, whether as a consul or for the rest of my life? But I have a great need of your wisdom to interpret what being 'of the people' truly means. For there is a widespread misunderstanding about this because of

the insidious lies of men who oppose and interfere, not only with the interests of the people, but with their welfare, and yet who still want to speak as if they were 'of the people'.

8. Citizens, I know the condition the Republic was in on the first of January: it was full of worry, full of fear. There was no evil or problem which decent people did not fear and disloyal ones look forward to. All sorts of destructive plans were being set in motion to destabilize the Republic and your peace (some were even said to have already been started the moment we were elected consuls[4]); it was not the blow of some new catastrophe that made business completely lose confidence but suspicions of and uneasiness about the courts and the annulment of legal verdicts. People thought that new forms of oppression and extraordinary powers – not those of commanders, but of kings – were being sought. 9. As I did not just suspect this but saw it clearly (it is not as if it was done in secret), I told the Senate right out that I would be a consul of the people during my term in office. What is better for the people than peace? This gives joy to all that lives and breathes – even to our houses and fields. What is better for the people than freedom? You can see that it is not just people who make this their main goal but animals too. What is better for the people than peace at home – something so wonderful that you, your ancestors and every truly brave man believe you should endure extreme labours so you may enjoy it one day, especially if it comes with power and status. This is why we should particularly praise and thank our ancestors: it was their hard work that ensured we now enjoy peace without risk. How could I not be a consul of the people, citizens, when I see all this: peace overseas, the freedom that is the birthright of our people and our name, peace at home, everything that you hold dear and think honourable – all entrusted to me and given to me as consul to protect.

10. Citizens, you should not think it wonderful or 'of the people' when someone waves about a handout which sounds good but can never become a reality without emptying our treasury. You should not think that the dealings in the courts which you are uneasy about – the annulments of verdicts and the restoration to full rights of the convicted[5] – are in the

interests of the people. They are the final stages of the ruin of crushed states, those which mark their death throes. Nor should you think it is in the interests of the people if men promise you land or play on your hopes with lies, even as they scheme something very different behind closed doors. To speak the truth, I cannot criticize every type of agrarian law. I remember that two very distinguished and brilliant Romans, both great friends of the Roman people, Tiberius and Gaius Gracchus, settled people on public lands which had been in the hands of private individuals. I am not a consul who thinks – as many do – it an unspeakable crime to praise the Gracchi; I see that their policies, good sense and laws reformed much of the Republic.[6]

11. Thus, right from when I was elected consul and it was announced that the newly elected tribunes of the plebs[7] were drawing up an agrarian law, I wanted to know what they were intending; I thought, since we were all magistrates in the same year, we should form an alliance to administer the Republic well. 12. When, as a friendly gesture, I tried to be a part of their discussions, I was kept in the dark and excluded. When I showed them that if I thought their law would profit the Roman people I would promote and help it, they still repelled my generous offer and said that I could never be induced to approve of a handout. I put an end to my offers for fear my persistence would seem duplicitous or rude. In the meantime, they kept on meeting secretly, inviting some unelected people, gathering at night and in isolated places. You can easily imagine how afraid I was from your own worries during that period,

13. At last the tribunes of the plebs take up their offices. As Rullus was the prime mover of the agrarian law and acted more aggressively than the others, people wait with baited breath for him to call his assembly. From the second he was elected, he carefully practised putting on a different expression, a different tone of voice and way of walking, and shabby clothes; he neglected his looks, his hair was longer and he grew a full beard[8] – as a result, his eyes and expression seemed to menace the Republic and he threatened to use the power of the tribunes at every turn. I eagerly awaited this person's law and assembly, but at first he proposed no law but ordered an assembly to be

convened on the twelfth of January. Everyone gathers in high anticipation. He unwraps a speech which is certainly long and very well expressed. There was only one thing I thought problematic: that among the immense crowd there was not a single person who could understand what he was saying. I have no idea whether he wanted to deceive or if he enjoys that style of oratory, but some people in the assembly who were a bit sharper than the others suspected that he intended to say something or other about an agrarian law. At long last, after my election, he published his law. I ordered a large number of clerks to assemble and bring me a copy of it.[9]

14. Citizens, I can honestly tell you what my frame of mind was as I sat down to read and familiarize myself with that law: I wanted to promote it and help it pass – *if* I thought it was suited to and profitable for you. The consulship is not inclined by its nature, by animosity or some deep-rooted, inherent hatred, to wage war with the tribunes, although some decent and brave consuls have stood up to subversive and worthless tribunes, and the tribunes have used their veto to block consuls whose appetites were out of control. It is not the difference in their powers but the distance between their minds that creates the gulf between them. 15. So when I picked up this law, my intention was to find it in line with your interests and of such a nature that a consul, who was in reality and not just in his rhetoric a man of the people, could honourably and happily defend it. Citizens, from the very first line of the law to the last, I saw that there was nothing else it thought of, planned and aimed at except appointing ten kings to rule over the treasury, the taxes, all the provinces, the whole of the Republic, allied kings, our free allies – that is the entire world – all under the lying name of an agrarian law. I tell you, citizens, that under this lovely agrarian law you, the people, receive nothing, while it gives everything to a few particular individuals, and it parades an offer of land for the Roman people while it steals your freedom; it increases the wealth of some private individuals but drains the Republic's and, even worse, it uses a tribune of the plebs, an office our ancestors established to protect and guard freedom, to set up kings over our community.

16. Citizens, if after I have laid it all out for you you still think my claims false, I shall follow your lead and change my opinion; but if you see that it sets traps for your freedom under the pretence of a handout, do not hesitate to defend, with a consul at your side, the freedom your ancestors bequeathed you, freedom they earned with their sweat and blood – it will cause you no trouble. The first clause of that agrarian law gives them a chance (or so they think) to make an easy trial of just how you will allow the erosion of your freedom. It orders the tribune who has passed the law to have seventeen tribes vote to set up a board of ten men, so whatever man nine tribes elect will be one of the ten.[10]

17. I ask him why the very opening words of his law and proposals deprive the Roman people of their right to vote. Every time an agrarian law has been created, there have been boards of three, of five or ten men. I ask this tribune of the plebs and man of the people why thirty-five tribes have always voted on their membership? Given that it is right that every position of authority, military command and membership of a board comes from *all* the Roman people, it is even more right that this should be the case for what is established in the interest of and to benefit the people; in this situation they all select the person they think will especially work on their behalf and every one of them eagerly votes to ensure that there will be a way to benefit himself. This tribune of the plebs took it into his mind to deprive the entire Roman people of their votes and to ask a few tribes to exercise their freedom to vote, not under the conditions our laws have set down, but as the gift of the chance falling of the lots.[11]

18. The next clause says, 'It will take place the same way as the election of the pontifex maximus.' He cannot even see that our ancestors were so concerned for the people that, although religious law did not allow the people to elect someone a pontifex, they still wanted to give more status to that priesthood by making candidates appeal to the people. Gnaeus Domitius,[12] a tribune of the plebs and a very distinguished man, passed a law for the other priesthoods; it ensured that although under religious law the people could not elect a priest, a part would be asked to do so, and whoever that portion chose would become a member of a priestly college. 19. See the great difference

between Gnaeus Domitius, a tribune *and* a high noble, and
Publius Rullus who – I think – tried your patience when he said
he was a noble.[13] Domitius went to great lengths to ensure that,
even though religious practice forbade the whole people to vote,
part of the people should gain the right as far as religious law
allowed it, while Rullus tried to rip from you and steal completely your rights, although it had always been the case that the
people should first grant the right to distribute land – something
that has always belonged to the people – a right no one has ever
infringed on or changed. The former managed in some way to
give to the people what could not be given; the latter is trying to
use some fixed scheme to steal what cannot be taken in any way!

20. Does anyone ask what he was aiming at with such insulting and shameless behaviour? He had a plan, but, citizens, he
certainly had no honest or good intentions towards the Roman
plebs and your freedom. He orders the same person who proposed the law to be in charge of the election and to set up the
board of ten. I shall speak more plainly: Rullus – a man without greed and looking for no reward – orders *Rullus* to hold an
election. I am not yet criticizing as there are precedents for
this – but see what he hopes to gain with this smaller part of the
people, something for which there is *no* precedent. He will hold
an assembly; he will want it to elect those for whom he is using
this law to seek royal power. He does not trust the entire
people – nor do those who are the real masterminds of his plan
feel that the people should be trusted. 21. The same Rullus will
cast lots for the tribes. He – Mr Lucky – will select the tribes he
wants. I shall show you that the ten men elected by the nine
tribes Rullus selects will be our lords and masters. To show
their gratitude and that they do not forget such kindness, the
men elected will admit their obligation to various notorious
men[14] from these nine tribes. As for the remainder – the twenty-
six other tribes – they will feel entitled to refuse them everything.
Who does Rullus want elected? He is top of the list. How is
that legal? We have ancient laws, the *lex Licinia* and the second
lex Aebutia; if it matters to you, these are not laws of the
consuls but laws of the tribunes, laws you and your ancestors
held dear. These forbid the person who passed a law about the

membership of a board or a special commission *and* his colleagues, relatives and in-laws from being appointed to such
boards or holding those commissions.[15] 22. If you are really
looking out for the interests of the people, remove all suspicion
that you will benefit; show that you are thinking of nothing
except what profit the people will reap, allow the power to go
to others – and the thanks for your gift to you. This behaviour
is scarcely that of a free people, scarcely that of people with
your courage and grandeur.

Who passed the law? *Rullus*. Who stopped the majority of
the people from voting? *Rullus*. Who presided over the election? Who called whatever tribes he wanted to attend it without
anyone keeping a watchful eye on the drawing of lots? Who
made whoever he wanted members of the board? The very
same – *Rullus!* Whom did he make the head of this board?
Rullus! By Hercules, I do not think he could get his slaves to
approve of this, let alone the people who are masters of the
whole world! And thus our best laws will be repealed – no
exceptions. The same man will seek membership of a board
under his own law, the same man will hold an assembly after
stripping the majority of the right to vote! He will appoint
whoever he wants to the board – himself among them! *Naturally*, he will not reject the co-sponsors of his agrarian law as his
colleagues, those men who may have allowed him to have his
name in the title and at the head of the law but who hope by
mutual guarantee to take an equal part of its rewards.

23. But look at Rullus' diligence – if you think that he
thought of this, or that any such idea ever crossed the mind of
a Rullus. The men who are engineering all this saw that if the
entire people had the power to choose, it would without hesita-
tion entrust everything which required integrity, honour,
character and authority to Gnaeus Pompey's leadership. They
knew well that after you chose one man alone and appointed
him to lead all your wars on land and sea against every nation,[16]
it was certain that when you were electing people for this board
you would give him a position there, either because you trusted
him or you wanted to confer an honour on him – and that was
only right.

24. Youth, legal issues, a current command or magistracy – which might be somehow handicapped by other responsibilities or the laws – not even being currently on trial: none of these are reasons that one cannot be a member of this board. But this is not so for Gnaeus Pompey, who cannot serve on the board with Publius Rullus (I am silent about other members). For Rullus orders him to declare himself a candidate in person,[17] something which has never been a legal requirement, not even for those magistracies we elect each year; this is so that if this law is passed, you will not give Rullus a colleague who can keep an eye on or punish his greed. Since I see that Pompey's position and the insult this law gives him is shaking you, I shall return here to my opening point: this law is raising up kings and destroying your freedom from the foundations upwards.

25. Did you think otherwise? Do you not see that after a cabal had run their eyes over all your possessions, they would first of all work to keep Gnaeus Pompey from guarding your freedom and watching over and looking after your interests in any way? They saw – *they see* – that if your lack of foresight and my lack of care resulted in you passing an unread law, as soon as you uncovered its traps and were electing the board you would realize you needed Gnaeus Pompey to protect you against all its criminal faults. Does it not convince you that a group of men are looking to oppress and rule the world, when you see that the only person they know who could protect your freedom cannot be elected to that board?

26. Learn now the power of this board – and how far it reaches. First Rullus honours the members with a *lex curiata*.[18] It is completely unheard of and without precedent for someone to become a magistrate under this law if an assembly has not previously elected him. He orders the praetor who is elected at the top of the polls to propose that law. Why?

'So that the men the plebs elected could become members of the board.'

He has forgotten the plebs elected none of them! Will a man who cannot remember in the third clause of his own law what was in the preceding one tie up the whole world with new laws? It is clear what legal rights your ancestors gave you – and what this tribune of the plebs has left you. Your ancestors wanted you to vote twice for each magistrate. They made sure that a *lex centuriata* is passed for the censors and a *curiata* for the other patrician magistrates; thus, if the people regretted their choice of whom they had given power to, they could vote again on the same men.[19] 27. Citizens, you still use the centuriate and tribal assemblies; the curial one is only kept for the taking of the auspices. But since this tribune of the plebs saw that no one could have civil authority without the express command of the people or the plebs,[20] he reinforced the authority of the board by the curial assembly – one in which you have no place – and took away your tribal assembly. And so, even though your ancestors wanted you to vote on each magistrate at two assemblies, this man of the people did not even leave you the power to vote at one!

28. Now look at his diligence and his respect for ritual. He realized that the board would not have authority without a *curiata*, since only nine tribes had established it; he orders a *curiata* passed for them; he commands the praetor.[21] It is no business of mine to comment on how very absurd this is. He orders the person who was elected praetor at the top of the polls to pass a *curiata* – and if he cannot do that then the praetor who was elected last should do it. It looks to me as if he has either been playing the fool in these momentous issues or has something else (gods know what) in view. But let us leave behind all of this; it is either as crooked as it is funny or as maliciously intended as it is unclear. Let us return to his respect for ritual. He sees that without a *curiata* the board of ten can achieve nothing. 29. What would be next, if this was not passed? Listen to his brilliance.

'The board', he says, 'will be as legal as those properly and legally appointed.'

If, in this community which has far, far freer laws than other communities, someone can hold military or civil power although there has been no election, what is the point of the third clause of the law which orders the passing of a *curiata*, when in the fourth you grant these men the same powers they would have held if the people had elected them legally? Citizens, they are setting up kings, not a board of ten. These arise from such beginnings and foundations that they will take away all your rights, power and freedoms, not from the start of their rule but from the very moment they are set up.

30. But see how carefully he retains the tribunes' right of veto. The tribunes' vetoes often stop the consuls as they are trying to pass a *curiata* – not that we complain that the tribunes have this power; it is only the case if any of them uses it at a whim we think them mad. But his *curiata* – the one the praetor is to pass – takes away the power of the tribunes to veto. But while we should blame him because as tribune of the plebs he diminishes the tribunes' power, we should mock him because he gives the consul – who cannot hold a military command without a *curiata* – and he gives the praetor – the man against whom he forbids anyone to use a veto – the power he would have held if the law had been passed, even if a veto is used! As a result, I do not understand why he forbids the use of the veto or thinks anyone will use a veto, as it will only show the stupidity of the person who uses his veto and will not stop anything.

31. So, let there be a board of ten created, not by a real election, that is, by the votes of the people or by the assembly[22] the lictors call for form's sake, so that it can take the auspices according to ancient custom. See how he rewards the men – to whom you have granted no power – with far more honours than we – to whom you have given the highest powers – possess! He orders the ten men in charge of the sacred chickens[23] to take the auspices to establish colonies 'under the same right', he says, 'as the board of three had under the *lex Sempronia*'.[24] Rullus, do you really dare to bring up the *lex Sempronia*, a law which should remind you that their board of three was elected by all the thirty-five tribes? And even though you are so very far removed from Tiberius Gracchus' sense of justice and shame, do you really think we should consider a law passed so differently from his to be a law just as his is?

32. He also gave them what he calls praetorian authority, but which is actually royal authority; he says it will end in five years, but makes it eternal by strengthening it with such resources and troops that it can never be taken away against their will. He decks them out with assistants: secretaries, clerks, heralds, architects – *and* mules, tents, meal allowances and furniture. All are paid for by the treasury and supplied by the allies; there are two hundred surveyors from the equestrians, twenty attendants for each one of them – all ministers and minions of their power. Citizens, until now you have seen the very shape and appearance of tyrants; you see the trappings of power – but not yet the extent of their power. Does someone ask, 'How do these secretaries, lictors, heralds and chicken-keepers harm me?' Citizens, if someone has all these rights through no vote of yours, he must look like an unendurable king or an insane private individual.

[*Throughout the remainder of this speech, Cicero continues to stress the extent of the board's powers. He next turns to discussing the lands they will be able to sell, although the law was apparently silent on the specifics. In fact, one of the issues Cicero repeatedly brings up is how vague and general the law is, something which (according to Cicero) gives them the right to sell off most of the Roman empire. His rhetorical strategy of showing the people the extent of their power, and suggesting how much of the land they currently hold will be lost by these sales, is very effective. The speech concludes by discussing the planned colony at Capua, which he says will become a challenger to Rome's power.*]

95. Citizens, do you not think we must worship and honour our ancestors, who foresaw all this, as if they were immortal gods? What did they foresee? Please pay attention and learn about it. It is not their blood or their origins that make men behave as they do, but what nature supplies to shape how we live our lives, the things that nourish us and allow us to live. The Carthaginians were not deceivers and liars by nature; that was caused by their location: their many ports lured them to

have a passion for deceit and for profit by the doubletalk of merchants and strangers. The Ligurians[25] are hard, rough men: their own land has taught them to be so by producing nothing unless they extract it with intensive farming and hard labour. The Campanians have always been proud because of the high quality of their fields and crops and the healthiness, location and beauty of their city. It was that abundance and their bounty on all fronts that first bred the arrogance which demanded that our ancestors make one of the consuls a Capuan[26] and the luxury which conquered Hannibal – a man until then unconquered in war – by the pleasures it provided. 96. When that board has settled 5,000 colonists there in accordance with Rullus' law and established 100 decurions,[27] ten augurs and six priests, what sort of pride, hostility and arrogance will they have? They will laugh at and despise Rome, placed as it is in the middle of mountains and valleys, with its miserable attics perched over its streets, its rather dreadful roads and narrow alleys, when they compare it with their Capua laid out on a wide plain and in a very beautiful location. Oh yes – they will not think our Vatican and Pupinian fields comparable with their rich and fertile plains![28] For a good laugh they will compare a number of our neighbouring towns; they will compare Veii, Fidenae, Collatia, and even, by Hercules, Lanuvinium, Aricia, Tusculum with Cales, Teanum, Neapolis, Puteoli, Cumae, Pompeii and Nuceria.[29] 97. There will be no controlling them once they are exalted and inflated with all these thoughts; perhaps it will not happen immediately, but it will happen if they take on even a little of their historical strength. They will advance and will carry all before them. A single private individual, unless he has great wisdom, can scarcely be held back by the boundaries and limits that duty sets if he experiences great good fortune. It is even less likely that after Rullus has stationed in Capua – that residence of pride and headquarters of luxury – colonists he has ferreted out and hand picked, who resemble him, that they will not immediately look to commit crimes and offences. Or, should I say, they will be even keener to do so than the old, genuine Campanians, who, born and raised in the lap of their ancient wealth, were corrupted by sheer excess. The new residents, taken from the depths of poverty to that profusion of wealth, will be overcome not only by the size of that wealth, but by its unfamiliarity.

98. Publius Rullus, you have preferred to follow the footsteps of Marcus Brutus' crime[30] rather than the wise examples our ancestors have left; you and your supporters have devised a plan to raid our taxes, try out new ones, set up a new city to rival Rome and subjugate under your law, control and power cities, tribes, provinces, free peoples, kings – in short, the entire world. All this so that when you have drained all our money from the treasury, used up all our taxes and exacted every penny from each king and nation and from our commanders, you will gesture for them to pay more; so you can palm off to the Roman people, at whatever price you decide on, noxious lands bought from the occupiers Sulla settled on them, and deserted and disease-ridden ones bought from your cronies – and even yourselves; so you can occupy all the municipalities and colonies of Italy with your new colonies; so you can station them wherever and however you please; 99. so you can surround the entire Republic with your soldiers, cities and garrisons and keep it ground down; so you can keep Pompey himself – a man to whom the Republic has so often turned to defend herself against her bitterest enemies and most worthless citizens – away from our citizens and from his victorious army; so that you will have complete control over everything that gold or silver can pervert, a mass of votes confiscate and violence and force destroy; so you could romp through nations and through each kingdom with your all-important military authority, your never-ending legal powers and massive piles of cash; so you could enter the camp of Gnaeus Pompey and even sell it off if you could turn a profit; so that, exempt from all our laws and unafraid of any court, you can demand that all the other magistrates appear before you; so no one could bring you before the Roman people, take you to court or force you to face the Senate; and so no consul could curb you and no tribune of the plebs restrain you.

100. Rullus, given your stupidity and lack of self-control, I do not wonder that you wanted all this, but I am utterly aston-

ished that you hoped to gain it while I was consul. Each consul should take great care in guarding the Republic; this is even more true of those who are not elected consul in their cradles but on the Campus Martius. I had no family predecessors to vouch for me to the Roman people: it was all down to belief in *me*. And you, the people, should demand that I personally repay what I owe you. When I was running for consul, no ancestors recommended me; as a result, if I fall short in any way, I cannot summon up their ghosts to plead my case with you. Citizens, if I live long enough (and I shall try to guard my life from their criminal traps), I promise you this on my word of honour: you have entrusted the Republic to a bold man, not a timid one, to a conscientious one, not a lazy man. 101. Am I, the consul, to fear an assembly, to tremble before a tribune of the plebs, to repeatedly shake in my boots for no reason, to fear that I may end up in jail if the tribune of the plebs orders it?[31] Armed with your weapons, outfitted with the high insignia of my position, commanded and authorized by you, *I* am not scared to march to this platform; with your help, citizens, I can resist Rullus' depravity and I shall not fear that these men can conquer and crush a Republic protected by such forces. This assembly and the people who stand before me have taken away any fears I may have had before today. Has anyone who argued in favour of an agrarian law found as supportive an assembly as I have while arguing against this bill? That is, if what I have done here is to argue against it and not bulldoze it into the ground.

102. Citizens, remember this from all I have said: there is nothing more in the interests of the people than what I, a consul of the people, present you with this year – peace overseas, tranquillity at home. I have taken resolute steps to make certain that what you feared when we were elected consuls will not happen. It is not just that you will experience domestic tranquillity – your ever-present wish – but I shall make those who hate that completely calm and peaceable, for it is disturbances and civic unrest which usually raise such men to public office, power and wealth. You, whose influence comes from your votes, whose freedom comes from our laws, whose legal rights come from the courts and the justice of the magistrates,

and, finally, whose wealth comes from peace, should fight for domestic tranquillity in every way you can.

103. Consider this: if men who, simply out of apathy, live in tranquillity and still relish it, even as they wallow in their laziness, will you not be blessed if you preserve your domestic tranquillity – which was not something you sought because of your laziness but was the child of your courage? I have made sure that I and my co-consul are of one mind – something the men who said we would be enemies to one another do not like at all – I have taken precautions against all possible outcomes, I have made plans in the case of a rise in the cost of corn, I have brought back integrity and I have warned the tribunes not to spark trouble while I am consul. But, citizens, the greatest and most solid protection that all our fortunes in this community could have is that you should behave in the future just as you did today in this great assembly convened for your welfare. I promise, I guarantee, I assert to you all that I shall make sure that the men who were bitter when you raised me to this office will one day confess that in electing me you all showed great foresight.

First and Second Catilinarians

CATILINARIAN I

Delivered on 8 November 63 to
the Senate in the temple of Jupiter Stator

Lucius Sergius Catilina, more commonly known as Catiline, was to provide Cicero with one of the defining moments of his career – and threaten his life. All of our sources on Catiline are hostile (even those that are also hostile to Cicero), but there is no reason to doubt most of the salient facts, even if some of his aims and motivations are harder to understand. Born c. 108, he was the product of an ancient patrician family, the gens Sergia, which had given its name to one of the Roman tribes; this, if the epic poet Virgil can be believed, traced its roots back to the Sergestus who came to Italy with Aeneas after the fall of Troy. We know little of Catiline's very early career; he first enters history as one of Sulla's minions after Sulla's blood-drenched return to Italy in 83–82. He even stooped to killing his own brother (Plutarch, Life of Cicero 10.3) during the proscriptions of 82, adding his name to the proscription lists after the event to avoid prosecution. Another murder of a family member followed, this time that of his brother-in-law Quintus Caecilius, also hunted down in Sulla's proscriptions. As if this were not enough murder and mayhem, the ancient sources tell us that after torturing Marcus Marius Gratidianus in November 82, he cut off his head and carried it back to Sulla. To add to a charming reputation, in 73 he was prosecuted (and acquitted) for seducing the Vestal Virgin Fabia (Cicero's wife's half-sister). It is hardly an unblemished record by any means, but Catiline was not alone in taking part in the blood-baths that were periodic events in the 80s, and it certainly did not stop him from being elected praetor for 68.

After his term as praetor he was appointed governor of the province of Africa, where – like many other governors – he sought to recoup the costs of his campaign and gather money for a run for consul. When the consuls elected for 66 were convicted of electoral bribery and were disqualified from taking office, Catiline decided to make his first attempt at the position. However, the consul Lucius Volcatius Tullus refused to allow him to run, either because he had not run in the initial election or was being prosecuted for extortion (Cicero initially thought of defending him). It was during this year, according to Cicero, that he first hatched his plans to overthrow the Republic, standing armed in the Forum on 31 December and organizing a gang to kill the newly elected consuls, along with other important citizens (see chapter 15 below). It is hard to see why Catiline would have been driven to such drastic measures at this stage in his career and most people agree that this so-called 'first Catilinarian conspiracy' is pure invention.

In 65 Catiline was still being prosecuted for his extortionate practices in Africa and thus could not run for consul. His turn came at last in 64; the slate of seven candidates included only three with a fighting chance: Catiline, Gaius Antonius (who had also enriched himself during the proscriptions) and Cicero. Antonius and Catiline formed an electoral alliance; it also seems that Catiline had the backing of Marcus Licinius Crassus, Rome's wealthiest man, and Julius Caesar. Over the year, their support waned as did that of other nobles, perhaps thanks to Cicero's scathing invective. In the end, it was the newcomer, Cicero, who won, taking office along with Antonius. In 63 Rome was in the grip of a fiscal crisis; now that Pompey had defeated the pirates and the war against Mithridates in Asia was reaching its end, money was flowing out of Italy to be invested overseas. The result was a lack of cash in Rome and increasing demands on debtors. The urban plebs were also in a state of unrest (something Publius Rullus' agrarian bill tried to capitalize on; see On the Agrarian Law*). Catiline made his final bid for the consulship; his platform included cancellation of the debts, mulcting the wealthy and also distributing offices among his supporters. While this appealed to heavily indebted members of the elite and Sulla's veterans, to a wider public it was great cause for concern. When the elections eventually took place, Cicero attended dressed in a very visible breast-plate out of concern for his safety. Catiline was once more defeated; he knew there would be no third chance – hence his conspiracy to overthrow the Republic. Everything we know about the conspiracy comes from hostile sources, but there is little reason to doubt that Catiline was up to something: he had little left to lose, much to gain. And there were many others in Rome and Italy in a similar situation; a change in the leadership of Rome and the cancellation of debts would be very welcome. Their strategy to obtain this is unclear; it certainly included Sulla's veterans in Etruria, some arson in the city (though burning down all of Rome, which Cicero alleges was one of their plans, seems rather counter-productive) and the murder of Cicero and several other important citizens.*

Cicero had spies in Catiline's camp and knew some of what was afoot; on 19 October he called a meeting of the Senate and argued (on rather weak evidence) that Catiline's associate Manlius was gathering forces for a revolution in Etruria. On the 21st he presented more evidence to the Senate, so alarming it that it passed the senatus consultum ultimum, *the ultimate decree of the Senate, a type of emergency powers act which authorized the consuls 'to see that the state took no harm'. (The extent of the powers it actually invested in the consuls was rather murky, something that would return to haunt Cicero.) Catiline called another meeting of his associates on the night of 6 November where, among other things, he found two equestrians who agreed to murder Cicero in his home the next day. Forewarned by his spies, Cicero refused entry to the would-be murderers. On the next day, the 8th, he called a meeting of the Senate in the temple of Jupiter Stator to try to force its hand with Catiline; here this speech was delivered – originally in an impromptu performance of great brilliance.*

Despite his confident tone, Cicero was on very unstable ground. Catiline may not have won the consulship and might have somewhat dubious connections, but he was still one of them. Many senators were suspected of being part of the conspiracy (including Caesar and Crassus) and would hardly be willing to turn on their co-conspirator. There are conflicting stories of Catiline's reaction: according to some, he left the Senate without a word; according to others, he argued his case and denied the existence of any conspiracy. Whatever his reaction in the Senate was, he left that night to join Manlius at Faesulae.

1. Answer me, how long, Catiline, will you abuse our patience? How much longer will this madness of yours mock us? To what purpose will your unbridled insolence fling itself again and again? Do you feel nothing at seeing a nocturnal guard on the Palatine, nothing at the vigilance in the city, nothing at the people's terror, nothing at this gathering of every decent man, nothing at this heavily guarded meeting-place of the Senate, nothing at seeing the faces and expressions of these men? Do you not understand that your plans are exposed? Do you not see that our knowledge of all this shackles your conspiracy? What you did last night, what the one before, where you were, the men you met, the plans you hatched – who here do you think is ignorant of these? 2. That our age, our behaviour is reduced to this! The Senate understands all this, the consul sees it: yet Catiline still lives! He lives? Worse: he even enters the Senate, takes part in our measures for the state's safety, and with his glance notes and marks for butchering each one of us. But we, brave men that we are, we think that we look as if we have done enough for the Republic if only we escape his rage and assaults. Catiline, you ought to have been led off to die by a consul's order long ago; the ruin which you have been engineering against all of us should have recoiled on you.

3. Did not a very great man, the pontifex maximus Publius Scipio, even though he held no political office, kill Tiberius Gracchus though he was only chipping away at the stability of

the Republic? Will we, the consuls, put up with Catiline aching to ravage the world with slaughter and fire? I pass over antiquated examples such as Gaius Servilius Ahala killing Spurius Maelius – a man eager for revolution – with his own hand.[1] There was – yes, there was – once such *courage* in this Republic of ours that brave men would cut down destructive citizens with sharper punishments than they would use on their bitterest enemy. Catiline, we hold against you a powerful and weighty decree of the Senate; the leadership and guidance of this order does not fail the Republic; I declare openly that we fail her, we the consuls. 4. The Senate once decreed that the consul Lucius Opimius should see that 'the Republic would take no harm':[2] not even a night passed and Gaius Gracchus, the son, the grandson and the descendant of most noble men, was killed on *suspicion* of treason, as was Marcus Fulvius[3] – along with his children! The Senate entrusted the Republic to Gaius Marius and Lucius Valerius under a similar decree; did the Republic's punishment – death – of the tribune of the plebs Lucius Saturninus[4] and the praetor Gaius Servius wait even for a day? But we now permit the twentieth day[5] to blunt the point of the Senate's leadership. We possess a decree of the Senate like those I have mentioned, but it lies buried in our records as if sheathed in a scabbard. This decree of the Senate, Catiline, authorizes your immediate execution. You go on living – living not to decrease but to increase your recklessness. My desire, members of the Senate, is to be merciful; my desire is not to be delinquent in the face of these huge dangers to the Republic; but already I find myself guilty of laziness and negligence. 5. Camps aimed against the Roman people have been placed within Italy in the pass of Etruria, the number of the enemy grows day by day, and so we watch the general of their camp and the leader of the enemy daily engineering some internal ruin for the Republic inside our walls – even here in the Senate. I imagine, Catiline, that if I order your arrest or execution now, what will happen is *not* that all decent men will say that I acted too late, but that not a single person will say that I acted with uncalled for cruelty! But here is the reason why I am not yet convinced that I should do what should have been done long ago: you will

finally be put to death when and only when there is no one left
so shameless, so ruined, so like you, that they will not admit
that it was done justly.

6. And now as long as there is a single man who dares to
defend you, you will live, and you will live as you are living:
surrounded by many unshakeable defences which prevent you
from moving against the Republic. Even though you are unaware
of them, many eyes and ears will continue to spy on and guard
against you, as they have done until now. What can you hope
for now? Neither night with its shadows can hide your perverse
gatherings nor a private residence[6] contain the sound of your
conspiracy; all these are lit up and out in the open. Believe me
when I say this: change your plan and forget about slaughter
and arson. You are checked on all sides and your plans are
clearer to us than daylight. And now, if you would, kindly
review them with me. 7. Do you not remember that I said in the
Senate[7] on the 21st of October that Gaius Manlius, the accomplice and assistant to your arrogance, would take up arms on a
prearranged day before the 27th of that month? Surely, Catiline, not only was I right about such an important matter, so
shocking and so incredible, but about something more astonishing – the day? I also said in the Senate that you had appointed
the 28th of October for the murder of our finest citizens, a day
when many of our leaders fled from Rome, not so much to save
their lives as to thwart your plans. Are you honestly able to
deny that on the very day my guards carefully encircled you
and prevented you from moving against the Republic, you said
that although some had left you would be content with the
slaughter of the remainder? 8. What? When you were confident
that you could occupy Praeneste on the first of November using
a night-time attack, did you not learn that this colony was
protected on my order by my defences, guards and vigilance?
There is nothing you do, nothing you engineer, nothing you
think about which I shall not only hear of but also see and have
full insight into.

Review with me the night before last and you will understand that I keep a sharper eye on the safety of the Republic
than you do on her destruction. I assert that on the night before

last you came into the Scythe-makers Street – no, let me be plain about it – into the house of Marcus Laeca, and that many partners in your criminal insanity met with you in the same place. Surely you do not dare to deny it? Why are you silent? I shall win my case if you deny it, for I see that there are men here in the Senate who were there with you. 9. Immortal gods! Where on earth are we? What Republic is this? In what city are we living? Here, there are *here*, members of the Senate, in the most sacred and august council the world possesses, those who plot the destruction of us all, the ruin of this city and the whole world. I, the consul, see them and I ask their opinion about public business and yet my words do not lash men whom the sword should cut to pieces.

So, Catiline, you were at the house of Marcus Laeca on that night; you portioned out Italy; decided where you wanted everyone to march; selected those you would leave at Rome, those you would lead out with you; and parcelled out what parts of the city to burn. You confirmed that you yourself were about to leave, but there would be a slight delay because I was still alive. Lo and behold, you found two equestrians[8] who would free you from that worry and who promised that they personally would kill me in my bed shortly before dawn. 10. *I* was the one who discovered all this although your gathering had scarcely been disbanded. I fortified and protected my house with more guards. And when the very men had come, whose arrival I had already predicted to many of our senior states-men, I denied entry to those you had sent to 'pay their respects' to me early in the morning.[9] Since this is the case, Catiline, con-tinue on as you have begun and – finally – leave the city. The gates gape wide – go. For too long that Manlian camp of yours has sighed for you to be its general. Lead out with you all your followers too, and if not all, then as many as possible. Purify the city. You will relieve me of great fear once the city wall lies between the two of us. You cannot reside among us any longer; that I cannot, will not, *shall not* tolerate.

11. Great thanks must be offered to the immortal gods and to the most ancient guardian of this city, Jupiter Stator[10] – he who is right here – that we have already so many times escaped

a disease so vile, horrible and virulent. Rarely is the health of
the Republic endangered by one man! As long as you plotted
only against me as the consul-elect, I defended myself not with
a public guard but with personal carefulness. When at the most
recent consular elections you wished to kill me (the consul!)
and your rivals, I checked your unholy efforts with guards and
an army of friends without provoking a public commotion. In
short, as often as you have attacked me I have thwarted you,
although I saw that my own destruction would mean the Republic's absolute downfall.[11] 12. But now you take open aim at the
entire Republic, you call to catastrophe and devastation the
temples of the immortal gods, the houses of the city, the life of
every citizen and, finally, all Italy. Because I still hesitate to take
the best course of action, one which would be in line with the
authority I have been granted and the lessons provided by our
ancestors, I shall do what is more lenient than severity requires
but more useful for our common well-being. For if I order you
to be killed, the remnants of your conspirators will subside into
the sludge of the Republic; but if you leave – as I have been
urging you to do for so long – then that deadly scum will be
flushed out of Rome.

13. What is it, Catiline? Surely you do not hesitate to do as
I order – after all, you were about to do it voluntarily. The consul orders an enemy out of the city. 'Into exile?' you ask. I do
not order that, but if you are asking me, I advise it. What pleasure now remains for you in this city, Catiline? Here everyone
who has not joined your conspiracy of losers already fears and
hates you. What personal disgrace[12] is not branded on your
face? What financial failure is not part of your reputation?
When have you torn your eyes from sex, your hands from
crime or your body from a degrading act? To what precious
young man now entangled in your seductive nets have you not
provided tools for his crimes or a light to shine on his lechery?
14. What more? Just now, when you made your house free for
a new bride by the death of the old wife, did you not then pile
another unbelievable crime on that crime?[13] But I pass that by
and willingly suffer it to go unsaid for fear that it will look as
if in this city a crime of such immensity could happen – or go

unpunished. I pass over the collapse of your fortunes, all of which you will be aware must be handed over on the 15th of the month.[14] Now I come to what pertains not to the personal disgrace of your vices, not to your financial difficulties and indecency at home, but to the supreme crisis of the Republic and to all of our lives and safety.

15. Can it possibly be that you find the light or the breeze from this sky pleasant, when you know that not one of these men here is unaware that on the 29th of December, in the year of the consulship of Lepidus and Tullus, you stood in the assembly *armed*,[15] that you readied a gang to murder the consuls and our senior statesmen and that nothing – not a change of plan or your fear – except the good fortune of the Roman people thwarted your mad crime? But as your plots are well known and you've committed more since then, I shall skip over how often you tried to kill me when I was the consul-elect *and* consul. How many of your thrusts – so well aimed that they seemed unavoidable – have I escaped (as the saying goes) by dancing out of the way. You have no success, you gain nothing, but you do not stop wishing or trying. 16. How many times has your blade been ripped from your hands, how often has it fallen or slipped from them by some blunder! Yet you cannot live without it. I cannot imagine with what ritual it has been consecrated and dedicated that you think it is necessary to plunge it into the body of a consul.

What sort of life do you have these days? For I shall now so speak with you that I shall not appear to be provoked by hatred – as is my right – but by pity, not a scrap of which you deserve. A little while ago you entered the Senate. What man from this massive crowd and among your many friends and connections paid their respects? If *no one* has experienced this within living memory, do *you* wait for my insults when the momentous judgement of their silence crushes you? What shall we say of the fact that at your arrival those benches around you were emptied, that all men of consular rank (so often marked by you for murder) left your section bare and empty as soon as you sat down? Tell me, how do you think you should bear this? 17. By Hercules, if my *slaves* feared me in the way all citizens fear you, I'd reckon it time to leave home. And do you not think you should leave this city? If I saw myself wrongly suspected and so offensive to my fellow-citizens, I would prefer to be out of their sight rather than be the focus of their hostile eyes. Since the guilty awareness of your crimes ensures you understand everyone's justified, overdue hatred, do you hesitate to avoid the sight and company of those whose minds and feelings you torment? I presume that if your parents feared and hated you, and you could not please them at all, you would have taken yourself somewhere out of their sight. As it is, your country, the father we all share, hates and fears you, and he has long since judged that you think only about his parricide. Will you not respect his authority, follow his advice or tremble at his power?

18. He now pleads with you and speaks in his own silent way:

'For some years now there has been no crime committed except through you, no abuse without you. You alone went unpunished and free from any consequence for the murders of many citizens, for the harassment and plunder of our allies; you have succeeded not only in sneering at laws and courts, but even in overturning and shattering them. I endured these crimes as best I could, although I should not have had to endure them. But that I live in complete fear because of you alone, every sound brings fear of Catiline, that no plot can be hatched which your criminal nature shrinks from – that must not be endured. For this reason, depart and remove my fear. Then, if my fear is *real*, I shall not be taken by surprise, but if it is false, it will have an end.'

19. If your country were to speak as I have just spoken, surely it should prevail, even if it could not use force? What of the fact that you surrendered yourself for house arrest and said you wished to live in Manius Ledipus' house to avoid suspicion?[16] And when he would not take you in, you even dared to come to me and ask me to keep an eye on you at my home! And when you got my reply that there was no way I could be safe shut up in the same house as you, given that I was already in

great danger because we were inside the same city, you went to Quintus Metellus,[17] the praetor. After he rejected you, you departed for your companion, Marcus Metellus,[18] that most excellent man, who (of course!) you thought would be the most diligent person to guard you, the quickest to suspect you and the most forward in punishing you. Do you think it right that a man who thought he should be under house arrest is nowhere near a prison and chains?

20. Given this situation, Catiline, if you are unable to die with dignity, why do you hesitate to go abroad and entrust the life you have snatched from thoroughly deserved punishment to a lonely flight? 'Bring the matter before the Senate,' you say. You demand that, and you insist you will obey if this body decrees your exile. I shall *not* bring this matter before the Senate: it is inconsistent with my character. Nevertheless, I shall make you understand what these men think about you. Leave the city, Catiline, free the Republic from fear. Go – you are awaiting that word. What is it, Catiline? Are you paying any attention? Have you noticed these men's silence at all? They permit this speech – they are silent. Why do you await their spoken command when you can clearly see their silent desire? 21. But if I had said the same thing to that peerless young man Publius Sestius[19] or to that very brave man Marcus Marcellus,[20] by now this Senate would, and with complete justification, have laid violent hands on me, the consul, in this very temple. But in your case, Catiline, their lack of reaction is their judgement, their tolerance of my words their vote and their silence their outcry. And it is not just these men, whose guidance alone (naturally!) is as dear to you as their lives are cheap, but also the equestrian class – honourable and peerless men – and the rest of the brave citizens who surround the Senate, the crowd whose size you could see, whose enthusiasm you could view and whose voices you could hear just a moment ago. It will be easy for me to convince men, whom I have been hard put to keep from attacking you, to escort you right up to the city gates, as you leave behind all you have been straining for so long to destroy.

22. Why do I even bother speaking? As if anything would break you, or you would ever straighten yourself out, contemplate

flight or consider any form of exile! If only the immortal gods could grant you that! Still, I see that even if in terror at this speech you made up your mind to go into exile, how great a storm of ill-will threatens to rain down on me – not now because of the fresh memory of your crimes, but later. However, I would still consider this worthwhile, provided that it is just *my* private catastrophe and is separate from the dangers to the Republic.

But we must not expect you to be swayed from your vices, to dread legal punishment or yield to the needs of the Republic! Catiline, you are not a man to allow a sense of shame to pull you back from indecent behaviour, or fear from danger or reason from insanity. 23. This is why you should leave as I keep telling you to, and if you wish to fan hatred for me as your enemy – as you declare you do – go directly into exile. Surely I shall hardly be able to endure men's gossip if you do so or sustain the weight of ill-will if you go into exile *at a consul's order!* However, if you want to help my reputation, leave with your vicious gang of criminals, take yourself off to Manlius, stir up ruined citizens, separate yourself from the decent ones, wage war on your country, relish your treacherous, outlaw life. Then it will not look as if *I* exiled you to live among strangers, but that your own people invited you to live with them. 24. But why should I 'invite' you to leave? I know that you have already sent men ahead who are to await you armed near the Forum Aurelium,[21] I know that you have agreed upon a particular day with Manlius and that you have sent ahead that silver eagle[22] (which I am confident will be fatally destructive to you and all yours), the eagle for which you set up a shrine at your house. How can you stand to be any longer without it – that object you worshipped before you headed out to slaughter and from whose altar you often raised your unholy right hand to murder citizens?

25. You will finally go where your unrestrained, mad lust began dragging you long ago – an outcome which does not bring you pain but a type of unimaginable pleasure. Nature created you, your inclination trained you and fortune kept you safe for this insanity. It is not just that you never wanted peace, you did not even want a war unless it was perverted. You

acquired a gang of deviants welded together from complete losers, men entirely abandoned by fortune *and* hope. 26. Given this, what happiness will you savour, what joys boast of and what gratification get drunk upon when among your huge crowd of followers you will not see nor hear a single decent man? This is the life for which you undertook your so-called 'training'. You slept on the ground not just to position yourself for sex but to be on call for crime; you kept watch not only to plot against husbands' sleep but also peaceable citizens' property; now you have an opportunity to show your famed endurance of hunger, cold and complete deprivation – and you will see how quickly they wear you out.

27. Even if I accomplished nothing else when I defeated you at the consular elections, I ensured that you would make an attempt on the Republic as an exile rather than harass it as a consul, and what you had criminally undertaken would be called terrorism rather than war. Members of the Senate, I beg you now to listen carefully to what I shall say next and lay it deep within your hearts and minds so that I can avert from myself the almost (if I may say so) legitimate complaint of my country through prayer and pleas. Suppose my country – which is much dearer to me than my own life – and all Italy and the entire Republic were to speak thus with me: 'Marcus Tullius, what are you doing? Will you allow a man – whom you have discovered to be an enemy, and see will be a general in this war, who is awaited as a commander in the camp of the enemy, is the instigator of crime, a leader of a conspiracy, a recruiter of slaves and ruined citizens – to leave so that he may look not like someone you have sent out of the city but as one sent against it? Will you not order this man to be cast into chains, to be dragged away to die, to pay the ultimate price? 28. What exactly is impeding you? Our traditions? But in this Republic even private citizens have frequently punished destructive ones with death. Or is it the laws which have been passed regarding the punishment of Roman citizens? But in this city laws have never preserved the rights of citizens who have abandoned the Republic. Maybe you fear posterity's hatred? Naturally! Repay the remarkable favour you owe the Roman people for raising

you – a man famous through his own efforts and not those of his ancestors – at such a young age[23] through each successive political office, until you reached their apex, by neglecting the safety of fellow-citizens because you fear danger or being hated. 29. But if you have some fear of being hated, is hatred which you have incurred through rigour and courage something you should fear more deeply than that which comes from being lazy and worthless? Or, when Italy is devastated, her cities ravaged and her houses burned by war, do you think that you will not then be consumed by a fire-storm of hatred?'

I shall respond briefly to these, the Republic's sacred words, and to the thoughts of those of you who feel the same way. I, members of the Senate, had I been of the belief that it was the best thing to do to punish Catiline with death, would not have given one hour's grace to that gladiator. For if our greatest men and most prominent citizens did not so much stain as grace themselves with the blood of Saturninus, the Gracchi, Flaccus and many before that, surely I should not fear that any hatred will overwhelm *me* after this murderer of his fellow-citizens is killed. But even if this should threaten me, I have always been of the mind that hatred born from a courageous act is in reality glory.

30. And there are many, not just among the perverse but also the naïve, who have followed their leadership. Some have nourished Catiline's ambitions with their soft attitudes, encouraging the growing conspiracy by not believing it existed. Many, not just among the perverse but also the naïve, have followed their leadership, and so if I had punished Catiline they would say that it had been done cruelly and despotically. I understand now that if he arrives at his destination, Manlius' camp, no one will be so stupid that they will not see that a conspiracy has been formed, or so perverse that they will not admit this. But if he alone is killed, I know well that this cancer of the Republic can only be checked for a little, not suppressed forever. But if he banishes himself, takes his followers with him and gathers up into one place other washed-up characters from all over, not only will we eradicate and wipe out this full-grown cancer, but even the root and seed of all evils. 31. For a long time we have

been susceptible to dangerous plots from the conspiracy, yet somehow or other all his crimes and his long-standing madness and arrogance came to a fever-pitch in my consulship. If he is the only one removed from this pack of outlaws it will look for a brief time as if we are relieved of worry and fear, but the danger will linger, buried deep in the Republic's blood and guts. Just as when men are seriously ill and are racked with a fever's heat, they often seem to be relieved at first if they drink cold water, but then are afflicted more seriously and more violently, so this sickness which infects the Republic will grow worse if the rest remain alive, even if it will be relieved by Catiline's punishment.

32. For this reason let evil men leave; separating themselves from the decent, let them herd together in one place. Let them finally (as I have often said before) be divided from us by the city walls, cease plotting against the consul in his own home, surrounding the tribunal of the city praetor,[24] besieging the Senate house with swords in hand and preparing grenades and torches to set fire to the city. Let every man carry branded on his forehead what he feels about the Republic. Members of the Senate, I promise this to you: we, the consuls, will take such great care, you will hold such authority, the equestrians such bravery and all decent men have such consensus, that by Catiline's departure all will be laid wide open, made clear, crushed – and punished. 33. Catiline, with these omens, and attended by your ruinous cancer and the destruction of those who have joined you, head out to disloyal and sacrilegious warfare, and in doing so vastly improve the Republic's health. Jupiter, you who were established with the same auspices as this city,[25] whom we call truly the guardian of our city and empire, will you ward off this man and his allies from your temples and those of the other gods, from the houses and walls of the city and from the life and fortunes of all citizens? Will you afflict those who are hostile to decent men – enemies of the state, united in a criminal alliance and in an unspeakable association as outlaws to all Italy – with eternal punishment, whether living or dead?

CATILINARIAN II

Delivered on 9 November 63 to
the assembly of the people

This speech was Cicero's response to Catiline's departure from Rome; its ringing invective was meant both to assure the people that they had just seen the end of a dangerous threat to Rome and to portray the conspirators as evil incarnate, yet ready to collapse once the appropriate pressure was applied. Although the speech speaks for itself, it cannot tell the future. Here, then, is what came after it was delivered.

It was several weeks after the speech before Cicero could move further against the conspirators. A Gallic tribe, the Allobroges, gave him the means to do so; envoys of this tribe had come to Rome looking for relief from tribute and moneylenders, and were a natural target for the conspirators. On being approached, however, they went to their tribe's patron, Quintus Fabius Sanga, who consulted Cicero. Cicero asked them to play along with the conspirators and request written proof of the conspiracy as a condition for their help. Rather astonishingly, the conspirators did so and wrote incriminating letters. As arranged by Cicero, the envoys were arrested on 2 December 63 while leaving the city with the letters; on the 3rd those conspirators still in Rome were arrested, brought before the Senate and confronted with the letters. They confessed all and were handed over to the custody of various leading citizens. That evening Cicero delivered his Third Catilinarian. *On the 5th the Senate met again to debate the fate of the conspirators, but could not bring itself to vote for their deaths. Cicero delivered his* Fourth Catilinarian *and clearly showed that he favoured execution for the arrestees. That night the five of them (Lentulus, Cethegus, Gabinius, Statilius and Ceparius) were strangled in the Tullianum, the state prison on the Capitoline Hill. Catiline tried to lead his army into Transalpine Gaul but found the passes blocked by Metellus Celer. On 5 January 62 he met with Cicero's co-consul Gaius Antonius at the foot of the Apennines near Pistoria (modern Pistoia). His army was wiped out and he himself killed – according to tradition, while fighting furiously.*

The fall-out from the execution of the conspirators haunted Cicero and eventually led to his exile. The lex Valeria *of 509 stated that no magistrate should execute or whip a Roman citizen without allowing an appeal to the people; this meant that only the centuriate assembly could pronounce a death sentence within the walls of Rome; in 121 Gaius Gracchus passed a plebiscite stating that no trial at which the life of a Roman citizen was at stake could take place without the consent of the people. In Cicero's view, the ultimate decree of the Senate superseded that right and gave the consuls the authority to execute the conspirators without a trial, and that as they had been declared enemies of the state they had lost their rights as citizens. These were dubious legal grounds, however, and the cracks in Cicero's position showed even before the conspiracy was crushed for good. On 10 December, Quintus Caecilius Metellus Nepos took office as one of the following year's tribunes of the plebs; he then declared that anyone who had executed Romans without a trial should not be allowed to address the people. He was as good as his word: when Cicero stood to give the traditional oration on the last day of a consul's office, Metellus stopped him. Always quick on his feet, Cicero used his departing oath to declare that he alone had saved the Republic. Despite the trouble which was to follow, it seems appropriate to leave Cicero in his greatest moment of triumph: the evening of 5 December 63, when the crowd of Rome escorted him home, hailing him with the title of* pater patriae, *father of his country.*

1. Citizens, we have finally thrown out or, rather, dismissed and wished bon voyage to Lucius Catiline, raving with recklessness, panting out crime, scheming unholy ruin for his country and threatening you and Rome with fire and the sword. He left. Exited. Escaped. Erupted. Now that ill-omened monster will

not plot destruction for our city from within. What is more, we have defeated that singular general of civil war without a fight. His dagger will not be twisted in our ribs, whether we stand in the Campus Martius, the Forum or the Curia;[1] we shall no longer tremble in our homes. He was dislodged from his position when he was driven out of Rome. Now, without hindrance, we wage open war with the enemy. There is no doubt that we destroyed him and gained a brilliant victory when we forced him from hidden plotting into open outlawry. 2. Tell me, what do you think might be the depth of overwhelming sorrow he feels now, since he did not achieve his desire and carry off with him a sword dripping with my blood as he departed? Or because I tore the sword from his hands and he left citizens unharmed and Rome still standing? Now he lies in the dust and understands that he is beaten, rejected; I am sure he often twists his gaze back to Rome and laments that she was snatched from his jaws. When I look at Rome, she looks as if she is rejoicing because she vomited up and spat out such a great cancer.

3. Citizens, if there is someone (and, in fact, this is how everyone should think) who would attack me vigorously on the very subject on which I now exultantly triumph – my failure to arrest and my release of such a deadly enemy – well, that is not my fault but that of our times. Lucius Catiline ought to have felt our heaviest punishment and died long ago; tradition, the uncompromising nature of my position and the Republic all demanded that. How many people do you think there were who did not believe my reports, or who even defended him, who did not even think there was a conspiracy, because of their stupidity, or who actually favoured him because of their own depravity? But if I had honestly thought that with him gone you would be in no danger, I would have taken out Lucius Catiline a long time ago, even if I was risking not just hatred but my own life. 4. Since I saw that some of you were not convinced of the facts, and that I would have been crushed by hatred if I had punished him with the death he deserved – an outcome that would ensure I could not pursue his accomplices – I took the matter this far so that you could do open battle with

him, as with an open enemy. Citizens, understand from my next statement how strongly we should fear this enemy now that he is flushed out into the open: I am annoyed that he left the city with just a meagre escort. If only he had taken out *all* his forces with him! Lucky for me he took Tongilius, a man he began to love while still wearing his boy's toga,[2] *and* Publicius and Minucius,[3] men whose bar bills would hardly cause chaos in the Republic – and left behind men with huge debts, the powerful and the noble.

5. When I compare them with our Gallic legions, the recent military levy which Quintus Metellus held in Picenum and Gaul[4] and the troops which we are assembling every day, I thoroughly despise his army of desperate old men, cloddish wasters and country bankrupts, consisting of people who have chosen to forfeit their bail rather than positions in his army. These will collapse if I show them a praetor's edict,[5] let alone our army's battle line. I would prefer that he had taken with him as soldiers the men I see hanging around the Forum, standing near the Curia, and even coming into the Senate all slick with hair oil and gleaming with purple.[6] If they remain here, just remember that the army he has now is not as terrifying as one made up of its deserters. In fact, they are even more terrifying because they are aware that I know what they are thinking, and even that has no impact.

6. I see who was allocated Apulia, who has Etruria, Picenum or Gaul, who demanded as his share plotting, slaughter and arson within Rome herself. They see that all their plans from the night before last[7] have been reported to me; I made that clear in the Senate yesterday. Catiline himself feared and fled – so what are *they* waiting for? They are certainly mistaken if they hope that my previous gentleness will continue forever. I achieved what I was aiming at: that all of you would see that a conspiracy against the Republic has been openly created – unless there is someone who thinks that men who resemble Catiline do not agree with him? There is no longer a place for gentleness; this situation demands no mercy. But even now I shall grant one thing: they can leave and go on their way and stop poor Catiline from withering away with desire for his

men. I shall point out the path; he went along the Aurelian Way[8] – if they want to hurry, they will catch him by evening.

7. The Republic is fortunate if she has in fact spat out this scum of Rome. By Hercules, I think the Republic is lighter and refreshed since we flushed away Catiline. Is there an evil or crime which can be dreamed or thought up which he did not come up with? Can we find in any part of Italy any poisoner, any gladiator, any outlaw, assassin, parricide, forger of wills, con-man, glutton, prodigal, adulterer, woman without a decent name, corrupter of the young or corrupted loser who does not confess that he was intimate friends with Catiline? In recent years, what murder was committed without him, what perverse sexual act without his help? 8. Was there ever anyone who was as attractive to young men as he was? He loved other men in a most disgusting way and degradingly played the slave's part to other men's love;[9] he promised some the satisfaction of their desires, others the death of their parents – and did not just encourage but *helped*. How quickly he collected a huge number of losers, not just from the city but even from the countryside! There was not a single person crushed by debt in Rome or any Italian backwater that he did not admit to his unbelievable criminal alliance.

9. Now take a look at his various tastes in different spheres. Every member of a gladiatorial school who, even by the standards of gladiators, is overeager to commit crime, admits he was extremely close to Catiline. Every more than normally worthless and useless actor brags of being his crony. It was these sorts of people who called him brave, because his workouts in sexual offences and crimes made him a hard man, able to endure cold, hunger, thirst and sleepless nights. But the truth was, he was wasting whatever profit his hard work and courage brought him in sex and wild behaviour. 10. If his true comrades follow him, if that infamous herd of hopeless men leave Rome – lucky us! Fortunate Republic! How my consulship will be praised! Already their lust is extraordinary, their arrogance inhuman and unendurable. They think of nothing except slaughter, arson and looting. They have run through their inheritances, mortgaged their estates; their money ran out long ago – their credit

only recently. And still the desires they had in their days of prosperity remain the same. If they only looked for good times and
whores as they drank and gambled, we could despair of them
but still find them tolerable. But who could tolerate cowards
plotting against the brave, idiots against the wise, the drunk
against the sober and the comatose against the conscious? Men
who recline at feasts, clutching whorish women, limp from
wine, stuffed with food, crowned with garlands, smeared with
perfumes and worn out from sex, belch out as conversation the
murder of decent men and the burning of Rome.

11. I am confident that their doom hangs over them and that
the penalty, which has for a long time been due to depravity,
excess, crime and lechery, is now at hand or, at the very least,
draws near. If my consulship gets rid of them (since they cannot
be cured) then it will have extended the Republic's life, not for
some brief moment but for many generations. We do not tremble before any other nation, there is no king who could start a
war with the Roman people. Everything beyond our borders
has been pacified, on sea and land, by the mastery of one man.[10]
But an internal war remains, there is treachery at home, a pent-
up danger – an enemy. We must go to war against excess,
insanity, against crime. Citizens, I declare myself your general
in this war. I take up this feud with ruined men. I shall cure
what can be cured however I can. I shall not allow what must
be cut away to remain and ruin our community. So, then, let
them leave or be peaceable. And if they stay in the city while
keeping their old frame of mind, they should expect to get what
they deserve.

12. Citizens, there are still those who say that I sent Catiline
into exile. If mere talk could achieve this, I would also exile
those who make this comment. *Naturally*, such a timid and
extremely retiring man could not bear the consul's voice; as
soon as he was ordered off into exile, he obeyed and went. Yesterday, citizens, a day on which I was nearly killed in my own
home, I called a meeting of the Senate in the temple of Jupiter
Stator and reported the whole business to the members of the
Senate. When Catiline arrived, was there a senator who would
use his name or greet him? Was there a single one who saw him

as anything other than a ruined citizen or, should I say, as a completely vicious citizen? In fact, even the leading members of that body left the sections of benches he had approached bare and empty. 13. Then I, the famously violent consul, who exiles citizens with just a word, I asked Catiline whether or not he had been at the nocturnal meeting at Marcus Laeca's. Since he, although he has plenty of nerve, was overcome by the consciousness of his guilt and was silent at first, I laid out the rest. I laid out what he had done that night, where he had been, what he had decided on the next night, how he had drawn up the whole plan of his campaign. When he stammered, when he was trapped, I asked why he hesitated to head out for the place he had been for a long time preparing to go to, since I knew that weapons, the rods and axes,[11] trumpets, military standards and that silver eagle (for which he had even set up a shrine in his house!) had been sent ahead. 14. Was I trying to exile a man who I knew had already started a war? And I suppose that centurion Manlius, who placed a camp in the Faesulan region and declared war on his own account against the Roman people, and his camp, are not awaiting Catiline as their general? I suppose that when Catiline is exiled he will take himself off to Massilia[12] like they say instead of heading to Faesulae? The miserable task of administering *and* saving the Republic falls to me! Even now if Lucius Catiline, surrounded and crippled by my planning, my efforts and my threats, suddenly became fearful, changed his mind, abandoned his followers, cast aside his intention for making war and went into exile, instead of continuing in his career of crime and his war path, people will not say that I disarmed his aggressiveness, stopped him dead and terrified him by my diligence or drove him out from his hopes and schemes. Instead, they will say that the violent threats of a consul sent him into exile as an unjudged and innocent man. There will be those who will wish *him*, if he does this, to be judged wretched rather than perverse and *me* a thoroughly vicious tyrant rather than an extremely diligent consul!

15. Citizens, I am happy to accept this groundless hatred and injustice if it means I can avert the threat of unholy, horrific war from you. He can be called 'exiled' – provided that he goes

into exile. But – trust me with this – *he has no intention of going.* I shall never hope that, just to lessen people's hatred of me, the immortal gods make it so you hear that Catiline is flying to his weapons and marching at the head of an enemy army. Yet within three days you *will* hear this. I fear this more: that people will hate me because I let him go instead of banishing him. But since there are people who say that now he has gone he was 'banished', what would they say if he had been killed? 16. The truth is that those who keep saying that Catiline is going to Massilia fear that more than they are complaining about it. There is not one of them so full of pity that he would not prefer him to go to Manlius rather than Massilia. But, by Hercules, *he*, even if he had never planned his current actions, still prefers to die while living as an outlaw rather than to live as an exile. Now, since nothing has happened to him that is different from what he wanted or planned (except that he has left Rome while I still live), let us hope rather than complain that he is going into exile. 17. But why am I spending so long talking about one enemy? And about an enemy who now confesses that he *is* an enemy, and whom I do not fear since there is a wall between us – the very thing I have always desired? Do I say nothing about those who mask their treachery and remain at Rome among us? But if it is at all possible, I am eager to restore them to their true selves and to reconcile them to the Republic rather than punish them. I am at a loss to see how that cannot be achieved, if they would only listen to me. Citizens, I shall explain to you from what types of men his army is made up; then I shall treat each one with a dose of my advice and oratory.

18. One type is made up of those who, although in great debt, have property that is even greater than their debt but cannot be persuaded to get rid of it because they love it so. As they are wealthy, this is a respectable-looking group of men, but their intentions and principles are totally shameless. Do you people, with your abundance of land, buildings, silver plate, slaves – in fact, everything – hesitate to sell off part of your property and regain some credit? What are you hoping for? War? What then? Do you think that when everything else is plundered, your property will remain sacrosanct? Maybe the

cancellation of debts?[13] Those who hope Catiline will grant them that are mistaken; but with *my* help debts will be paid off – with auctions. There is no other way for property owners to become debt free. If they had been willing to act earlier and not stupidly struggle on, using the profits from their estates in a vain attempt to pay interest, we would find them richer and better citizens. I think we should not fear this group a great deal; we shall change their minds or, if we do not, I think they are more likely to rely on prayers than be slayers.

19. The next type are men who, despite being squeezed hard by debt, still hope for absolute power, who want to control everything. These think that when the Republic is in crisis they can gain the political offices that they despair of ever getting when it is at peace. As with the others, I must advise them that they should give up hope of achieving their aims. First, I myself am on guard and at hand and looking out for the Republic. Second, there are decent men with great courage here, and the masses stand in unity with us. Third, we have a large military force. Finally, the immortal gods will personally aid us, an unconquered people, a splendid empire and a most beautiful city, in the fight against such criminal violence. But even if these men were to attain their totally insane desires, surely they do not imagine that, standing in the ashes of their city and in the blood of its citizens, as their criminal and unholy minds long for, they will become consuls, dictators – or even kings? Do they not see that if they attain their desire, they will have to hand it over to some runaway slave or gladiator?

20. The third type is weakened by age, but keeps its strength up through training. Manlius, the man Catiline now replaces, is from this group. These are men from the colonies established by Sulla; I am aware that the members of these colonies are normally the best and bravest of citizens, but there are colonists who have flounced about too extravagantly in their unexpected and sudden wealth. While they built like the rich, enjoyed choice estates, great numbers of slaves and magnificent banquets, they fell into debt – and to become free of debt they must raise up Sulla from the dead.[14] These men have even incited some poor, poverty-stricken peasants to join them in

their hopes for the looting of the old days. I place both colonists and peasants into the same class of looters and plunderers, but I warn them to stop their madness and their expectations of dictators and proscriptions. The pain of those days scarred our community so much that I think it is not only men but even the animals in the fields that will not tolerate their return.

21. The fourth type is made up of varied, heterogeneous troublemakers. They are men who were crushed long ago and will never rise again, who stagger under old debts incurred partially through their laziness, partially through mismanaging their affairs and partially through extravagance. They are the men who, exhausted by posting sureties, by court cases and by the public sales of their property, are said to be taking themselves off in large numbers from city and countryside to Catiline's camp. I do not consider these so much eager soldiers as unenthusiastic defaulters. Let these men fall as soon as possible if they cannot stand on their own two feet – but fall so that not only Rome but also our close neighbours do not feel it. What I do not understand is why, if they cannot live honourably, they want to die disgracefully, or why they consider that they will die in less distress if they die alongside others and not alone.

22. The fifth type consists of parricides and assassins – in short, every other type of criminal. I do not want these back from Catiline. They cannot be torn from him and, for all I care, they can die as outlaws since there are so many of them that prison cannot hold them all.[15] This last type is not just *last* in my list but last in character and way of life: they are Catiline's own, his favourites, those he is closest to and fondest of. You see them, all slick with their groomed hair, clean-shaven or with a neatly trimmed beard, dressed in long-sleeved, ankle-length tunics and wearing see-through gowns, not togas.[16] All their effort and hard work at staying awake is put to use at all-night dinners. 23. This herd contains every gambler, adulterer, soiled and whorish man. These oh-so-charming and delicate boys have learnt not only how to get it but give it up, to dance and sing *and* shake their daggers and mix poisons. Understand this: unless they leave, unless they die, this will be a nursery for

Catilines remaining in our midst, even if Catiline dies. What do those wretched men want? Do they really intend to take their little whores with them into camp? Yet how will they do without them, especially on these nights?[17] How will they survive the Apennines and their legendary frost and snow? Perhaps they think that they will find it easier to endure winter because they learnt to dance naked at their get-togethers?

24. Yes, that is a war we *really* should fear, since Catiline will have this bodyguard of male whores! Citizens, draw up now your defences and armies against Catiline's truly magnificent forces. First, array your commanders and consuls against that used-up and wounded gladiator; then lead out Italy's combined and flourishing strength against that washed-up and crippled band of shipwrecked men. Then the towns of colonists and the municipalities will face off against Catiline's wooded hills. I really should not compare the rest of your forces, military equipment and defences with that outlaw's needy poverty. 25. But even if we set aside what we are well supplied with and he lacks – the Senate, the equestrians, Rome, the treasury, our revenues, all of Italy, every province, foreign allies – even if we omit all these and send our opposed 'principles' to battle among themselves, we will understand how very weak they are. On our side, the combatants are a sense of shame, decency, honesty, loyalty, resolution, honour, self-control; on theirs, shamelessness, indecency, deceit, betrayal, insanity, dishonour and permissiveness. So, justice, moderation, courage, wisdom and all the virtues struggle against injustice, excess, cowardice, recklessness and all the vices. In short, plenty collides with poverty, good principles with corrupt, sanity with insanity and high hopes with complete despair. Surely, in a contest or battle of this sort, even if human enthusiasm were to flag, the immortal gods would ensure that so many great vices were overcome by these splendid virtues?

26. Citizens, since this is the case, as I just explained, use your vigilance and guards to defend your houses; I have taken care to ensure that the city is well defended without involving or disturbing you. I have informed the colonies and municipalities of Catiline's journey last night and they will easily

defend their towns and borders; the gladiators that he thought would form a highly reliable gang (although some of them are more loyal than some patricians) will be confined by my authority.[18] I foresaw all of this and sent Quintus Metellus ahead into Gaul and Picenum; he will either crush Catiline or check all his movements and forays. As for the rest, I shall call the Senate together and put before it what we must decide upon and quickly act on. 27. As for those who have remained in Rome or, rather, were left by Catiline to plot against Rome's and your well-being, although they are now enemies, since they were born citizens I want them to be given this earnest warning: if I seemed a little lax and gentle to anyone before now, I was only waiting for what was hidden to break out into the open. As for the future, I cannot forget that this is my country. I am the consul of the men here and I must live with them or die for them. There is no guard on the gate, no ambush set on the way; if anyone wants to leave, I can turn a blind eye. But if anyone makes a move in the city, I shall detect not just his actions but anything begun or attempted against my country. He will learn that this city possesses vigilant consuls, outstanding magistrates, a brave Senate, weapons and a prison which our ancestors wanted as punishment for unholy and flagrant crimes.

28. Citizens, all this will be arranged to ensure the following: that the most important affairs will be settled with the least disorder, the biggest threat with no disturbance and the most vicious and greatest internal and civil war within living memory with me alone as your general and commander, wearing not armour but a toga. I shall manage all this so that – if it is at all possible – not even a disloyal citizen of Rome will suffer the punishment his crime deserves. But if the enormity of his open recklessness or the danger threatening our country forces me from my previous gentleness, I am still sure I shall achieve the near impossible: that no decent citizen will die and the punishment of a few men will make all of you safe. 29. Citizens, I promise this to you, not relying on my wisdom nor on human counsel, but on many sure signs from the immortal gods. With them as my guides, I have begun to hope and believe that they do not defend us from a foreign, distant enemy, as in the past,

but are among us and protect with their divine power and aid their own temples and the houses of Rome. Citizens, you should pray to, beseech and beg them that, after overcoming all your enemies on land and sea, they will defend this city from the unholy crimes of one absolutely corrupted citizen, this city which they wish to be the most beautiful, the most flourishing and the most powerful in the world.

In Defence of Archias, the Poet

Delivered in 62 in the court on Roman citizenship

In 1333 the poet Petrarch rediscovered Cicero's speech in defence of Archias (or Aulus Licinius Archias to give him his full Roman name); Petrarch and other poets would find inspirational its spirited defence of the nature of the poetic vocation and the services that a poet could do for the state. In truth, even if this is nominally a defence speech for a man accused of illegally claiming Roman citizenship, it is much, much more than that. Cicero spends remarkably little time refuting the charge and considerable time not only praising Archias' remarkable abilities but celebrating the role poets play in a community and delivering a panegyric on the wonders of a literary education – not an easy task in a culture that was often suspicious of the type of education Cicero commends here.

Cicero's praises speak for themselves but a few words on the law and the background are necessary. We know little of Archias beyond this speech (all of the poems that Cicero speaks of are now lost to us). He was born in Antioch around 120 and arrived in Rome shortly before 100; this was a period in which Roman statesmen were looking for people to herald their accomplishments and military achievements. Although he counted many of the elite among his audience, his primary patron was the great general Lucius Lucullus, who helped Archias become a citizen of the municipality of Heraclea, a Greek town in Magna Graecia.[1] Archias' friendship with Lucullus meant that, as is often the case with Roman politics (and not just Roman), Lucullus' enemies were his enemies. And one of those enemies was Gnaeus Pompey, better known as Pompey the Great. The prosecution of Archias was probably initiated at his desire, although it was handled by Grattius. (He is another person we know nothing of beyond this speech.) By attacking Archias, Pompey was also attacking Lucullus; if Archias lost his citizenship and was forced to leave Rome, besides losing a friend and panegyrist, Lucullus would also suffer from the disgrace of being unable to protect his client. Cicero's decision to take on this case was, however, not necessarily motivated by irritation or anger with Pompey; it is clear that he felt a great deal of affection and respect for Archias, who had been his teacher. He also clearly hoped that Archias would write an epic poem on his triumph over Catiline; this was never to materialize.

The laws under which Archias was eligible for Roman citizenship were two: the lex Julia de Civitate Latinis *of 90 which gave Roman citizenship to all citizens of every Italian municipality which had not rebelled against Rome in the Social War and the* lex Plautia Papiria de Civitate Sociis *of 89 which gave citizenship to an individual under three conditions:*

1. *That he was a citizen of a city allied to Rome;*
2. *That he maintained a permanent residence at Rome;*
3. *That he presented himself before a praetor within sixty days of the passing of the law.*

Archias was probably prosecuted for violating the lex Papia de Peregrinis *of 65, passed by the tribune of the plebs, Papius, under the guidance of the Senate, which challenged false claims to citizenship (charges could be laid by individuals, as in this case, or by communities; we know of four court cases from this court, one of which,* In defence of Balbus, *was also argued by Cicero. The case against him appears to have been based on four grounds: that there was no official record of him becoming a citizen in Heraclea; that he did not maintain a permanent residence in Rome; that the praetors' records of 89 on which Archias' name appeared were unreliable due to corruption and incompetence; and that his name did not appear on the census records during the period Archias claimed residence in Rome. Cicero's responses to these are given in the speech below; it is also clear that he had little trouble dismissing these charges.*

1. Jurors, I am aware of how meagre my natural ability is, but however much I possess of it or any training in speaking (something I admit I have spent some little time on[2]) or strategy drawn from my studies and training in what is the most superior of skills (something I confess I have never held back from at any time of my life), I would in justice owe the rewards of all these to Aulus Licinius[3] above all people. As far back as I can cast my mind over the extent of my life, even calling up my earliest childhood memories, looking back I see he is always the prime mover who stands out and explains why I began and continued in these pursuits. If my voice, the voice he shaped with his encouragement and mentoring, ever helped anyone, surely I ought to give, to the best of my ability, help and safety to the man who gave me the skill which has enabled me to help and save others. 2. If anyone here is wondering why I am presenting my case like this, given that Archias' talent is very different from mine and he has not my technique or training in public speaking, let me say that not even I have entirely devoted myself to this one pursuit. The fact is that all the cultural arts have some common bond and are, as it were, connected to each other by kinship. 3. But if some of you find it strange that in a court of law and in a public court,[4] when the case is being conducted before a praetor[5] of the Roman people (a very excellent man), before very severe jurors and in the middle of a great crowd, I employ a style of speaking that is hardly typical of normal legal practice, I ask you to pardon it here. It is appropriate for this defendant and, I hope, not a trouble for you to allow me, as I speak in defence of a great poet and a very learned man, before a gathering of highly educated men – all cultured people – and *this* praetor, to talk a little more freely about cultured pursuits, and adopt a persona, which because of the time and study required is rarely introduced in courts and trials, and to use a new and unusual style of oratory.

4. I believe that if you reward me by granting me this privilege, I shall ensure that you think Aulus Licinius here should not only *not* be struck from the number of Roman citizens (where he belongs) but should also be made one even if he were not. For as soon as Archias left childhood behind and first moved

from the studies which shape, train and culture the young to honing his skill at writing, in Antioch[6] – the birthplace of this noble man – his fame began to surpass everyone else's in that once bustling and populous city, a city then teeming with highly educated men and cultured pursuits. From then on, his appearances in other parts of Asia and throughout Greece were so packed that the anticipation of his arrival surpassed even his reputation, and the admiration after his actual appearance surpassed the anticipation!

5. Greek arts and training were then common in Italy and were cultivated in Latin towns more enthusiastically than is now the case. Even here at Rome, the tranquillity of the Republic meant they were not neglected. Thus the people of Tarentum, Locris, Regium and Neapolis[7] gave Archias citizenship along with other rewards, and everyone who had some ability to judge talent considered him worthy of recognition and hospitality. After his fame had spread so far and wide that he was already a household name, even to those who had never met him, he came to Rome in the consulship of Marius and Catulus.[8] In Marius he discovered a man who provided him with great deeds to write about, in Catulus one who supplied him not only with achievements but an enthusiastic pair of ears. Although Archias was still wearing his boy's toga,[9] the Lucullan family immediately took him into their home.[10] That the same house which supported him as a young man held him close in his old age shows the brilliance of his genius and education *and* his nature and character.

6. During that period he was on friendly terms with the famous Numidicus Metellus[11] and his son, 'the Loyal'. He counted Marcus Aemilius[12] among his audience. And he lived with Quintus Catulus – both the father *and* the son.[13] Lucius Crassus[14] cultivated him. Since he held the Luculli, Drusus, the Octavii, Cato and the entire household of the Hortensii bound by the ties of friendship, both those who cultivated him because they wanted to learn or hear something useful and those who pretended to desire the same treated him with great respect. Then, when some time had passed and he had travelled to and from the province of Sicily with Marcus Lucullus, he arrived in Heraclea.[15]

Since this community had full civic privileges under its treaty with Rome, he wanted to become a citizen there. He managed this not only because the Heracleans thought he personally merited it but also because of Lucullus' prestige and influence there.

7. He was granted citizenship under the law of Silvanus and Carbo which states:

'Roman citizenship is to be granted if any man has been given citizenship in the federated states provided that when this law was passed they had a domicile in Italy and had declared themselves before the praetor within sixty days.'[16]

Since he had had a residence at Rome for many years, he made his declaration before the praetor Quintus Metellus, his very dear friend. 8. If I said nothing more about the legality of his citizenship, I could say nothing more convincing. The case is over. Grattius, which of these facts can you refute? Will you deny that he became a citizen of Heraclea? Marcus Lucullus, a respected and trustworthy man of immense prestige, is present and tells you not of what he thinks but what he knows, not of what he heard but what he saw, not that he was present but *that he performed the action*. Most honourable ambassadors from Heraclea are present just for this trial; they are here in their official capacity and with a declaration from their city: they say he is a citizen of Heraclea.

Grattius, here is where you demand the public records of Heraclea, records we all know were lost when the registry was burned in the Italian War.[17] It is ridiculous not to respond to the evidence we possess but instead ask for what we cannot possibly have, to be silent about testimony men have given and demand testimony from documents and – even though you have here a great and respected man and the trustworthy oath of an exceedingly incorruptible town – reject what no one could regard as false and demand records when you are the same person who insists that they are habitually tampered with!

9. Did Archias – a man who made Rome home to all he possessed and his wealth many years before he became a citizen – not have a residence in Rome? Is it that he did not make a public

declaration? On the contrary, he made his public declaration in
registers which alone of all the registers from that board of
praetors still retain the authority which public records should
have. Although the registers of Appius are said to have been
kept without proper caution, and Gabinius' carelessness before
he was convicted and his disgrace after his conviction meant
his registers had no credibility, Metellus was a very honest and
scrupulous man and someone of such diligence[18] that he came
to Lucius Lentulus and the jurors and said he was disturbed by
the erasure of one name.[19] In these registers you can see that the
name of Aulus Licinius is *not* erased.

10. Given this, what doubts can you have about Archias'
citizenship, especially as other cities had made him a citizen? I
suppose during a period when the Greek cities of Italy made a
practice of presenting citizenship for no reward to many ordinary men and even to those without an art or a humble one, the
Rhegians or the Locrians or the Neapolitans or Tarentines
would not have wished to give it to such a famous individual –
although they lavished it on actors! What? When others – not
just after our citizenship was expanded but even after the *lex
Papia*[20] – crawled their way somehow into the registers of those
towns, will you reject as a citizen this man, a man who did not
even make use of the other citizenships he held because he
always wanted to be considered a Heraclean?

11. *Naturally* you ask for the Roman census reports! Is it
somehow unclear that during the most recent census he was
with the army of that famed commander Lucius Lucullus? Or
that during the census before he was also with Lucullus when
he was a quaestor in Asia;[21] and in the one before that (that of
Julius and Crassus) there was no census of any part of the
population.[22] But the census does not confirm citizenship; it
only indicates that whoever happened to be recorded on it was
behaving then as if he were a citizen – and during the times you
charge that he did not even think about exercising the rights of
a Roman citizen, he made several wills[23] according to our laws,
was named as an heir to various Roman citizens and Lucius
Lucullus gave his name to the treasury along with others he
recommended for rewards. 12. Try and dig up other evidence,

if you can; Archias and his friends always acted as if he were a citizen.

Grattius, you will ask us why we get such pleasure from this man. It is because he provides refreshment for minds exhausted by the uproar of the courts and respite for ears tired by quarrels. Or maybe you think it possible for us to supply ourselves with subject matter on a daily basis for all our different law cases without using these studies to cultivate our minds? Or that our minds could bear such great strains without the same studies relaxing them? Personally, I confess that I have given myself to these studies; let other people be ashamed if they have buried their noses so far in book learning that for all their work they contribute nothing to the common good and produce nothing that sees the light of day. But why should I feel ashamed of them, since I have lived my life for many years so that leisure never kept, pleasure distracted or even a need for sleep slowed me from giving help to anyone in their hour of need? 13. So who would rebuke me or in justice be angry with me if I have used the time others are granted to take care of their own affairs, attend games on feast days, for other pleasures or simply to relax their minds or bodies – or even the time others give to all-day banquets, to dice- or ball-playing – to pursue these studies? I should be granted that privilege even more because they nourish my oratorical skill. To the best of my abilities that skill has never been slow in meeting dangers to my friends. I know for certain from which sources I draw what really matters, even if *some* people think they are rather unimportant.

14. If the teachings of so many people and much reading had not convinced me from my adolescent years that there is nothing finer one can seek in this life than glory and honour, and that to achieve them I should disregard all agonies of the body and all danger of exile and death, I never would have taken so many great risks or exposed myself to the daily attacks of corrupt men on your behalf.[24] Philosophers, the past and all books speak of and are full of paradigms – and all these would be shrouded in darkness if the light of literature did not shine on them! Greek and Latin authors have sculpted many

representations of remarkably brave men, not just as a legacy to look at but one to imitate; I keep these always before me as I go about public business; I formed my heart and mind through reading about outstanding men.

15. Suppose someone asks, 'What? Were our great men, the men whose character our records describe, educated in the disciplines you have extolled?' I know what my answer should be, even though one cannot be sure about this in the case of every individual. I admit that there have been many men who have possessed outstanding minds and characters but who have lacked formal education; with these it is almost as if the divine character of their inborn qualities impelled them to become self-controlled[25] and great with no outside help. Let me also add that it is more common that inherent quality without learning produces a reputation for excellence than learning without inherent quality. But I also insist that when systematic training is added to a remarkable and brilliant personality, something splendid and exceptional usually emerges. 16. From this number came the superhuman Africanus[26] of our fathers' day, from this Gaius Laelius and Lucius Furius, highly self-controlled and restrained men, and the bravest and most learned man of their time, the famous Cato the Elder.[27] They would never have devoted themselves to the study of literature if it had not helped them acquire and develop their character.

But even if we did not look for such a great reward from studies and they only gave us delight, I believe you would still vote that the mental relaxation they provide is the most civilized and refined one you can find. Other forms of relaxation do not suit all times, ages or places, but these studies give youth its edge, amuse us in old age, enhance prosperity, delight us at home, do not weigh us down when we are away from home, supply us with a refuge and comfort in bad times, fill our nights, travel with us, even follow us to our country villas. 17. Even if we cannot touch or taste them with our senses, we should still admire those arts when we see them in others. Who in Rome was such a clod or so insensitive that the recent death of Roscius[28] did not move him? Although he was an old man when he died, it still seemed that his brilliant charm and skill should have made him immortal. We all loved him a great deal because of the movement of his body – are we to ignore the incredible movement of the mind and its natural quickness?

18. Jurors, I have often seen Archias here – for I shall exploit your kindness since you are listening so attentively to this new type of oration – I have often seen this man here, although he had not written down a single word, spontaneously reciting many very brilliant improvised verses on subjects we had just been talking about. And then, when he was called back for an encore, he recited again on the same subject but with different words and phrasing. I have seen what he had written with care and thought so applauded that he was praised as people normally praise ancient writers. Should I not hold him dear? Not admire him? Should I not think that I must defend him every way I can? We have learnt from very great and scholarly men that the study of other subjects rests on instruction, teaching and skill, but that the poet draws his power from nature herself and is ignited by the power of the mind and inspired as if by a divine spirit. For this reason, our famous Ennius[29] calls poets 'holy' – as he has the perfect right to – for it seems that the gods entrusted them to us as a gift or reward.

19. So, jurors, as men of great culture consider the name of poet holy, a name no barbarian has ever desecrated. Stones and wild places respond to his voice, monstrous beasts are often stopped in their tracks by his singing:[30] will the voice of poets not move us, even though we have been instructed in the best teachings? The Colophonians say that Homer was a fellow-citizen, the Chians claim him as theirs, the Salaminians want him returned but the Smyrneans insist he was one of their own, and so have even dedicated a shrine to him in their city – and there are many others who fight and argue over him.[31] They desire a dead foreigner because he was a poet; will we spurn a living poet, ours under our laws and by his own free will, although he has given all his energy and talent to glorifying and praising the Roman people? As a young man he dealt with the Cimbrian campaign[32] and charmed Gaius Marius himself, a man who appeared somewhat unmoved by things like poetry.

20. There is no one so estranged from the Muses that he

would not be happy to have poetry eternally broadcast his deeds. They say the famous Themistocles,[33] the greatest man in Athens, when asked what entertainment or whose voice he would most like to hear, said, 'The voice of the man who would do the best job of proclaiming my heroism.' Likewise, Marius valued Lucius Plotius so highly because he thought his talents would most celebrate his accomplishments.[34] 21. But Archias treated the Mithridatic War, a great and difficult war waged over many different lands and seas, from start to finish;[35] his books not only made the brave and distinguished Lucius Lucullus famous but also the name of the Roman people. For under Lucullus' command the Roman people opened up Pontus, a region previously protected by royal wealth and by its terrain; under the same leader a tiny Roman army routed the innumerable forces of the Armenians.[36] It is a glory for the Roman people that Lucullus' strategy snatched and saved Cyzicus from every royal attack and from the mouth and jaws of war.[37] People will always call ours the victory in that great and incredible naval battle Lucullus fought near the island of Tenedos, when he sank the enemy's fleet and killed their generals:[38] they are *our* trophies, *our* monuments, *our* triumphs. Those whose talents extol these events spread the fame of the Roman people far and wide.

22. Our own Ennius was dear to Scipio Africanus the Elder;[39] for that reason it is even thought that a marble statue of him was set up in the tomb of the Scipios. His praises not only enhanced Scipio's name but that of the Roman people. He praised Cato, the great grandfather of our Cato, to the heavens *and* greatly honoured the deeds of the Roman people. Finally, we all have a share in the praise he gave those Maximi, the Marcelli and the Fulvii.[40] This was why our ancestors made him, a man from Rudiae, a citizen. Will we cast out from our city a Heraclean whom many cities wanted but who became a legal citizen of ours?

23. Anyone who believes Greek poetry brings us less glory than Latin is terribly mistaken. Nearly all races read Greek books; Latin ones stop at our very narrow boundaries. So if our achievements are only bounded by the limits of our world,

we should want our glory and fame to spread as far as our weapons have. Not only do these rewards give great honour to those whose deeds have been written about, but we can be sure that they spur on those who risk dangers and even their lives for glory. 24. Alexander the Great is said to have travelled with a coterie of chroniclers to record his achievements,[41] but when he stood in Troy before the tomb of Achilles, he said, 'Fortunate youth to find a Homer to spread your heroic deeds!' Did he not speak the truth? For if the *Iliad* did not exist, the same tomb which covered Achilles' body would also have buried his name. And did not our own Pompey the Great, a man who made his good luck equal to his heroism, give citizenship to the chronicler of his deeds, Theophanes[42] of Mytilene, before an assembly of the army? And did not our own brave men – farmers and soldiers – moved by the charm of his praise, and as though they shared in that same praise, approvingly and wildly applaud Pompey's action?

25. I suppose that if Archias were not legally a Roman citizen, he could not have managed to get some commander to grant him citizenship? Although Sulla[43] granted it to Spaniards and Gauls, I suppose he would have rejected Archias if he were seeking it. Sulla, a man we have seen in an assembly ordering an immediate reward be given, from whatever auction he was holding, to some dreadful poet from the rabble who handed him a little poetry book because he had written an epigram on him, even though it was in alternating couplets of odd lengths! Of course, there was a condition – that he not write anything again. Would a man who thought the labours of a terrible poet merited some reward not have sought out the genius, ability and prolific talent of Archias? 26. To go on: would Archias have failed to become a citizen through his own influence or that of the Luculli or through Quintus Metellus Pius, a very close friend – and someone who made many men citizens? Especially, when Metellus looked so hard for someone to write about his own deeds that he even paid attention to poets born at Corduba,[44] although they sounded rather awkward and strange. Here is something we must not lie about, cannot hide, must admit: we are all drawn by our longing for praise, and the

better a man is the more he is led by the search for glory. Well-known philosophers even put their own names on the pamphlets they write on how glory should be despised – in the very books in which they look down on public fame and high reputation, they wish to be famous and have their names remembered!

27. Decimus Brutus, a great man and great general, decorated the entryways of his temples and monuments with the poems of Accius,[45] his close friend. Furthermore, the famed Fulvius,[46] who fought the Aetolians with Ennius by his side, did not hesitate to vow the spoils of Mars to the Muses. And so in our city – a city where generals almost while still dressed for war honoured the name of poets and the temples of the Muses – jurors dressed for peace should not hesitate to honour the Muses and save poets. 28. To make you more willing to do so, I shall testify and confess to you about what you might almost call my passion for glory – which is perhaps too keen but is still honourable. For this man has touched on and begun a work on the actions I took during my consulship in alliance with you to save our empire, the lives of the citizens and the entire Republic.[47] After I heard his verses, I gave him the means to finish the task because I thought it was a great and agreeable subject. For courage desires no other reward for its labour and dangers except that of praise and renown, and when that is taken away, what is there left in our narrow and brief span of life for which we should exert ourselves?

29. It is certain that if our minds did not look to the future and were bound by the same limits which circumscribe our lives, they would not break themselves with such efforts nor torment themselves by so many cares and sleepless nights, nor fight so often for life itself. All great men possess a certain noble instinct which goads their minds day and night with the prospect of glory, and reminds them that the memory of their names ought not to be lost with the end of their lives but should live on for all time. 30. Should we be so small-minded, we who spend our time working for the Republic among the dangers and troubles of public life that, even though up to our final moments we shall have drawn no calm nor leisurely breath, we think everything perishes at the moment we die? Have not

many great men taken pains to leave statues and death-masks, images not of their minds but their bodies? Should we not prefer to leave representations of our character and aims written and polished by the greatest talents? At the very moment I was performing my deeds, I thought I was planting them in the world's undying memory. Whether this will have no effect on me after death or – as the very wise think – some part of me will then still sense it, the thought and hope of it still delights me at this moment.

31. Jurors, this is why you should save a man of such decency, a man you see validated not just by the position of his friends but by the length of their friendship; it is right that talent so great be valued because – as you can see – men with excellent judgement seek him out. The law favours his case as does Heraclea's standing, Lucullus' testimony and Metellus' records. Jurors, we ask you, since talent as great as this should show not just heaven's seal of approval but *man*'s, to receive as a fellow-citizen someone who has always celebrated your generals and the achievements of the Roman people, who has even promised to write of our recent domestic dangers (something that will ensure that they are remembered for all time) and who is one of the poets, one whom all people have always considered holy. Show that he was freed by your sense of culture, not broken by your severity.

32. Jurors, I have spoken about the facts of the case briefly and simply, as is my custom, and I have complete faith that you approve of all I have said. However, I have spoken about the genius of this man and his studies in a way that differs from normal judicial practice. I hope you have received these in good part; I know that the person who presides over this trial certainly does.

On his House (extracts)

Delivered on 29 September 57 to
the college of the pontiffs[1]

When Cicero was exiled in 58, he lost his rights and status as a
citizen – and his property. It was a terrible fall from grace for
the man who only five years before had been acclaimed as the
father of his country. The prime mover of his disgrace was Publius Clodius, the patrician who had been adopted by a plebeian
young enough to be his son, so he could stand for tribune of the
plebs (see chapters 34–8). On becoming tribune of the plebs,
Clodius wasted no time; among his first acts was the passing of
a bill which declared that anyone who had executed a Roman
citizen without a trial was not to be allowed fire and water
within 400 miles[2] of Rome; this was clearly aimed at Cicero
and his actions during the Catilinarian conspiracy (several conspirators were executed without trial). Although Clodius had
not yet named him or charged him in court, Cicero fled into
exile; he was later to portray this choice as a heroic attempt to
avoid violence in the city, but at the time it felt like (and was
seen as) a shameful retreat.

The most visible sign of Cicero's fall was the fate of his
beautiful house on the Palatine Hill, which was ransacked and
levelled (for good measure several of his villas were also set on
fire). He had bought this house from Marcus Licinius Crassus in
62 while still awash with the triumph of his consulship and victory over Catiline; it cost 3.5 million sesterces, a sum Cicero
could only scrape together by borrowing heavily from a client.[3]
But it was in a prime location, overlooking the Forum and –
even more importantly – entirely visible from there (in fact, it
had been designed to be so by a former owner, the tribune Mar-

cus Livius Drusus[4]). For someone who lived and breathed the
Forum, it was perfect. By purchasing the house, Cicero also took
on some of the lustre of its previous owners and the nobility who
crowded the Palatine: the man from Arpinum had finally arrived,
even if some still thought him a jumped-up provincial.

Losing such a place would be a blow hard to bear; even
harder was the symbolic meaning of its demolition. Such treatment was the typical punishment for those aiming at tyranny – a
deliberately cruel blow for a man who saw himself as a champion of liberty and believed that he had saved Rome and the
homes of its citizens from the tyranny of Catiline. To rub salt
into the wound and to ensure that Cicero would never get the
land back, Clodius then turned a portion of the site into a
shrine to the goddess Freedom (Libertas), using his brother-in-
law the pontifex Pinarius Natta to consecrate the site. Even
after Cicero's triumphant return to Rome in September 57, he
could not feel himself fully restored until he could regain and
rebuild his house. For it to remain as it was would be a perpetual reminder of his disgrace and, even worse, tie him forever to
that most fearful of Roman bogeymen: the man who would be
king. Cicero's arguments for the return of his house (or, rather,
the site, as there was nothing of the house left) are more than
words over a piece of property; they are a speech about what
lasting memory Rome will have of his name. Would people
pass Clodius' shrine for years to come and whisper his name as
one of shame? Or would Cicero's restored house show that
once more the saviour of his country was back in Rome? Nothing less was at stake.

Because the house was now the site of a religious shrine, it
was a matter for Rome's religious authorities, and the speech
was delivered to the members of the college of the pontiffs.
Cicero was successful in part: the site was returned but he only
received 2 million sesterces in compensation. And just to make
sure he knew that his old enemy still had teeth, on 3 November
Clodius drove away the men who were rebuilding the house
and destroyed it once more. To drive his point home, he then
set fire to Quintus' house next door.

1. Members of the pontifical college, even though our ancestors created and established many miraculous institutions, none of these is as striking as their desire that the same men preside over the worship of the immortal gods and the vital interests of the state, so the highest and most distinguished of our citizens would protect that worship by governing the Republic well and protect the Republic by wisely interpreting religious ritual. If ever the priests of the Roman people had the authority to judge an important case, this is that case. It is so important that the position of the entire Republic, the safety, the lives, freedom, the hearths and homes, gods, fortunes and residences of all our citizens have been entirely entrusted to your wisdom, integrity and authority. 2. Today you must decide whether you prefer to strip insane and ruined magistrates of the protection of perverse and unholy citizens or hand them the extra weapon of religion. For if that disgrace and inferno of the Republic[5] uses religion to defend his pestilent and deadly tribuneship – a term in office indefensible under the rules of human justice – we shall have to look for other religious ceremonies, other priests of the immortal gods and other intermediaries between us and the gods in our rituals. But if your authoritative and wise voices overturn all that the madness of disloyal men has achieved in our Republic – a Republic some crushed, others abandoned and still others betrayed – it will give us reason to feel entitled to praise the decision of our ancestors to select men of the greatest importance for priesthoods.

3. But since that lunatic is under the impression that by denouncing the proposals I recently made in the Senate on the state of the Republic he will win your attention, I shall depart from my plan for this speech: I shall not reply to that madman's 'oratory' (since he is incapable of oratory) but to his abuse, a skill which he has made his own not just by his unbearable insults but by his endlessly continuing freedom from reprisals. But first, I ask you, you deranged lunatic of a man, what great nemesis of your outrageous crimes made you believe that men like these – men who keep the Republic great not just by their good sense but by their ceremonial grandeur[6] – are angry with me because I made a proposal which connected the safety of

citizens with an honour for Gnaeus Pompey?[7] Or that they feel differently now about matters of great religious importance than they did when I was not in Rome?

4. He says, 'Then you had more authority among the pontiffs, but now you have switched sides and become a man of the people you must have less standing.' *Really?* Would you dress these men in the worst faults of the ignorant masses, their mercurial and inconstant nature and their shifting outlook, which changes like weather in a storm? Would you do that to men whose character keeps them from being inconstant? Men whom the fixity and precision of religious law, historical precedent and the authority of documents and records keep from impulsive shifts in opinion? He says, 'Are *you* the person the Senate could not do without, whom decent men mourned, the Republic longed for, whose restoration we thought would bring back the Senate's authority – and who betrayed it the moment you returned?' I shall not give my response yet: first I shall reply to your shameless assertions.

[*In the section following this, Cicero yet once more tries to justify his actions and his reasons for leaving Rome to go into exile before he was tried. Then follows a subject Cicero was never tired of: invective against Clodius' every action, in great and excruciating detail. In the section below Cicero begins by using the device of* praeteritio, *'passing over' – pretending to skip over various egregious faults and actions of an opponent while still mentioning them. The centrepiece of his attack is Clodius' adoption by Fonteius, one which was certainly risible and probably illegal under religious law. However, one element of his adoption that was perfectly ordinary was that he was adopted as an adult; the Romans did not as a rule adopt children.*]

34. You do see, do you not, that I am not trying to rip up from their roots all your accomplishments entirely, nor am I arguing that you never, ever did anything lawfully (although that is pretty obvious) or were a tribune of the plebs *and are still a patrician?* I am addressing the pontiffs; there are augurs present; I am dealing with a fundamental point of public law.

Members of the college, what is our law on adoption? Clearly, that people adopt who can no longer have their own children and who tried to have them while they were still able. This body usually looks into the reason for an adoption, what type of family it involves, what is its standing and how the adoption affects their sacred rites.[8] Which of these was examined in the case of your adoption? A man of twenty (perhaps even younger) adopts a . . . senator.[9] Does he want children? But he can have them: he has a wife and will raise the ones she bears him. By adopting, he will disinherit his future sons. 35. Why should you work so hard to ensure the sacred rites of the Clodii die out? This should have been the focus of the pontiffs' investigation when you were adopted – or maybe they asked you whether you wanted to use your violent treachery to throw the Republic into complete disorder, and if the reason for your adoption was not to become his son but tribune of the plebs and destroy the Republic from its foundations. I imagine you replied that this was what you wanted. The pontiffs thought it was a good reason. They gave their approval. No one asked the age of the adopter, as they did in the case of Gnaeus Aufidius and Marcus Pupius[10] who were (as I recall) very old when the first adopted Orestes and the second Piso; those adoptions, along with countless others, were followed by the adoptees taking on the names, the property and the sacred rites of their new fathers. You have not become a Fonteius as you should have, you are not the heir of your 'father', nor have you given up your own inherited rites to take up those of your adoptive family. So, having thrown into total disorder those rites, created a mess of the family you deserted *and* the new one you polluted, and having abandoned the legal rules for citizens on guardianship and inheritance, you sacrilegiously gave yourself a father who was young enough to be your son.

36. Speaking before the pontiffs, I deny that your adoption was legal under pontifical law. The first reason is that because of your ages, the man who adopted you could have been your son, or whatever relationship the two of you have.[11] The second is that normally the pontiffs ask why a man is adopting, to make sure that he is seeking something under pontifical law

which he cannot achieve naturally, ensuring the adoption does
not threaten the honour or ritual obligations of two families.
But the main reason is so that no cheating, no fraud and no
trickery can be used and the fiction of adopting a son can, as
far as is possible, mimic the acknowledgement of legitimate
children. 37. What greater example of cheating is there than a
boy without a beard, married and in excellent health, coming
here and saying he wants to adopt as his son a Roman senator,
all while everyone sees and knows that Clodius was adopted
not to fill the position of a son, but so he could stop being a
patrician and become a tribune of the plebs? He hid nothing;
he was emancipated right after he was adopted so he would not
stay in the power of the man who adopted him.[12] Why was
there even an adoption? Approve of this type of adoption: soon
no family rites – rites you are supposed to protect – and no
patrician will be left. Why would anyone wish to be ineligible
to become a tribune of the plebs? To have a fainter chance of
becoming a consul?[13] To be blocked from holding a priesthood
as it is not the time for a patrician to hold one?[14] Whenever it
happens to be more convenient for someone to be a plebeian,
he will be adopted using a similar scheme.

38. And so in a short time the Roman people will not have a
rex sacrorum, *flamines* or *salii*, will lose half its remaining
priests[15] and have no one who can oversee the centuriate or
curial assembly; if patricians are not elected magistrates, the
auspices of the Roman people must of necessity die out since
there will be no *interrex*, given that he has to be a patrician and
be nominated by patricians. I have stated before the pontiffs
that your adoption was not approved by any decree of this college, took place in opposition to every law the pontiffs possess
and must be considered null and void – and that you must
understand your term as tribune has been entirely invalidated.

[*In the omitted section, Cicero (as before) defends his decision
to depart from Rome rather than face a trial, and pours abuse
on Clodius' actions and life. His arguments also revolve around
what (he says) was the illegality of Clodius' bill which exiled*

*him, the destruction of his property and the creation of a shrine
to the goddess Freedom on the site.*]

100. Members of the college, it is your verdict that will mark
my true return. If you give me back my residence, an outcome
which you have always worked towards with your energy,
counsel, influence and words, I shall know that I have been
truly restored. But if instead of returning my home to me you
allow my enemy to keep his memorial of my humiliation, his
crime and our public disaster standing, everyone will think that
this is not a return from exile but eternal punishment.

Members of the college, nearly all Rome could see my house.
If it remains not a monument of the city but her tomb inscribed
with the name of my enemy, I must leave rather than live in a
city where I shall see trophies set up to commemorate my
defeat – and that of the Republic. 101. Could *I* have a mind so
hardened and eyes so shameless that I – someone the Senate
and the entire community voted many times had saved the
city – could look upon my demolished home, a home destroyed
not by *my* personal enemy but by *our* common adversary? Or
look at the shrine he erected and placed in full view of our community so decent citizens would never be able to dry their tears?

Spurius Maelius wanted to be king and so his house was levelled; the justice of that punishment is seen in the name the site
now holds, Aequimaelium,[16] or 'What Maelius deserved'. For
the same reason, Spurius Cassius' home was demolished and the
temple of Tellus[17] built on the site. The home of Marcus Vaccus
used to stand in Vaccus' meadows; it was confiscated and levelled and now his crime is remembered by the name of the
place.[18] Marcus Manlius drove the Gauls back from the slopes
of the Capitoline Hill,[19] but was not content with the glory that
came from his achievement; he was convicted of seeking to
become a king. Today you can see the two groves of trees planted
on the site of his demolished house. Our ancestors thought this
the greatest punishment that could be inflicted on unholy and
criminal citizens; will *I* experience the same punishment so our
descendants will not see me as someone who quenched a criminal conspiracy but as its mastermind and leader?

102. Members of the college, while the Senate lives and breathes and you lead our public policy, can the honour of the Roman people carry the stain of the incongruous disgrace of Marcus Tullius Cicero's home being a permanent memorial of the state's punishment as Fulvius Flaccus' was? The Senate decreed that Flaccus was to die because he and Gaius Gracchus[20] had committed an offence against the Republic's well-being. His home was confiscated and demolished and later Quintus Catulus used spoils from the Cimbri to set up a portico on the site.[21] When that fury and incendiary of his country captured, occupied and ruled over the city with Piso and Gabinius[22] at his side, in one moment he wiped out that memorial to a distinguished dead hero by yoking my home with that of Flaccus! And all so that, after he had crushed the Senate, the man the Senate had voted was his country's guardian would suffer the same punishment as someone they thought had plotted its demise. 103. Will you allow Clodius' portico to remain on the Palatine, the most beautiful part of our city, as an eternal memorial to all the people of the world of a tribune's insanity, the consuls' crime, the cruelty of the conspirators, the Republic's disaster and my suffering? The love you hold and always have held for the Republic would fill you with a desire to tear down his portico not just with votes, but even with your hands if the need should arise – unless, by some chance, a superstitious fear about its dedication by that purest of priests deters you.

104. Now, *that* is an outcome that weak-minded men will never stop laughing about, but people who think more seriously will never hear without pain! Did Publius Clodius, a man who desecrated the house of the pontifex maximus,[23] consecrate mine? Will you – you the high-priests of our rites and rituals – consider him your guide and teacher in matters of public religion? Immortal gods, I call upon you to hear this: does Publius Clodius care for your rites, tremble before your power or believe that all human concerns are intrinsically bound to your worship? Or, pontiffs, is it not rather that he mocks the authority of all the distinguished men who are assembled here and he abuses your dignity? Clodius, can a religious word really fall or slip from *your* mouth? You used that

same mouth to launch the foulest and vilest abuse on religion when you attacked the Senate for issuing a severe decree on that topic.[24]

105. Pontiffs, take a good look at this highly religious man and tell him, like good pontiffs, that there is some limit to religious feeling; it should not go so far as to become superstition. Mr Religious Fanatic, I ask you, what old womanish superstition made you intrude on a sacrifice in a stranger's home? Was your mind so feeble that you thought the gods would not be happy unless you got involved in women's rituals? Did you ever hear of a single one of your ancestors – men who performed their private rites and held public priesthoods – attending the ritual for Bona Dea? No! Not even the blind one[25] did so! This shows us how often popular belief is wrong: the man who never willingly looked on something unholy lost his sight; the man who not only polluted it with his gaze but with his sacrilegious and criminal sexual indecency went and lost his mind instead of his vision! Members of the college, you must be *deeply* moved when such a pure, religious, holy and pious source tells you that he tore down the home of a great citizen with his bare hands – and used the very same ones to consecrate it.

106. Let us look at your style of consecration. 'I had passed a law,' he says, 'so it was legal.' *What?* Did you leave out the clause that says, if a law contains anything contrary to our laws it cannot be passed? Does everyone here think that it is lawful if all your houses, altars, hearths and household gods are at the mercy of the appetites of the tribunes? That it is lawful for the home of a man, assaulted and attacked by a crowd someone has incited, not only to be knocked down in a moment of temporary insanity which rose like a sudden storm, but to be tied up forever with a religious prohibition? 107. I have always understood, members of the college, that the most important thing in undertaking some religious act is to decipher what the gods wish, and that we cannot show piety towards them unless we have an honourable understanding of their will and intent. We should seek nothing from them that is unjust or dishonourable. Even though at the time Clodius had everything under his control, that stain of an individual could find no one who

would buy, receive or take my house as a gift. Although he was burning with desire for my house – that was the only reason this *decent* man wanted to use his deadly law to set himself up as a master over all my possessions – even he, despite being deep in the grip of his madness, did not dare to occupy the very place that had sparked his desire. Do you really think that the immortal gods wanted to move to the home of a man – a home that a great criminal had demolished with his unholy terrorism – who kept their temples safe by his hard work and policy?

108. Not one citizen among our vast population laid a finger on my property or did not try to defend me as much as he could in that crisis – except, that is, Publius Clodius' polluted and bloodstained gang. And public and private opinion punished anyone who contaminated themselves by touching the loot as his partner or purchaser. So did the immortal gods want my home even though everyone thought that any man who even as much as touched my possessions was an out-and-out criminal? Did your beautiful goddess of Freedom drive out my household gods so that she could station herself in a captured house? 109. What could be more inviolable, more guarded by all religious principle, than the homes of each and every citizen? They contain our altars, our hearths, our household gods, our family rites, our religious ceremonies. Everyone considers a home a refuge so inviolable that they think it is sacrilege to rip someone from there. That is why you should drive the words of his madness from your ears; he is a man who, in defiance of all religion, undermined everything that our ancestors wished religion to keep safe and inviolable, *and* who overturned it in the name of religion!

110. And who is that goddess? She must be *bona fide* since *you* set her up in her shrine.[26]

'She is Freedom.'

So you stationed freedom in my home after you took it away from Rome? Even though your colleagues held the highest power, you would not allow them to be free men; you allowed no one access to the temple of Castor[27] when, in the hearing of the Roman people, you ordered your men to trample all over this man here, this highly distinguished and high-born man, one who had enjoyed the highest gift the people can give, a pontiff, an ex-consul and an exceptionally good and restrained person[28] – I have no words to express my astonishment that you can even meet his eyes. To go on: when using that tyrannical law you passed against me alone, you hustled me out of the city even though I had had no trial,[29] when you kept the leader of the whole world[30] shut up in his home, when you occupied the Forum with your armed hordes of losers, did you then try to station a statue of Freedom in the very house which was itself an indictment of your vicious oppression and the wretched slavery of the Roman people? Should Freedom have driven out from his own home the man who more than anyone else had ensured that our entire community did not fall under the power of your slaves?

111. Where did you find that Freedom of yours? I have looked into this very carefully. It is said that a certain whore lived in Tanagra and a marble statue of her was erected on a tomb not far from there. A certain noble – not totally unconnected with our devout priest of Freedom – carried this statue off to enhance his time as aedile[31] as he planned that the splendour of his games would outshine all previous ones. He was certainly thrifty in carrying off to his own home (for the sake of the Roman people, of course) all the statues, paintings and art treasures that remained in shrines and public places throughout Greece and the islands. 112. Later, when he understood that he could defraud the Roman people of his aedileship and be elected as praetor by the consul Lucius Piso if there was a rival who shared his initials,[32] he put his aedileship in two places: his safe and his gardens. He gave this stolen representation of a whore to Clodius, not so that it could represent Rome's Freedom but the brothers' to do whatever they wanted with. Is this a goddess anyone should fear to insult: a whore's image, a tomb's decoration – stolen by a thief and erected by a desecrator? Is it she who will drive me from my home? Will this conqueress of a crushed community be decorated with the spoils of the Republic? Will she rest, perched on her monu-

ment, as evidence of the Senate's humiliation and an eternal
reminder of our disgrace?

113. Quintus Catulus! But should I call up the father first or
the son?[33] The son first: our memory of the son is fresher and
he was more closely associated with my achievements. Were
you so terribly mistaken when you thought that every day
would bring me greater rewards in public life? You said that it
was against the laws of the gods that this community could
have two consuls who were enemies of the Republic. And lo
and behold there were two consuls[34] who handed over a Senate
bound hand and foot to a raving lunatic of a tribune who used
edicts and their authority to forbid the members of the Senate
to plead with and beg the people on my behalf,[35] who looked
on as my home was ransacked and demolished, and, to cap
that off, who ordered the charred remains of my possessions to
be carried to their own homes.

114. I come now to the father. Quintus Catulus! You wanted
the home of Marcus Fulvius to be a monument for your war
spoils even though he was your brother's father-in-law; your
aim was to erase from the sight and minds of men all memory
of one who had plotted the destruction of the Republic. What
would you have replied if someone had told you as you were
building your portico that there would come a time when a
tribune of the plebs, who had ignored the authority of the Senate and the opinions of all decent men, would tear down your
monument as consuls not only looked on but *helped*? *And* that
they would treat the home of a citizen who had defended the
Republic, in the name of the Senate, just as badly? I think you
would have replied that this could not happen while our community still existed.

115. Now, look at how that person's intolerable nerve is
combined with headlong and unbridled greed. Did he ever plan
to build a monument or anything religious? He wanted to live
luxuriously and magnificently – and to combine two large,
noble mansions. Right at the very second my departure robbed
him of an excuse to shed blood, he pressured Quintus Seius[36] to
sell him his home; when he refused, Clodius threatened to
block the light to his windows by building up around them.

Seius insisted that while he was alive Clodius would never gain possession of his house. Clodius is a sharp youngster and so he understood what he had to do: he barefacedly poisoned Seius and, after he had worn down the other bidders, he bought the house for almost 50 per cent more than it was worth.

Where am I heading with all of this? 116. Nearly all of the site of my home is free for building on, as barely a tenth of it was added to Catulus' portico. The walkway and the monument and the Tanagrean Freedom (although he had demolished freedom) were all an excuse. He wanted a portico on the Palatine, 300 feet long – all paved – with a lovely view and with rooms, a massive peristyle and with everything necessary to far outdo everyone else's house in size and status. When Mr Religion was selling *and* buying my house, even he did not dare to put his name down as buyer: the whole business was shrouded in darkness. He put Scato in place, a man whose character kept him poor; Scato, a Marsian,[37] who did not even have a roof in his home town to keep out the rain, went around saying he had bought an extremely noble house on the Palatine. Clodius allotted the lower part of the site, not to his own Fonteian clan but to the Clodian one he had abandoned; yet out of all the many Clodians, no one handed in his name there unless he had fallen on hard times or was living the hard life.[38] Members of the college, will you sanction such a mix of strange inclinations, shamelessness, recklessness and desire?

[*The speech continues with further discussion of the dedication of the site (well, what Clodius called a dedication and Cicero called a perversion of one), before Cicero concludes with a plea to the college.*]

In Defence of Sestius (extracts)

Delivered in March 56 before
the court on public violence

Cicero's restoration from exile left him with many debts – and grudges. The grudges included, as always, Publius Clodius; but he also harboured bitter feelings towards the two consuls for 58, Lucius Piso and Aulus Gabinius, who had stood by while Cicero's life was destroyed, his property confiscated and his home demolished (to say nothing of the trouble his family went through). Chief among the debts was one to Publius Sestius, tribune of the plebs in 57. In 63 (the year of Cicero's consulship), Sestius was quaestor and was assigned to Cicero's co-consul, Gaius Antonius. During this period, Sestius seems to have served as Cicero's eyes and ears in Antonius' camp. He is mentioned in Catilinarian I *(chapter 21) in generous terms, and during that crisis he was dispatched first to secure Capua; after he managed this, he joined up with Antonius to face Catiline in Etruria. In 62 he was Antonius' proquaestor while he governed in Macedonia, probably remaining there until 60 when Antonius returned (and was promptly tried and convicted, despite Cicero's efforts in his defence). In 58 and 57 Sestius worked tirelessly for Cicero's recall, drawing considerable hostility from Cicero's foes; that hostility did not vanish with Cicero's return. On 10 February 56, a Marcus Tullius (no relation to Cicero) charged Sestius with public violence (Latin, vis) under the* lex Plautia de vi. *This law was used when violence was perceived to be against the state's interest and in the case of any violence which was aimed at the community as a whole; it seems clear that Sestius, like many other politicians, had formed an armed gang: that in itself was not illegal – but using it for violent acts against the public interest was.*

Sestius was clearly able to summon powerful help besides Cicero; Marcus Licinius Crassus, Gaius Licinius Calvus and Quintus Hortensius all spoke before Cicero – all of them more than able orators. They appear to have argued that Sestius had committed the acts he was accused of, but that his actions were not against the Republic's interests. Perhaps they covered the subject so thoroughly that Cicero felt free to spend remarkably little of what is an extremely long speech talking about anything to do with Sestius or the charge. He probably also felt it necessary to speak at considerable length about his own exile as Sestius was clearly being targeted because he had aided Cicero's recall, and this was as much as anything a political trial. Of course, as one of Cicero's favourite subjects was himself, this was probably not a chore.

There are two extracts translated here: the first where Cicero describes the many vicious acts done in 58, including but not restricted to his exile. The second is Cicero's famous discussion of the consensus ordinum *(the agreement of the orders): his vision of a settled, peaceful balance of the various orders or classes that made up Rome, all under the guidance of the* optimates, *the self-styled finest citizens. In this, Cicero represents politics in Rome as a struggle between these and the* populares, *the men of the people. It is impossible to translate these two words into modern terms; neither of them was a political party in our sense, as they had no manifesto or clear single leader. While the* optimates *were conservative, they were so in the sense that they wanted the Senate to hold the power. And while the* populares *are sometimes described as democrats or left wing, it is always worth remembering that while they may have aimed at some reforms of the state, many of them were completely self-serving. After all, Caesar, perhaps the ultimate* popularis, *was not a democrat but ended up ruling Rome as a perpetual dictator. On the other hand, the* populares' *strategy of turning to the assemblies rather than to the Senate to have legislation passed did invest a great deal of power in the hands of the people. Whether or not one thinks this part of the speech is a serious exercise in political thought, it is still worth reading as Cicero's optimistic view of who the best men might include.*

Sestius was unanimously acquitted and was elected praetor in 54 – and was then immediately prosecuted for electoral bribery. During the civil war, he went over to Caesar's side after his victory at Pharsalus; however, he was still close to Cicero and served as a mediator between the two. He survived Caesar's assassination and was still active in the Senate until 39. In the last we hear of his family, his son Lucius became consul in 23.

[*Prior to this section Cicero has described the emotional circumstances of his exile and the agony he felt. He represents his decision to go into exile as one taken to avoid bloodshed in the Republic (something he repeats elsewhere) rather than a cowardly decision chosen over the more honourable option of suicide. Here, he returns to a discussion of the year of his exile and to the crimes (in Cicero's eyes, at least) of the consuls, Gabinius and Piso – and those of Clodius.*]

53. Let me return to the year 58 when the criminality of the consuls[1] overwhelmed the Republic with all manner of possible misfortune. First there is that day, which was for me almost like that of my death and for decent men one of tragedy, the day I tore myself from the arms of my country and your sight. The day I yielded to the criminality, missiles and threats of a madman, fearing the danger to you – not to myself – and left my beloved country because I loved it.[2] A day when not only the people but the houses and temples of Rome mourned my misfortune. A day so monstrous, so harsh, so sudden, that none of you wanted to gaze on the Forum, the Curia or the light of the day. On the day itself[3] – but why speak of a 'day'? No, I mean the hour, the second when my destruction, the Republic's and Piso's and Gabinius' provinces were all put to the vote. Immortal gods, our city and empire's sentinels and safe-keepers, what abominations and crimes you saw then in this Republic! They drove out a citizen who, along with all decent citizens, had the Senate's authority to defend the Republic – and that was the very charge they used to drive him out! They drove him out without

a trial – but with violence, stones, swords and a frenzied bunch of slaves. They passed a law in a desolate and abandoned Forum, now the home to assassins and slaves, passing it even though the Senate had dressed in mourning in an attempt to prevent it.

54. Even though our community was in such commotion, the consuls did not even allow one night to pass between my destruction and their prize: as soon as I was down, they swooped in to drink my blood and drag off their spoils from the gasping Republic. I pass over the congratulations, the feasts, the parcelling out of the treasury, the rewards offered, the hopes, the promises, the pickings and the joy of a few men in the midst of everyone's grief. My wife was harassed, my children's lives threatened[4] and a consul – a *Piso* – kicked away my son-in-law[5] – a *Piso* – from his feet as he lay there as a suppliant, my property was looted and brought to the consuls, my home on the Palatine burned. And all as the consuls *feasted*. Even if they revelled in my misfortunes, they should still have been shaken by the danger to the city.

55. Moving away from my case, remember the other outbreaks of that year; then you will see very clearly how many different treatments the Republic needed the next year's magistrates to prescribe. Remember the sheer number of laws that were proposed and passed? They were passed while these consuls were – is the word I am looking for 'silent'? No! It is 'approving'. These laws abolished the censor's black mark,[6] the most serious sanction that the holiest office, our Republic, possesses; they threw away almost a fifth of our tax revenue by reducing the price of grain by six and one third asses;[7] that gladiator[8] responsible did not just restore the old associations in defiance of a senatorial decree, but formed countless new ones. Instead of Cilicia, the province it had been agreed was to be his if he betrayed the Republic, Gabinius was granted Syria – and so a law was passed to allow a pig of a man the power to decide twice on the same topic and use a new law to switch his province. 56. I skip over the law which in one stroke wiped out all the rules for ritual, the auspices and the powers of magistrates, all the laws about the rules and the times for putting a law to a vote.[9] I skip over the disasters at home; we grew famil-

iar with seeing even foreign nations staggered by the madness
of that year.[10] A tribune's law drove out and robbed the well-
known priest of the Magna Mater at Pessinus[11] of his priesthood,
and the site of that holiest and most ancient of cults was sold
for a great price to Brogitarus – an appalling man, unworthy of
that sacred office – even though he wanted to hold it not in
order to respect it but to desecrate it. The people gave the title
of king to men who had not even approached the Senate; convicted exiles were recalled to Byzantium, even as they were
exiling unconvicted citizens from our community.[12]

57. King Ptolemy,[13] even if the Senate had not yet given him
the title of ally, was the brother of a king to whom the Senate
had already given that honourable title[14] and was from the
same family, of the same ancestry and had the same historical
relationship with us – in short, he was a king who even if he
was not yet an 'ally', at least was not our enemy. He was peaceful, causing no trouble and trusting in the Roman people's
empire and he enjoyed full ownership of his ancestral kingdom
in royal tranquillity. He was anticipating nothing, suspecting
nothing, as Clodius' operators were voting that he should be
put up for public auction even as he sat crowned (the mark of
kings) with his purple robes and sceptre. By the command of
the Roman people – a people accustomed to restore kingdoms
even to defeated kings – a friendly king was sold off, along with
all his property, although no one could bring up any injury to
us and we made no demand for reparations. 58. That was a
year of many cruelties, disgusting acts and riots; but still I think
I am right to say that this was only second to the cruelty done
to my person.

After defeating Antiochus the Great in a large-scale war on
land and sea, our ancestors ordered him to stay on as ruler
south of the Taurus Mountains; they punished him by giving
Asia to Attalus.[15] We ourselves waged a long, hard war against
Tigranes, the king of Armenia, as we thought his injuries to our
allies amounted almost to a declaration of war against us.[16] He
was a violent person and an intensely hostile enemy to our
empire, using all his kingdom's resources to defend Mithridates
after he lost Pontus; although Lucius Lucullus, a very great

man and general, beat him, he clung on to what was left of his army – and his previous hostility to us. When Gnaeus Pompey had him as a grovelling suppliant before him in his camp, he raised him up and replaced the crown, the mark of royalty Tigranes had flung from his head, and, giving him specific commands, Pompey ordered him to be a king again. He thought that setting up a king brought more glory to him and our empire than shutting one up in prison.

59. So it is that a man who was an enemy of the Roman people, who harboured our bitterest enemy in his kingdom, who fought us, met us on the battlefield – and almost replaced us as an empire – rules today and, by his prayers, achieved the title of 'ally and friend' which he had abused by taking up arms against us. But that poor king of Cyprus, who was always our friend, always an ally, about whom the Senate and our commanders never heard any truly serious suspicions, got a spectator's seat (as the saying goes) as he was sold off lock, stock and barrel. Jurors, why should other kings consider their positions safe when they have the precedent of that deadly year right at hand and see that some tribune with his innumerable operators could rob them of their fortunes and strip them of their kingdoms. They even wanted to use the affair to smear Marcus Cato's good name. Clearly they do not know the true strength that character, honour, greatness of mind – in short, being a real man – have. Men like this are calm in a wild storm, are a beacon in the dark and, although driven from their ground, they still cling firmly to their country, shine out under their own power and are never soiled by others' filth. Their intention was not to honour Marcus Cato but to banish him, not to entrust him with this business but to burden him with it, since they openly boasted in an assembly that they had ripped out Cato's tongue, a tongue which had always spoken out freely against special commissions.[17] My hope is that they will soon feel that that free tongue of his still works and is made even stronger – if such a thing were possible! When even Marcus Cato despaired that he might achieve anything using his personal influence, he still raised an indignant outcry against these consuls, and weeping over my misfortune and the Repub-

lic's after my departure, he attacked Piso with such language
that he, even though he was a thoroughly corrupt and shameless man, nearly regretted what he had done to get his province.

61. 'But why did he obey?'

As if before that occasion he had not sworn to obey other laws
he thought were illegally passed![18] He will not offer himself up
at the altar of their rash decisions when it will deprive the
Republic of a citizen like himself and gain the Republic nothing.
During my consulship, when he was tribune of the plebs elect,
he risked his life and made an unpopular argument even though
he knew that it was so unpopular he was putting his head on
the block.[19] He spoke passionately, acted energetically and
never hid his thoughts. He was a leader, the mover and shaker,
on that occasion; he was well aware of the risk he was running,
but as that great storm lashed our Republic, he thought nothing
was worth considering except the dangers to our country.

62. Then followed his term as tribune. What can I possibly
say about his unique greatness of mind and his remarkable
heroism? You all remember the day when his colleague seized a
temple and we feared we were about to lose a man and a citizen
of such calibre, while he entered the temple with total self-
possession and silenced the shouts and attacks of disloyal men
with his sheer presence and by acting like a true hero.[20] He
confronted danger then, but there is no need for me to talk now
of how important was the reason he confronted it. And it was
not as if there would have been less disgrace attached to the
Republic if he had not obeyed that thoroughly criminal bill
concerning Cyprus, for it was not until after this kingdom had
been confiscated that the bill naming Cato was put to a vote.
Are you in any doubt that if he had refused, force would have
been used to make him agree, since it was he alone who looked
capable of undermining all their actions that year?

63. Cato also saw that, as no one could wash away the stain
that was attached to the Republic from the confiscation of
Cyprus, it would be better for him to preserve what good could
come to the Republic from this evil than for someone else to

throw it away. And even if in those days some other form of violence had driven him from Rome, he still could have lived with it – for, after all, he had stayed away from the Senate in the previous year[21] (although, had he come, he would have seen that I was still an ally of his public policies). Could he have remained calmly in Rome when I was exiled, given that although it was my name that was being mentioned, it was his argument and the entire Senate who were the ones condemned?[22] In reality, like me he yielded to the times, to the same lunatic, to the same consuls, to the same threats, plots and dangers. I drank more deeply of grief; he no less of mental agony.

[*The speech continues with a list of harms done to various people, starting with those outside the Roman community but still under her protection: kings, allies and other communities. Cicero presents a picture of Rome completely under Clodius' domination until the sleeping giant of Gnaeus Pompey wakes and there is movement to recall Cicero from exile. There are, of course, twists and turns: the consuls Gabinius and Piso still stick cravenly to their bargain with Clodius, while a conspiracy hatched against Pompey's life causes him to retreat. However, the tide still remains firmly in Cicero's favour when Sestius (newly elected to the office of tribune, but yet to take it up) petitions Caesar on Cicero's behalf. It is only at this late stage (chapter 71 of the speech!) that Cicero announces plans to talk about Sestius' period as tribune of the plebs. Quite remarkably, it is the first time he has mentioned Sestius since chapter 15. However, the story of the efforts to have Cicero recalled from exile still stays front and centre. Finally, Cicero begins the famous digression on the two different factions in the Republic: the* optimates *and* populares. *Cicero's description of the* optimates *basically includes anyone who is not a criminal or a lunatic actively seeking to harm the Republic. It is hard to say how sincere he is here – this is a defence speech, after all, and his aim was to have his client acquitted. However, it has been argued that this is a serious political statement which was added to the speech when Cicero revised it for publication.*]

96. Here we come to the heart of why you made a particular point of asking me in your prosecution speech what I mean by the phrase 'clique of the finest citizens'[23] – your term. Your question touches on a subject which is a splendid one for the young to learn about and one I find it no hardship to teach. So, jurors, I shall say a few words; I do not think they will be out of order since I believe they will help the general audience, you in your duty in this case and the case of Publius Sestius. Our community has always had two types of people eager to engage with and take a prominent part in politics: one group wants to be called 'men of the people',[24] the other to be called and actually *be* the 'finest citizens'. Men who wanted everything they did and said to be appealing to the masses were considered to be men of the people, while those who tried to ensure that their policies found favour with all the finest people were thought to be the finest citizens.

97. 'How then are you defining a "fine" citizen?'

Since you ask, there is no end to this class – if there were, Rome would fall apart. They are our senior statesmen and those who follow their lead. They are those who are of the highest rank to whom the doors of the Curia are open. They are citizens of Roman municipalities and peasants. They are businessmen. There are even freedmen who are the finest citizens. As I said, their number includes men of different types who are spread far and wide. But in case there is any possible misconception, here is a quick definition and description of them as a class: a fine citizen is anyone who is not a criminal, perverted in nature, insane or hobbled by personal financial difficulties. Thus it is that those whom you have called a clique are those who are ethical, sane and keep their personal finances in good shape. The men who steer our Republic in conformity with this group's wishes, interests and expectations are those we count as their protectors – and are themselves the most important of the finest citizens and greatly distinguished men, leaders of our community.

98. What port should those who steer the Republic keep their eyes upon and direct their course towards? The one which

those who are sane, decent and prosperous consider the best, more desirable by far than any other: peace with honour. All those who want this are considered our finest citizens; those who make it happen are great men and saviours of our community. For men should not get so carried away by the honour of a public position that they do not care for peace, or embrace any peace which is not compatible with honour.

These are the foundations, these the elements of peace with honour, these what the Republic's leaders should defend and protect with their lives: our rites, the auspices, the powers of magistrates, the authority of the Senate, the laws, our traditions, the courts and their verdicts, our integrity, provinces, allies, respect for our empire, the military and the treasury. 99. A great spirit, great talent and great firmness are needed in those who are protectors and guardians of so many important responsibilities. This is because among our multitude of citizens there is a mass of men who look for revolution and political upheaval, either because they fear punishment or feel guilt because of their sins, or who feed off subversion and civil conflict because of some congenital insanity, or who, because of their financial difficulties, prefer to burn with everything else rather than alone. When such people have found leaders who will shield their vicious cause, the Republic is tossed on the waves, and those who guide their country must stay alert and struggle, with all their skill, to hold to their course and sail into that port of peace with honour – all while preserving those foundations and elements I just mentioned.

100. If I were to deny, jurors, that this is a rough, steep and treacherous path to tread, I would be lying, particularly since this is not only something I have always known but have experienced more than other people. Greater forces attack the Republic than defend her, since reckless, ruined men need only a tiny sign to egg them on – or even move against the Republic at their own initiative. But decent people are unfortunately slower to act and they ignore the start of the problem; it is only an actual crisis that finally gets them moving. The result is that even though they are willing to enjoy peace without honour, their delays and sluggishness sometimes lose them both.

101. The self-styled defenders of the Republic defect if they cannot stay the course and falter if their courage fails; the only people who stand firm and endure everything for the Republic are men like your father was, Marcus Scaurus,[25] who stood his ground[26] against subversives from Gaius Gracchus to Quintus Varius; he was a man no violence, no threats and no risk of unpopularity ever shook. Or men like Quintus Metellus, your mother's uncle, who as censor tried to expel from the Senate Lucius Saturninus, a prominent man of the people, and faced down a violent, inflamed mob to strike off the register of citizens that fake Gracchus.[27] He was the only person to refuse to swear to abide by a law he thought had been passed illegally, preferring to be forced out of our community rather than from his beliefs.[28] Leaving behind ancient examples – and there are as many of these as our empire is great – and without using the name of anyone still alive, they were like the recently deceased Quintus Catulus.[29] Neither fear of a storm of dangers nor hope of a favouring breeze could ever blow *him* off his course.

102. By the immortal gods, everyone here who seeks honour, praise and glory should imitate these men! They are honourable, they are divine, they are immortal. Such examples are what make our fame, are written about in histories and handed down from generation to generation. I admit this takes effort. I confess it involves great risk. Here is a truthful line: 'There are many traps for decent men.'[30] But we should also remember, 'It is a fool's errand to demand what many envy, what many want – unless you bring along with you all your effort, all your care.' I wish the author had not said elsewhere the phrase which perverse citizens seize upon, 'Let them hate, as long as they fear,' for the rest of it was good advice for the young.

103. There was a time, however, when using principle as one administered the Republic was extremely dangerous, as there were many subjects on which the mob's passions and the people's 'interests' were out of tune with what was good for the Republic. Lucius Cassius passed a law on the secret ballot: the people thought their freedom was at stake. The leaders of our state disagreed as they were particularly afraid that the whims of the mob and the wild use of the secret ballot would be used

against our finest citizens.[31] Tiberius Gracchus proposed an agrarian law: the people liked it as it seemed to give more financial stability to the poorer classes. The finest citizens resisted it since they saw that it would stir up conflict and thought the Republic would lose her defenders as it evicted the wealthy from property that they had held for a long time.[32] Gaius Gracchus proposed a grain law: it appealed to the plebs because it would give them plenty of food with no effort. Decent people opposed it because they thought it seduced the plebs to abandon hard work and saw it would empty the treasury.[33]

104. There have also been many examples in our lifetime when the desires of the people were at odds with the policies of our leading citizens – these I intentionally omit. But now there is no reason for the people and elite and leaders to disagree; the people make no demands, do not itch for revolution and find equal pleasure in their own peace, the honour of the best men and the reputation our entire Republic enjoys. These days, men who want subversion and riots, unable to use handouts to cause trouble since the plebs embrace peace and want no more violence or civil unrest, hire people to attend their assemblies. They have no intention of saying or proposing anything the attendees actually want to hear; instead, they use bribery and graft to make sure that those there fake a desire to hear whatever is said.

105. Do you seriously believe that the Gracchi or Saturninus or anyone from the past who was thought to be a man of the people ever paid anyone to come to an assembly? Not one of them did; it was their handouts and the expectation of profit that incited their mass audiences to turn up for nothing. In those days, the men of the people offended steady and honourable men, but the masses went wild for them in every way they could. They were applauded in the theatre and had no trouble finding the votes to support anything they wanted; men loved their very names, speeches, expressions, their style of walking. The members of their opposition, who were considered important and steady men, and who held considerable influence in the Senate and even more with decent men, had no appeal for the masses. They could find no votes for proposals they wanted –

and if any of them were ever applauded, they were afraid that they had done something wrong. Yet, despite all this, on any issue of significance they still held the most authority with the people.

106. But now – unless I am mistaken – our community is in such good shape that, ignoring the hired gangs, we all think as one about the Republic. There are three particular places where the Roman people can express what they want and what they think: the assembly, the elections and at dramatic and gladiatorial shows. Has there been in recent years any assembly – I talk of real assemblies not hired ones – where you cannot clearly see the Roman people's collective desire? That crime-soaked gladiator[34] held many assemblies about me, assemblies that not one unbribed or ethical person attended, for no decent person could look at his revolting face or listen to his maniacal voice. Those assemblies of losers had, by necessity, to be riots.

107. The consul Publius Lentulus also held an assembly on my fate;[35] the Roman people gathered; all the classes, all Italy stood together in that assembly. He pleaded his case with such weight and eloquence, and there was such intense silence and universal approval for his words, that it seemed as if the Roman people had never heard anything they considered so related to their interests. He then led forward Gnaeus Pompey, who not only lent his weight to my cause but prostrated himself[36] before the Roman people. Pompey's oratory had always had weight and influence with the assemblies, but I contend they never before thought that his opinions and eloquence held such authority or found them so pleasing. 108. There was great silence as the rest of the senior statesmen of our community spoke about me. I shall not name names here for fear that by not praising someone enough I shall look ungrateful – and to speak of all of them as they deserve would be an infinite task.

Now I remind you of the time my enemy addressed a true assembly of the people about me in the Campus Martius. Did anyone there approve? Instead, didn't everyone consider it a shocking offence that he was alive and breathing, let alone speaking? What attendee did not think that Clodius' voice contaminated the Republic, and that by listening he would become

an accomplice in Clodius' crime? 109. I come now to the
assemblies that elect magistrates or pass laws.[37] We see laws
voted on all the time (I am excluding those passed at assemblies
where barely five men – and those are not even in their right
tribes – can be found to vote). He, the Republic's nemesis, says
that he passed a law on me, a man he used to call a tyrant and
the thief of freedom. Can you find anyone who confesses he
voted *against* me and *for* that law when it was passed? But
when, in accordance with a decree of the Senate, another law
about my situation was proposed at the centuriate assembly,
could anyone be found who did not openly confess that he had
voted for my restoration? Which of these assemblies should be
considered popular: the one in which all our community's honourable members – no matter what age or class they are – come
together as one, or that in which frenzied Furies flock together
as if over the carcass of the Republic?

[*Much of the rest of the speech attacks Cicero's many enemies
by name in rather juicy terms and describes shows of support
for him in various public arenas, including the theatre. He then
turns to his recall from exile, before ending with a rousing plea
to save Publius Sestius.*]

In Defence of Milo

Delivered on 7 or 8 April 52[1] before
the court on public violence

On the afternoon of 18 January 52, two men and their escorts
met on the Appian Way at Bovillae near a shrine of Bona Dea
(the 'Good Goddess'); one man walked away from the encounter, the other's corpse was brought back to Rome to be mourned
by his wife and mother. These were not ordinary men and the
aftershocks of this roadside murder reverberated through Rome
and Roman politics: the dead man was Publius Clodius Pulcher,
Cicero's inveterate enemy and the architect of his exile, the sur-
vivor was Titus Annius Milo, who had fought hard to have
Cicero recalled. Both were currently up for election; Clodius
was running for praetor and Milo for consul, and both controlled large urban gangs. Instead of Clodius being buried and
mourned in traditional fashion, the Curia, the meeting-house of
the Senate, became his funeral pyre, the wood supplied by
benches and furniture from the house, mixed with documents
from the Senate's clerks. The riots lasted for days as Clodius'
gangs fought it out with Milo's, and an already explosive situation devolved into utter chaos. The situation was intolerable
as Rome was ripped apart by street violence on a daily basis.

Unable to hold the already severely delayed elections, the
Senate appointed a series of interreges to oversee the elections
but to no avail. In the end, Gnaeus Pompey was appointed sole
consul (he was then proconsul and the only figure of authority
near the city) and Milo was prosecuted for his actions under a
new law passed by Pompey on public violence[2] and in a new
court. Milo immediately chose Cicero to speak for his defence.[3]
Cicero, bound by ties of obligation and friendship, delivered
his defence speech in a Forum ringed with soldiers, while

Pompey looked on and Clodius' supporters jeered from the sidelines. Not surprisingly, this was not one of Cicero's better performances, though it is doubtful that even at his finest he could have altered the outcome of this trial. Milo was exiled and went to live at Massilia, modern Marseilles (quite comfortably it must be said); Cicero, unhappy with the speech he had delivered, later published the considerably revised version we possess and which is translated here.

The speech is, to put it frankly, a tissue of lies. If we were to rely on Cicero to reconstruct events, we would picture a villainous Clodius, a monster compounded of every vice known to the Romans, lurking in wait on a high spot outside his estate for an innocent and virtuous Milo, travelling with his wife and a few men and slaves – slaves who heroically killed Clodius while believing Milo dead. However, we are lucky enough not to have to rely on Cicero for the reconstruction of the encounter. An ancient commentary by Asconius from the first century CE survives and gives a very different account. He tells us (and we have no reason to doubt his veracity or reliability) that when Clodius and Milo encountered each other, both were heavily guarded – normal in those days, when the Appian Way could be a dangerous place to travel. Clodius had thirty armed slaves and three friends; Milo was accompanied by his wife, Fausta (the daughter of the dictator Sulla), armed slaves and several gladiators, including the famous Eudamus and Birria.[4] A scuffle broke out between the escorts as they passed each other, and when Clodius turned around to glare at the brawl, Birria threw a spear which pierced his shoulder. The wounded Clodius was taken to a nearby tavern. However, Milo, deciding that a wounded Clodius was more dangerous than a dead one, ordered him to be dragged out and killed. His battered body was left in the street for a passing senator, Sextus Teidius, to pick up and have brought back to Rome. When it arrived, Clodius' wife, Fulvia, and his mother took it in all its bloody state to the Forum where it was exhibited to the crowd.

Fired up by the sight of the dead body and by speeches given by Clodius' supporters and Milo's opponents, the crowd rioted and burned the body in the Curia; the flames did not just destroy the building but spread to the nearby Basilica Porcia. Not content with this, Clodius' supporters then attacked Milo's house and that of Marcus Lepidus, who had been appointed interrex. *They then marched to the homes of Quintus Metellus Scipio[5] and Publius Plautius Hypsaeus (both of whom were running for consul against Milo) and, for good measure, to Pompey's suburban residence demanding him as consul or dictator. Milo, rather incredibly, continued to canvass with extensive bribery for consul even though elections were clearly impossible in the chaos. Faced with anarchy, the Senate called upon the* interrex *at the time, the tribunes of the plebs and Pompey to ensure the safety of the state. At the end of February, one of Pompey's first moves (he was now sole consul) was dealing with the fallout of the murder of Clodius, which he did by passing the* lex Pompeia de vi; *this established a new court with the primary (or perhaps sole) intent of trying this particular case. It was under this law that two nephews of Clodius prosecuted Milo. Not only were the facts of the case against Milo but he had garnered enormous unpopularity because of Clodius' death, and Pompey himself appeared extremely hostile. Milo was convicted by 38 votes to 13; he was later tried and convicted on several other charges, including electoral bribery.*

Cicero has often been criticized for choking on the day of the trial and our extant speech is quite different from that which was delivered before a hostile audience. In fact, Milo joked that had Cicero delivered it as it was published, he would never have had the chance to enjoy the excellent seafood of Massilia. We know that a version of Cicero's delivered speech was in circulation, taken down by shorthand writers on the day of the trial, perhaps prompting him to publish the revised version. Even if it is mainly constructed of lies, the speech is a literary masterpiece and a fascinating record of the chaos and instability of the 50s, where political violence was an everyday occurrence. Rome's electoral machinery had ground to an almost complete halt in the face of enormous bribery and violence.

1. Jurors, I fear it is shameful for someone starting the defence of a very brave man to be afraid. It is also very inappropriate, when Titus Annius Milo is himself more troubled about the Republic's safety than his own, that I cannot bring to his cause an equal strength of mind. Still, this novel form of a novel court brings terror to my eyes;[6] wherever they fall, they seek the old familiarity of the Forum and how our trials were conducted in the past. It is not your usual audience that surrounds you; the familiar crowd does not encircle me. 2. The guard you see in front of all the temples, even if it is stationed there against the threat of violence, still inspires some fear in a speaker. And even in the Forum and this court, although we are surrounded by guards to ensure our safety, we cannot be without fear even though we have been freed from our fear. If I thought that they were placed there to threaten Milo, I would yield to the situation, jurors, judging that there is no place for a speaker among armed men. But Gnaeus Pompey's good sense gives me fresh courage. He is a very wise and just person and would *never* have thought it compatible with his sense of justice to surrender to soldiers a defendant he had handed over to a court to be judged, or with his wisdom to make a gift of the state's approval for the whim of a whipped-up mob to use as a weapon.

3. These weapons, centurions and cohorts are here not to threaten but to protect. They encourage me to be composed *and* brave. They promise help and silence as I make my case for the defence. The rest of the crowd or, at least, the part made up of fellow-citizens, is completely on our side. Among the men you see everywhere – that is, wherever you can catch a glimpse of the Forum – watching and waiting the outcome of this trial, there is not one who does not applaud Milo's courage or think our struggle today is for himself, his own future and that of his children and country. Only one type of person is opposed and hostile to us, he whom Publius Clodius' madness fattened with looting, arson and everything devastating to the community. Just yesterday they were incited in an assembly to dictate to *you* what your verdict should be. Any noise coming from that side should be your cue to hold on to, as your fellow-citizen, a man who always ignored the great commotion that sort make

when he weighed it against your well-being. 4. So collect yourselves, jurors, and lay aside any fear you may have. If it was
ever in the power of a select group of our most distinguished
classes[7] to judge the case of decent, brave men and of deserving
citizens or to use their verdict to declare their active support for
brave, decent citizens (a support you have often hinted at in
expressions and stray words), you have it in your power now.
You can decide whether we unfortunates, who were always
devoted supporters of your authority, will mourn our lot or,
though long the subjects of attacks from ruined citizens, will
finally gain new life from your integrity, courage and wisdom.
5. Can you imagine or describe anyone more long suffering,
harried and plagued than Milo and I? The allure of great
acclaim led us to serve the Republic; now we live in fear of
vicious punishment. I always thought that Milo had to weather
other tempests and storms in the troubled waters of the assemblies because he had sided with decent citizens against disloyal
men. I never considered that in a court, and before a jury made
up of distinguished men drawn from all classes, his enemies
could hope not only to destroy his standing, but crush his reputation. 6. And yet, jurors, we shall not use Titus Annius' work
as tribune, and all he has done to keep the Republic safe, as a
defence against the charge. Unless you can see with your own
eyes that Clodius laid the ambush, we shall not plead with you
to forgive this crime because of Milo's many remarkable services to the Republic. Nor will we demand that if Publius
Clodius' death saved you, you attribute that to Milo's heroism
rather than the Roman people's good fortune. But *if* Clodius'
ambush is made as clear as day, *then* I shall beg you, jurors,
even if we have lost everything else, to leave us with the right to
defend our lives, without fear, against wild attacks.

7. But before I come to the specifics of this case, I believe it
is necessary for me to refute the accusations that Milo's enemies
have tossed about in the Senate as disloyal types have in the
assembly and as did the prosecutors only a little while ago.
Once I have cleared away misconceptions, you will be able to
see what lies at the heart of this trial. *They* say it is not right
that someone who confesses to murder still looks on the light

of day. In what city are these idiots arguing their case? In the city whose first capital trial was that of our bravest hero, Marcus Horatius, who was set free in a still unfree state by an assembly of the Roman people, although he confessed he had killed his *sister* with his own hand![8] 8. Is there anyone who does not know that in a homicide trial it is normal for defendants either to deny completely that they committed the murder or argue it was a moral and legal action? Unless you think that Publius Africanus[9] was out of his mind when he replied to a question about the death of Tiberius Gracchus posed by the subversive tribune of the plebs, Gaius Carbo, at an assembly, that he believed Gracchus had been killed legally. Servilius Ahala, Publius Nasica, Lucius Opimius,[10] Gaius Marius (familiar examples) or even the Senate, when I was consul, would be considered evil, if it were evil to kill criminal citizens. Jurors, there is a reason why erudite writers have handed down to us the legendary story of how, when the jury was deadlocked, it was not just any deity but the wisest goddess who voted to acquit a man who had killed his mother to avenge his father.[11]

9. If the Twelve Tables[12] have decreed that a thief in the night can be killed with impunity, no matter what the circumstances are and 'by any means', and one in the day if he defends himself with a weapon, is there any man who thinks – seeing as the laws themselves sometimes hold out a sword for us to kill with – that a man should be punished if he has killed 'by any means'? If there is a right time to kill a man legally (and there are many right times), then that time is when it is not just legal but *necessary* to respond to violence with violence. When a military tribune in the army of Gaius Marius – and one who was a close relative of Marius – violated a soldier,[13] he was killed by the very man he forced. That soldier, a decent young man, preferred to risk danger rather than accept disgrace. Marius, who was a great man, acquitted him as he had committed no crime. 10. What death can be illegal when it is dealt to an outlaw and ambusher? Why else do we have escorts and swords? Surely they would not be permitted if we were never allowed to use them? There is an unwritten and instinctive law, one we did not learn, inherit or read, but grabbed, devoured

and pulled from nature herself. We are not educated but made for it, not trained in it but immersed in it. It tells us that if we are violently attacked by enemies or outlaws, whatever we do to survive safely is honourable.

11. Laws are silent in the middle of a fight and do not demand we wait for them, since someone who waited would suffer injustice before they could seek justice. The law[14] very wisely and tacitly gives us the right to self-defence; it does not say that we cannot kill but that we cannot have a weapon concealed with the intent of killing. When at a trial people look at motive not action, it is the case that someone who used a weapon in self-defence is ruled not to have possessed the weapon with the intent to kill. So, jurors, let that be considered a settled matter in this case. I do not doubt that I shall prove my case to you if you do not forget the unforgettable: it can be lawful to kill a man who ambushes you.

12. The next issue is a frequent comment of Milo's enemies, which is that the Senate ruled that the bloodshed in which Publius Clodius was killed was an action harmful to the Republic. But the Senate voted enthusiastically in approval of his death; I have spoken many times in the Senate on that topic and received the loud and open applause of the entire body! When, even in an extremely packed Senate, could one find four or, at the most, five men who did not approve of Milo's case? The extinguished assemblies of this singed tribune of the plebs[15] declare the same, assemblies in which that tribune daily and maliciously accused me of having too much power, saying that the Senate voted not as it felt but as I wished. If you must call what I possess 'power', rather than the normal influence which one gets in return for working hard to support decent causes or the influence my dutiful efforts have gained me among decent men, then, for all I care, let it be called that – I only care that I use it to protect the decent against the insanity of the corrupt.

13. But the Senate never thought this court – even if it is just – should be established. There were already laws and courts that dealt with murder and assault, and the death of Publius Clodius did not bring the Senate such distressing grief that we needed to establish a new court. Given that the Senate

lost the power of determining the jury which would vote on Clodius' sacrilegious indecency, who could believe that it thought that a new one should be set up to rule on his death?[16]

So why then did the Senate vote that the burning of the Curia, the besieging of Marcus Lepidus' house[17] and the bloodshed we are discussing here were harmful to the Republic? It is because in a free state no violence can take place between citizens and *not* harm the Republic. 14. Although it is sometimes necessary to defend oneself against an assault, it is never desirable. Or maybe you think the day on which Tiberius Gracchus was killed, or the one on which his brother was or the day the weapons of Saturninus[18] were crushed (even if they were crushed for the public good), brought no harm to the Republic? When it was clear that there had been bloodshed on the Appian Way, that was why I did not vote that the man who had defended himself had done so 'to harm the Republic'; instead, as there had been violence and an ambush, I censured the act but reserved the question of guilt for the courts. If that mad tribune of the plebs[19] had allowed the Senate to act as it thought right, we would never have had this new court – for it was in the act of voting that the trial should take place under our established laws but should be given priority. Then, at someone's request (do I really have to identify *everyone*'s outrageous actions?), the motion was split into two parts.[20] And just like that, a bought veto stripped what remained of the Senate's authority.

15. But someone will say that Gnaeus Pompey in his bill ruled on the facts and how the case would be judged. He said there should be a trial about the bloodshed on the Appian Way in which Publius Clodius had been killed. What did he propose? Clearly, *that there should be a trial*. Next, what should a trial investigate? Whether there was bloodshed? But that is clear. Who was responsible? That is obvious. He saw that even when someone has confessed, he can still plead justification; unless he knew that a man who confessed could still be acquitted, he never would have ordered a trial when he saw we confessed to what had happened – nor would he have given you the power to acquit as well as convict. I think that Gnaeus Pompey did not weigh in harshly against Milo; I also think he

considered what you should think about when deciding on your verdict. Someone who did not punish a confession but allowed it a defence considered you should investigate *why* the death happened, *not* the death itself. 16. I am sure he himself will tell us whether he did so on his own initiative as a tribute to Publius Clodius or because the situation demanded it.

Marcus Drusus, a tribune of the plebs and a most noble man, the Senate's defender – and in those days what we might call its protector – and the uncle of one of today's jurors, Marcus Cato (another very brave man), was killed in his own home. In the case of his death, no bill was put before the people and the Senate voted for no special court. Did our fathers not tell us of the great grief in Rome on the notorious night Publius Africanus was violently attacked in his home while he slept?[21] Was there anyone who did not cry out? Was there anyone who did not burn with sorrow that there was someone who would not wait for Africanus' natural death – Africanus, a man everyone would have wished to be immortal if it were possible. Was there any 'special court' for his death? Of course not! 17. Why not? Because the murders of a great man and an unknown one are not considered different crimes. There should be a difference between the position of the great and the low during life; however, when they are murdered, they should be judged under the same laws and with the same penalties. Or maybe we think a man more of a parricide if he kills a consular 'father' than an unimportant one? Or – their frequent allegation – the death of Publius Clodius is more shocking because he was killed on the Appian Way, his ancestor's monument?[22] I guess Appius Caecus built that road not so that the people might use it, but so his descendants might ambush people there with impunity? 18. I suppose that when Publius Clodius killed that highly honoured Roman equestrian Marcus Papirius[23] on the same Appian Way, that crime did not need to be punished since an *aristocrat* killed a Roman *equestrian* in the middle of his own family road.

And what tragic scenarios does the name 'Appian Way' inspire! No one mentioned it when an honourable and innocent man was murdered, but now they keep mentioning it since it has been drenched with the blood of an outlaw traitor. Why

am I even bringing this up when Publius Clodius' slave, whom
he had placed there to kill Gnaeus Pompey, was arrested in the
temple of Castor? The blade was ripped from his hands as he
confessed. After that, Pompey kept away from the Forum, the
Senate and the people, using his door and walls to protect himself – not the laws and courts. 19. Was a bill proposed then? Or
a new court voted for? But if any situation, any man or any
crisis was ever worthy of one, then all these events were. An
ambusher had been stationed in the Forum, on the very doorstep of the Senate; death was plotted for a man on whose life
the community's well-being depended. If Pompey had died in
that critical moment, it would have been the end not just of this
community but of all of them. Did we not punish that action
because it was not carried out? It seems, then, as if the laws
avenge the results of men's actions, not their plans. Even if we
felt less pain because the crime was not carried out, still the
punishment should not have been less.

20. Jurors, I myself have frequently escaped the attacks and
bloody hands of Publius Clodius. But if my good fortune or the
Republic's had not saved me, tell me, who would have proposed a new court about *my* death? But I am a fool for daring
to compare the cases of Drusus, Africanus, Pompey and myself
with that of Publius Clodius. Those events could be tolerated:
no one can possibly bear the death of Publius Clodius with res-
ignation. The Senate mourns, the equestrians weep, the entire
community is broken down in grief, the municipalities are
bereft, the colonies crushed – even the very fields feel the loss of
so generous, so useful and so kindly a citizen!

21. I am sure that was why Pompey recommended a special
court should be set up! No: he did so because, as a wise man
endowed with a noble and almost prophetic mind, he foresaw
a great deal. Clodius was his enemy, Milo his close friend; if he
personally took part in the joy everyone felt, he was afraid that
belief in the sincerity of his reconciliation with Clodius would
waver. The chief of what he foresaw was this: however harsh
his proposal, your verdict would reveal your independence.
And so he selected the stars of our most important classes. And
he did not, as some people say over and over again, exclude my

friends when selecting the jurors. A man so supremely just would not think like that (not that he could have achieved it, even if he had wanted to, since he was selecting *decent* men). *My* influence is not confined to my close friends, of which there cannot be many since intimacy is not possible with a great number. Anything I achieve, I achieve because the Republic associates me with decent men; when Pompey was choosing the best men from that group – he considered his selection particularly reflected on his integrity – he could not help but choose my supporters. 22. In this he particularly wished you, Lucius Domitius, to preside over this trial,[24] he pursued nothing other than justice, character, human decency and integrity. I believe he ruled that the president of the court had to be an ex-consul because he considered it is the duty of our leading men to stand up to the unstable mob and heedless, ruined men. He appointed you in preference to the other ex-consuls, as even from your youth you showed great evidence of how you cared nothing for 'popular' mania.

23. Jurors, let me bring us at last to the real issue to be decided here. If the admission of the deed is not at all unusual, the Senate has not ruled on our case other than we could have wished, if the person who proposed the law-court, even though there was no dispute about the actual deed, still wished there to be a discussion about the law, if the jurors have been selected, and the man who has been appointed the president of the court is someone who will decide on these matters justly and wisely: well, what remains, jurors, is for you to discover which of the two men laid an ambush for the other. Please pay careful attention while I briefly explain to you what happened so it is easier for you to see the truth.

24. When Publius Clodius decided he would torment the Republic with every sort of crime after he was elected praetor, and saw that the elections had been delayed so much that he would not be praetor for long, being a man who did not care about advancing through the offices as other men do but wishing to escape having Lucius Paulus (a man of singularly proper behaviour) as a colleague, and wanting an entire year to rip the Republic apart – well, he suddenly dropped the idea of running

in his year and transferred to the next.[25] It was not for some religious reason[26] as is usual, but, as he himself admitted, so he would have an entire year to be praetor – that is, to destroy the Republic. 25. He realized that while he was praetor he would be thoroughly hamstrung if Milo were consul, and that Milo was on the way to becoming consul with the unanimous vote of the Roman people. Clodius took himself off to Milo's competitors but personally and single-handedly directed the course of the entire election (even against the candidates' wishes) and, as he said again and again, shouldered the weight of the entire election. He called together the tribes, acted as electoral agent and enlisted a new Colline tribe[27] of absolutely ruined citizens. The more agitation Clodius caused, the stronger Milo grew. And when Clodius, someone prepared to commit every crime in the book, saw that a real man and his greatest enemy was quite certain to be elected consul, and understood that the Roman people often declared so not just with words but with votes, he began to act publicly and openly say Milo must be killed. 26. He had brought down from the Apennines the rough, barbaric slaves you saw, slaves he had used to pillage the public forests. (I am not speaking of obscure details here.) He repeated constantly that although the consulship could not be snatched from Milo, his life could. He often hinted at this in the Senate but said it outright in public assemblies. When a courageous man by the name of Marcus Favonius asked him what he was aiming at by using such violence while Milo was still alive, he replied that he would be dead in three or, at the most, four days – a comment Favonius reported at once to Marcus Cato here.

27. Since Clodius knew (not that it was *hard* to know it) that, as Lanuvium's dictator,[28] Milo needed to make his annual, lawfully mandated journey there to nominate a priest, he suddenly set out the day before to lay an ambush for Milo outside his country estate – as events show us. And he left in such a hurry that he missed a turbulent assembly which felt the loss of his ravings and was held *on the very day* of the murder, an assembly he would never have missed unless he had wished to be in the right place at the right time for his crime. 28. Meanwhile, Milo had been in the Senate on that day until it was

dismissed and then came home. He changed out of his formal clothes,[29] waited for a little while his wife got herself ready – you all know how that goes – and set out at the hour when Clodius, *if* he had been planning on coming back to Rome that day, would have returned. An unencumbered Clodius met him on the way: *he* was on horseback, with no coach, baggage or Greeks (his usual companions) and without his wife (a rare occurrence). Milo, the ambusher, who had set out on that journey to do murder, was travelling with his wife, in a coach, wearing a travelling cloak, with a great deal of baggage and a soft, feminine escort of maids and boys. 29. He encountered Clodius outside his estate around 3 p.m. or so.[30] At once several men attacked with missiles from above. Some in front killed the driver of the coach. But when Milo leapt down from the coach, threw his cloak back over his shoulders and put up a fierce defence, the men who were with Clodius drew their swords. Some ran to the coach so they could attack Milo from the rear, while others, thinking he had already been killed, began to slaughter the slaves behind him. Among these there were some loyal to their master and ready to fight: some were killed and the others, when they saw the fight at the coach, were prevented from helping their master. After hearing it from Clodius' own lips they thought Milo had really been killed. Then Milo's slaves – I say it outright, not to divert the responsibility for the crime, but as it is a fact – without the command, knowledge and presence of their master, did what everyone would wish their own slaves to do in such a situation.

30. Events unfolded just as I have explained. The ambusher was overcome, violence was defeated with violence – or, should I say, a wild assault was crushed by the actions of a *man*. I say nothing about the gain to the Republic, to you and all decent men. For all I care, let it be no profit to Milo that it was his fate to be born incapable of saving himself without saving you and the Republic at the same time. If he could not do what he did lawfully, I have no defence. But if reason has dictated to civilized men, need to barbarians, tradition to all mankind and nature herself to wild animals that they should always react to all violence to their persons, rights and lives by defending

themselves however they can, you cannot rule Milo's action to be morally wrong without ruling at the same time that all those who fall among outlaws must fall either by their weapons or by your verdict. 31. If Milo had believed that to be the case, it would have been better for him to offer his throat to Clodius – and it was not the first time it had been Clodius' target – than to have it cut by you for *not* baring it to him. But if none of you think this way, the question to be decided here is not whether Clodius was killed (we admit that), but whether he was killed lawfully or unlawfully, a question which has often come before the courts. It is clear that an ambush was set, and that the Senate judged it was set to harm the Republic, but who set it is in question. It is concerning this point that this court is in session. The Senate has identified the issue, not the person responsible, and Pompey proposed this court to examine the *legality* of the action *not* the action. Surely what this court is examining is whether one of them set an ambush for the other? Nothing else! If Milo set it for Clodius, punish him; if the reverse, acquit him.

32. How can we prove that Clodius set the ambush for Milo? It is enough to demonstrate in the case of that reckless, evil monster that he had a strong motive, great hopes and that he gained considerable advantage from the death of Milo. Let Cassius' well-known question, 'Who benefited?',[31] carry weight in this case: although there is no reward that can make decent men commit a crime, perverse men will often do so for a small one. With Milo dead, Clodius was likely to achieve the following: as praetor he would not have him as consul, impeding his crimes, but would have consuls[32] with whose connivance (if not aid) he hoped to have free play for his insane plans. He calculated that even if they could, they would not want to check his attempts, since they would believe they owed him for his great favour, and even if they wanted to they could hardly check the outrageous actions of a long-hardened criminal.

33. Jurors, can you be the only people who do not know this? Are you visitors to Rome? Has your hearing taken a holiday? Have you not heard what is said everywhere about the laws (if they must be called laws and not torches to burn Rome and cancers on the Republic) that man was planning on impos-

ing and branding on all of us? Sextus Cloelius![33] Exhibit, I beg,
exhibit that case containing the laws, which they say you
snatched from Clodius' home in the night and took from the
middle of an armed mob as if it were the Palladium[34] – all so if
you ran into some tribune who would operate under your direction you could give it to him as a *truly* magnificent decoration
for a tribune's outfit. Look! His glance is just as it is when he
threatens all kinds of harm to everyone. How that *burning*
light of the Curia affects me! What? Do you think that I am
angry with you, Sextus? You punished my bitterest enemy far
more cruelly than my sense of human decency could demand.
You dragged out the bloody corpse of Publius Clodius from his
home. *You* flung it into public view. *You* stripped it of the
masks of his ancestors, mourners, the funeral procession and
the eulogy. *You* left his corpse half-burned by cursed wood, to
be ripped apart by dogs in the night.[35] Although I cannot praise
you, I certainly should not be angry even if what you did was
unholy, since you put your cruelty to use against my enemy.

34. You have heard, jurors, how big an advantage for Clodius
it was to have Milo killed: turn your attention now to Milo.
What advantage did Milo gain from the death of Clodius? Why
would Milo want (I shall not say 'consider') such a thing?

'Clodius stood in the way of Milo's hopes for the consulship.'

But he was on the verge of being consul despite his opposition –
or, should I say, *because* of it; Clodius was a better canvasser
for him than I. Jurors, you placed great importance on Milo's
services towards me and the Republic. The same was true of
my prayers and tears; I know these moved you to an amazing
degree. But far stronger was your fear of the looming threat.
What citizen could picture to himself the unfettered praetorship
of Publius Clodius without fearing a coup? But you saw it would
be unfettered unless there was a consul who would dare to and
could restrain it. Since the entire Roman people understood that
Milo alone was that man, was there a single person who would
hesitate to use his vote to rid himself of fear and the Republic
of such a threat? But now, since Clodius is no longer with us,

Milo must struggle to defend his position by the usual means. That exceptional glory – granted to him alone – which grew greater every day he checked Clodian insanity, disappeared with Clodius' death. *You* gained freedom from fear of any citizen; *he* lost scope for exercising his courage, a canvasser for his candidacy and an eternal source of glory. So Milo's consulship, which could not be undermined when Clodius was alive, has begun to be attacked only now he is dead. Thus, not only has the death of Clodius not benefited Milo, it has impeded him.

35. 'But his hate made him do it.' 'He did it in anger.' 'He did it because he was his enemy.' 'He did it to get justice for an injury.' 'To get revenge for his private grievances.'

What? If I do not just say that these were stronger motives for Clodius than Milo, but that for Clodius these were everything, for Milo nothing – what more will you ask for? Why should Milo have hated Clodius, who gave him such fertile ground and raw material for fame, beyond, that is, the hatred a normal citizen has for all perverse men? But Clodius had reason to hate Milo. First, Milo protected my well-being, tormented his madness, tamed his weapons and, finally, even prosecuted him: as long as he lived, Clodius would be in danger of prosecution by Milo under the *lex Plotia*.[36] Tell me, how do you think the tyrant took that? How great and how justified was his hatred, even for a man without any sense of justice?

36. It remains for Clodius' nature and way of life to defend him and convict Milo! Clodius never did *anything* using violence; Milo everything. *Really?* Jurors, when *I* left Rome amid your distress, was I afraid of a trial?[37] Or was it slaves, weapons and violence? What was the just reason for my restoration, other than that I had been unjustly exiled? I suppose he had named the day of my trial, proposed a fine, begun an action for high treason against me? *Naturally*, I should have feared a trial as it was my 'poor' case not your splendid one that was on trial. I did not wish my fellow-citizens to be endangered by weapons wielded by slaves, the poverty-stricken and criminals, when I had, at great personal risk, used my wisdom to save them.

37. I saw – yes, actually saw – Quintus Hortensius,[38] that star and ornament of the Republic, nearly killed by a band of slaves when he was acting on my behalf. In that riot his companion, the senator Gaius Vibienus and the best of men, was so roughed up that he lost his life.[39] After that, when did Clodius' dagger – his inheritance from Catiline – rest? It pointed at me and I would not suffer you to be endangered by it for my sake. It lay in ambush for Pompey; it bloodied the Appian Way – the monument holding his family name – with the murder of Papirius. Then, after a long pause, he directed the same dagger at me, and – as you know – not long ago it nearly finished me off at the palace of Numa.[40]

38. How does this resemble Milo? This was always the aim of Milo's 'violence': stopping Publius Clodius, since the courts could not deal with him, from controlling a state overwhelmed by his violence. If Milo *had* wanted to kill him, he had many splendid opportunities. Could he not have lawfully got his revenge when he was defending his home and household gods from attack?[41] Or when that outstandingly brave citizen, his colleague Publius Sestius, was wounded? Or when Quintus Fabricius,[42] best of men, was driven away as he was proposing a law regarding my recall from exile and a vicious blood-bath in the Forum followed? Or when the home of Lucius Caecilius,[43] that extremely just and brave praetor, was attacked? Or on the day when the law on my restoration was passed, and, inspired by my recall, all Italy gathered and would willingly have claimed as its own the fame from Clodius' murder? Then, even if Milo had done the actual deed, the whole community would have claimed the glory. 39. What an opportunity that was! The consul Publius Lentulus was in office, a very illustrious, brave man, who was Clodius' enemy and punished his crimes, championed the Senate, defended your decisions, guarded the state's unanimous wish *and* restored me from exile.[44] There were also seven praetors[45] and eight tribunes of the plebs who opposed Clodius but defended me. *And* there was Gnaeus Pompey, Clodius' enemy, who instigated and led the movement for my restoration; he spurred on the Roman people, and the whole Senate supported the powerful and magnificent

speech he gave on the subject of my recall. When he passed a decree at Capua on my situation, he personally gave a signal to the whole of Italy (eagerly begging for his aid) to come together to restore me to Rome. If anyone had killed Clodius then, when every citizen burned with hatred for him because of how much they missed me, the issue would not have been how to let him off but how to reward him.

40. Still, Milo restrained himself and took him to court twice, never turning to violence. When he was a private citizen and Publius Clodius prosecuted him before the people, and Gnaeus Pompey was attacked as he was speaking in his defence, *that* was not just an opportunity but even a good case for crushing Clodius![46] By the immortal gods, what an opportunity he had not long ago when Mark Antony[47] brought great hope of safety to decent men and he – a most noble young man – bravely took up a very important public duty by trapping that monster as he was wriggling free of the nets of justice. When Clodius, as he fled from Antony, hid himself in the dark under the stairs, was not that a great chance for Milo to eradicate this cancer without bringing hatred on himself and, instead, bringing greater glory to Mark Antony? 41. Milo often had the power to eradicate Clodius at the elections in the Campus Martius. There was the time Clodius forced his way into the voting enclosures[48] and made sure swords were drawn and stones thrown;[49] then, utterly terrified by the expression on Milo's face, he suddenly fled to the Tiber while you and all decent men prayed that Milo would be allowed to unleash his heroic nature.

Although he refused to kill Clodius when everyone would have thanked him for it, did Milo decide to do so when some would complain? Although he did not dare to do it when he had the right, the opportunity and the time to do so with impunity, can we think he killed him unlawfully, with no good opportunity, at an unsuitable time and at the risk of his life? 42. Unlikely, jurors, seeing as the day of the elections, the day of contest for the consulship, was near. I know how timid and worried a candidate is and how great is his ambition to be consul. You fear everything – not just what people will criticize in public, but what can be secretly mulled over, trivial rumours and invented tales. We candidates watch everyone's face and eyes. For nothing is so fragile, so delicate, so brittle and so easily altered as the goodwill and feelings our fellow-citizens have for us: they do not just get angry with candidates' scandalous acts but are often even offended by proper ones. 43. Did Milo, as he pictured to himself a hoped- and longed-for election day, plan on arriving at the critical auspices taken for the elections, confessing his crimes and with his bloody hands showing his offence? How can you believe this? How can you not consider it in the case of Clodius, as he thought he would rule like a king after Milo's murder? What? Jurors, is not that the source of reckless behaviour? Who does not know that the hope of sinning with impunity is the greatest attraction to do so? For which man is this true? Milo, who now is a defendant for what was a splendid deed or, without a doubt, a necessary one? Or Clodius, who so despised courts and punishment that he enjoyed nothing that nature or divine law permits?

44. But why am I still arguing? Why do I continue to make a case? I call on you, Quintus Petilius, best and bravest of citizens. I call on you, Marcus Cato,[50] as a witness. For it almost seems as if the gods have given you to me as jurors. You heard from Marcus Favonius – you heard it while Clodius was alive – that Clodius had said to him Milo would be dead within three days. And three days later, events unfolded as he had said. When he did not hesitate to talk openly about his plans, can you hesitate to believe his actions? 45. How did he pick the right day? As I just said, it was no trouble to learn the days the dictator of Lanuvium had to perform a sacrifice. He knew Milo had to set out on the very day he did – so he acted first. And what day was it? The one I just mentioned, when a mercenary tribune of the plebs whipped up that insane public assembly. He never would have missed that day, that assembly and that uproar if he were not hurrying off to a premeditated crime. He did not even have an excuse for his journey – but he had one for staying. It was not in Milo's power to stay; he not only had a *reason* to go but *had* to go.

But if Clodius knew that Milo would be on the road that day, could Milo not suspect the same about him? 46. First, I ask how Milo could have known this. That is something you can have no doubt about in Clodius' case; even if he had asked no one except Titus Patina, his very close friend, he could have found out that on that very day Milo as the dictator of Lanuvium had to nominate a priest. But there are many others from whom he could very easily have learnt it. Who would Milo have asked about the return of Clodius? Let us take it as fact that he asked. See how generous I am: let Milo have bribed a slave as my friend Quintus Arrius said. Read the testimony of your own witnesses. Gaius Causinius Schola of Interamna, Clodius' very close friend and his companion on that particular day – and the man whose testimony long ago put Clodius in Interamna and Rome at the same time[51] – said that Publius Clodius had been intending to stay in his Alban villa that day but was suddenly informed that his architect, Cyrus, was dead. So he unexpectedly decided to set out for Rome. Gaius Clodius, another companion of Publius Clodius, said the same. 47. Jurors, look at what important facts their testimony established. The first is that Milo is acquitted of setting out with a plan to ambush Clodius on the way, since it was highly unlikely that Clodius and he would encounter each other. The second is this (for I do not see why I should not also do myself a good turn here): you know, jurors, that there have been those who, as they pushed for this trial, said[52] that although Milo shed the blood, he did it on the advice of a more senior person. Naturally, these abandoned losers hinted that the outlaw assassin was . . . me. Those who say that Clodius would not have planned to return to Rome on that day unless he had heard about Cyrus are floored by their own testimony. I can breathe again; I am acquitted. I am no longer afraid of appearing to have based my plans on a circumstance of which I was entirely ignorant. 48. Now I shall examine the rest of their allegations. Here is one:

'Clodius had not even thought about laying an ambush, since he was planning on staying in his Alban villa.'

That is true – if he had not been planning on leaving the villa to commit murder. I know the man who 'reported' the death of

Cyrus did not bring news about that but about Milo's approach. For why would he bring news about Cyrus, a man Clodius had left dying as he departed from Rome? I witnessed Cyrus' will along with Clodius; I was in the same room: he had made an open will[53] and made Clodius and me his heirs. Since Clodius left Cyrus breathing his last the day before at nine in the morning, was news of his death going to be reported to him the next day at two in the afternoon?

49. Let us say it happened as they suggest. Why would he hurry back to Rome? Or rush off at night? Was he in such a hurry because he was an heir? First, there was no reason for such a rush; second, if there was any reason, tell me what he could have gained that night which he would have lost if he had arrived in Rome early the next day? Should he not have avoided arriving in Rome at night instead of trying to do so, given that Milo the 'ambusher' would have lain in wait for him had he known that? He would have killed him at night and killed him in a place ripe for an ambush and full of thieves. 50. Given that everyone now wants Milo acquitted, even though he confesses the murder, they would have believed him if he had denied it. The place itself,[54] a site that conceals and harbours thieves, would have helped him, as the mute isolation of the site and the blackness of the night would have hidden him. As would those who would have been hauled up as defendants: the many who had been abused, robbed and driven from their properties; the many who were afraid of even falling into suspicion – and the whole of Etruria.

51. It is certain that Clodius stopped at his Alban villa on his return from Aricia.[55] Even if Milo knew Clodius had been in Aricia, his logical deduction should have been that even if Clodius wanted to return to Rome that day, he would have planned on staying at his own villa, which lay right alongside the road. Why did he not meet him there and stop him staying at his villa? Or lurk where he was likely to pass during the night?

Everything is clear to this point:

1. Clodius alive was useful to Milo.
2. Milo's death was the pinnacle of Clodius' desires.

3. Clodius had a strong hatred for Milo, but Milo had none for him.

4. Violence was a perpetual state of being for Clodius, while Milo only sought to defeat it. [52.]

5. Clodius threatened and openly spoke about Milo's death; nothing of the sort was ever heard from Milo.

6. The day of Milo's departure was known; the date of Clodius' return was unknown.

7. Milo's journey was necessary; Clodius', on the other hand, was inconvenient.

8. Milo had talked openly about the day on which he was planning to leave Rome; Clodius hid the day on which he was planning to return.

9. Milo did not change his mind on the subject; Clodius made up an excuse to change his mind.

10. Milo, if he were planning an ambush, should have waited near Rome for nightfall; Clodius, even if he were not afraid of one, still should have been afraid to arrive there at night.

53. Let us now look at the main point: for which one of them was the actual spot where they came to blows more convenient? Jurors, is that something that we need to hesitate on or mull over any longer? Did Milo think he would win a fight outside Clodius' estate, where his crazy building plans kept easily 1,000 strong men employed? Or on a raised, high spot belonging to his enemy? Did he select that location (above all others!) for a fight? Or did a man who planned to make his attack there because of the advantage of the location lie there in wait for him? Jurors, the facts speak for themselves – always the most important thing. 54. Even if you were looking at a picture of this rather than hearing about it, it would still be clear who was the ambusher and who plotted nothing, since Milo was enswathed in travelling clothes and driving a coach, accompanied by his wife. Which of these was not a serious impediment? His clothing? Vehicle? Companion? What could be less convenient for a fight: his entanglement in his travelling clothes, the impediment of the coach or that he was nearly as much tied up by his wife's presence?

Now look at Clodius. First, he suddenly sallies out of his villa. Why?

'It was evening.'

What made that necessary?

'He was late.'

How does that make sense, especially at this hour?

'He made a detour to Pompey's villa.'

To see Pompey? But he knew that he was in Alsium.[56] Or was it to look at his villa? He had been there a thousand times. It was all delay and equivocation. He did not want to relinquish his position before Milo arrived. 55. Now! Compare with Milo's impediments how this unencumbered outlaw was travelling. Before this, Clodius always travelled with his wife; now he was without her. Before, he never travelled except in a carriage; now he was on horseback. He always went around accompanied by his little Greeks, even when he was rushing to his strongholds in Etruria;[57] but now none of that rubbishy sort was part of his escort. Milo was for the first time in his life by chance at the head of a herd of boy singers and maids. Clodius, who always was the kind of person who travelled at the head of a pack of prostitutes, man whores and streetwalkers, then had no one – except those you would call an elite corps. Then, why did he lose? Because a traveller is not always killed by an outlaw: sometimes the outlaw is killed by the traveller. Because, although Clodius was prepared and attacked unprepared men, he was still a woman attacking *men*.

56. Besides, Milo was never so unprepared for Clodius' attacks that he was not prepared to some degree. He always kept in mind what a great advantage it would be for Publius Clodius if he, Milo, died, how much hatred Clodius had for him and how far he would go. For this reason, he never put his life in danger without protective guards, as he knew it had been

more or less auctioned off and sold for a great price. Add chance, the uncertain outcome of a fight and the impartiality of Mars – a god who often destroys someone even as he is already stripping a corpse and boasting about it – using the defeated to crush the attacker. Throw in the incompetence of a well-fed, half-drunk and half-asleep leader, who, after he left his enemy cut off from the rear, gave no thought to his companions who were still on the outside. When, enflamed with anger and despairing of their master's life, they encountered him, he was stopped dead by the penalties faithful slaves seek in return for the life of a master.

57. Why did Milo free those slaves? *Oh yes* – he dreaded that he would be betrayed, that they would not be able to bear the pain and would be forced under torture to confess that Publius Clodius had been killed by Milo's slaves[58] on the Appian Way. What need for fear? Is your question whether Milo killed him? He killed him. Lawfully or unlawfully? A torturer does not care about that: one asks about facts on the rack, about legality in a court. So, let us delve here into what is relevant to this case. We admit whatever you would discover by torture. But if you would rather ask why he freed them than why he only gave them part of their proper reward, you do not understand how to criticize an enemy's actions. 58. Marcus Cato, always a steady and brave speaker, said the same thing and in a rioting assembly (which was calmed by his presence): slaves who had defended their master's life should not only receive their freedom but every reward. And what reward can be enough for slaves so unselfish, good and faithful and who have saved your life? And even that was not as important as the fact that it was they who ensured that his vicious enemy did not get to gorge his eyes and mind on Milo's bloody wounds. If he had not freed them, the torturer would have got his hands on these men who had saved their master, punished a crime and protected his life. But there is nothing among his troubles which gives him as much comfort as the knowledge that whatever happens to him, they have received in full the reward they deserved.

59. 'But the inquisitions held recently in the temple of Freedom are a threat to Milo.'

Whose were the slaves?

'Publius Clodius'.'

Who demanded the inquisition?

'Appius.'

Who produced them?

'Appius.'

Where did they come from?

'From his house.'

Good gods! What could *possibly* have been done more rigorously? Clodius has come close to the gods – closer even than when he penetrated their inner sanctum, since the inquiry about his death is like the one about the violation of religious ceremonies.[59] Our ancestors refused to question slaves against their masters, not because it would be impossible to discover the truth, but because it seemed shocking and more dreadful than the actual deaths of their masters. When the prosecutor's slave is tortured to disadvantage the defendant, can the truth be discovered? 60. But how did the questioning go?

'Hey! You! Rufio!' (to pick a random name). 'Be careful you don't lie. Did Clodius lay an ambush for Milo?'

'He did.'

'Crucifixion for sure.'

'He did not.'

'There is hope for freedom.'

What could produce better results than this? Even when slaves are seized for questioning without warning, they are separated from each other and thrown into cells so they cannot communicate. *These* slaves, however, spent a hundred days in the house of the prosecutor and were produced from there by the same prosecutor. What could be more ethical or above board?

61. But if you have not examined the evidence enough yet – although it is quite clear and absolutely proven that Milo returned to Rome with a clear and open conscience, free from criminal intent, neither terrified by fear nor paralysed by a guilty conscience – remember, by the immortal gods, how quickly he returned, how he entered the Forum as the Curia was in flames, his strength of mind, his appearance and his words. He placed himself not just in the hands of the people, but the Senate; not just in the hands of the Senate, but armed state guards; and not only in these but in the power of a man in whose hands the Senate had placed the entire Republic, all the manpower of Italy and the weapons of the Roman people. Surely he would never have handed himself over to Pompey unless he was confident of his case, because at that time Pompey gave a hearing to every rumour, found many of them frightening, was wary of some and believed others. The conscience has great power, jurors, and it has great effect on the innocent and the guilty: the guilty visualize their punishment, but the innocent have no fear.

62. The Senate had good reason to support Milo's cause. As men of great wisdom, they saw the reasoning behind his action, his resolve and his unfaltering defence. Or have you actually forgotten, jurors, when news of Clodius' death was still fresh, not just what Milo's enemies gossiped about and waited for him to do, but even those ill-informed about his character? 63. They said he would not return to Rome, as – whether or not he had acted in an angry and desperate state of mind, and butchered an enemy while enflamed with hatred – he thought the death of Clodius so important he would be resigned to exile

because he had gorged his hatred on the blood of an enemy. Or, if he had wished to free his country by killing Clodius, as a brave man he would not hesitate to bow resignedly to the laws, since at great personal risk he had brought safety to the Roman people, and would carry away everlasting glory, leaving us with the benefits he had allowed us to enjoy! Many people even brought up Catiline and his freaks, saying, 'He will revolt! He will seize some position and attack his country!'

Sometimes, citizens who deserve the Republic's greatest rewards are to be pitied, as people not only forget their most splendid deeds but even suspect them of evil ones! 64. Those accusations, which would very obviously have been true if Milo had been guilty of something he could not defend honourably and truthfully, were all lies. What about the charges piled on him after that? Immortal gods, he did not waver even though they would have crushed a conscience guilty even of a minor offence. Did not waver? More truthfully: he despised those charges and considered them nothing, although they were charges no guilty man could have sneered at – and no innocent one, unless he was very brave. One charge was that a mass of shields, swords, spears and even harness for horses would be seized. People said that there was no neighbourhood of Rome, no back alleyway, in which a house had not been rented in Milo's name; weapons had been brought down the Tiber to his villa at Ocriculum;[60] his house on the Capitoline Hill was stuffed with shields and there were incendiary devices for burning down Rome everywhere.

These charges were not just reported to Pompey but almost believed, and he did not reject them before he investigated. 65. I praised the incredible care he took, jurors, but I shall speak as I feel. Men who have the Republic in their care must listen to too much – how could it be otherwise? But it got so that the butcher Licinius[61] from the Circus Maximus (or someone like that) merited a hearing when he said Milo's slaves had become drunk in his house and confessed to him that they had conspired to kill Pompey, and afterwards one of them had struck him with a sword so he would not betray them. This was reported to Pompey in his suburban residence. I was among the first to be sent for, and following the advice of his friends he brought the matter before the Senate. I could not but be paralysed at suspicion coming from a man who was my protector and also that of my country. But I was astonished that a butcher was believed, the confession of Clodius' slaves was given a hearing and a side wound, which looked like a pin-prick, became proof of a gladiator's blow.

66. But, as I understand it, Pompey was not frightened; he was wary not of what you *should* be afraid of, but all you *might* be. It was reported that the home of Gaius Caesar,[62] that splendid and brave man, was under attack for a large part of the night. Even in such a busy place no one had heard or known about it – still, the story found an audience. I cannot suspect Gnaeus Pompey – a man of exceptional courage – of fear; I thought that a man who had been placed in charge of the Republic[63] could not take too much care. Not long ago, in a packed meeting of the Senate on the Capitol, a senator was dug up who said Milo was carrying a weapon. He stripped himself in that holiest temple, since even the life that a citizen and a man such as he had led could not ensure that the facts would speak for themselves if he kept his silence.[64]

67. These accusations were discovered to be treacherously invented lies. Still, even if Milo is still feared, the charge of Clodius' murder does not scare us – but, Gnaeus Pompey, it is your, yes, *your* suspicions that I really dread. I name you loudly enough so you can hear me.[65] If you are afraid of Milo, if you think he is now plotting against your life or has ever schemed in some way against it; if (as some of your recruiting officers have said repeatedly) your levy of Italy, these weapons, these Capitoline cohorts, sentries, watchmen, this select group of young men who protect you and your home is armed to fend off an attack by Milo: if all these preparations have been stationed against and watch for Milo alone, then he must certainly possess great power and unbelievable courage. Certainly, they are not the powers and resources of a mere individual if our pre-eminent commander has been chosen and the entire Republic armed in order to fend off one man.

68. But is there anyone who does not understand that every

diseased and failing part of the Republic was entrusted to you so that you could use these weapons to cure them and make them strong? If Milo had been given the chance, he would certainly have proven that no one ever loved another man as he did you, that he had never fled from any danger while defending your honour, and there were numerous times when he fought that vile cancer to protect your glory. His term as tribune was devoted to my recall; in that he was governed by your wishes since I was so very dear to you. Afterwards, you defended him when his life was in danger and aided him when he was running for praetor. He always hoped that he had very good friends in both of us: you because of your services to him and I because of his toward me. If he could not prove that and if your suspicions had become so deeply entrenched that there was no way they could be rooted out, and Italy would never have peace from levies and Rome from armed men without his destruction, then it cannot be doubted that he, a man who was born for and naturally inclined to such sacrifice, would have left his country voluntarily. But Pompey the Great, before he left, would have appealed to you – as he does even now: 69. You see how untrustworthy and changeable life is, how haphazard and unreliable good fortune, how unfaithful friends can be and how they adapt their excuses to the situation, and how in dangerous times those closest to you flee in great fear. Although I hope all your affairs prosper, there will certainly come a time and a day will dawn when perhaps, after some national crisis – which our experience should tell us is a frequent occurrence – you will feel the loss of a dear friend, the faithfulness of a very steady man and the great courage of the bravest person ever born.

70. Who would believe that Gnaeus Pompey, a man highly familiar with constitutional law, our traditions *and* the administration of the Republic, to whom the Senate gave an army and turned to 'see that the Republic took no harm'[66] – a sentence which had always armed the consuls well even when they were not given arms – would wait for a decision by a court to punish a man who was planning to use violence to get rid of those very courts! Pompey judged to his satisfaction that those

charges were brought falsely against Milo and he proposed his law, by which – or so I think – he wants you to acquit Milo (a result everyone hopes for). 71. When he sits there, surrounded by his army of public guards, is he not making enough of a declaration that he is not trying to strike terror into all of you? For what could be less worthy of him than forcing you to condemn a man whom he could have dealt with using tradition and the laws? The soldiers are there to allow you to give a free verdict despite yesterday's assembly.

72. I am not disturbed by the charge of Clodius' murder, nor so demented, unaware of or unfamiliar with your feelings that I do not know your reaction to his death. As for that, if I were unwilling to refute the charge (something I have just done), Milo could still shout out loud and without fear of reprisal this glorious lie: 'I did not kill a Spurius Maelius who seemed too popular with the common people and was suspected of trying to become a king by squandering his property to make corn cheaper. I did not kill a Tiberius Gracchus who stripped legal authority from a fellow magistrate through subversive means, whose killers have made the whole world ring with their glorious names. I have killed a man' – for he would dare to say this as he had risked himself to free his country – 'whose unholy adultery right there, among the sacred couches of the gods, our noblest women detected. 73. A man whom the Senate had often voted to punish so they could purify those solemn rites. A man about whom Lucius Lucullus[67] had said – and on oath – that after a private investigation he had been discovered to have committed unholy incest with his own sister. A man who, using armed slaves, banished a fellow-citizen that the Senate, the people of Rome and all peoples declared was the saviour of Rome and citizens' lives.[68] A man who handed out kingdoms and took them away, who distributed the world to whomever he wanted. A man who, when he had done slaughtering people in the Forum, forced a citizen of exceptional courage and fame from his home by violence and weapons, who never thought anything sacrilegious, whether he was committing a crime or indulging his appetites. A man who burned the temple of the Nymphs so he could destroy the census records in our public

archives. 74. In short: a man who heeded no law, no codes of conduct or rules of ownership; who sought others' estates, not using insulting lawsuits, unlawful claims and oaths, but camps, an army and military assaults; who tried to take by military force not just the property of the Etruscans (he despised them from the bottom of his heart) but that of one of our jurors, Publius Varius, the bravest and best of citizens. A man who crisscrossed a multitude of villas and parks with his architects and measuring poles and wanted his property to stretch from the Tiber to the Alps. Who, when he could not get that splendid and brave Roman equestrian Marcus Paconius to sell him his island on the Prilian lake, suddenly transported lime, stones and sand there, not hesitating to build on another man's property even as its owner watched from the opposite bank. 75. Who said to Titus Furfanius – to one such as he, immortal gods – I shall not waste my time repeating what he said to that poor little woman Scantia, or to the adolescent Publius Apinius.[69] He threatened both of them with death unless they handed over their parks. But he actually dared to say to Furfanius that if he did not hand over the amount he was demanding, he would carry a corpse into his house and use that to stoke up blazing hatred for him. This was a man who forcibly occupied the estate of his brother Appius (a man I was a close friend to)[70] while he was away. Who decided to build a wall through his sister's forecourt and lay its foundations in such a way that he not only deprived his sister of her forecourt but any access or entrance.'

76. Even if he attacked the Republic, private citizens, those distant and close, strangers and family without distinction, we could almost endure all that. I do not know how, but our unbelievable submissiveness had through familiarity hardened and coarsened us. Yet how could you endure or avert what threatened on the horizon? If Clodius had acquired power over the military – forget the allies, foreign nations, kings and tetrarchies – you would have prayed that he would attack them rather than your property, your houses, your wealth. Wealth? As a god is my witness, even your wives and children would have been the object of his unchecked and uncontrolled appetite. Do you think these are inventions? They are obvious,

widely known and proven facts. Clodius had an army of slaves he was about to sign up who would give him possession of everything in public and private ownership. 77. Would Titus Annius have felt any fear about our community's reaction if he had shouted, 'Citizens, I beg you to come here and listen. I killed Clodius! My sword, my right hand deflected his frenzy from your throats, a frenzy we could not rein in by any law or court. I alone have allowed our community to retain any justice, equity, laws, freedom, purity and decency!' all while clutching a bloody sword? For who now does not approve of or praise him? Who does not say or think that, alone of all men in living memory, Titus Annius has benefited the Republic the most, has given great, great joy to the Roman people, all Italy and every nation? While I cannot judge how much delight the Roman people of the past would have felt, I can say that although our times have seen many splendid victories from great generals, none of those brought us a joy that lasted so long or was so great.

78. Jurors, I hope that you and your children will enjoy many good times in our Republic, and that in those moments you will decide you would never have seen them if Publius Clodius were still alive. I have complete faith that under the consulship of this great man, Pompey, we have reason to have a *very* reliable and well-grounded expectation that this year will be a healing period for our state, since wild behaviour will be curbed, selfish greed checked and the laws and courts reformed. Is there anyone so demented that he considers this could have been achieved if Clodius were alive? What? What part of your personal property – something securely in your possession – could you have hung onto when that madman ruled over us? Jurors, I am not afraid that I will look as if I am spewing these charges with more enthusiasm than fairness, enflamed by personal hatred for Clodius. Even if that should be beyond the norm, he was such an enemy to everyone that my hatred was almost equalled by everyone else's. One cannot speak or even reflect enough about the sheer volume of crime and destruction contained in that man.

79. Jurors, imagine this scenario – for our imaginations are free and can visualize whatever they want, allowing us to cre-

ate mental pictures – so just imagine the possibility of Milo's acquittal, but only on the condition that Publius Clodius would live again. Why the terrified expressions? What effect would the living Clodius produce on you when the mere thought of him dead appalled you? What! If Gnaeus Pompey himself, who possesses such courage and good fortune that he has always achieved what no one except him could have achieved, had the choice between a trial on the death of Publius Clodius or raising the man himself from the dead, which of the two do you think he would prefer? Even if their friendship made Pompey wish to summon him from the dead, consideration of the Republic would have stopped him. You sit here now to avenge the death of a man whose life you would not restore even if you thought it possible. We have voted to have a trial for the death of a man whose resurrection, under the same law that established this court, would never have been approved. If someone were his killer, should he, as he confesses, fear punishment from the people he freed? 80. The Greeks treat heroes who have killed tyrants like gods[71] – I have seen this for myself in Athens and other Greek cities. The divine homage such men enjoy! The songs! The poetry! They are immortalized with festivals and reverence close to what is given to immortals. Will you allow a man who saved our glorious people and punished great criminality not only to receive no honours but to be dragged off to his execution?

I tell you, he would confess the deed; if he had done it, he would happily and bravely confess that he had done so to preserve everyone's freedom. And this is something he ought not just confess, but honestly boast of. 81. However, if he admits an action for which he looks for no reward beyond a pardon, would he hesitate to admit one for which he should look for accolades? Unless he thinks you will be more grateful to him for defending his life rather than yours, despite the fact that if you were of a mind to be generous, his confession would be followed by the highest possible honours. And if you did not approve of his action? (But how could anyone not approve of their own deliverance?) Still, *if* the heroism of a truly brave man had failed to prompt the gratitude of his fellow-citizens, he would leave an ungrateful state with a brave, steady heart. And what could be more ungrateful than others rejoicing as the man, who alone made their joy possible, mourns?

82. We have always thought that since the glory that the crushing of traitors brings is ours alone, so too should be the danger and ill-will. What praise would I have deserved, when I dared so much for you and your children during my consulship, if I had thought I could achieve my goal at no risk to myself? What *woman* would not dare to kill a criminal and destructive citizen, if she were not afraid? A man who does not slacken in his defence of the Republic though he knows the risk of hatred, death and punishment – that is whom we should consider a real *man*. A grateful people should reward citizens who have done well by the Republic. A brave man should not let even potential punishment make him regret his bravery. 83. For this reason Titus Annius can confess what Ahala, Nasica, Opimius, Marius and I could. If the Republic were grateful, he would rejoice, if ungrateful, his conscience could still give him comfort even in the middle of serious misfortune. But the fortune of the Roman people, your good luck and the immortal gods believe you owe them gratitude for this service. How could anyone think otherwise unless they believe there is no divine authority or power, or they are left unmoved by the greatness of empire, the sun, the orbit of the stars and sky, the changes and order of nature – or even (the most important thing) the wisdom of our ancestors, who themselves scrupulously observed religious rites, ceremonies and auspices and handed them down to us, their descendants. 84. There is beyond doubt a divine power: it cannot be that there is something in our weak bodies which lives and feels and does not also exist in the vast, splendid dance of the universe. Unless, perhaps, people do not believe in this because it cannot be seen and measured – as if we can see clearly or understand what is the nature of, or where exists, that which makes us wise, able to foresee things, or act or speak as we are doing right now. This is the power which has often brought incredible good fortune and wealth to this city, a power which extinguished and destroyed that source of destruction by inspiring Clodius to

aggravate with his violence and enrage with his sword a truly brave man; and the result was his defeat at the hands of a man whose own defeat would have ensured that Clodius was never punished or restrained again.

85. Human planning did not make this happen – instead, the gods showed more than their usual concern for us. By Hercules, it is as if the very places which saw that monster fall stirred themselves and upheld their personal claim against him. You, Alban hills and groves, I now call you as witnesses and beg your help. I also call you, the overturned altars of Alba, partners of, and equally as ancient as, the rites of the Roman people, altars which Clodius, as he rushed headlong in madness, crushed under the insane weight of his buildings after butchering and levelling your holy groves. Then you demanded atonement; your power prevailed, power he had polluted with every manner of crime. Holy Jupiter of Latium,[72] whose lakes, woods and territory he had often stained with every form of unholy, obscene, sexual indecency and crime, at last on your high Alban mountain you opened your eyes and punished him. As all of you watched, he paid a long-overdue but just penance. 86. That is, unless we say it was pure chance that after starting the fight he received his first wound – and the one which brought him his disgraceful death – right before the shrine of Bona Dea which is set on the estate of Titus Sergius Gallus (a young man who stands out even among the honourable and honoured): I repeat, it was *right before Bona Dea herself*. All so it would not look as if he had been acquitted by his unholy trial, but instead was destined for this symbolic punishment.

It was the same wrath of the gods that inspired such insanity in his minions that his body was left half-burned – unaccompanied by the death-masks of his family, music, funeral games, procession, lament, eulogies, a funeral – smeared with blood and dirt and robbed of that last day's congregation, something even one's enemies normally respect. I believe it would have been sacrilegious for the effigies of illustrious men to bring some honour to that utterly vile parricide, and there was no better place for his dead body to be ripped to shreds than where the living one was found guilty. 87. As a god is my witness, I thought it was a harsh, cruel fate for the Roman people to have allowed him to trample all over the Republic for so many years. He had indecently polluted our holiest rites, demolished the authority of important senatorial decrees, openly used bribery to escape justice, tormented the Senate while tribune, he had undone measures to aid the community that all the classes had agreed on, had driven me from my country, looted my possessions, burned my home, tormented my children and wife, declared unholy war on Gnaeus Pompey, slaughtered magistrates and private citizens, burned down my brother's home, devastated Etruria and dispossessed many of their residences and wealth.

On and on he threatened and menaced. Our community, Italy, the provinces and foreign kingdoms could not contain his insanity. Already at his home he was engraving laws to enslave us to our slaves. He thought that any property which caught his fancy, no matter who owned it, would be his this year. 88. No one stood in his way – except Milo. Clodius considered that the man[73] who could have stood in his way was tied to him by their new friendship; he claimed Caesar's power as his; and in the case of my exile, had despised what decent men had wanted. Milo alone was a threat.

And, as I said before, it was then that the immortal gods gave this ruined lunatic the idea to lay an ambush for Milo. There was no other way that cancer could perish; the Republic would never have got revenge on him in a law-court. *Right* – I suppose the Senate would have been able to keep him in his place when he was praetor, though it could never manage to do so when he was a private citizen. 89. And the consuls would have bravely curbed a praetor! With Milo dead, he would have had his own consuls. And what brave consul would have faced him when he was a praetor, remembering that as tribune he had cruelly tormented a consul who had acted heroically?[74] He would have controlled, owned and held on to everything: under a new law found in his house, along with the rest of the Clodian laws, he would have made our slaves his freedmen.[75] Finally, if the immortal gods had not put it into his mind that, despite being an effeminate creature, he should try to kill a brave, real *man*, you would today have no Republic.

90. Would he have done no evil while alive and a praetor, or later as a consul (in the unlikely event that these temples and walls lasted until his consulship), although it was one of his minions who instigated the burning of the Curia when he was dead? Have we ever seen a more wretched, bitter or tragic sight? It was not an ignorant mob (though that would be miserable enough) but *one* man who burned, destroyed and desecrated the temple of morality, dignity, enlightenment, statesmanship, the head of the world, the altar of our allies, a safe harbour for all peoples and a place the entire population had granted to one class. A person who dared that much to cremate a dead man would dare anything as he raised the standard of a living one. He chose the Curia over all other buildings so that in death Clodius could burn what he had destroyed when alive. 91. Are there people who complain about the Appian Way but are silent about the Curia? Who thinks the Forum could have been defended against him while he was still breathing, when the Curia could not stand against his corpse? Raise him from the dead! Raise him, if you can! Will you defeat him when alive, when you could barely hold your ground against his Furies when he was an unburied corpse? Did you hold your ground against the men who ran with their torches to the Curia, with sledgehammers to the temple of Castor or dashed through the Forum with their swords? You saw the Roman people butchered and swords break up their assembly when Marcus Caelius' speech was being silently listened to – he, a tribune of the plebs, a brave statesman, incredibly loyal to any cause he has taken up, dedicated to the wishes of decent men and the authority of the Senate, and who is behaving with a superhuman and incredible faithfulness in Milo's remarkable unpopularity[76] – though perhaps I should call that his remarkable good fortune.

92. But I have already said enough about the case – and even perhaps much that did not need to be said. What remains except for me to pray to and beg you, jurors, to give a very brave man the pity *he* does not beg for, but which I – even as he resists it – plead with you for? Do not be any less sparing of Milo if you have not seen him cry even while we all weep, if his expression has always stayed the same, if his voice and his

speeches were steady and unchanging. Whether you should help him because of that or not, I do not know. But if it is acceptable to loathe gladiators and men from the dregs of society – men who are cowards and beg for mercy – while wanting to save the brave and courageous ones who willingly and eagerly risk death, and to feel more pity for men who do not ask for pity than those who demand it – well, should we not do this even *more* for our bravest citizens?

93. Speaking for myself, jurors, I can tell you that every day Milo's words undo me. 'I hope they thrive,' he says. 'I hope my fellow-citizens thrive, live in safety, flourish and are prosperous. And however badly they have treated me, I hope this splendid city and my country – so dear to me – live on. As I shall not be allowed to enjoy it with them, may my fellow-citizens enjoy a tranquil state without me, but *because* of me. I shall yield. I shall leave. If I shall not be allowed to enjoy good government, at least I shall not have to experience bad government and will take my rest in the first free and civilized state I encounter. 94. In vain were my labours! Vain my treacherous hopes and empty plans! When I was tribune of the plebs, the Republic lay crushed. So I dedicated myself to the Senate's cause, which lay in tatters when I took office, to the faltering power of the Roman equestrians and to decent men, whom the armed thugs of Clodius had pressurized to abandon their authority entirely. Would I have thought then that decent people would not protect me? When I' – we talk of this frequently – 'brought you home, did I ever suppose that there would be no place here for me? Where now is the Senate I supported? Your supporters, the Roman equestrians? The support of the municipalities? Or Italy's voice of protest? Where is your voice, Marcus Tullius, the one which has so often defended and helped others? Am I the only person – I who have so many times risked death for your sake – that it cannot help?'

95. Jurors, he does not cry as he says this, as I do now. He has the exact expression you see right before you. He denies – yes, denies – that his fellow-citizens are ungrateful for his actions; he does not deny they are scared and glance around at every danger. He reminds you that he made your lives easier by

binding the plebs and the poorest part of the masses to him, men who under Publius Clodius' leadership threatened your fortunes. He did not just sway them with his character but softened them by spending three inheritances.[77] He is not worried that as he was appeasing the plebs with games he failed to win your favour by his exemplary services to the Republic. He says that even now he has often seen the Senate's goodwill towards him, and whatever fortune may have in store for him he will take with him the memory of the respect you and your class have shown him, your support and your words. 96. He reminds himself that the only thing missing in his life was the voice announcing him as consul – his smallest regret. The whole population, united in one desire, voted him consul.[78] Finally, if this trial goes against him, it will be the suspicion of criminal intent, not any guilt attaching to his actions, that works against him.

He adds these words which are certainly true: brave and wise men usually want the knowledge that they behaved properly *more* than they want the rewards for doing so; throughout his life, he did nothing which was not splendid; and if there is nothing more important to a man than freeing his country from danger, then he is blessed whom his fellow-citizens honour for such actions – but those who surpass fellow-citizens in their services should not be pitied. 97. Still, if we think of the past and its rewards, then the greatest reward that acting heroically can bring is glory. This alone consoles us for our short life by promising us that we shall be remembered, and ensures that even when we are gone we are present, and, although dead, we live. It is the rungs of glory that make men seem to ascend to heaven.

98. 'The Roman people', he says, 'will always speak of me, as will all peoples; history will never forget me. Even at this very moment, as my enemies fan the flames of hatred towards me, whenever men are gathered, they celebrate me through their thanks, good wishes and by talking about me.' I say nothing about the festivals Etruria has already celebrated or established. This is the hundredth dawn since the death of Publius Clodius – and perhaps the hundred and first. On that day, it was not just the report of the event which reached as far as

the borders of the Roman empire stretched, but the joy that sprang from it. It was this that made him say, 'I do not care where I end up since my name already has and always will have glory throughout the world.'

99. Milo, you often said such things to me when these men were not present; but *I* say them to you in their hearing. Since you have such courage, I cannot praise you enough; but the more superhuman your heroism, the greater the pain I feel at being torn from you. Nor, if you are ripped from me, will complaints – all I have left – be able to console me; I cannot be angry with those who gave me such a blow. For it is not my enemies that rip you from me, but my closest friends; they are not men who ever deserved evil from me, but always the best. Jurors, you will never cause me such searing agony – I could feel no greater one. But not even this experience will make me forget how you have always treated me. And if you have forgotten that or have taken some offence at me, why is it not *my* head on the block rather than Milo's? If something happens to me before I witness such a terrible outcome, then that will have been a good life.

100. Titus Annius, my only consolation now is that I failed you in nothing my affection, support or gratitude owed you. I have sought the animosity of the powerful for your sake. I have often risked life and limb in the face of your enemies' weapons. For your sake, I have thrown myself at the feet of many and begged for mercy. I have devoted my possessions and wealth and those of my children to your use in your time of need. If there is any violence at hand on this day, or any personal risk in future, I demand my share. What is left now? What can I do in return for your services to me, except consider that your fate is mine? I do not object. I do not reject it. I plead with you, jurors, either add to the services you have already done for me by acquitting him or realize that in destroying him they vanish.

101. Milo is not shaken by my tears for he has incredible strength of mind. He thinks that to live where there is no place for heroism is exile, and that death is not punishment but simply an end to life. He was born with such an attitude; let

him always hold it. And what of you, jurors? Tell me, what will
be your feelings? Will you keep Milo in your memory, but exile
the man? Will there be any place on this earth worthier to
receive this hero than the one which gave birth to him? You! I
call upon you, bravest of men, you who have shed much blood
to defend the Republic; I call upon you, the centurions and you
the soldiers, in this moment of danger for an unconquered citizen: will you stand armed around this court and watch a true
man driven out, banished and cast from Rome?

102. How miserable am I! How unlucky! Milo, these men
helped you bring me home – will they not let me keep you here?
What will I say to my children who think of you as a second
father? What will I say to you, my brother Quintus, who, although
now absent, suffered with me in those times? Could I not keep
Milo safe by appealing to the very men who helped him save me?
What was the reason? One every race approved of. Who would
not give me an acquittal? Those whose lives the death of Publius
Clodius made so much easier. Who pleaded the case? I did. 103.
Jurors, was I guilty of some enormous crime or did I commit
some great offence when I tracked down, made known, laid out
and removed the seeds of our community's destruction? That is
the source of all my troubles and those of my friends. Why did
you want to bring me back from exile? Was it so that while I
looked on, you would exile the very man who restored me to
citizenship? Do not – I plead with you – allow my return to be
more bitter than my departure. For how can I think that I have
been fully restored to my rights if I am dragged from those who
brought about my restoration? I wish the immortal gods had
granted – I beg your pardon my country, I fear that as I speak
what is my duty towards Milo I speak what is harmful to you –
I wish not only that Publius Clodius were still alive, but that he
were praetor, consul, dictator, rather than see this! 104. Immortal gods! Jurors, *you* must save this brave man.

'Not that, not that,' he says. 'Let Clodius have paid the price he
should have and, if necessary, I shall pay one I should not.'

Will *this man*, born to serve his country, die anywhere else except in his country? Or, perhaps, *for* his country? Will you keep the testament of his courage, but allow no tomb for his body in Italy? Will anyone vote to exile him from Rome, when after his exile all other cities will invite him in? 105. Happy the land which will take him in! Ours will be ungrateful if she casts him out and pitiable if she loses him.

Let there be an end. I cannot speak any more because of my tears – and he forbids the use of tears in his defence. I pray to you, I beg you, jurors, that as you give your verdicts, you vote as you feel. Believe me: Pompey, who in selecting jurors chose the best, the wisest and the bravest, will particularly approve of your courage, justice and integrity.

First and Second Philippics

PHILIPPIC I

Delivered on 2 September 44 before the Senate

On the 15th (the Ides) of March 44, despite the worries and premonitions of his wife Calpurnia, Julius Caesar set out for a meeting of the Senate to be held in the Curia Pompeia (part of Pompey's theatre/temple complex). He never returned. As he entered, one of his friends and trusted officers, Gaius Trebonius, detained Mark Antony outside, while the conspirators waited inside. It was another 'friend', the Caesarian Publius Servilius Casca who struck the first blow. Before Caesar breathed his last, at the foot of a statue of Pompey (in what may perhaps be one of the greatest moments of historical irony ever), over twenty dagger wounds were added to this first blow. The extent of the conspiracy and the wide-ranging nature of those who joined it show how far Caesar had alienated many of his former followers. More than sixty men, many of whom, like Marcus Junius Brutus, were bound to him by close ties of friendship (and in Brutus' case, it was rumoured, very close blood-ties) or obligation, came together to strike him down. Cicero was not one of them.

The immediate result was chaos, followed by even more chaos. The senators who were not part of the conspiracy fled, the 'Liberators' retreated to the Capitoline Hill, defending it with a force of gladiators, while Marcus Lepidus, Caesar's master of the horse, brought a legion into the Forum. On 17 March, Mark Antony defused the tense situation somewhat when he convened the Senate; at that meeting a compromise was hammered out, with the Senate granting amnesty to Caesar's assassins and ratifying all of Caesar's acts – something that was to come back to haunt them when Antony began to forge documents and claim that favours he was selling were part of that agreement. As far as we know, this was the last time that Antony and Cicero met face to face. Civil war was temporarily averted but Rome's turmoil was not.

Shortly after this meeting, Caesar's will was read out and the Roman people learnt of their legacies from him. On the 20th, Mark Antony's funeral oration turned Caesar's funeral into a riot. The crowd seized the body and burned it on a funeral pyre they erected in the Forum (mimicking the earlier 'pyre' of Clodius in the Curia); the action was shocking and against religious law and is one of the subjects that Cicero brings up in Philippic I (chapter 5: 'that unceremonious death ceremony'). More worryingly for the Liberators, the mob turned from burning Caesar's body to trying to burn down the houses of various conspirators; faced with hostility, they retreated from Rome. Over the next few weeks, Antony stepped into the power vacuum and restored some order, making compromises that pleased the anti-Caesarian faction. This included the abolition of the office of dictator (the position Caesar had held, and which was only meant to be a six-month office used in times of crisis), limiting some of Caesar's contemplated but not passed projects and executing a slave claiming to be Marius' son, who was backed by a mob and had built an altar on the site of Caesar's funeral pyre. Although in Philippic I (chapter 6) Cicero argues that Antony's actions up to the beginning of June were commendable, only reverting to type after that date, we know from various letters of April and May that he thought quite differently. In one letter to his close friend Atticus we find that Antony had already begun to embezzle money from the temple of Ops, which Caesar had been using as his treasury before Cicero left (Letters to Atticus 14.14); in others, we see that by the middle of April Antony was already selling various political favours and pushing them through by using forged documents. However, Cicero attempted to retain a good rela-

tionship with Antony, who in turn consulted with him on various issues.

Antony himself left Rome around the end of April (perhaps the 25th) to do a tour of the colonies of veterans in Campania and to found new ones. (Caesar's great-nephew and heir, Octavian, was currently also in the region.) In Antony's absence, his co-consul Publius Cornelius Dolabella – who was Cicero's erstwhile son-in-law – pulled down the monument to Caesar in the Forum and acted viciously against those who were attempting to make Caesar a god. Antony, faced with Dolabella's actions and Octavian's return to Rome (where he promised to pay all the legacies in Caesar's will to the Roman people), came back to Rome around 18 May, bringing with him a personal bodyguard drawn from Caesar's veterans. A deal was quickly made with Dolabella, and Octavian's request for the money he was owed from Caesar's will was refused. Caesar's veterans continued to flock to Rome, increasing the tension and possibility for violence; as a result, when the Senate was convened on 1 June, many senators, including the consuls-elect for 43, did not attend. In response, Antony went to the assembly and managed to have them pass a resolution that both he and Dolabella would be granted the power to govern provinces for five years after their term as consuls; Antony also swapped the province he had already been assigned (Macedonia) for Gaul, while still retaining five of the legions which were then stationed in Macedonia. Further, as Antony's governorship was to begin before that of Decimus Brutus ended in 43, this would strip the Liberators of the support of three legions in Gaul and the only standing army in Italy. On 5 June, the Liberators faced even more trouble: Marcus Brutus and Gaius Cassius were assigned by the Senate to head an overseas grain commission. (The assignment was an insultingly minor one for Roman praetors.) Towards the end of June, Antony went on (with Dolabella's support) to pass an agrarian law to distribute land in Italy. The board of seven that oversaw this included his brother Lucius as chairman along with Dolabella, Antony himself and other supporters. This act conferred enormous power on the group, further weakening the anti-Caesarian faction.

This faction responded as best it could: from 6 to 13 July, Marcus Brutus held lavish games for the Games of Apollo; as we hear in the Philippics, *they were accompanied by public demonstrations in Brutus' favour. The anti-Caesarians also attempted to give a show of strength in a meeting of the Senate on 1 August, but on that occasion (as Cicero laments below) the only person bold enough to speak against Antony was Lucius Piso, Caesar's father-in-law, himself a former target of Cicero's invective. Failing to gain any support, Piso did not attend the Senate the next day. And adding to their troubles was the appearance of a comet during the seven days of the games Octavian held in July to honour Caesar, a phenomenon no one could have foreseen. This was interpreted as indicating Caesar's deification, thus further burnishing Octavian in his role as his heir. Although relations between Antony and Octavian were frosty, under pressure from Caesar's veterans they formally disavowed their previous hostile relationship. Marcus Brutus left for Greece; along the way he met with Cicero in Velia on 17 August.*

What had Cicero being doing during these months? One would like to be able to say he had been heroically resisting Antony in Rome, but the truth is that like many others he had left the city. As senators were restricted in their movement, Cicero had to wait until he was granted an honorary position as Dolabella's legate on 3 June before he could leave Italy. He attempted to sail to Greece from Rhegium (modern Reggio di Calabria) but was foiled by bad weather. On receiving reports in early August that relations between Antony and the Liberators had improved, and hearing additionally that his behaviour in fleeing the country was being seen as pure cowardice and a desertion of the Republic in her hour of need, he decided to return to Rome. He took his time about it, only arriving in the city on 1 September. He did not attend the Senate even though it was meeting that day to vote on a public thanksgiving for Caesar; Antony took great umbrage at this, publicly threatening him at the meeting. Antony did not attend the next day – but Cicero did and delivered Philippic I. *It was to be the opening salvo in an epic set of speeches which featured Cicero's only*

*remaining weapon, his rhetoric, at its finest. Although this first
speech is relatively mild, as he delivered it Cicero must have
known that he was risking Antony's hatred. While Cicero can
and has often been criticized for his cowardice, he cannot be on
this occasion. With Antony's responding invective against him
on 19 September, the gloves were off. In total, Cicero would
write at least fourteen Philippics[1] – Antony's faults provided
Cicero with a lot of ammunition. All, except the second, were
delivered between April 44 and September 43.*

*Modelled after the Greek orator Demosthenes' speeches
against Philip of Macedon (hence their name),[2] the Philippics
are more than just speeches: they are the foundation for Cicero's
posthumous reputation. Generations of Roman schoolboys
would pretend to be Cicero, hesitating on whether to burn the
Philippics to save themselves from Antony (not that Antony
offered Cicero that chance) or to refuse heroically to abandon
their post as the Republic's last and greatest defender. But for
all of the vigour (and frequent viciousness) of Cicero's rhetoric,
there is an elegiac sadness behind these speeches; the Senate as
a body had lost ground to men whose legitimacy came from
armies, not the old Republic. It was never to gain it back.*

1. Members of the Senate, before I can say what I believe must
now be said about the Republic, I shall briefly explain why I
left Rome and then turned back. I, when I hoped that at long
last the Republic had been returned to your counsel and guidance, made up my mind that I must remain, just as if, as an
ex-consul and as a senator, I was on guard duty. The truth is
I never deserted, never dropped my eyes from the Republic
from the day we were assembled at the temple of Tellus.[3] To the
best of my ability I laid in that temple the foundations of a
peace such as Athens once had.[4] Reviving her ancient example,
I made constant use of the Greek word she had used when
settling her civil conflict and recommended that eternal obliv-
ion should wipe out all memory of our conflict. 2. Then came
Mark Antony's splendid speech and his exceptional display of

goodwill; finally, he securely established peace with pre-eminent citizens through his child.[5] The rest matched these beginnings. In the discussions he used to hold in his home regarding the Republic, he consulted with leading citizens. He reported to this body his highly commendable decisions; at that time nothing, unless everyone already knew about it, was discovered in Caesar's journals and Antony replied with absolute directness to the questions he was asked.

3. Were any exiles restored?[6] One, he said, but no one else. Were exemptions from taxes granted? None, he replied. He even wished us to endorse a motion of Servius Sulpicius, an extremely illustrious man, that no decree or grant of Caesar should be posted[7] after the Ides of March. I pass over many other splendid actions; my speech hurries on to a particularly exceptional one. He completely abolished the office of dictator, which had now gained the force of royal power – on this topic we voted without debate. He presented a written motion to the Senate stating that wish; after it was read out we followed his guidance with great enthusiasm and used a senatorial motion to give thanks to him in highly complimentary language. 4. It felt like a light washing over us, since he removed not just what we had endured – royal rule – but even the fear of it. By completely abolishing the title of dictator[8] – an office often legitimately held – because of our fresh memories of a never-ending dictatorship, it looked as if he gave a great guarantee to the Republic that he wished it to be a free state. 5. A few days later, he freed the Senate from the fear that senators would be slaughtered when the runaway slave who had usurped Marius' name[9] had the hook rammed into him. All of this he did in tandem with his co-consul; there are a few other actions which were Dolabella's alone, but I believe if Antony had not been absent[10] they would have done them together. For when evil without end was slithering through the city and oozing further every day, as the men who had carried out that unceremonious death ceremony for Caesar were setting up a tomb in the Forum,[11] and ruined men along with slaves like themselves were threatening more and more of the city's houses and temples every day, Dolabella punished the arrogant, criminal slaves and the corrupt, perverse

freemen[12] and he levelled that cursed monument with such severity that I find the difference in his actions since then astonishing.

6. Look at how everything changed on the first of June,[13] the day they had proclaimed we were to attend the Senate: no legislation passed through the Senate, but much legislation of importance was passed by the people – an absent, an unwilling people. The consuls-elect[14] said that they did not dare to come to the Senate and the Liberators of our country were not in the city[15] from whose neck they had lifted the yoke of slavery – and yet those were the men the consuls themselves constantly praised in public and private. The veterans, whom Antony had called upon and whose interests this body had most carefully looked after, were incited not to preserve their own property but to hope for new loot. As I preferred to hear about these things rather than see them, and I had an honorary commission as a lieutenant,[16] I left with the intention of attending the Senate on the first of January, a day I thought was the first real chance of it being convened.

7. I have explained, members of the Senate, the reason why I set out. Now I shall briefly explain why I turned back, something you may find more surprising. Since I had good reason to avoid Brundisium, the usual route to Greece, I came to Syracuse on the first of August, as people recommend the crossing from there to Greece. Even that city, so closely connected to me,[17] could not hold on to me for more than one night despite her wishes, as I was afraid that, if I delayed, my sudden arrival would bring some suspicion upon my friends. After the winds blew me to shore from Sicily, to a promontory near Rhegium called Leucopetra, I set out from there in hope of crossing, but I had not sailed at all far when a stormy wind drove me straight back to the place from where I had set out. 8. Since it was then the dead of night, I stayed in the villa of my companion and friend Publius Valerius. I remained there the next day[18] waiting for a favourable wind when many citizens of the municipality of Rhegium came to me. Among these were some who were fresh from Rome and from these I first got the speech of Mark Antony; this pleased me so much that after I had read it I began

for the first time to think about returning. Not long after this I was given the edict of Brutus and Cassius;[19] this – perhaps because I love these men even more for what they have done for the Republic than because of our close friendship – seemed to me *extremely* fair. As it is generally the case that those who wish to bring some good news embellish it to make their news more welcome, they added that an arrangement would be reached, that on the first of the month there would be a full meeting of the Senate and Antony, who had spurned his evil advisers, had given up the Gallic provinces[20] and was about to listen again to the Senate.

9. I was then fired with such a desire to return that there were neither oars nor wind that could bring me back fast enough – not because I thought that I would not arrive in time but because I did not want to be slower than my desire to wish the Republic well. After I sailed to Velia I saw Brutus; I cannot express what anguish that meeting was. It seemed shameful for me to dare to return to the city from which *Brutus* was withdrawing and wish to live safely where he could not. But I did not see that man distressed as I myself was. He stood tall with the knowledge of his own great and glorious deed, and uttered no word of complaint about his own misfortune – but many about yours. 10. It was from him I first learnt the nature of the speech Lucius Piso[21] had given in the Senate on the first of August. Although he had little support from those who ought to have given it, Piso seemed to me to have covered himself in glory; this was something I first heard directly – and most importantly – from Brutus and then from everyone I saw later. So I hurried here to support Piso, as those who were present had not, not to do some good (of *that* I had no hope, knowing it was beyond my ability) but so that if the sort of accidents that happen to men should happen to me (and much that is neither nature nor fate's work seems to threaten me), at least the Republic might have my speech this day as a witness of my goodwill towards it.

11. Members of the Senate, since I am confident that you have approved of the reason for my decisions to leave *and* return, I shall complain a little about Antony's insult yesterday before I move on to talking about the Republic. I am his friend

and I have always admitted that I owe it to him because of a service he did me.[22] Then what was the reason I was pressured so brutally to attend the Senate yesterday? Was I the only person absent or have you not often had less well-attended meetings? Was the debate of such importance that even sick men should be carried in? I suppose Hannibal was at the gates or we were debating about peace with Pyrrhus, in which case tradition has it that even old Appius the Blind was carried in.[23] 12. Public thanksgivings[24] were under discussion, a topic for which senators are not usually absent. For they are pressured not by the threat of fines but by the influence of whoever's thanksgiving is being debated – it is the same when the subject is the granting of a triumph. The consuls worry so little on these occasions that it is pretty much up to a senator to be present or not. Since I knew this custom and was tired from my journey and felt unwell, out of a sense of friendship I sent a man to tell Antony this. But in your hearing, he said with excessive anger and vehemence that he would come with workmen to my house. Does any wrongdoing carry such a punishment that someone would dare to say before this body that he would smash up, using *public* workmen, a home built in accordance with a senatorial vote, at *public* expense?[25] Who has ever forced a senator to attend by imposing such a massive penalty or by anything beyond a fine or a fee? But if he had known what I was planning on saying, he would certainly have reduced the harshness with which he was pressurizing me. 13. Do you honestly think, members of the Senate, that I would have voted in favour of the resolution you had unwillingly supported, that the festival of the dead[26] be mingled with public thanksgivings, that sacrilegious practices would be introduced into the Republic or that public thanksgivings would be decreed for a *dead* man? I shall say nothing about who he was. But suppose he was the legendary Brutus, the very man who freed the Republic from royal oppression and who produced almost 500 years later an heir similar in courage and deeds – I still could not have been led to connect any dead man with a ritual meant for the immortal gods, so we would end up with public thanksgivings addressed to a man who does not even have a tomb where rites for the dead can be held! I certainly would have said what I am saying now – a statement I could easily have defended before the Roman people if a more serious misfortune had befallen the Republic, be it war, plague or famine (some of which are already here and some I fear are on the horizon). But I wish for the immortal gods to pardon for this decision both the Roman people, who did not approve of it, and this body, which reluctantly voted for it.

14. What? Am I not allowed to speak about the other evils that the Republic has experienced? Yet I am allowed and always will be allowed to protect my standing and scorn death. Just give me the power of entering this place and I shall not turn from the danger of speaking! Members of the Senate, if only I had been able to be present on the first of August! I know I could not have achieved anything, but I wish that on that day more than one ex-consul might have been found worthy of holding that position and worthy of the Republic.[27] I feel great anguish that men who have enjoyed the greatest benefits the Roman people can grant did not support the leadership of Lucius Piso in his noble proposal. Did the Roman people elect us to the consulship so that, having been granted so high a position, we should consider the Republic as nothing? Not only did no ex-consul verbally support Piso, no one supported him *even by a look*. 15. For pity's sake, what is this voluntary slavery? I admit you had to do *something*; I do not require that those who speak from the ex-consuls' bench do as I am doing.[28] Those whose silence I forgive are a different case from those I ask to speak out; I feel sorrow that the Roman people are beginning to think those men suspect, not because they were afraid to live up to their position (which itself would be shameful) but because they all did so for different and individual reasons. This is why I am expressing the immense gratitude I feel to Piso, a man who thought not about what he *could* do for the Republic but what he personally *ought* to do.

Now I ask you, members of the Senate, even if you will not quite dare to follow my line of argument and guidance, to grant me the same ready hearing you have done until now. 16. Therefore, first I recommend that the acts of Caesar should be preserved; this is not because I approve of them (who could do that?) but because I consider that our guiding principle must above all be the need for peace and calm. I would wish that Mark Antony were present – but without his 'legal team'[29] – though I think he is allowed to be a little under the weather, even if he would not grant the same right to me yesterday. If he were here he would instruct me, or rather you, members of the Senate, how far he himself defends Caesar's acts. Are the acts of Caesar to be approved, whether they are in his notes, scrawled down or in his journals and produced on Antony's authority alone – and sometimes not even produced, but only quoted? Is what Caesar inscribed on bronze, where he wished the people's commands and laws to remain forever binding, to be considered as nothing?

17. My opinion is that nothing should be thought to be more truly the acts of Caesar than the *laws* of Caesar. So, will whatever he has promised to anyone be ratified even if he was not able to fulfil it? He has left unkept many promises to many people, and yet far more of these have been discovered since his death than the favours he committed himself to and granted while he was alive. But I am not meddling or interfering with *those*; I defend his splendid acts with all my energy. If only his money had remained in the temple of Ops![30] It may be blood-stained but we need it now since it cannot be returned to its former owners. If that is what his acts say, let that money have been already squandered. 18. But is there anything which can be more appropriately called the act of a man who, although a civilian, held both civil and military power, than a law? If you ask for the acts of Gracchus, the Sempronian laws are brought out. If Sulla's, the Cornelian laws.[31] Where can we find the acts of Pompey's third consulship? Is it not in his laws? If you could ask of Caesar himself what he had done in Rome when a civilian, he would reply that he had passed many splendid laws – but he would either alter or not produce his handwritten notes, or if he produced them he would not consider them to be part of his 'acts'. I shall allow you those handwritten notes – I can even wink at them – but I think we must not allow the acts of Caesar to be annulled on the most important issues, the laws.

19. What law was better, more useful, more longed for even in the glory days of the Republic, than the ruling that praetors were not to govern their provinces for more than one year and consuls for more than two?[32] If this law is set aside, does it seem that Caesar's acts can be preserved? Is it not the case that the law which was made public regarding the third jury panel annuls all Caesar's laws about the courts?[33] And are you who defend Caesar's acts the same as those who overturn his laws? Unless, by some chance, anything on which he wrote notes to jog his memory later will be numbered among his acts and be defended no matter how unjust and pointless it might be, while whatever he brought before and had passed by the people in the centuriate assembly will not be considered Caesar's act? 20. But what is that new third jury panel of yours?

'One formed of centurions.'[34]

Was not service as a juror open to that group under the *lex Julia* and before that under the *lex Pompeia* and *lex Aurelia*?

'Their property qualification was predetermined.'

But that is the case not only for a centurion but even for an equestrian; so the bravest and most respectable men who have acted as centurions both *are* and have been jurors.

'I am not looking at *them*: whoever has been a centurion, let him be a juror.'

But if both you and Dolabella were to propose this for people who had served in the cavalry – a higher class of service – you would find nobody to approve of it, since we should consider both fortune and position in a juror.

'I am not looking for such qualities. I am adding as jurors foot-soldiers from a legion of Gauls,[35] for our people say that is the only way they can get acquitted.'

What an insulting honour for those unsuspecting men you call
to be jurors! For the aim of this law is that the men who will
form this jury panel will not dare to vote freely. Immortal gods,
see the great error of the men who contrived that law! For
whenever someone thinks he is stained by his low birth, he will
try to wash away his stain by freely handing out harsh judge-
ments in an effort to appear to be more worthy of being classed
among honourable jurors than properly considered someone
from a disreputable class.

21. They made public another law, one which says that those
condemned of violence and treason could appeal to the people[36] if they wished. Is this a law or the annulment of all laws?
Who benefits today if that law of yours stands? There is no current defendant under the laws we have and no one we think
will become one. For one thing is certain: the gains achieved by
weapons will never end up in court.

'But it is an issue in the people's interest.'

If only both of you wanted anything that was in the *people*'s
interest! For now all citizens have one mind and one opinion
about the safety of the Republic. So what is this desire to pass
this law, which has such a foul reputation and brings you no
credit? For what could be more disgusting than that a man who
committed violent treason against the Roman people, and was
condemned by a court, can resume the very violence for which
he was justly condemned? 22. But why do I keep talking about
this law? As if its objective is for anyone to appeal: its objective
and what it will achieve is that no one at all will ever be able to
be prosecuted under *your* laws. Will we find any prosecutor so
insane that, after a defendant is condemned, he will be willing
to throw himself in front of a paid mob? What juror will dare
to condemn a defendant so that he himself can immediately be
hauled in front of hired thugs? This law does not give the right
of appeal, but abolishes two particularly beneficial laws and
courts. What does that do except encourage young men to wish
to be wild, to be treasonous, to be destructive citizens? Since
the two courts for violence and treason have been abolished, is

there any malign end that the tribunes' madness cannot now be directed at?

23. What! Does this not replace the laws of Caesar which order men condemned for violence and treason to be exiled? When these men are granted the right of appeal, surely the acts of Caesar are voided? Members of the Senate, I, who never approved of those acts, still so strongly considered that they should be preserved for the sake of peace that I thought not only that the laws which Caesar had passed when he was alive should be retained, but even those which were produced and posted after his death. 24. Many men have been recalled from exile – by a dead man; citizenship has been given not only to individuals but to whole tribes and provinces – by a dead man; revenues have been lessened by endless exemptions from taxes – by a dead man.[37] So we defend these laws which were produced from his private home by the authority (but an exceptional authority) of one man, laws which, while we looked on, he himself read out, published, passed, over whose passage he was triumphant, thinking that the Republic's safety rested on them. I ask you, can we who defend the acts of Caesar think that his laws about the provinces and about the courts should be overturned? And yet we can at least complain about the laws which have been made public; we are not permitted to say anything about those which have been passed already. 25. For without any announcement, they were passed before they were even written down. But I ask why this is, why I or any one of you, members of the Senate, should fear bad laws while we have decent tribunes of the plebs? We have men ready to use their veto, to defend the Republic by invoking a religious prohibition:[38] we should be free from fear.

He says, 'What are vetoes to me? What is a religious prohibition?'

They are what the health of the Republic rests on.

'I disregard them and consider them far too antiquated and idiotic. The Forum will be surrounded, every entrance will be closed, armed men will be stationed all around on guard.'

26. What then? Will what has been achieved like this, will that be law? I suppose you will order inscribed on bronze this formula:

> THE CONSULS CONSULTED THE
> PEOPLE AS IS THE LAW.

Is this the way of consulting the people, 'as is the law', which we inherited from our ancestors?

> AND THE PEOPLE ADOPTED IT AS IS THE LAW.

What people? The ones kept from the Forum? Under what law? Is it that which has been set aside by armed violence? But I speak about the future, because it is the duty of friends to speak in advance about what can be avoided; if it does not turn out like this, my speech will be proven false. I speak about laws which have been made public, about which you are free to act. I point out their faults: erase them! I denounce your violence and your weapons: remove them!

27. Dolabella, neither of you should be angry with me for speaking in the defence of the Republic – although I do not think *you* will be (I know your easy-going nature). They say that your co-consul in the middle of what he considers his good fortune, but what I would think more truly fortunate (although I have no intention of speaking harshly) if he imitated the consulship of his uncle and grandfather – well, I hear he has been made angry. But I see how unpleasant it is to have someone angered with you *and* armed, especially when there are no consequences at all for using the sword. But I shall propose what I think is a reasonable ground rule, one which I do not consider Mark Antony will spurn. I, if I speak insultingly about his life or his morals, shall not object to him becoming my greatest enemy. However, if I stay true to the way that I have always acted in regard to the Republic, that is, if I speak *freely* what I think about the Republic, I beg him in the first place not to be angry. Then, if I cannot achieve this, I ask that he is only angry with me as with a fellow-citizen. Let him use weapons, if it is as necessary as he says it is to defend *himself*; let these weapons

not harm those who have spoken in defence of the Republic about the situation as they saw it. What petition could be made more reasonably?

28. But if, as some of his close friends have told me, every speech which opposes his will offends him deeply, even if it contains no insult, I shall not quarrel with a friend's nature. But the same men also say: 'You will not as Caesar's adversary be given the same licence as will be granted to Piso, his father-in-law.' At the same time, they will warn me about something which I shall beware of: 'Death will be an even better reason for not coming to the Senate than illness.'

29. But, by the immortal gods, as I look on you, Dolabella, a man who is very dear to me, I cannot be silent about the error that you both are making. For I believe that you are men of noble birth, setting your sights on great goals, not – as some overly credulous people believe – money (an object which has been despised by every great and illustrious person), or violently obtained wealth, or oppression (which the Roman people never tolerate), but fame and the affection of your fellow-citizens. But fame is the praise given to great and deserving actions on behalf of the Republic, a truth confirmed not only by the statements of the best men but even by those of the crowd. 30. I would tell you, Dolabella, what the reward is for good actions, if I were not aware that you more than other men experienced what that was like for a short time. What day in your whole life can you recall as having been more brilliant with joy than the one when – after you had cleaned up the Forum, broken up a gathering of disloyal men, punished the ringleaders of crime and freed this city from fear of arson and murder – you went home? Who was there from any level of society, family or wealth who did not show their enthusiasm for your actions with praise and thanks? Decent men even thanked and congratulated me in your name because they thought that you had acted under my leadership. Dolabella, I beg you to remember the day when that audience, forgetting all of your previous actions which had offended them,[39] unanimously showed that they gave up the memory of their former bitterness because of this new service of yours.

31. Could you, Dolabella (and it is agony for me to say this), could you, I ask, throw away such a great honour with an untroubled mind? But Mark Antony (for I address you, although absent), do you not prefer that one day on which the Senate met in the temple of Tellus to all these months when some, whose opinion is vastly at odds with mine, think you have been happy? What a speech you gave then about unity! How you freed the Senate from fear and the state from great disquiet when you said – casting aside your hostility, forgetting the auspices which you as an augur of the Roman people personally announced[40] – you wished Dolabella to be co-consul with you, and you sent your little son to the Capitoline Hill as a token of peace. 32. Was there ever a day that gave the Senate and the Roman people more joy? They have certainly never crowded any meeting more. Then we seemed finally to have been freed by those remarkably brave men,[41] since, as they had wished, peace followed freedom. On the next day, on the day after that, and the one after that and all the days that followed you did not stop presenting daily a fresh gift to the Republic. But the greatest gift was that you abolished the title of dictator. You, yes, *you*, I say, burned a mark of disgrace on the dead Caesar forever. Just as, because of the crime of one particular Marcus Manlius, it was decreed by all the Manlians that no patrician Manlius could be called Marcus, so you, because of the hatred of one particular dictator, utterly abolished even the title of the office.

33. Is it even possible that, after you had accomplished these great feats for the good of the Republic, you were dissatisfied with your fortune, your prestige, your prominence and fame? From where then did this great change suddenly spring? I cannot be led to believe that you have been ensnared by the lure of money. People can say whatever they want: we do not have to believe it. I have never known anything low or ignoble in you. Even though family are sometimes a source of corruption, I know your strength of character. If only you had been able to avoid not just that failing but even the suspicion of it! But I am particularly afraid that, ignorant of the true path to glory, you may consider that it is more glorious for you to have more

power than everyone else together and prefer to be feared rather than respected by your fellow-citizens. Yet, if you think like this, you are entirely ignorant of the road to glory. When a citizen is loved, has done well by the Republic, is praised, honoured and respected, it is glorious; being feared and hateful is repellent, detestable, fleeting and precarious. 34. We even see this in the play where the very man who said 'Let them hate, as long as they fear'[42] was ruined by his own maxim. If only, Mark Antony, you would remember your grandfather's example! Yet you have so often heard me talking about him. Do you think he would have wanted to be worthy of immortality at the price of being feared because he could use weapons without consequences? To him this was life, this was good fortune: to be equal in freedom to others, but first in position. And so, to speak no more of the successes of your grandfather, I say that I should prefer that most bitter day of his passing than the oppression of Lucius Cinna who most inhumanely murdered him.[43] 35. But why should I try to move you by my speech? If the death of Caesar cannot ensure that you prefer to be loved rather than feared, no speech can manage that nor have any power over you. Those who think that he was happy are themselves miserable; no one is happy whose life is lived by this law: not only can someone kill him with impunity, but the killer gains enormous fame from the deed. For this reason, I beg you to alter your ways, look back at your lineage and govern the state so that your fellow-citizens rejoice at your birth. Without that, no one can be happy, prominent – or safe.

36. Indeed, both of you have much evidence of this from the Roman people and it troubles me very much that it does not affect you enough. What else were the shouts of countless citizens at the gladiatorial games? The popular songs? The endless applause given to the statue of Pompey or for the two tribunes of the plebs[44] who are opposed to the pair of you? Does this not communicate enough the unbelievable, unanimous desire of the entire Roman people? And? Was the applause for the Games of Apollo[45] – or rather I should say the testimony and judgement of the Roman people – not enough for you? They were happy

men[46] who, although they were not allowed to be present in person because of the threat of violence, were still held deep within the hearts of the Roman people. Unless, perhaps, you were thinking it was Accius they applauded and awarded victory to sixty years after his play was first performed, rather than the Brutus missing at his own games? At this lavish spectacle, the Roman people showed their fervour for him even though he was absent, and quenched their desire for their liberator with endless clamouring applause. 37. Certainly, I am a person who has always despised applause when it is given to those who chase after popularity, but when it is granted by those of the highest, middle and lowest ranks all at the same time, when it is given by absolutely everyone, and those, who before used to chase after the people's approval, now depart the audience, I consider that not applause but a real verdict. But if these actions, which carry great meaning, seem so unimportant, surely you do not even now disregard your own observation of how dearly the Roman people held the life of Aulus Hirtius?[47] It was enough for him to be (as he is) respected by the Roman people, to be more pleasing to his friends than anyone else and loved by his relatives most dearly. But do we remember decent men worrying or everyone fearing so much for the health of anyone else? No, we do not.

38. What then? By the immortal gods, can you not interpret the signs? What? Do you not consider how those, who hold so dear the lives of the men who they hope will respect the Republic, think about *your* lives? Members of the Senate, since I have reaped the rewards of my return, whatever misfortune I may encounter, I have said words which stand as testimony of my steadfastness and you have heard them with attentive kindness. And if the power to speak out frequently falls to my lot, without danger to you or me, I shall use it. If not, to the best of my ability, I shall hold myself in reserve for the Republic rather than for myself. It is enough for me that I have lived long enough for a decent lifespan and to achieve my own fame; if any extra time is granted, it will not have been granted so much to me as to you and the Republic.

PHILIPPIC II

Immediately after Philippic I, *Antony made a public declaration of his hatred for Cicero and demanded that he attend the Senate on 19 September. Antony then retired for two weeks to a villa at Tibur which had been the property of Metellus Scipio, Pompey's father-in-law. (Naturally, this provided Cicero with further fodder for his invective.) He took with him Sextus Clodius, a teacher of rhetoric, to prepare what he thought would be a devastating reply which would crush Cicero forever. This speech, which is no longer extant, was delivered on 19 September and was a vicious attack on Cicero's entire life. However, Cicero was lucky enough not to be in the audience. To ensure complete intimidation, Antony also surrounded the temple of Concord, where the Senate was meeting, with armed soldiers and even brought them into the temple itself. Not content with this, he had the doors of the temple closed, to ensure the maximum terror: no one would be walking out of his speech. We do not know its exact contents, though we can guess at some of its charges from Cicero's responses; presumably, as consul, he charged Cicero with ingratitude, misbehaviour and murder of Roman citizens, responsibility for Clodius' murder, for Caesar's murder and, in a move that might surprise us, his terrible poetry (see the response to this in chapters 40–42 below). Antony left Rome for Brundisium on 9 October; on the 25th Cicero sent his response to Antony's speech in draft form to his friend Atticus (*Letters to Atticus 15.13.1); it appears that he did not expect it to ever reach wide circulation until Antony had been crushed. However, Cicero seems to have circulated a revised version of the speech which incorporated Atticus' suggestions after Antony left Rome for Cisalpine Gaul at the end of November. Precisely when Cicero decided to throw caution to the winds cannot be known for certain, though perhaps it was after he delivered the* Third Philippic *on 20 December. In terms of invective this is a work of genius; on no grounds does Cicero spare Antony. While not all of the charges have the same resonance today (though it* *must be said that throwing up in front of an electoral assembly is as disgusting to us as it was to the Romans), in terms of Roman culture and morality this is a devastatingly complete character assassination. This is the longest by far of the* Philippics, *giving Cicero plenty of space to review all of Antony's many misdeeds over his entire career.*

Throughout this speech, Cicero maintains the fiction that he is speaking directly to the Senate, with Antony in attendance, complete with reaction shots of Antony recoiling from Cicero's barbs.

1. Members of the Senate, why is it my fate that everyone in these past twenty years who was an enemy of the Republic at the same time publicly declared war on me? I do not even have to name anyone – you yourselves remember them. Those men paid a heavier price than I would have wished and I wonder, Antony, that as you imitate them you do not dread their end. But I wondered less that others did this. For not one of them was my enemy voluntarily; I challenged them all for the sake of the Republic. But you, although I have injured you not even with a single word, voluntarily challenged me with your abuse so you could look more reckless than Catiline and more insane than Clodius, thinking your estrangement from me would be your recommendation to disloyal citizens. 2. What should I think? That he despises me? I do not see what there is in my private life, in my influence, in my official actions, or in my pedestrian talent which can be looked down upon by *Antony*. Did he believe that it would be so easy to attack me in the Senate? This body has put on public record that many illustrious citizens have achieved much for the Republic – but that I alone saved it. Did he wish to fight it out to the bitter end with me in a debate? Such a kindness! What subject could I find more full of material, more fruitful than to speak for myself and against Antony? That's it! He did not think that he could prove himself to be an enemy of his country to men like himself unless he was hostile to me.

3. Before I answer him on other subjects I shall say a little about the friendship he has accused me of abusing, something I consider to be a very serious charge. He complained that I appeared against him in court at some time[1] (who knows when). Should I not argue a case against a stranger for a close friend? Should I not argue a case against influence gained not by a belief that one should act like a proper man but from the attractions of youth?[2] Should I not plead a case against a wrong he inflicted by the gift of a completely unjustified veto from a tribune instead of the precedents of the praetor's court? But I think you brought this up so you could recommend yourself to the dregs of society; all of them remember that you were the son-in-law of an ex-slave and your children the grandchildren of Quintus Fadius, an ex-slave.[3] But you handed yourself over to me for training (that is what you said) and were always visiting my house. *If* you had done so, you would have kept your reputation and body cleaner. You did not – nor would Curio[4] have given you permission even if you had wanted to.

4. You said you gave up your candidacy for the augurship[5] for me. What unbelievable arrogance! What a shameless statement! When the entire college of augurs sought me out, and Gnaeus Pompey and Quintus Hortensius nominated me since it was not permitted to be nominated by more, you were bankrupt and thought that you could be solvent only after the Republic was destroyed. Were you able to run for augurship at a time when Curio was not in Italy? And when you finally became an augur, were you able to carry a single tribe without Curio's help? Even his close friends were charged with electoral violence because they had been too enthusiastic on your behalf.

5. But you did me a favour. How? I have always admitted openly the act you reminded us of. I have preferred to confess what I owed to you rather than look even a little ungrateful to the uninformed. But what is that favour? That you did not kill me at Brundisium?[6] Could you have killed a man whom the conqueror himself (who had plucked you out to be a commander-in-chief of his outlaws, something you yourself were always gloating about) had wished to save, and whom he had ordered to return to Italy? Let us suppose it had been possible. What is

the kindness of outlaws, members of the Senate, other than their ability to remind us that they gave life to people from whom they did not steal it? But if it were a favour, those who killed a man who had saved them[7] and whom you like to term 'very illustrious men' would never have achieved such great fame. But what sort of kindness is it to refrain from a perverse crime? I ought to find it less pleasing that I was not murdered by you than miserable because you could have done it without any consequences.

6. But suppose it is a kindness, since there is nothing better one can get from an outlaw, how can you call me ungrateful? Should I not have complained about the death of the Republic so you would not think I was ungrateful to you? But what was in my sad and forlorn complaint – except what I had to say in return for the position to which the Senate and people of Rome once elected me – which was insulting, which was not restrained and friendly? Complaining about Mark Antony without using abuse – that took some self-control! Especially when you had devoured the last scraps of the Republic, when everything was for sale at your home in a most disgusting traffic, when you confessed that laws, which had never been made public, were proposed both *for* you and *by* you, when as an augur you had abolished the auspices, as a consul the right of veto, when, repulsively, you were surrounded by an armed guard, when, limp from wine and sex, daily you sampled every type of obscenity in your filthy house.

7. But I – as though it were a disagreement between me and Marcus Crassus, with whom I had many great disagreements of this sort,[8] not with this almost uniquely worthless gladiator – said nothing about him personally while I protested about the state of the Republic. So today I will make sure that he understands what a great favour I did him then. Why, the man even read out a letter, which he said that I sent to him, being completely unaware of civilized behaviour *and* ignorant of how people deal with each other.[9] What man who was even marginally familiar with the way decent men behave ever made public and openly read out letters sent to him by a friend because there was now some quarrel between them? What does

this do except to take away from life that which binds us together, to take away conversation with absent friends? How many jokes do letters normally contain, which, if they were published, would look awkward? How many serious comments which still should never, ever be made public?

8. Let us accept that he has the manners of an animal; take a look at his astonishing stupidity. What do you have to reply with, Mr Eloquence, as Seius Mustela and Numisius Tiro[10] call you? Since these men are standing right now with their swords in view of the Senate, I also will consider you eloquent, if you show how you would defend them in a murder trial. But how could you reply if I were to deny that I had ever sent that letter to you? With what evidence could you convict me? By the handwriting? You have a profitable knowledge of that.[11] As they were written by a secretary, how could you manage that? I envy your teacher who, for an enormous fee, teaches you to know nothing – a subject I shall soon discuss. 9. What is less like a human being (I cannot say orator) than for a man to accuse his opponent of a charge which, if he denies it at all, stops his accuser in his tracks? But I do not deny it; in fact, on this very point I convict you not just of having the manners of an animal but of insanity. What word in that letter is not full of refinement, service and kindness? But this is your entire accusation: that I do not judge you badly in that letter, one I wrote as if to a fellow-citizen, as if to a decent man, *not* to a criminal and an outlaw.

But *I* – even if I have the right to do so since you have torn into me – shall not read out your letter, a letter in which you seek to have my permission to recall someone from exile and swear that you will not do so if I am unwilling. That's what you asked of me. Why was I to stand in the way of your arrogance, something neither the guidance of this body nor the opinion of Roman people nor any law could ever curb? 10. Why did you ask this of me if the man about whom you inquired was recalled by Caesar's law?[12] But, no doubt Antony wanted me to have the credit in a case where not even he could get any credit if a law had been passed.

But, members of the Senate, since I have to say a great deal in my defence and against Mark Antony, I ask first that you listen sympathetically when I speak in my defence – I shall ensure you listen attentively when I speak against him. At the same time I beg for this: if you have known my restraint throughout my life and my decorum when I speak, do not think that I have forgotten myself when I reply to him today as he has provoked me to.[13] I shall not treat him as a consul, just as he did not treat me as an ex-consul. And even if he is in no sense a consul, either in his life-style, his governing of the Republic or the way he was elected,[14] I am without debate an ex-consul.

11. To make clear to you what sort of consul he voluntarily admitted he was, he flung in my teeth my consulship, a consulship, members of the Senate, that was mine in name, but in reality yours. What did I decide on or achieve that was not done with the advice, guidance and will of this body? Did you dare to denounce those actions, Mr Wisdom (not just Mr Eloquence!), in front of those whose advice and wisdom made them happen? And beyond yourself and Publius Clodius, has anyone been discovered who would denounce my consulship? His fate awaits you as it did Gaius Curio, since you have at home what was fatal to both of them.[15]

12. My consulship does not please Mark Antony. But it pleased Publius Servilius, to name him first as the most recently deceased from the ex-consuls of that time. It pleased Quintus Catulus, whose guidance always will be alive in this Republic. It pleased the two Luculli, Marcus Crassus, Quintus Hortensius, Gaius Curio the senior, Gaius Piso, Manius Glabrio, Manius Lepidus, Lucius Volcacius, Gaius Figulus – and Decimus Silanus and Lucius Murena, who were then consuls-elect. The consulship which was pleasing to those ex-consuls pleased Marcus Cato – luckily for him, his departure from this life meant he did not see you as consul.[16] But in particular, Gnaeus Pompey approved of my consulship, and when he saw me as he was returning from Syria he embraced and congratulated me and said that he would see his country again because of my service.[17] But why should I remind you of them individually? It pleased a full Senate so much that there was no one who did not thank me as they would a father, credit me with his life, fortune, children and the Republic.

13. But since the Republic has been robbed of that multitude of great men which I have named, let me move on to the living, to the two who are left from the ranks of the ex-consuls. Lucius Cotta, a very wise, very brilliant man, decreed a thanksgiving in the most complimentary wording because of those very achievements you are criticizing. The other ex-consuls I just named *and* the entire Senate voted in agreement an honour which no civilian before me received in the history of this city. 14. With what a speech of firmness and weight of authority did Lucius Caesar, *your* uncle, deliver his vote against his sister's husband, *your* stepfather.[18] Although you should have held him as a guide and mentor in all of your decisions and in the way you lived, you preferred to be like your stepfather rather than your uncle. I as consul, although unrelated to him, made use of his advice – did you, the son of his sister, ever consult him about anything at all to do with the Republic? By the immortal gods, did you consult anyone other than the men whose birthdays we are forced to hear about? 15. Today, Antony does not appear in public. Why? He is throwing a birthday party in his suburban residence.[19] I shall name no one: consider that one day it is for some free-loader, a Phormio, or a Gnatho or even a Ballio.[20] How outrageously repulsive he is! How unbearably shameless, worthless, lecherous! Can you, though you have a leading senator and exceptional fellow-citizen as a close relative, never turn to him about the Republic, but instead turn to those who have nothing of their own and suck you dry? No wonder, then, that *your* consulship is 'beneficial', but mine was 'destructive'. Have you so completely lost your sense of shame that you dared to say those words in the temple[21] where *I* consulted a Senate (then so flourishing!) which used to govern the entire world, but where *you* stationed men – all losers through and through – with their swords.

16. And you even dared – but what would someone like you not dare – to say that under my consulship the Capitoline Hill was packed with armed slaves! I suppose I was planning to use force on the Senate so that those nefarious senatorial decrees would be passed! You miserable individual, to speak so shamelessly among men like these, whether you are unaware or aware

of the facts (but in truth, you know nothing decent)! For what Roman equestrian, what young man of noble birth (except you!), what person of any rank who remembered that he was a citizen did not put down his name to serve on the Capitoline Hill when the Senate was then sitting in this temple? There were not enough scribes or tablets to take down their names. 17. And, indeed, when evil men, forced by evidence given by their accomplices, by their own handwriting, by their letters almost speaking out against them, confessed that they had plotted to murder their country, to burn the city, to slaughter fellow-citizens, to devastate Italy, to wipe out the Republic – who would not be roused to defend our common good? Especially when the Senate and the Roman people then had such a leader that, if his like existed now, the same fate which befell them would have happened to you.

He says that I did not hand over the body of his stepfather for burial. Not even Publius Clodius ever said that, and I am sad to see that in every vice you have surpassed him, my legitimate enemy. 18. How did it ever enter your mind to remind us that you were brought up in the house of Publius Lentulus? Were you afraid that we would consider you had turned out so evil by nature alone had training not been added to the mix? But your speech was so senseless that throughout it you struggled only against yourself and said things that not only made no internal sense but were self-contradictory and inconsistent; in the end it was not so much a clash with me as with yourself. You confessed that your stepfather was involved in that massive conspiracy and you complained that he was punished for it. So you praised what I achieved but criticized what was entirely the work of the Senate. For the arrest of the guilty was my work, their punishment the Senate's. But Mr Eloquence here does not understand that he is praising the man he speaks against and denouncing those among whom he is talking!

19. Now that is something – I do not say 'shocking' as he wants to be shocking – stupid, in which he exceeds everyone, to mention the Capitoline Hill, when armed men are stationed among our benches, when, by the gods, men with swords stand placed in this chamber of the goddess Concordia, a place where,

during my consulship, words which brought safety were
spoken, thanks to which we have survived to this day. Accuse
the Senate, accuse the equestrians, who were then united with
the Senate, accuse everybody and every citizen, provided that
you also confess that at this very moment Ityraeans[22] surround
this body. You say these things so shamelessly, not because you
are reckless, but because – as a man who does not see how these
things are inconsistent – you are a total fool. For what is more
insane than when you yourself have seized weapons to ruin the
Republic you then object that another took them up to save it?

20. And, dear gods, you even wished to be witty at one point,
something which does not suit you. In this you should accept a
certain amount of blame, for you could have acquired some wit
from your mime-actress wife.[23] 'Let weapons yield to the toga.'[24]
And? Surely they yielded then! But later the toga yielded to your
weapons. Let us ask, therefore, whether it was better if weapons of criminals yielded to the freedom of the Roman people or
our freedom to your weapons? But I shall not respond more to
you about my poetry; I shall only say briefly that you do not
understand it, or any literature at all. I have never failed the
Republic or my friends, but in every genre of the writings I
completed in odd scraps of time, I have worked so that what I
wrote in hours while others slept would bring some praise to
Rome and be something of use to our youth. But this is not the
moment for that subject; let us look at more important subjects.

21. You said that Publius Clodius was killed by my design.
And what would men think if, as the Roman people looked on,
he had been killed when you pursued him with a sword and
would have closed that negotiation if he had not flung himself
under the stairs of a bookshop and checked your attack by barricading them?[25] For my part, I admit that I indeed applauded
your action in this, although not even you say that I suggested
it. However, I was not able to applaud Milo's plan, for he did
the deed before anyone could suspect that he was going to do
it. But I suggested it! Oh yes, such was Milo's spirit that he was
not able to aid the Republic without suggestion. But I rejoiced!
What of it? Would it have been appropriate for me to have
been the only sad person while the whole state was jubilant?

22. Although that court on the death of Clodius was not established very wisely (what did it achieve to hold a trial under a new law for the person who had killed him when there was already a court established?), there was still a trial. What then – have you uncovered someone to say something after so many years, although no one spoke against me when the case was under investigation?

23. You also dared to say – and at length, too – that I worked hard to break off Pompey's friendship with Caesar, and for that reason I am culpable for spawning the outbreak of the Civil War. In this you were not wrong about the entire matter but, crucially, you were wrong about the timing. In the consulship of that most outstanding citizen, Marcus Bibulus,[26] I omitted nothing that lay in my power to draw Pompey from his connection with Caesar. Caesar was luckier on this front, for *he* broke off Pompey's close friendship with *me*. Afterwards, when Pompey surrendered himself entirely to Caesar, why would I have tried to drag them apart? It would have been the act of a stupid man to hope for it and of a shameless one to suggest it.

24. Still, there were two occasions on which I suggested something to Pompey against Caesar's wishes. I would like you to criticize these if you can. The first was for him not to extend Caesar's command for five more years, the other for him not to allow Caesar to be considered as a candidate for office while absent.[27] If I had managed to persuade him on either occasion we would never have fallen into this miserable situation. But also, when Pompey had conferred all resources – both his and those of the Roman people – on Caesar, and began too late to understand that an unholy war was being prepared for our country (something I had long foreseen), I never ceased to be an agent of peace, harmony and settlement between the parties. My refrain on that point was well known:

'I wish, Pompey, either that you had never joined forces with Caesar or never separated from him! One of these would have been in keeping with your firmness of character, the other with its prudence.'

This was always my advice, Mark Antony, both for Pompey and the Republic. If it had been successful, the Republic would still stand, but you would have fallen because of your outrageous behaviour, poverty and infamous reputation.

25. Those are old charges, but this one is new: that Caesar was killed on my advice. Members of the Senate, I am afraid that I shall appear now to have done something loathsome and set up a fake prosecutor against myself,[28] one who will not only load me with praises due to me but add those belonging to other people. For who has heard *my* name among those who joined in that most glorious deed? Is the name of anyone who was part of that group a secret? I say 'secret', but is it not the case that their names were almost immediately made public? Is it not more the case that some uninvolved people went around boasting of it so that they would appear to have been involved, instead of anyone who was involved trying to keep that concealed?[29] 26. Besides, how likely is it, among so many men – some who were obscure and some young, unable to keep quiet about anyone's involvement – that my involvement could have been concealed?[30] And if men had been needed to urge on the liberation of the country, could I have compelled the Bruti?[31] One of them saw the death-mask of Lucius Brutus every day in his home, the other that *and* Ahala's! Were men of such ancestry to seek advice from people outside their family, rather than their own kin, or from those outside rather than inside their home? What about Gaius Cassius? The family into which he was born was not just unable to endure oppression but even any individual's dominance. Did he who, even without the help of splendid men, would have finished that deed off in Cilicia at the mouth of the River Cydnus – if only Caesar had directed his ships to the bank he had originally intended and not to the one he did – did he need my guidance?[32] 27. Was it my guidance, rather than the killing of his father – splendid man – or the death of his uncle,[33] or the stripping of his social standing, that inspired Gnaeus Domitius to recover his freedom? Or did I persuade Gaius Trebonius?[34] I would not even have dared to prompt him! For this reason the Republic owes him more gratitude, because he placed the freedom of the Roman people above

the friendship of one man and preferred to drive out oppression than share in it. Or did Lucius Tillius Cimber[35] follow my guidance? I admired him more for having done that deed than thought he would do it. I also admired him more because, forgetting Caesar's services to him, he remembered his country. And as for the two Servilii[36] – should I call them Cascas or Ahalas? – do you reckon that they were more inspired by my guidance than love for the Republic? It would take a long time to go through the rest: that there were so many of them is their glory and a magnificent thing for the Republic.

28. Recall how that sharp man proved me guilty. 'Right after Caesar was killed,' he said, 'Brutus, as he held high his bloody dagger, cried out the name of Cicero and congratulated him that freedom had been restored.' Why me in particular? Because I was in on it? Perhaps he named me because, having achieved something very like my past achievements, he wanted me in particular to witness that he had rivalled my fame. 29. But you, since you are the stupidest man alive, do not understand that if (as you allege) it is an offence to have wished for Caesar's killing, it is also an offence to have rejoiced at Caesar's death. For what is the difference between someone who suggests something and someone who applauds it? What does it matter whether I wanted it done or am delighted that it was done? Is there anyone, with the exception of those who were happy that he was our king, who did not want it done or disapproved that it was done? Everyone is at fault, then. Indeed, all decent men, as far as they could, killed Caesar; some may have lacked a plan, others courage, and still others the opportunity, but *no one* lacked the desire.

30. But look at how that man (or should I call him a dumb animal?) stumbles around. For so he spoke:

'Brutus, whom I name with all respect, holding the bloody dagger cried out Cicero's name, from which it should be understood that he was an accomplice.'

So I, a man you suspect suspected something, am called a criminal by you, but you name the one who raised the dripping dagger before him 'with all respect'? So be it: stumble in your speech – you do that even more in your actions and opinions! Consul, rule the case of the Bruti, Gaius Cassius, Gnaeus Domitius, Gaius Trebonius and the rest to be what you want it to be; sleep off or work off your drinking binge. Or must we prod you with a torch to wake you up as you sleep through such an important case? Will you never understand that you must rule whether the men who did that deed are murderers or freedom's champions?

31. Pay attention for a moment and try to think like a sober man for a little while. I, as I confess, am a close friend of these men, and, as you accuse, their ally; I say there is no middle way. I absolutely confess that they, if they are not liberators of the Roman people and saviours of the Republic, are worse than assassins, worse than murderers, worse even than parricides, since it is more terrible to kill the father of your country than your own. What do you say, you wise and thoughtful man? If they are parricides, why did you name them 'with all respect' both in this body and before the Roman people? Why was Marcus Brutus freed from legal restriction and allowed by your motion to be out of the city for more than ten days?[37] Why were the Games of Apollo celebrated with incredible tributes to Brutus? Why were provinces granted to Brutus and Cassius? Why were they given extra quaestors? Why was the number of their staff increased? These things were accomplished through you. Therefore they are not murderers. And so it follows that it is your judgement that they are liberators, since there is no third option.

32. What is it? Surely I am not upsetting you? Perhaps you do not properly understand either/or arguments. But this is the sum total of my conclusion: since you freed them from a criminal charge, by that same action you judged them very worthy of our fullest rewards. And so now I retract what I said. I shall write to them, asking them not to deny to anyone who might ask whether what you state about me is true. I am afraid that it might appear to be dishonourable for them that they hid their conspiracy from me, or loathsome for me to have run away when I was invited. By holy Jupiter, was there ever a greater,

more glorious deed more deserving of men's eternal remembrance, done not just here in Rome, but anywhere? Do you wish to shut me up with the leaders as a partner in their plan as if we were all in the Trojan Horse? 33. I do not object; in fact, I thank you for doing so, whatever your reason is. For that act was so great that I cannot compare the malice you wish to incite against me with the praise it brings. For who can be happier than those men whom you declare you expelled and banished? What place is so deserted or uncivilized that it does not seem to greet or even seek them out whenever they approach? What men are so crass that, whenever they catch sight of them, they do not think that they have reaped life's greatest reward? What future age will ever be found that is so unmindful, or what literature so begrudging, that it will not glorify them forever? Go ahead! Enrol me in their ranks!

34. But I am afraid that you may not approve of this one thing: if I had been with them, I would have not only taken out the king but also his power. Trust me: if, as you say, that had been my pen at work, I would not only have finished off the one act but the entire play. Although, *if* it is a crime to have wanted Caesar killed, I beg that you, Antony, see what your future will be, since it is very well known that you hatched a plot with Gaius Trebonius in Narbo, and that it was because of your partnership in this that we saw Trebonius calling you aside when Caesar was being killed.[38] But I (see how I deal with you as a friend!), I thank you because for once you thought properly and did not give the plot away, and I forgive you for not actually doing the deed. That required a *man*.

35. But if someone should take you to court[39] and use Cassius' well-known question 'Who benefited?', I beg you not to freeze up. Although that deed was (as you used to say) good for everyone who did not wish to be a slave, it was especially so for you, a man who is now not only *not* a slave, but a king, who has freed himself from enormous debt using the temple of Ops,[40] who has squandered uncountable amounts using those same account books, who has carted off so much from Caesar's house and whose own house contains a highly profitable workshop for fake journals and signatures and a completely outrageous

sales office for land, towns, tax exemptions and taxes.[41] 36. What could have relieved your needs and debts *except* the death of Caesar? You seem a little bit disturbed. Is it possible that you are secretly afraid that my charge may stick? I shall relieve your fear: no one would ever believe it – it is not your way to do well by the Republic. The Republic knows that our most splendid men were the authors of that glorious deed. I only say that you rejoiced at it; I do not allege that you *did* it.

I have responded to your most serious charges, now I must respond to the rest. 37. You have flung at me what happened during my time in Pompey's camp. As I said, if my advice and guidance had won out, today you would be a pauper, we would be free men and the Republic would not have lost so many generals and armies.[42] I confess that when I foresaw events would turn out as they did, I felt the same grief as all other pre-eminent citizens would have done had they foreseen them as well. I grieved, members of the Senate, I grieved because the Republic, which had once been saved by the decisions you and I took, would soon fall. I was not so uninformed and unfamiliar about how things work that I was crushed because of a desire for a life which would only wear me out with its agonies, as long as it lingered, but once it was cast aside would free me from all troubles. I wanted those most outstanding men, the Republic's stars, to live – all those ex-consuls,[43] ex-praetors, most honourable senators, the very pick of our nobility and youth, armies of our pre-eminent citizens – for if these had lived, even in an unequal state of peace (for peace with fellow-citizens seemed considerably better to me than civil war), we would still have a Republic today.

38. If my opinion had won out and men I wanted to live had not so strongly opposed me, carried away by the hope of victory, you (I shall pass over the rest) certainly would never have remained a member of this body – or, rather, of this city. But 'my speech estranged me from Pompey'.[44] Was there anyone he respected more or with whom he shared conversation or plans more often? This was a great thing: that we, who disagreed about the fortunes of the Republic, remained in a constant friendship. I saw what he felt and was aiming at and he did the same with me.

My first concern was for security now and honour afterwards – his was honour now. We could tolerate our differing opinions because each knew what goal he should pursue.

39. Those who followed his flight from Pharsalus to Paphos know what that exceptional and nearly superhuman man thought about me. He never mentioned me without honour, without being full of friendly longing; he confessed that I had foreseen more but he had hoped for better results. Do you dare to abuse me by using the name of a man whose friend you think I was and whose property you were a bidder for? But let us say no more about that war in which you were too lucky. I shall not even respond on the subject of the jokes you said that I made in his camp. Certainly, that camp was full of anxiety, but even when they are in troubled situations, men, if they are human, still relax their minds from time to time. 40. But that the same man criticizes my despondency *and* my humour is a great argument that I was moderate in both.

You have said that I have come into no inheritances. I wish that had been your offence – then more of my friends and connections would still be alive. But what made you think of that, for I have received more than 20 million sesterces in inheritances?[45] However, I confess that in this you have been luckier than I. None but a friend made me his heir, so that sorrow would be joined to benefit – if one could call it a benefit. But Lucius Rubrius of Casinum made you an heir although you never set eyes on him. 41. And see how much he loved you, he a man who did not know whether you were white or black: he passed over his brother Quintus Fufius' son, although his brother was a very honourable Roman equestrian and a great friend of his, and after he had declared openly his nephew was his heir, he did not even name him in his will. However, he made you, a man he had never seen or even said hello to, his heir. I should like you to tell me, if it is not a trouble, what Lucius Turselius looked like, how tall he was, what was his home town and what his tribe. You will say, 'I know nothing beyond what estates he owned.' So, did that man, disinheriting his brother, make you his heir? Additionally, as if he were the proper heir, Antony has seized a great deal of money from other totally unconnected men after the true heirs were removed by force.

42. I was particularly astonished you dared to bring up that you were claiming inheritances, when you yourself would not accept your inheritance from your own father.[46] You utter lunatic, was it to gather these points together that you spent so many days rehearsing in another man's villa?[47] Although, as your closest friends often say, you normally rehearse not in order to sharpen your talent but to work off your wine. Certainly, for the sake of a joke, you and your fellow-drinkers voted to invite in as your chief a rhetorician, a man (and to be sure a very witty one) whom you allowed to say whatever he wanted against you. But it is easy to gather material for words about you. And look at what a difference there is between you and your grandfather. *He* spoke slowly that which would help his case; *you* speak rapidly what is not relevant.

43. What a huge fee you have paid this rhetorician! Listen, members of the Senate, listen and understand the wounds Antony has inflicted on the Republic. You granted 2,000 acres of land around Leontini[48] to your teacher, Sextus Clodius, and you granted it tax free so that the Roman people could pay a great price for you to learn nothing. Was this too in Caesar's journals, you totally brazen-faced man? But I shall speak later about the Leontine and Campanian regions, where that man has polluted lands stolen from the Republic with the most loathsome tenants. Now, since I have responded sufficiently to his charges, something must be said about our pedant and reformer himself. I shall not bring up everything to ensure that, if we have repeat engagements, I shall always come to battle with fresh weapons – something the multitude of his vices and sins will give me in abundance.

44. Do you want us to look over your character from childhood? I think so – let us start from the beginning. Do you still remember that you declared bankruptcy while a boy? You will reply, 'That is the fault of my father.' I concede that. Indeed, that is a very dutiful and filial defence. However, it was your personal arrogance that made you sit on the fourteen benches[49] kept for equestrians, although the *lex Roscia* allocated a spe-

cific place to bankrupts, even if one has declared bankruptcy
through fortune's fault and not one's own. You put on a man's
toga and right away you exchanged it for a woman's.[50] At first
you were a common prostitute and charged a fixed fee (and not
a small one!) for your degradation. But Curio quickly intervened, stole you away from your whore's trade and, as if he
had made you a proper wife, set you up in a long-lasting marriage. 45. There has never been a boy bought to satisfy lust
who was as much in his master's power as you were in Curio's.
His father kept throwing you out of his home and stationing
guards so that you would not get through the door; you lowered
yourself through his roof, night your accomplice, lust urging
you on – not to mention your fee. In the end, his home could
not stand it any longer. You do know I am speaking about a
subject I am very familiar with? Remember when Curio the
father was lying grieving in his bed and the son was prostrating
himself at my feet, weeping, entrusting you to me, praying that
I would protect him against his father if he sought the six million sesterces[51] (for he said that he had pledged security for that
amount)? But he himself, burning with love for you, kept insisting that he could not endure the sorrow of separation and that
he would go into exile with you.

46. I resolved – or should I say removed – so many evils
from that very distinguished family at this time! I persuaded
the father to pay off his son's debts and use his family's resources
to redeem a young man of great promise, gifted both in spirit
and talent, and to prohibit him by a father's right and authority[52] not only from close friendship but even from casual
meetings with you. Since you remember that I made that happen, would you have dared to provoke me with abuse unless
you trusted in the swordsmen we are looking at now? 47. But let
us pass over your sexual escapades and other degrading acts:
they are such that I cannot honourably speak of them. You,
however, have more freedom here because you have consented
to things you cannot hear from an enemy with a proper sense
of decency.

Now look at the rest of his career, which I shall briefly
scratch the surface of. My mind races on to what he did in the

Civil War, in the middle of the Republic's greatest miseries – and what he does every day. I ask you to listen to these as attentively as you are now, although you know them far better than I do. In such situations, it is not just the knowledge of actions that stirs one's mind, but the act of recalling them – however, I think I should cut it short or it will be late night before we arrive at his most recent activities. 48. He, the man who mentions his kindnesses towards me, was intimate with Clodius during his tribuneship, was the spark for all of his fiery schemes, although he even had a little something going on in his home.[53] (He knows what I am talking about.)

There was then a trip to Alexandria in opposition to a decree of the Senate, but he had as his leader Gabinius, a man who allowed him a free rein to do whatever he wanted.[54] How and by which route did he return? On leaving Egypt, he first made a stop in farthest Gaul before coming home. But what home? Although in those days everyone occupied his own home, there was no home you could call yours. I say 'home' but where on earth could you set your foot on your own property except your place in Misenum, which you owned with partners as if it were a time-share?[55]

49. You came from Gaul to seek the quaestorship. I dare you to say you visited your mother before me. I had already received letters from Caesar asking me to accept that you had made enough amends to me, and I did not permit you to speak about the favour I granted you. Afterwards, you cultivated me and received my assistance in your campaign for quaestor. Indeed, in this period you tried to kill Publius Clodius in the Forum – to the approval of the Roman people – and even though you attempted that feat of your own free will and not at my instigation, you still said publicly that you did not think you could ever make amends for the wrongs you had done to me until you had killed him. Because of this, I have no idea at all why you say that Milo killed him at my instigation, when I never encouraged you as you tried voluntarily to render that same kindness to me. Although, if you were going to persevere in *that*, I preferred it to redound to your credit rather than my influence.

50. You became quaestor. Next thing, at once, without a senatorial decree, without being selected by lot, without legal authorization, off to Caesar you ran. You thought that was the only place in the world to escape from poverty, from debt and from criminality since you had squandered all your own money. There, when you had stuffed yourself by his generosity and your own looting – if stuffing oneself is swallowing what you at once vomit up – off you flew, broke, to the tribuneship so that while holding that magistracy you could try and be just like your husband.[56] I beg you to listen now not to how he shamelessly and indecently damaged himself and his personal honour, but how he damaged us all and our fortunes – or should I say the entire Republic. You will discover that it was his crime that spawned the start of all our troubles.

51. When on the first of January, in the consulship of Lucius Lentulus and Gaius Marcellus,[57] you, the Senate, wished to prop up the tottering and nearly collapsing Republic and to look after Caesar's personal interests (as long as he was in his right mind), Antony blocked your plan with a tribuneship purchased and under new ownership, exposing his neck to the axe which has killed many for lesser sins. A whole Senate, its stars as yet undimmed, passed against you, Mark Antony, the decree which it is traditional to pass against a traitor. And did you dare to speak against me among these men, when they have judged me to be the Republic's saviour and you her betrayer? We may have stopped talking of your crime, but we shall never forget it. As long as humankind exists, as long as the name of the Roman people remains (a name which will be eternal, if only you allow it), that fatal veto will be named as *yours*. 52. What was the Senate doing unfairly or rashly when you alone, a young man, not just once but repeatedly, prevented this entire body from passing a decree on the safety of the Republic and would not allow it to plead with you about its authority? What were they pleading for except for you *not* to wish to overthrow and reduce the Republic to rubble? When senior statesmen, your elders or a full house could not move you from the vote you had sold off at auction, whether it asked or threatened, it was only then after many efforts had been made that they had

to deal that blow to you,[58] a blow inflicted on few before you –
none of whom escaped unharmed. 53. Then this body armed
the consuls and the remaining magistrates with military and
civilian power against you. If you had not taken yourself off to
Caesar's army, you would never have escaped.

You! You! *You*, Antony, were the leader who gave Caesar, a
man desperate to throw everything into disorder, an excuse for
war and for attacking his own country. What else did he say,
what other excuse did he give for his completely insane decision
and actions, except that the Senate ignored *your* veto, abolished
the tribunes' power and impeded *Antony* as he tried to exercise
his powers? I pass over how false, how trivial, these excuses
were, especially since there can be no just cause for anyone to
take up arms against their own country. But I say nothing about
Caesar: surely you must confess that you personally provided
him with an excuse for this appallingly damaging war.

54. You miserable individual, if you understand – and even
more miserable if you do not – that this is recorded in documents, published in writings, and generations to come will
never forget that the consuls were driven from Italy and with
them Pompey, who brought honour and light to the empire of
the Roman people, *and* all the ex-consuls who were healthy
enough to survive that disastrous flight, praetors, ex-praetors,
tribunes of the plebs, a huge part of the Senate and all our stock
of young men. In short, the Republic was cast out and banished
from its own home. 55. Seeds possess something which can
produce trees and plants; like them you were the seed of this
tragic war. You all mourn for three armies of the Roman people
killed – Antony murdered them. You long for those most illustrious citizens – Antony snatched them from you. The authority
of this body has been crushed – Antony crushed it. Finally, all
we have seen since then (and what terrible things have we not
seen?), we shall, if we are thinking properly, lay at Antony's
feet alone. What Helen did to the Trojans, *he* did to our
destroyed Republic. The rest of his tribuneship was like the
start: he did everything the Senate had made impossible to do
as long as the Republic was whole.

Now I shall tell you of a crime piled on these crimes. 56. He

gave back their rights as citizens to men who had suffered misfortunes, without bothering to mention his own uncle.[59] If he is
severe, why not to all? If merciful, why not to his own family?
But – passing over the others – he did the same for a fellow
gambler, Licinius Denticulus.[60] He had been convicted for gambling; Antony pretended he restored him because he was not
permitted to play with a condemned man, but the real reason
was so that he could use a legal favour to pay back his gambling losses. What reason did you give to the Roman people
why he should get those rights back? I suppose you said that he
was absent during the case, the case was judged without being
given a hearing, that there had been no legally constituted court
regarding gambling, that he was pressured by violence or weapons and – what was said about your uncle – that the court was
corrupted by bribery?

Nothing of the sort!

But he is a decent man and worthy of the Republic! That would
not have any relevance, but if he were so, I would pardon him,
since his conviction is considered unimportant. Does not a man
who has restored to full rights the most worthless man of the
lot, one legally convicted for gambling – and a man who would
not hesitate to play *in the Forum* – does he himself not bla-
tantly declare his own passion?

57. In the same tribuneship, after Caesar, on his way to
Spain, handed over Italy to him to grind underfoot, how he
travelled, how he made his tour of the municipalities! I know
that I am dwelling upon subjects everyone talks about, and that
everyone who remained in Italy knows more about the events I
am talking about and will talk about than I who was away.
Nevertheless, I shall single out for mention some individual
events, even if my speech cannot match your expert knowledge.
Has anyone ever heard that such outrageous behaviour, such
grossness, such lack of decency took place anywhere else? 58.
A *tribune of the plebs* travelled around in a *carriage*, while lictors with laurels preceded him, and in the middle of these,
carried in an open litter, was a mime actress – a woman whom

honourable men from the municipalities, turning out on the
road from necessity, hailed, not by her familiar professional
name, but as Volumnia.[61] A coach followed carrying pimps, a
completely worthless crew, while his rejected mother followed
the girlfriend of her infamous son as if she were her daughter-
in-law! Ah, the fatal fertility of that miserable mother! That
man stamped the marks of these offences onto all the municipalities, the towns, the colonies and, in the end, onto all Italy.

59. Criticizing the rest of his actions, members of the Senate,
is extremely difficult and dangerous. He was busy with war,
glutted himself with the blood of fellow-citizens unlike himself:
he was lucky – if there can be any luck in crime. But since we
wish to respect the veterans, although your situation and that
of the soldiers is different – they followed, you sought a leader –
nevertheless, so that you will not stir up hatred for me among
them, I shall say nothing about what sort of war you waged.
Victorious, you returned from Thessaly to Brundisium with the
legions. There you did not kill me. A great favour! – I confess
you could have done so. Although not one of the men with you
then thought that I should be killed. 60. For people have such
a great love of their country that I was untouchable, even to
your legions, because they remembered that I had saved Rome.
But let us grant that you gave to me something you did not
steal and that I have my life because *you* did not take it. Could
I have regarded this as a 'favour' (as I used to) after you insulted
me, especially when you knew that you would get this response?

61. You came to Brundisium to the breast and embrace of
your little actress. What is it? Surely I am not lying? How miserable it is not to be able to deny what it is so disgusting to
confess! If you were not ashamed among the municipalities,
were you not ashamed before your veteran army? Was there a
single soldier who did not see that woman in Brundisium? Was
there anyone there who did not know that she had made such
a long trip to congratulate you? Was there anyone there who
did not feel deep anguish because he knew too late how worthless a man he had followed? 62. There was another lightning
tour of Italy with the same actress as your companion; in the
towns there was a cruelly wretched quartering of the soldiers,

in Rome a revolting scrambling for gold, silver – and especially
wine. It happened that the services of his friends (without
Caesar's knowledge, since *he* was in Alexandria) enabled him
to be appointed master of the horse.[62] As a result, he thought it
only right to live with Studs[63] and handed over horses which
were the property of the state to the mime actor, Sergius.[64]
Then he selected for himself not the house which he is now no
easy owner of but the home of Marcus Piso[65] to live in. What
can I say about his decrees and thefts? Or the estates he awarded
and stole from their heirs?[66] Poverty drove him as he had
nowhere to turn. He had not yet received a massive inheritance
from Lucius Rubrius or from Lucius Turselius, not yet, as an
impromptu heir, had he taken the place of Pompey and many
others then absent. He had to live like a thief, 'owning' only
what he could grab.

63. But let me say no more about the activities of his more
mature depravity; let me speak, rather, about the most excessive
example of his lack of respect. That throat of yours, those lungs
of yours, that whole body of yours with its gladiator's strength,
sucked down so much wine at Studs' wedding that you had to
vomit it up in the sight of the Roman people *the next day*.[67]
What a revolting thing not just to see, but to hear about! If this
had happened to you at a feast right in the middle of those famous giant drinks of yours, who would not have thought it
disgusting? In a gathering of the Roman people, as he was dealing with public business, the master of the horse – for whom it
would be disgusting even to belch – *he* filled his lap and the
whole platform, vomiting wine mixed with chunks of putrid
food! But he admits this himself, along with his other sins – so
let us come to his more splendid activities.

64. Caesar left Alexandria.[68] He thought he was fortunate,
although in my opinion no one can be fortunate who is so
*un*fortunate for the Republic. The sign for an auction[69] was
placed in front of the temple of Jupiter Stator and the goods of
Gnaeus Pompey – my misery, for although all my tears have
been used up, I cannot shake this deep-rooted grief from my
mind. The goods, I say, of Gnaeus Pompey the Great went
under the harsh voice of the auctioneer. Forgetting its slavery,

in this one case, our community groaned. For although everything was controlled by fear and their courage was enslaved,
still the groan of the Roman people was free. As everyone
waited to see who would be so faithless, so insane, so much an
enemy to gods and men that he would dare to bid at that crime
of an auction, no one except Antony could be found, even
though there were many men at that sale who would dare to do
anything else. One man alone was found who would dare do
what the nerve of all the others had shrunk away from and fled.
65. Were you possessed by such great stupidity – or, to put it
more truly, such great madness – that, although you were a
high-born bidder and a bidder on *Pompey*'s property, you did
not realize that you would be cursed by and detestable to the
Roman people, and that it would make all the gods and all men
your enemies, now and for all time? How arrogantly did the
waster seize on the fortune of a man whose courage had made
the Roman people more terrifying to foreign peoples – and
whose justness made them more loved. The moment he got to
wallow in that man's wealth, he leapt with joy, like the character from a mime who was once poor and is now suddenly
wealthy. But, as some poet (whose name escapes me) says, 'Evil
profits become evil losses.'[70]

66. It is astonishing and like an omen just how (and in how
few days – not even months!) he ran through so much. There
was a huge quantity of wine, an immense amount of the finest
quality silver, precious cloth, much elegant furniture and many
magnificent possessions all around the place – not those of a
man who loved luxury but of a rich one.[71] In a few days nothing
was left. 67. What Charybdis[72] is so voracious? I say Charybdis, but if she existed she was only one animal; the ocean, as the
gods are my witnesses, scarcely could have devoured so many
things or swallowed up so quickly so much from so many different places. There were no locks, no seals, no inventory.
Whole warehouses of wine were given away to absolutely
worthless men; actors grabbed some, actresses other stuff; the
house was packed with gamblers and bursting at the seams
with drunks, there was drinking every day and everywhere.
Gambling losses were piled on top of this – for he was *not*

perpetually lucky. You would have seen the slaves' beds in their
nooks strewn with Pompey's purple coverlets! So, stop wondering that this wealth was so quickly consumed. Such great
excess could not only have devoured the property of one man
so quickly, no matter how ample (as his was), but even that of
cities and kingdoms. As for Pompey's houses and gardens – the
immense nerve of it! 68. Did you even dare to enter that home,
to cross its most holy threshold, to show your filthy face to
its household gods? For a long time no one was able to see or
to pass by his home without tears. Are you not ashamed to
squat for so long in a home which cannot give you any pleasure, although you are a man incapable of sensitivity? Or do
you, whenever you catch sight of the naval trophies[73] in the
forecourt, think you are entering *your* home? Impossible!
Although you are brainless and senseless (and you are), you
know yourself, your achievements and your family's. Nor do I
honestly believe that your mind can be at ease awake or asleep.
It must be the case that although you are a violent madman
(and you are), when Pompey's ghost drifts before you you start
awake, terrified, or that often, even while awake, you rave like
a lunatic.

69. I pity the very walls and roof of that home! For what had
it ever seen except what was seemly, except what was done in
the most well-mannered way and the most orderly, decent conduct? For Pompey was, as you know, members of the Senate,
prominent in public life, admirable at home, never praised
more for any achievement overseas than he was for his private
life. Now, in his house, instead of bedrooms there are whore-
rooms, instead of dining rooms, bar-rooms. And yet he denies
it now. Ask no more – he has become thrifty. He divorced his
little actress, kicked her out, took away her keys as the Twelve
Tables[74] allow. How fine a spectacle of a citizen he is, how
respected! There was nothing more honourable in his entire life
than this divorce from his actress.

70. But how often did he repeat in his speech, 'I am both a
consul and an Antony!'[75] That is to say: both a consul and a
man without shame, both a consul and a man worth nothing.
For what else is Antony? If social standing were shown by a

name, your grandfather, I believe, would sometimes have called himself 'both a consul and an Antony'. He never did. Even my co-consul, your uncle, would have said it – unless you are the only Antony. But I say no more about these sins, which do not belong to the part you played in harassing the Republic. I return to that part, to the Civil War, which was caused, born and brought home through your efforts. 71. Although you did not take part in the war in Africa, not just because of your cowardice but also because of your lechery, you had already tasted citizen blood – or rather you had been soaked in it. You had been a leader in the battle of Pharsalus, you killed Lucius Domitius, an illustrious and noble man, and you pursued and cruelly butchered many others who had fled from battle and whom, perhaps, Caesar would have spared, as he had others. Having accomplished great deeds like these, what was the reason you did not follow Caesar to Africa, especially when such a great part of the war was still to be fought? What position around Caesar did you obtain after his return from Africa? What rank did you hold? You who had been his quaestor when he was general, his master of horse when dictator, a man who was the principal excuse for war, the author of its cruelty, his accomplice in plundering, who, as you yourself used to say, held a son's position in his will – you were summoned to pay what you owed for the house, for the gardens, for your purchases at auction.

72. At first you replied quite defiantly and spoke reasonably and justly (in case I seem only to be attacking you on all fronts):

Caesar wants money from me? Why should I not want it from him instead? Did he win without me? He never would have managed it! *I* gave him the excuse for civil war, *I* proposed destructive laws, *I* took up weapons against the consuls and generals of the Roman people, against the Senate and the Roman people, against my country's gods, altars, homes, *against my country*. Surely he did not win for himself alone? Why should those who shared in the crime not also share in the plunder?

You demanded your due, but that was not the point. He had more power. 73. And so, after your mutterings had been brushed aside and he sent soldiers to you and your guarantors, then that splendid sales list of yours was posted. How men laughed! The sales list was so long and had so many different items – and the man who was auctioning the items off could only claim as his own a piece of land at Misenum. What a miserable sight that auction was: some clothes belonging to Pompey (and stained, too!), some battered silver plate of his and a few bits of sad-looking slaves; the result was we felt sorry that there was anything left which we could see. 74. Still, the rightful heirs of Lucius Rubrius stopped this auction by a decree of Caesar. That good for nothing man was at a loss; he had nowhere to turn. And it was at this very time that an assassin with a dagger, said to have been sent by Antony, was arrested in Caesar's home; Caesar complained about this in the Senate, openly attacking you. He set out for Spain, granting you an extension of a few days to pay off your debts because of your financial difficulties.[76] You did not even follow him then. Did such a fine gladiator pack up his weapons so quickly? Will anyone tremble before a man who was so timid in defending his side, that is to say, his property?

75. At long, long last he set out for Spain, but he was not able to reach it safely, or so he says. How then did Dolabella get there? You should either not have supported Caesar's cause, or when you had supported it, you should have defended it to the very end. Three times Caesar fought battles with fellow-citizens, in Thessaly, in Africa and in Spain. Dolabella was present at all these battles, and he was even wounded in the Spanish one. If you ask my opinion, I wish he had not been there, but while his decision from the start should be criticized, still his consistency should be praised. But you – *what are you?*

Pompey's children were then trying to reclaim their country.[77] So be it: let us allow that this was an issue for everyone in your party. They were trying to reclaim their country's gods, altars, homes, their own homes – all of which you had seized possession of. When they sought by force what was theirs by law, who was the only fair person (even if nothing can be fair in these unfair circumstances) to fight a battle with Pompey's children? Who? You, who bid on it. 76. Or, as you were vomiting over the tables of your hosts in Narbo, was Dolabella to fight on your behalf in Spain? And how you returned from Narbo! Antony actually asked why I had so suddenly turned back in the middle of *my* journey. I have explained recently, members of the Senate, the reason for my return. I wished, if I were able, to be of help to the Republic even before the first of January. To answer your question of how I returned: I returned in the daylight, not in the dark, in boots and a toga, *not* in Gallic flip-flops and a cape. But even now you look at me and appear angry. Surely you would return to our friendship if you were aware how ashamed *I* am of your excesses – something you yourself feel no shame at. I have neither seen nor heard of anything so outrageous anywhere – not anywhere. Though you thought of yourself as master of the horse, although you were campaigning for (or, I should I say, asking for the gift of) the consulship for the following year, you, with your Gallic flip-flops and cape, raced through the towns and colonies of Gaul, whose votes we used to seek, when the consulship was something to be campaigned for and not given as a gift.

77. But look at the man's lack of respect: when in late afternoon he had got as far as the Red Rocks,[78] he skulked in some grubby bar and, hiding out there, he drank heavily until evening. Then, getting into a fast carriage, he hurried to the city; upon his arrival at his home he covered his face. The doorman asked, 'Who are you?' 'A messenger from Mark.' At once he was led to the woman[79] who had been the reason for his journey and he handed over a letter. When she had read it, she wept (for it had been written passionately and its gist was that in the future he would have nothing to do with his actress and had abandoned love in that quarter and now lavished it on her). And when the woman cried freely, that kind-hearted man could not bear it; he revealed his face and threw himself upon her neck. You worthless man – what? Should I call you something else? I cannot think of a fitter expression. And thus, so you could show yourself off before you were expected, so your woman could see her catamite sooner than she had hoped, you

unsettled the city with terror that night and Italy with fear for many days.[80] 78. At home you had the excuse of love, in public one even more disgraceful – to stop Lucius Plancus[81] selling the property of your guarantors. But after you were produced in a public meeting by one of the tribunes of the plebs, and replied that you had come because of private 'business', you managed to become the people's laughing-stock.

But I have spent too long on silly subjects – let me come to the more important ones. You went a very long way[82] to meet Caesar as he was returning from Spain. You were quick coming and going so that he would know that even if you were not brave, at least you were energetic. *Again* you became a close friend of his – I have no idea how. This was Caesar's way: whoever was clearly ruined, in debt and poverty stricken, he quite happily made him a close friend if he knew the same person to be worthless and reckless. 79. You, being exceptionally well recommended because of your situation, were ordered to be elected consul – and as his colleague, too! I have no complaint about Dolabella who was then encouraged to run, was led on – and cheated. Who does not know about your treachery towards him in that situation? Caesar led him on to seek the consulship as something promised and guaranteed; then he did an about-face and transferred it over to himself. *You* passed off your wish as *his* treachery. The first of January arrives. The Senate is convened. Dolabella delivers a diatribe against Antony, far more extensive and prepared than the one I am now delivering.

80. By the gods, how enraged was Antony's response! First, after Caesar had made clear that before he left Rome he would order Dolabella to be made consul (and they say that this man who was always saying or doing things like this was not a king!) – but after Caesar had said it, then this good augur here said that he had been granted by his priesthood the right to obstruct or invalidate the election results[83] and vowed that he would do so. Learn from this just how unbelievably stupid he is. 81. So – what you said that you could legally do as a priest, could you not have done as a consul, even if you were not an augur? Would it not have been even easier? We augurs can only announce the taking of the auspices, but consuls and other

magistrates *do* the taking. So be it: you spoke in ignorance – we should not look for intelligence from a man who is never sober. But look at his lack of shame! Many months before, he said in the Senate that he would use the auspices to prevent any assembly to elect Dolabella from gathering or he would do what he actually ended up doing. Can anyone prophesy the auspices will be unfavourable unless he has already decided to look for them? This is not legally permitted at the assembly, and if someone has looked for the auspices before the assembly is in session, he must announce that beforehand. But his lack of shame is intertwined with his ignorance; he neither knows what an augur does nor does what is appropriate for someone with a sense of decency.

82. Remember his consulship from that day right up to the Ides of March? What assistant was ever so submissive or so subservient? He could do nothing on his own; he used to beg for everything, and sticking his head into the back of his colleague's litter[84] he asked for favours to sell. The day of Dolabella's election arrives! The first voting century is selected:[85] Antony is quiet. The result is announced: he is silent. The first class is called, then the *suffragia*[86] as is customary, then the second class is called – and it happened faster than I have described.

83. When the business has been concluded, our good augur (you could call him Laelius the Wise[87]) said, 'Not today.'[88] Now, that *is* an exceptional lack of shame! What had you seen? Observed? Heard? You did not say then that you were 'scanning the sky' – and you do not say it now. So an unfavourable auspice occurred which you had foreseen already on the first of January and had predicted long before. By Hercules, you have lied about auspices – something I hope will prove to be *your* great misfortune rather than the Republic's. You tied up the Roman people with the help of religion, as an augur you impeded an augur and as a consul, a consul. I do not wish to continue in case I appear to be undermining Dolabella's acts, acts which must be brought before our college someday. 84. But learn about Antony's arrogance and insolence. When you want it, Dolabella is an 'irregularly elected' consul; then, when you want it, he was 'elected under good auspices'. If it does not matter when

an augur uses the words you used, why do you not confess that
when you said 'not today', you were not sober? If there is some
meaning in these words, then I as an augur ask of him as an
augur what it was.

But so that this speech does not accidentally skip over Mark
Antony's single most charming act, let us move on to the Lupercalia.[89] He is not hiding it, members of the Senate, it is clear
that he is disturbed – he sweats, he grows pale. Let him do
whatever he wants, as long as he does not throw up like he did
in the Portico of Minucius. What defence can there be for such
disgusting behaviour? I am all ears; I really want to see where
your teacher's enormous fee, that land of Leontini, makes an
appearance. 85. Your co-consul was sitting on the speaker's
platform dressed in his purple toga, crowned on his golden
throne. Up you climb, approach the throne (and, although you
were a priest of the Lupercalia, you should have remembered
that you were also a consul) and show the royal crown. The
whole Forum groans. Where did you get the crown? You did
not just pick one up lying around: you brought it from home –
a premeditated and considered crime. You kept trying to crown
him as the people wailed; he kept rejecting it as they applauded.
So it was that you, you accursed person, were alone exposed as
a kingmaker, who had as a fellow-consul a man you wanted as
your master, and who also tested how much the Roman people
could suffer and bear.

86. But you even tried to win his pity by grovelling at his
feet. Seeking what? Slavery? You should have sought that for
yourself alone, you who lived from childhood as a passageway
for all, as a natural slave. You certainly had no instructions
from the Senate and the Roman people. That was some remarkable eloquence when you addressed the people *naked!*[90] What
was more disgusting than this, more revolting or more deserving of every type of punishment? This speech would have
gnawed at and clawed at you, if you had any scrap of feeling. I
am afraid that I may diminish the glory of very heroic men, but
I have to say that grief moves me now. What could be more
outrageous than that the man who placed the crown on Caesar
still lives, although everyone admits that the man who rejected

it was justly killed? 87. But he even ordered it inscribed into the record under the date of the Lupercalia that 'The consul Mark Antony offered royal power by the command of the people to Gaius Caesar, dictator for life, and Caesar refused it'!

I am less astonished now that you have disturbed the public peace, that you have come to hate this city and even daylight itself, that it is not only from early in the day that you drink with a bunch of loser outlaws but *all* day. Where can you find peace? What refuge can you find in laws and in the courts, given that you have destroyed as many of those as you could with your oppression? Was Lucius Tarquinius driven out, Spurius Cassius and Marcus Manlius killed, so that after many generations Mark Antony could in an act of sacrilege set up a king?

88. But let us return to the auspices, a subject Caesar was planning to bring up in the Senate on the Ides of March. What would you have done? I heard a few times that you had come prepared because you thought that I would speak about how, although the auspices had been a lie, they still had to be respected. The Republic's good fortune put an end to that day – and did not the death of Caesar put an end to your opinion about the auspices? But I have reached a period that I *must* deal with before I go on to these subjects. How you feared and how you fled on that magnificent day! How you gave up all hope of living because of your guilty conscience and crept secretly home. It was only the kindness of men who wanted you to be safe, if you were sane, that got you away from the site of the assassination.

89. In vain have I always been a prophet! When our Liberators stood on the Capitoline and wanted me to go to you and urge you to defend the Republic, I told them over and over that you would promise anything as long as you were afraid, but the moment you stopped being scared you would return to your usual habits. As the other ex-consuls went to and fro, I stuck to my opinion. I did not see you that day or the next, and I believed that no treaty could forge an alliance between the finest of citizens and an absolutely implacable enemy. Two days later I unwillingly came to the temple of Tellus[91] where armed men surrounded every entrance.

90. What a day you had then! Although you have suddenly revealed yourself as my enemy, I still pity you because you have done yourself a great wrong. By the immortal gods, what a great man you would have been if only you had been able to hang onto the mind-set you had that day! We would have held on to the peace which was made that day through that noble boy hostage, the grandson of Marcus . . . Bambalio.[92] Although fear (not a long-lasting teacher of one's duty) was making you a decent person then, your arrogance, which never leaves you as long as fear is absent, has made you shameless. And it was just when everyone thought you were an upstanding individual (my opinion was somewhat different) that you behaved so atrociously at the funeral[93] of the tyrant – if anyone could call that a funeral. *You* gave the eulogy, *you* led the lamentation, *you* provided the provocation.

91. You – yes, you – lit those torches, those which half-burned Caesar and those which burned down the home of Lucius Bellienus.[94] You unleashed those assaults that gangs of losers (almost all slaves) made against our homes, assaults we vigorously beat back with our own hands. But you looked like you had cleared the smoke after that and carried out those remarkable decrees of the Senate, the ones which said that after the Ides of March nothing should be posted which granted a tax exemption or a favour. You *do* remember what you said about the one that banished the title of dictator forever from the Republic? That action made it look as if you had taken such an enormous hatred of royal power because of our late dictator that you banished even the threat of it. 92. The Republic looked secure to others; *I* thought differently, as I could see its total shipwreck with you at the helm. Was I wrong? Or could Antony no longer escape his true self? As you all watched, tablets were posted over the whole Capitoline, tax immunities were sold, not just to individuals but to entire peoples, citizenship was not only given to individuals but to whole provinces.[95] And so, if things continue the same way – and the Republic cannot continue if they do – you have lost, members of the Senate, all the provinces. This man's private trading has not just diminished our revenues but the empire of the Roman people.

93. Where are the 700 million sesterces which are listed in the account books of the temple of Ops? That money was bloodstained, but if it is not going to be returned to its original owners, it would free us from war taxes.[96] Precisely how did you stop owing the 40 million sesterces you owed at the Ides of March fifteen days later? No one can tally the amounts paid for purchases made from your close connections[97] and with your full knowledge; the one real knock-out of a decree was the one posted on the Capitoline about King Deiotarus,[98] a great friend of the Roman people. After that went up, nobody could hold back a laugh even in the midst of their grief. 94. Did anyone ever hate another person more than Caesar did Deiotarus? It matched his hatred for this body, for the equestrians, for the people of Massilia,[99] for everyone he thought loved the Republic. King Deiotarus, a man the living Caesar never dealt with justly or fairly, whether he was present or absent, became popular with him when he was dead! Caesar had rebuked him when Deiotarus was his host, counted up what he owed, set up one of his Greek cronies[100] in one of his principalities *and* took away Armenia, a region the Senate had granted him. When alive he took these things away but gave them back when dead.

95. And how was the decree phrased? At one point that 'it seemed right', at another that 'it seemed not unjust'! A strange combination of words. But Caesar – and I always represented Deiotarus in his absence – never said that anything I asked for on Deiotarus' behalf 'seemed right' to him. His ambassadors, good men but scared and inexperienced, without my advice or that of any of the other friends of the king, signed a promissory note for 10 million sesterces in the lady's *boudoir*[101] where much was for sale and still is. I recommend you think carefully about what legal action you will take about this promissory note. At his own discretion (not at that of Caesar's 'journals'), as soon as Deiotarus heard Caesar was dead, he recovered his own land with his own military campaign. 96. He was wise enough to know that it had been always the law that men who have had possessions taken away by tyrants could recover their losses after the tyrants were killed. There is no legal adviser – not even the man who is a lawyer in your eyes only[102] and who

acts for you in all these cases – who will say that he has to pay anything from that promissory note for property he recovered before it came due. He did not buy his own property from you, but seized it before you could sell it to him. He was a *man*; we deserve to be condemned who hate the architect of all this but defend his actions.

97. What should I say about the endless journals, about the never-ending signatures? They even have their own sales-people, who sell them openly as if they were programmes for gladiator fights. As a result there are such huge piles of money heaped up at his house that it is weighed, not counted. But how blind is greed! Recently a notice was posted which freed the richest cities of the Cretans from tribute *and* decreed that after the proconsul Marcus Brutus' governorship, Crete is no longer to be a province. Are you in your right mind? Should we not lock you up? How could a decree of Caesar's have freed Crete 'from tribute' after 'Marcus Brutus had left the province', when Brutus had not been allotted the province of Crete when Caesar was alive? But by the sale of this decree – just in case you all here think no harm was done – you have lost the province of Crete. If Antony could find a buyer for something, he was not slow to sell it.

98. Did Caesar come up with the law you posted about the exiles? I am not hounding any unfortunate person; I am only complaining, first, about how the men Caesar recalled had their return to Rome tainted by being lumped in with the rest, and, second, about why you did not do the same for the rest of them. It is not as if there are more than three or four people left in exile. Why do you not pity in the same way all those who share the same misfortune? Why do you treat them like your uncle? You refused to pass a law for him when you were pass-ing one about the rest of the exiles; instead, you pushed him to seek the censorship[103] and arranged his campaign – something which made men laugh *and* complain. 99. But why have you never held that election? Why on earth did the tribune of the plebs announce that there had been a sinister flash of lightning? When it concerns your interests, no auspices are regarded, but when it concerns those of your family you observe them. What

else? Did you not also abandon your uncle in his campaign
for the Board of Seven?[104] I suppose someone came along whom
you feared and could not refuse without endangering your life?
You loaded insults on a man whom, had you any family loyalty, you should have respected as a father. You divorced his
daughter, your cousin,[105] after first seeking and investigating
another match. That was not enough: you alleged that she, a
highly decent woman, had strayed. Could you possibly top
that? Still you were not satisfied! When a packed Senate was in
session on the first of January, you dared to say *this* was the
reason you hated Dolabella: that you had discovered that he
had slept with your cousin-wife. Who could work out whether
you were more disrespectful since you were speaking in the
Senate, more offensive since you spoke against Dolabella,[106]
more appalling since her father was in the audience or more
inhuman since you showed such disloyalty in spewing filth
against that poor woman?

100. But let us return to the documents. What investigation
did you make into them? The Senate confirmed the acts of Caesar
for the sake of peace, but we meant those Caesar had actually
done, and not those which Antony *said* Caesar had done. Where
did they appear from? By whose authority are they published?
If they are false, why are they being approved? If they are real,
why are they for sale? The Senate had wanted you, Dolabella,
and a committee to start on the first of June to investigate
Caesar's acts. What did that committee look like? Did you ever
meet? Did you wait for the first of June? Was that the day
when, after you had travelled through all the colonies of veterans, you brought yourself back here surrounded by armed
men? Was that not a remarkable lightning tour you made in
April and May, when you even tried to found a colony at
Capua! We know how you retreated from there – or rather
how you *nearly* did not get to retreat.

101. Now you want to harm Capua! I wish you would try it
so that one day that 'nearly' would be no more! And what a
dignified journey you made! Why should I mention your preparations for lunches, your mad drinking? Those were your
losses – these are ours. We thought that the Republic had suf-

fered a great blow when the land of Campania was removed from the tax stream[107] so it could be given to soldiers – that was land *you* tried to divide among your drinking and gambling partners. Members of the Senate, I am speaking of actors and actresses stationed in Campania. Why should I now complain about the land of Leontini? I can, since these Campanian and Leontine lands were formerly part of the patrimony of the Roman people and considered extremely productive and profitable. You gave your doctor 3,000 acres – what would you have given had he restored your sanity? 2,000 went to your teacher of rhetoric – what would you have given if he had been able to make you eloquent?

But let us return to your trip – and Italy. 102. You founded a colony at Casilinum where Caesar had already founded one.[108] Yes – in the case of Capua – you only consulted me about whether you could legally found a new colony in a place where there was already one, but I would have replied in the same way about Casilinum. I said that in the case of a colony founded with proper auspices, you could not legally found a new colony there as long as it was still unscathed. My expert opinion was that new colonists could be added. But you were so inflated with contempt that, after you had disregarded everything due to the auspices, you founded a colony at Casilinum, all so *you* could raise your flag and mark out its territory with the plough. You nearly scraped the gates of Capua with it to make sure the territory of that flourishing colony would be reduced.

103. Then, disregarding all religious observances, you fly to Casinum, to the estate of Marcus Varro,[109] a spotless and unimpeachable man. What gave you the right? The nerve? You will say, 'It was the same that made me an heir to the estate of Lucius Rubrius, an heir to Lucius Turselius and innumerable other properties.' If you bought it at auction, let the auction be valid – provided that Caesar's records are valid, not yours, records under which you owe something, not those under which you've wriggled out of paying. Who says that Varro's estate was actually sold? Who saw the notice for the auction? Who heard the auctioneer's voice? You say that you sent someone to Alexandria to buy it from Caesar, as it would have been

too long a time to wait for Caesar himself. 104. Who ever
heard that any part of Varro's property – a man who had more
people worried about his safety than anyone – had ever been
confiscated? What? If Caesar actually wrote asking you to
return it, is it possible even to talk about such an enormous
lack of shame?

Remove these swords we see here for a little while and soon
you will understand that the case of Caesar's auctions is one
thing, that of your smug overconfidence another. For not only
will the owner evict you from that house, but so also will any
friend, neighbour, guest or property manager of his. How many
days did you spend getting disgustingly plastered in that villa?
From early morning there was gambling, drinking, vomiting.
How I pity the house itself which 'now labours under a different style of master'[110] – though how is he a 'master' in any
way – still it was held by a different style of master. Varro
wished that place to be a haven for study, not lechery. 105.
What subjects used to be discussed and mused over and what
literature was written in that villa – books about the laws of
the Roman people, the deeds of our forefathers and the structure of every type of philosophy and branch of learning! But
under your tenancy (for this is not ownership) everything
echoed with drunken voices, the floors swam with wine and even
the walls were soused with it. Well-born boys were mixed in
with the 'working' sort and whores with respectable mothers.
From Casinum, Aquinum and Interamna people came to pay
their respects: no one was admitted. That at least was right, as
these marks of respect are demeaned when given to such a disgusting man.

106. While he was heading to Rome, a very large crowd met
him on the way as he approached Aquinum, a heavily populated
town. But he was carried through that town like a corpse in a
litter, with curtains drawn. Stupid people of Aquinum – but at
least they lived along his route! What of the people of Anagnia?
Although they were not on his route, they came down to pay
their respects to him as if he were a consul. It is an incredible
thing to say but everyone agrees that he did not return anyone's greeting – even though he had with him two Anagnines,

Mustela and Laco. (One of these was in charge of his swords, the other his drinks.) 107. Why should I bring up the threats and insults he flung at the Sidicinans and harassed the Puteolians with because they had taken as their patrons Gaius Cassius and the two Bruti? They did this out of great passion, judgement, friendship and affection – not because of violent force, as in your case and that of Basilus and other men like you, whom no one would want as clients, let alone to be the client of. And while you were absent, what a day your colleague had when he destroyed that tomb in the Forum[111] you used to worship! Everyone who was there agrees that when you heard about that event you collapsed. I have no idea what happened after this but I suppose fear and weapons won out; you dragged Dolabella down from heaven and made him a creature who, although even now he does not resemble you, no longer resembles his true self.

108. After that how you made your return to Rome! What commotion there was in the whole city! We remembered that Cinna was too powerful; after him was the oppression of Sulla, and just now we saw Caesar's reign. There were swords then, but sheathed and not in such numbers. How massive and how barbaric was your return! Men followed in marching order with their swords drawn and we saw litters full of shields carried along. But we have become inured and hardened by familiarity even to such things. However, when we wanted to enter the Senate on the first of June (as had been decided upon), we suddenly fled in fear, utterly terrified. 109. But *he*, since he wanted no Senate, did not feel the loss and instead was delighted with our absence; then, right away, he did those marvellous misdeeds. Although he had defended Caesar's journals for his own gain, he dismantled Caesar's laws (even the good ones) so he could undermine the Republic. He extended the number of years one could govern a province and at the same time, although he should have been the defender of Caesar's acts, he dismantled their authority in both public and private business. In public business there is nothing which carries more weight than the law; in private business a will is our strongest protection. He set aside some laws without notice; he gave notice of

new laws so he could set others aside. He nullified a will, although a will holds authority even in the case of the poorest citizens. He carted off the statues and pictures Caesar had left to the people, along with his gardens; some went into the gardens of Pompey, the rest into the villa of the Scipios.

110. And are you the one who respects Caesar's memory and who loves him now he is dead? What greater honour had he acquired than to have a divine couch,[112] statue, temple and the priest of a god? As Jupiter, Mars and Quirinus have priests, so the Divine Julius has Mark Antony. But why are you not doing your job? Why are you not consecrated? Pick a day, look for someone to consecrate you: we are all colleagues – no one will refuse. Whether you are the priest of a tyrant or of a dead man, you are an accursed man! I ask you now whether you are unaware what day today is? Do you not know that yesterday was the fourth day of races for the Roman Games[113] in the Circus and that you personally proposed to the people that a fifth day be added as a tribute to Caesar? Why are we not dressed in our togas of office? Why do we allow the honour your law gave to Caesar to be abandoned? Have you allowed thanksgivings to be polluted by adding a day to them, but refused a sacred couch? Either abolish religious propriety entirely or preserve it whole. 111. You ask whether I am happy for him to have a couch, temple and priest. None of these makes me happy; but you, who defend the acts of Caesar, can you say why you defend some of them and do not care about others? Unless, by chance, you want to confess that your only measuring-stick is your gain, not his?

So, what is your reply to all this? I await your eloquence. I knew your grandfather,[114] who was a very skilful speaker; you bare yourself even more when you speak. He never addressed a public assembly naked, but we have seen your chest, which is that of a simple man. Will you reply to this? Dare you open your mouth at all? Can you discover nothing in this long speech which you feel you can reply to?

112. But let us forget the past. I shall speak of this particular day, today, in fact this very moment in which I am talking. Answer – if you can – why is the Senate surrounded by a ring

of armed men? Why does your bodyguard listen to me speaking with their swords drawn? Why are the doors of our meeting-place not open? Why do you lead your Ityraeans, the most barbaric men of all races, into the Forum with their bows strung? He says that he does it for his own protection. Surely it is better to die a thousand times than not be able to survive in one's own community without the protection of armed men? But, believe me, that is no real protection. You ought to be sur-rounded by the love and friendship of your fellow-citizens, not by weapons.

113. The Roman people will seize them from you – may we live to see the day! But whatever way you treat us, trust me that while you adopt these strategies you will not live long. Indeed, that very generous wife of yours – whom I have no intention of insulting – for too long now owes the Roman people her third 'instalment'.[115] The Roman people has men to whom it can hand over the reins of the Republic:[116] wherever these men are, there is every protection for the Republic, or, rather, there is the Republic herself, which has so far only just gained vengeance, not the restoration of her health. The Republic is sure of these most noble young men, her ready defenders. Although, as they desire peace they have faded into the background as much as possible, it will still recall them.

There is sweetness in the name of peace, and living in peace is beneficial, but there is a great difference between peace and slavery. Slavery is the worst of all evils and must be driven off by war – or even by death. 114. But if our Liberators have removed themselves from our sight, still they have left us the example of their action. They accomplished what no one had accomplished before. Brutus pressed Tarquinius hard with war, but Tarquinius was king when that was permitted in Rome. Spurius Cassius, Spurius Maelius and Marcus Manlius were killed on suspicion of seeking royal power. But the Liberators were the first to make an armed assault, not on one seeking to be king, but upon a king in power. That action itself is remark-able, divine and held up as our model, especially since they have won glory which almost seems to reach past heaven. For although the knowledge of having done such a magnificent deed was enough reward in itself, still I do not think that mortals should despise immortality.

115. Mark Antony, remember that day on which you abolished the dictatorship, set before your eyes how the Senate and people of Rome rejoiced, compare with this your own and your friends' trafficking: then you will understand what the gap is between gain and glory. But, doubtless, just as a person with an illness loses their sense of taste and does not feel how sweet food is, so the lecherous, the greedy and criminally minded lose their taste for true glory. And if that cannot tempt you to act properly, surely fear can divert you from your most revolting exploits? You do not fear the courts: if that is because of innocence, I praise you, but if because of coercion, do you not understand what a man like you who does not fear the courts *must* fear? 116. If you do not fear brave men and outstanding citizens because armed men keep them away from you, trust me on this: your own people will not endure you much longer. What sort of life is it fearing your own followers day and night, unless you have men bound to you by greater favours than the men Caesar had bound to him – and some of them killed him? Or is it that you are to be compared to him somehow? That man had brilliance, calculation, memory, literary ability, carefulness, thoughtfulness, precision. He was successful in a war, which, although it was disastrous to the Republic, was still great; for many years he aimed to rule and he achieved what he had planned with great effort and great risks. He softened up the ignorant masses with games, buildings, gifts and feasts. He bound his followers to himself with rewards, his opponents with the appearance of clemency. Why go on? He brought to a free state acceptance of slavery, partly through fear, partly through familiarity.

117. Although I can compare you to him in your lust for power, you cannot be compared to him in anything else. But, from the many evils which he branded on the Republic, this much that was good still came about: that the Roman people learnt how much to trust anyone, to whom they could entrust themselves and against whom they should be on their guard. Do you not consider this or do you understand that it is enough

for brave men to have learnt what a beautiful deed it is to kill a tyrant – and what benefit it brings and what glorious fame it gives? When men did not endure *him*, will they endure you? 118. Believe me: after this, men will stampede to the task and they will not wait for something as slow as opportunity. Even now, I beg, look around and consider from whom you came, not with whom you live. Treat me as you will – just make peace with the Republic. You look to *your*self, I shall speak for *my*self. As a young man I defended the Republic; I shall not desert her as an old man. I despised the swords of Catiline; I shall not tremble before yours.

119. I would also freely offer up my person if my death would immediately bring back freedom to our state, so that the anguish of the Roman people would give birth to what it has been carrying within for a long time. For, if almost twenty years ago I denied, in this very temple, that death could be premature for a man who had held the consulship, how much more truly will I deny it is premature for an old man. Members of the Senate, I should desire death after the political offices I have attained and the deeds I have done. I long for these two things only: one, that as I die I shall leave behind a free Roman people (there is nothing greater that the immortal gods can give to me); second, that everyone will get his just rewards for his treatment of the Republic.

Glossary of Names

A BRIEF NOTE ON ROMAN NAMES

The names of Roman males usually had three parts: praenomen, nomen and cognomen. Marcus Tullius Cicero's name thus breaks down into Marcus (praenomen), Tullius (nomen or family name) and Cicero (cognomen). Women took a feminized form of the nomen; thus Cicero's daughter was known only as Tullia. Occasionally extra honorific cognomina would be added to commemorate great achievements (and sometimes great failures): thus, when Publius Cornelius Scipio the Younger conquered Carthage in 146, he was given the cognomen Africanus. While it is usual to list Romans by their nomina, for ease of use here they are listed in alphabetical order by their cognomen, except where the person is better known by another name, such as Cato the Younger or Mark Antony.

Gaius Servilius **Ahala** Legendary figure of early Rome, he was master of the horse for Lucius Cincinnatus, dictator in 439. At Cincinnatus' order, he killed Spurius Maelius in the Forum when he refused Cincinnatus' summons.

Gaius 'Hybrida' **Antonius** The son of the famous orator Marcus Antonius, he served under Sulla and benefited by his proscriptions. After the censors expelled him from the Senate in 70, he went on to be elected praetor in 66. He was co-consul with Cicero in 63, despite making common cause with Catiline in 64. He was prosecuted for his time as the governor of Macedonia. He was recalled by Julius Caesar and eventually became censor in 42.

Marcus **Antonius** (orator) The grandfather of Mark Antony; he was praetor in 102 and consul in 99. A famous orator (he appears in Cicero's dialogue *On the Orator*), he also scored significant successes against the pirates during his time as praetor. He supported Sulla and was killed (in 87) by Marian supporters.

Mark **Antony** Born *c.* 83 to an old and distinguished family of plebeians. Quaestor in 51, tribune of the plebs 49 (when he supported
Caesar, to whose camp he fled after being threatened by the Senate),
consul in 44 (with Caesar). After the death of Caesar, he made common cause with Octavian and Lepidus, forming the second triumvirate
in 43. In 31 he committed suicide after his and Cleopatra's forces
were defeated by Octavian at the battle of Actium. For more on his
life and career, see the *Philippics* for a very biased perspective.

Marcus Junius **Brutus** Born *c.* 85. Quaestor in 53, praetor 44. He was
the son of Servilia (Caesar's lover; it was rumoured that Brutus was
actually Caesar's son) and Marcus Junius Brutus and was adopted
by his uncle Quintus Servilius Capio before 59. His ancestry
included the Brutus who had forced the kings out of Rome and
founded the Republic. In 49 he supported Pompey against Caesar
but was pardoned after the battle of Pharsalus; he seems not to have
been hostile to Caesar until Caesar became perpetual dictator.
(After Cato's death he married Cato's daughter Porcia.) He was a
leading member of the conspiracy to assassinate Caesar, but made
the error of sparing Antony's life on the Ides of March. Thereafter,
he and the other Liberators (the name the assassins gave themselves) were outmanoeuvred by Antony and Octavian. In 42 he and
Cassius fought Antony and Octavian at two battles at Philippi in
northern Greece. Although Brutus scored an initial and impressive
victory over Octavian, he was defeated in the second battle and
committed suicide. Antony is said to have covered the body with a
cloak in respect and allowed it an honourable burial.

Gaius Julius **Caesar** Born in 100 to a family that claimed descent
from Venus. Quaestor in 69, pontifex maximus 63, praetor 62, consul 59, 48, 46, 45, 44, governor of Gaul 58–49, dictator several
times from 49 to 44. His aunt married the *popularis* leader Marius,
and under Sulla Caesar was asked to divorce his wife, Cornelia (the
daughter of Cinna, an ally of Marius), but refused. He may have
supported Catiline and argued against the execution of the Catilinarian conspirators (he suggested life imprisonment in various
Italian towns). After a victorious campaign in Spain, he returned in
60, giving up his right to hold a triumph in order to run for the
consulship. He allied himself with Crassus and Pompey, forming
the first triumvirate. After being assigned a uniquely long period as
governor of Gaul, he conquered new regions of that territory for
Rome, killing something like a million Gauls in the process and
enslaving another million. This campaign gave Caesar massive
wealth (none of which the Roman treasury saw) and the loyalty of

his legions. In 49, he sought to run for consul *in absentia*; instead, facing recall by the Senate – which would lead to his prosecution – he invaded Italy on the pretext of defending the rights of the tribunes who had been forced out of Rome on pain of death. After his defeat of the Pompeian forces, he was awarded a perpetual dictatorship; this was cut short when he was assassinated by a collection of his friends on the Ides of March 44.

Cassius (Gaius Cassius Longinus) Quaestor in 54, tribune of the plebs 49, praetor 44. He fought with Crassus in Parthia, surviving the massacre that took Crassus' life. He sided with Pompey and the Senate in the Civil War with Caesar. Along with Brutus, he was one of the leaders of the conspiracy to kill Caesar. He killed himself after the first battle of Philippi in 42, unaware that Brutus had defeated Octavian.

Cato the Younger (Marcus Porcius Cato) Born 95. Tribune of the plebs in 62, praetor 54. The great-grandson of Cato the Elder (also called Marcus Porcius Cato), he was completely uncompromising in his principles, something that frequently frustrated Cicero, who thought his lack of realism was impressive but unworkable and damaging. He fought on Pompey's side in the Civil War with Caesar; after Pompey's defeat at the battle of Pharsalus in 48, he went to join the Pompeians in Africa. When they lost the battle of Thapsus in 46, he committed suicide rather than accept Caesar's pardon.

Quintus Lutiatus **Catulus** the Elder Consul in 102 (with Marius). He fought against the Cimbri and triumphed jointly with Marius in 101. He built a portico on the Palatine out of the spoils of this campaign (mentioned in *On his House*: chapter 102). He was a cultured man and befriended Archias when he came to Rome. He supported Sulla against Marius.

Quintus Lutiatus **Catulus** the Younger Consul in 78, censor 65. He was a supporter of Sulla and his reforms. He opposed the laws of Aulus Gabinius and Gaius Manilius which granted special commands to Pompey. He was defeated in the elections for pontifex maximus in 63 by Caesar and died soon after.

Appius **Claudius** Caecus (the Blind) Censor in 312, consul 307 and 296, praetor 295. A distant ancestor of Clodius. He went blind in old age (hence the *caecus*, Latin for 'blind'). While censor, he built the Appian Way from Capua to Rome and Rome's first aqueduct.

Publius **Clodius** Pulcher Born *c.* 92. Quaestor in 61, tribune of the plebs 58. A member of an old and aristocratic patrician family, he became a plebeian in 59 so he could run for tribune of the plebs. Despite supporting Cicero during the Catilinarian conspiracy, he became his inveterate enemy and was responsible for Cicero's exile in 58. For more on Clodius, see almost any of the speeches after 61; for his death (in 52), see *In Defence of Milo*.

Marcus Licinius **Crassus** (the triumvir) Praetor in 73, consul 70. He made a fortune during the Sullan proscriptions and fought against the slave army of Spartacus in 72–71. He is often called *dives*, wealthy, because he was immensely rich; he said that no one should be called rich unless they could maintain a legion out of their own resources. He supported Catiline during his run for consul and was perhaps one of the backers of Rullus' agrarian law (see *On the Agrarian Law of Rullus*). He was also one of Caesar's financial backers. He sold Cicero his house on the Palatine, but Cicero disliked him; Crassus appears to have returned the favour. A member of the first triumvirate, he died while campaigning in Parthia in 53.

Publius Cornelius **Dolabella** Born *c.* 69. Tribune of the plebs in 47. He was Cicero's son-in-law, marrying Tullia in 50, much to Cicero's dismay (in 46 he divorced her and never returned her dowry, which seems fairly typical of his character). During the Civil War between Caesar and Pompey, he fought on Caesar's side without much distinction. He was personally very charming and Caesar selected him to be consul after he left for the east on his campaign against Parthia, but Antony blocked this by using the auspices. He seized the consulship after Caesar's death and simultaneously wooed the Liberators *and* Antony, before eventually siding with Antony. He committed suicide in 43 in Syria after being besieged by the Republican Gaius Cassius Longinus.

Marcus **Fulvius** Flaccus Consul in 125. He held a triumph in 123 for a victorious campaign against the Salluvii. After this he became tribune of the plebs in 122 (an extremely unusual move). He supported Gaius Gracchus' reforms and he and his sons were killed along with Gaius in 122.

Gaius Sempronius **Gracchus** The younger brother of Tiberius Gracchus. Tribune of the plebs in 123 and 122. After passing several agrarian laws and reforms, he suggested expanding Roman citizenship; this was not popular with the urban plebs or the Senate. In 121, when he was no longer tribune, the Senate passed the first ultimate decree of the Senate (see Glossary of Terms) to deal with him. The consul Opimius, at the head of a senatorial party, killed him with Marcus Fulvius Flaccus and some 3,000 supporters.

Tiberius Sempronius **Gracchus** The elder of the two Gracchi brothers, both famous *populares* and sons of Tiberius Sempronius Gracchus, who was consul in 177; their mother was Cornelia, the daughter of

Scipio Africanus the Younger. Tribune of the plebs in 133. That year he proposed an agrarian law along with other reforms; facing hostility in the Senate, he had the law passed by the people before having it debated in the Senate. Facing the repeated veto of another tribune, Marcus Octavius, he had him removed from office. He was lynched by a group of senators led by Scipio Nasica while attempting to seek re-election (holding the tribuneship in successive years had no precedent).

Publius Cornelius **Lentulus** Sura ('Legs' Lentulus) Quaestor in 81, praetor 74, consul 71. He was Mark Antony's stepfather. When Sulla accused him in the Senate of embezzling public money as quaestor, he stuck out the calf of his leg (*sura* in Latin), in a disrespectful gesture imitated from ball games. Expelled from the Senate in 70 on moral grounds, he gained re-entry in 63 by being elected praetor for a second time. He was the most high-profile member of the Catilinarian conspiracy to be executed.

Marcus Aemilius **Lepidus** (the triumvir) Praetor in 49, consul 46 and 42, Caesar's master of the horse 46–44, pontifex maximus after the death of Caesar until 13/12. While praetor, he supported Caesar and after his death supported Antony, despite assuring Cicero that he would aid the senatorial party. In 43 Lepidus, Antony and Octavian formed the second triumvirate, though he was largely ignored when it was renewed in 37. He died in 13 or 12.

Spurius **Maelius** According to legend, he was a rich plebeian who used his property to buy and distribute grain during a famine in 439. In that year he was accused of aiming at being a tyrant and was killed by Ahala.

Marcus **Manlius** Capitolinus Consul in 392. Like Maelius, he is frequently mentioned by Cicero as an example of someone legitimately crushed by the Senate. He saved the city from a Gallic attack in 390 after he was woken by the sound of the goddess Juno's sacred geese on the Capitoline. In 385/4 he championed the cause of debtors and also accused the Senate of embezzling money captured from the Gauls. He was tried and despite popular support was convicted of aiming at tyranny. He was thrown to his death from the Tarpeian Rock. From then on, the patrician members of the Manlian *gens* were forbidden to take the name of Marcus.

Gaius **Marius** Born in Arpinum *c.* 157. Quaestor *c.* 123, tribune of the plebs 119, praetor 115, consul 107, 104–100, 86. Like Cicero, he was a 'new man', the first in his family to hold a consulship. He was one of Rome's great generals, fighting victorious campaigns in Africa (against Jugurtha) and various northern tribes. A *popularis*

hero, he reformed the army, admitting members of the urban prole-
tariat, and he worked initially with Saturninus to get land for his
veterans, though he turned against him in 100. He was also a fierce
foe of Sulla, fleeing Rome in 88, but returning in 87 when Sulla was
fighting in the east. Although his politics were not Cicero's, Cicero
admired him greatly, writing an epic poem on his achievements.
Marius was married to Caesar's aunt Julia.

Titus Annius **Milo** Tribune of the plebs in 57, praetor 55, candidate
for consul in 53. While tribune, he worked for Cicero's recall from
exile and also led armed gangs against Clodius. In January 52, the
men at his command murdered Clodius after the two encountered
each other on the Appian Way. He was exiled despite Cicero's
defence; he went to the Greek colony of Massilia. In 48 he tried to
lead a revolt against Caesar and was killed in the attempt.

Mithridates VI Eupator Born *c.* 133. King of Pontus and one of
Rome's most dangerous enemies, he fought three wars with Rome
(see Chronology). Sulla and Lucius Licinius Murena had command
of the Roman forces in the First and Second. The Third was initially
fought under the command of L. Licinius Lucullus but was transferred to Pompey the Great. He was said to have been planning an
invasion of Italy when his son led a revolt against him. He committed suicide in 63.

Octavian (later Augustus) Born in 63. Caesar's great-nephew, he was
adopted by him in his will and made his heir. His youthfulness at
the time of Caesar's assassination led to Cicero believing he could
be used and discarded; Cicero was soon to be disabused of this
notion. In 43 he formed the second triumvirate with Antony and
Lepidus. After his defeat of Antony and Cleopatra in the battle of
Actium in 31, he was sole ruler of the Roman Empire until his death
in 14 CE.

Lucius **Opimius** Praetor in 125, consul in 121. The Senate voted him
the ultimate decree of the Senate (see Glossary of Terms) to deal
with Gaius Gracchus. In 109 he was convicted of having accepted
bribes from the Numidian king Jugurtha and was exiled. He died in
exile in Dyrrhachium.

Lucius Calpurnius **Piso** Caesoninus Consul in 58. Father-in-law of
Caesar, he was a long-time political enemy of Cicero, who blamed
him for not attempting to restrain Clodius in 58. He was distantly
related to Cicero's first son-in-law, but would not help him prevent
Cicero from being exiled or aid in his recall. After Caesar's death,
he tried to restrain Mark Antony for a brief period.

Pompey the Great (Gnaeus Pompeius) Born in 106. Consul in 70 and

55 (with Crassus), sole consul 52 (he later appointed a co-consul). He took the title 'the Great' in 81 in imitation of Alexander the Great. Before this he had fought several victorious campaigns during the Social War and the Civil War between Marius and Sulla (Pompey fought on Sulla's side). He was sent in 77 to help deal with Sertorius in Spain and returned victorious in 71. On his return, he helped mop up what was left of Spartacus' slave army and held his second triumph in 70. Given command over the war with the pirates in 67 and the Third Mithridatic War in 66, he returned again in triumph in 62. Faced with an uncooperative Senate, he formed the first triumvirate with Crassus and Caesar in 60, marrying Caesar's daughter Julia to cement their alliance. After the collapse of the triumvirate and Caesar's invasion of Italy in 49, he led the Senate's forces against Caesar, losing to him at the battle of Pharsalus in 48. On fleeing to Egypt, he was assassinated as he landed on 28 September 48.

Lucius Appuleius **Saturninus** Tribune of the plebs in 103, 100 and elected for 99 (he never served because of his death). A supporter of Marius, he lost Marius' support in 100, the same year he had had a candidate for consul murdered at the elections. During his second term as tribune, the Senate declared him and the praetor Glaucia public enemies. He was murdered in the Curia in the autumn (or perhaps December) of 100 by tiles flung from the roof, a crime for which the elder senator Gaius Rabirius would be prosecuted in 63 (Cicero defended him).

Publius Cornelius **Scipio** Africanus the Elder Born in 236. Aedile in 213; in 210 the people granted him consular *imperium* for a campaign in Spain against the Carthaginians during the Second Punic War (despite the fact that he had been neither consul nor praetor). Consul in 205. He crossed over to Africa and defeated Hannibal in 202 at the battle of Zama, ending the Second Punic War. Massively powerful in Rome after this, he was elected censor in 199 and served as consul again in 194. However, facing trial in 184, he went into voluntary exile and died while still in exile in 183.

Publius Cornelius **Scipio** Aemilianus Africanus the Younger Born in 185/4, he was adopted as a child by the son of Scipio Africanus the Elder. When he stood in the elections for the position of aedile in 147, he was instead elected consul (this was against the law, but such was the popular demand the Senate permitted it). In 146 he captured Carthage and ended the Third Punic War. He razed Carthage and cursed the site. Consul again in 134, he fought successfully in Spain, capturing Numantia. He was an opponent of Tiberius Gracchus (his

cousin and brother-in-law) and became unpopular for approving of
his murder. He was found dead in 129; murder was suspected but
no one was ever charged. He was a highly cultured individual and
friend and patron of the Greek historian Polybius.

Publius Cornelius **Scipio** Nasica Serapio Pontifex maximus *c*. 140,
consul 138. He was a cousin of Tiberius Gracchus, whom he fiercely
opposed. When Tiberius sought re-election to the tribuneship in
133, with the help of a mob, Scipio, along with a group of senators
and their clients, lynched him.

Quintus **Sertorius** Quaestor in 91, praetor *c*. 85. He took command
of the Marian forces in Spain in 83/2, though he was driven out for
a brief period. A brilliant general of guerrilla warfare, he also gained
considerable support among the native Spanish. He proved the
hardest of the Marians to defeat and by 77 he held much of Roman
Spain. In 76/5 he formed an alliance with Mithridates, but after 75
he had less and less success in the field. He was assassinated by
Perperna, one of his lieutenants, in 73.

Publius **Sestius** Quaestor in 63; he served under Gaius Antonius
Hybrida in that year and in 62 in Macedonia. As tribune of the
plebs in 57, he fought hard for Cicero's return from exile. Following
Cicero's return, he defended Sestius in 56 (see *In Defence of Ses-
tius*). Praetor in 54, he was prosecuted for electoral bribery and was
defended successfully once more by Cicero. Although Cicero and
Sestius remained friends throughout their lives, Sestius defected to
Caesar's side after the battle of Pharsalus.

Lucius Cornelius **Sulla** Felix (the Lucky) Born *c*. 138. Quaestor in
107 (to Marius), praetor 97, consul 88. He was a devout conservative and fought successfully under Marius and Catulus the Elder.
When the tribune Publius Sulpicius Rufus tried to take from him
command of the war with Mithridates in 88, he marched on and
entered Rome at the head of his army (something no Roman commander had ever done before). After killing Sulpicius and trying to
hunt down the Marians (Marius fled to Africa), he left for the east
in 87. He was outlawed during this period when Marius and his
supporters retook control of Rome. In 83 he invaded Italy and took
Rome once more in 82; proscriptions and murders of Marius' supporters followed. Appointed dictator in 82 (a position he held until
79), he put considerably more power into the hands of the Senate
and stripped the tribunes of the plebs of much of theirs.

Terentia Cicero's first wife. They married sometime between 80 and
76. She was a wealthy woman and it was probably her dowry that
helped Cicero launch his public career. She bore him two children,

a daughter Tullia and a son Marcus. She aided him considerably in his exile, even risking personal harm. He divorced her (in an act that was much criticized) in 47/6 and married his young ward, Publilia.

Tigranes II King of Armenia and surrounding territories (reigned *c.* 95–*c.* 56). He was the son-in-law and ally of Mithridates. Lucius Lucullus defeated him at Tigranocerta (his capital) in 69 and stripped him of Syria, Phoenicia, Cilicia, Galatia and Sophene. Lucullus, however, experienced several mutinies in his army and Tigranes took advantage of his troubles to regain some territory. After Lucullus was replaced by Pompey, Tigranes surrendered to Pompey in 66 (Tigranes' son had defected to Pompey) and was given back Armenia as his kingdom, having agreed to pay a huge penalty and cede his other territories.

Tullia Cicero's only and beloved daughter; her birth date is uncertain. She married Gaius Piso Frugi in 63 or 62. On his death she married Crassipes; they divorced *c.* 52. She and her mother arranged her final marriage to the Caesarian, Dolabella, while Cicero was governing Cilicia in 51–50. It was not a happy marriage and it appears that Dolabella was frequently unfaithful. She died as a result of complications after childbirth in 45. Cicero was inconsolable, divorcing his young second wife, Publilia, because he thought she did not mourn Tullia properly.

Glossary of Terms

While I have avoided using Latin terms (except for laws) in this translation, it is useful to know some Latin for various English words in this Glossary, hence their inclusion after some entries.

aedile The second office in the *cursus honorum*; one had to be at least thirty-seven to hold the office. There were four in total, two curule and two plebeian, each with a different responsibility in the city of Rome. They presented public games, the cost of which mainly came from their own pockets.

auspices The interpretation of signs given by birds or weather (such as thunder and lightning). Fifteen (sixteen under Caesar) men made up the college of augurs (Cicero was elected to this college in 53 after the death of Publius Crassus in Parthia); they were considered the authoritative interpreters of the auspices. However, the taking of the auspices or 'watching the skies' for the auspices was normally the responsibility of magistrates, who could use this to disrupt actions in the various elections, assemblies and the Senate.

Bona Dea The 'Good Goddess', an enigmatic goddess who was honoured each year by a December ritual held in the home of the wife of the senior magistrate. Only women could attend and it was restricted to aristocratic women; during the festivities, unwatered wine was drunk but it was called 'milk'. Clodius was charged with profaning the ritual in December 62, when it was being held in Julius Caesar's home. He dressed up as a female entertainer but was quickly unmasked by Aurelia, Caesar's mother. Although it was suspected that he was involved in a relationship with Caesar's wife, Caesar did not move against him or accuse his wife of adultery, but divorced her with the words 'Caesar's wife must be above suspicion.' During his trial for sacrilege, Clodius claimed that he was out of Rome on that night, but Cicero testified that he had seen him in Rome. Clodius was acquitted after phenomenal bribery.

Campus Martius Literally, 'the field of Mars' from its original use as a place to marshal troops. It was a space outside the *pomerium*, inside which no armed forces were allowed, hence commanders waited here before they entered the city in triumph. It was also used for elections.

censor The highest office of the *cursus honorum*; two (normally ex-consuls) were elected for an eighteen-month term every five years by the centuriate assembly. They could expel from the Senate people who could no longer meet the property requirements or were considered morally unfit. Their other main responsibility was to conduct the census of Roman citizens.

centuriate assembly (*comitia centuriata*) This assembly could only be called by magistrates with *imperium*. As it was originally a military assembly, it could gather outside the *pomerium*, usually in the Campus Martius. Every century (there were 193 in total) had one vote, which was determined first by a majority of all the members present. This assembly elected the consuls, praetors and censors, and voted to declare war and to confirm the power of the censors. It was heavily weighted in favour of wealthier citizens, as those in the top census bracket supplied eighty centuries and those in the second twenty. The very lowest class (the *proletarii*) supplied only one century.

century The unit into which the Roman electorate was divided for the purpose of voting in the centuriate assembly.

city praetor (*praetor urbanus*) One of the eight praetors, whose main responsibility was to oversee Rome's courts.

client Rome was organized on the basis of patron–client relationships. A client turned to his or her patron for help with law cases and other issues and provided services in return. Freed slaves were automatically the clients of their ex-masters and whole peoples could be clients of powerful Romans who had some connection with their country or tribe. The more clients one had, the greater the prestige.

consul Two were elected annually; these were Rome's chief civil and military magistrates. There was a minimum age requirement of forty-two, though this rule was broken in the Late Republic to allow both Pompey and Octavian (the future Augustus) to hold office while still under the legal age. In Cicero's time, at least one of the consuls had to be a plebeian. If both consuls remained in Rome, they alternated control month by month. In their year of office, they either served in the city or were, as was frequently necessary, placed in charge of a military campaign. Like praetors, they normally served as governor of a province after their term in office.

Curia The Senate meeting-house, located in the Forum. It was burned down in 52 when it was used as a pyre for Publius Clodius but rebuilt by Faustus Cornelius Sulla. The one that stands today in the Forum is that begun by Caesar and finished under Augustus.

curial assembly (*comitia curiata*) Normally overseen by a consul or praetor (though the pontifex maximus took this role if it was meeting for a religious reason). It was formed of thirty *curiae*: three ancient clan tribes (the Tities, the Ramnes and the Luceres) supplied ten each. Each of these was represented by a lictor. It confirmed the *imperium* of magistrates or their right to take auspices (how necessary this was is problematic) and also confirmed adoptions and some wills. It met on the Capitoline Hill.

cursus honorum The course of various magistracies that were held on the path to the consulship. It ran quaestor–praetor–consul (followed sometimes by censor), though the aedileship could be held (and often was) after being quaestor. A public career could begin by running for tribune of the plebs before being quaestor.

curule magistrates These included the censors, consuls, praetors and curule aediles. They were so called from the curule chair which was one of their symbols of office.

dictator This office, used in times of crisis, spanned a maximum period of only six months (though both Sulla and Julius Caesar held the office for longer). A dictator was nominated by the Senate and appointed by a consul, praetor or *interrex*. While in office, he was all powerful, though he could be prosecuted afterwards.

equestrians (sing. *eques*, pl. *equites*) Often translated as 'knights' because they were originally the group that formed Rome's cavalry. In Cicero's day, however, it was a social and economic class and membership was based upon wealth – to be an equestrian one had to have property worth at least 400,000 sesterces. Traditionally, these have been seen as businessmen (they supplied many who oversaw the collection of Roman taxes, for example), though this is somewhat deceptive. Before they were entitled to enter the Senate as ex-quaestors, even the children of nobility were classed as equestrians.

finest citizens (*optimates*) Not a political party in our sense, though sometimes described as such, this group was basically conservative and aimed at maintaining the authority of the Senate. It was also fiercely hostile to various agrarian laws and to the tribunes Tiberius and Gaius Gracchus. Although this group traditionally only included nobility, Cicero claimed in *In Defence of Sestius* that it included all decent, right-thinking citizens, even down to freedmen.

imperium The supreme power to command legions and to interpret the law and inflict punishment (which included the death penalty). Only consuls, praetors, dictators and the masters of the horse held this power. It was symbolized by the *fasces*, the bundles of rods carried by lictors. When outside Rome, an axe was added to the *fasces*. While operating as governors or as commanders of armies, ex-consuls, ex-praetors and those appointed to special commands had *imperium*. Within Rome, certain limitations were placed on this power – one did not have the right to inflict the death penalty, for example.

interrex (pl. *interreges*) A position that appears to hark back to the days of the Roman monarchy (it literally means 'between the [reign of] kings'). The position was appointed by the Senate from ex-consuls of patrician rank to hold the elections for consul and praetor when the consuls were unable to do so. Each *interrex* held the office for five days in succession.

lictor Someone who accompanied those magistrates who held *imperium*, whether they were inside or outside Rome; the dictator was accompanied by twenty-four lictors, the consuls twelve and praetors six. They carried *fasces* (rods – an axe was added if the magistrate was outside Rome); their primary function was to clear people from a magistrate's path (with the exception of Vestal Virgins and respectable married women) and to symbolize and implement his power to command and punish. A separate group of lictors represented the ancient clan tribes at the curial assembly.

lieutenant (*legatus*) Someone who served on the staff of a commander or governor. While the Senate appointed them, it did so on the recommendation of the commander or governor they were to serve. However, Caesar and Pompey normally appointed their own lieutenants.

man of the people (sing. *popularis,* pl. *populares*) Not a political party, but an individual who (sometimes) aimed at reforms, particularly in the way public land was distributed. The archetypal *populares* were Tiberius and Gaius Gracchus and Gaius Marius. *Populares* used the various assemblies of the people to push through legislation that the Senate was hostile to; closely associated with this group were the tribunes of the plebs. However, many individuals could turn *popularis* to ensure that legislation of theirs was passed if it hit trouble in the Senate. While they are sometimes seen as democratic or left wing, they were not necessarily so; some were genuinely interested in reform, others were simply looking for power and a way to force through legislation.

master of the horse A position unique to and nominated by dictators; he represented a dictator's authority in war or at Rome.

military tribune There were six tribunes for each of Rome's four standing legions, all elected by the tribal assembly and all holding the most senior positions within those legions. The tribunes for any specially raised legion were chosen by the commander.

municipality (*municipium*) A largely self-governing town, originally not of Roman status (i.e., not holding Roman citizenship), but largely incorporated into the Roman state and operating under the umbrella of Roman law, while still retaining some local laws and magistrates. After the Social War (91–87) inhabitants could vote in Roman assemblies and run for office.

new man (*novus homo*) Sometimes used for the first man in a family to enter the Senate; it is more often used in Cicero for someone who was the first in his family to be elected consul.

optimates See *finest citizens*

patrician Thought to be descended from a member of the first Senate that advised Romulus. Initially, patricians alone were allowed to hold the higher public offices; by 394 this right had been lost. Only a patrician could be an *interrex* or hold certain priesthoods.

plebeian Initially meaning the mass of Roman citizens, as distinct from the patrician nobility, but in Cicero's day it included many noble and wealthy families (such as, for example, the Antonii). Only plebeians could be tribunes of the plebs, hence the patrician Publius Clodius had himself adopted so he could run for that office.

pomerium The sacred boundary of Rome; it did not spread over all seven hills but included the Palatine Hill and the Forum. Monarchs and commanders holding *imperium* were forbidden to cross its boundaries; one could also not carry weapons within it.

pontifex maximus Literally, the 'chief priest'; the holder was the high priest of the state and oversaw (among other things) the Vestal Virgins. Originally only held by patricians, after 300 it was also opened to plebeians. In the Late Republic it was an elected position, though only seventeen of the thirty-five tribes voted on it. Caesar was elected to the position in 63 after massive bribery.

popularis/populares See **man of the people**

praetor From 146 to 81 there were six praetors at any one time; Sulla increased their number to eight. During their term in office, their responsibilities were primarily legal and they presided over the various standing courts of Rome. After their term, they were frequently appointed as governors of various provinces.

proscription A list of those classified as enemies of the state and who hence could be legally killed (the Sullan lists contained 4,700 names). After the death of a proscribed person, part of their estate went to the state, the remainder to their killer, hence making proscription a profitable business for all concerned, except the victims and their families. It was primarily used by Sulla in 82/1 and by the second triumvirate in 43/2.

quaestor An annually elected magistracy, with a minimum age of thirty (however, many held the office earlier, due to special exemptions). There were twenty quaestors who were assigned by lot to various duties. Two administered the treasury, others the water and grain supplies. Several also aided consuls and governors abroad. After Sulla, election to this office gave one automatic admission to the Senate following one's year in office.

Rostra The speaker's platform in the Forum, so called from the ships' beaks (*rostra* in Latin) adorning it.

Senate The chief governing body of the Republic. Membership fluctuated between 300 and 600 (under Caesar the number crept up to almost 1,000). It controlled the Republic's finances, foreign relations, the allocation of provinces to various magistrates and the levy of military forces. However, the different assemblies had to confirm certain decisions, such as declaring war or ratifying treaties.

Social War Also called the Italian War, the War with the Allies or the Marsic War; it was fought between Rome and her Italian allies (*socii*, hence the name of the war) from 91 to 87. The war began with the concerns the allies had over the amount of manpower they were asked to supply to the Roman military without receiving an equal share of the profits of empire. As a result, many allies demanded full Roman citizenship; ultimately, after bitter fighting, Rome was forced to concede and expand her citizenship to the allies.

tribal assembly (*comitia tributa*) Made up of thirty-five tribes (four urban, thirty-one rural), there were two forms this assembly took. One form was presided over by a consul or praetor and occasionally the curule aedile; it elected the curule aediles, quaestors, some military tribunes and granted special commissions. In this form it included both plebeians and patricians. In the second form (the *concilium plebis*), it was only open to plebeians and was presided over by a tribune of the plebs or a plebeian aedile. It elected the tribunes of the plebs and plebeian aediles and voted on any laws the tribunes proposed (such as the Manilian law); in this form it normally met in the Forum.

tribune of the plebs Ten were elected annually from the ranks of the plebeians only; their term of office started on 10 December and their persons were sacrosanct. Their primary responsibility was to safeguard the interests of the people; in doing so, their primary weapon was the veto (only dictators and the *interrex* were exempt from this). Sulla stripped them of this power in 81 and also forbade anyone who had held this office from being elected to a higher magistracy. In 75 they were once more allowed to run for higher office, and their right of veto was returned to them under legislation passed by Pompey in 70. They could also introduce legislation to the *concilium plebis* (a subset of the tribal assembly: see above).

tribuni aerarii Literally, 'the tribunes of the treasury'; originally, perhaps, assistants to the quaestors and responsible for paying soldiers. However, in Cicero's day they appear to have been a distinct census class (with incomes close to that of the equestrians) and after 70 comprised a third of juries in criminal cases.

triumph After a significant victory over foreign enemies, a Roman general who held *imperium* could, if voted one by the Senate, hold a triumph. On such occasions the general led his troops (along with any spoils taken in the campaign) into the city through the triumphal gate and ending at the Capitoline Hill.

triumvirate A board of three men, better known as the title given to the unofficial alliance of Caesar, Crassus and Pompey in 60 (though it was not termed such at the time) and the official alliance of Antony, Octavian and Lepidus in 43.

ultimate decree of the Senate (*senatus consultum ultimum*, often abbreviated to SCU) Sometimes translated as the 'final decree of the Senate', it was a type of emergency powers act. It authorized the consuls to 'see to it that the state took no harm'. This meant that consuls need not fear prosecution for their actions during the emergency; however, the limits on their actions were somewhat murky. It was first passed in 121 against Gaius Gracchus, and was later passed in 100 (against Saturninus) and 63 (against the Catilinarian conspirators), in 62, 52 and 49 (the latter against Caesar), and in 48, 43 and 40.

Maps

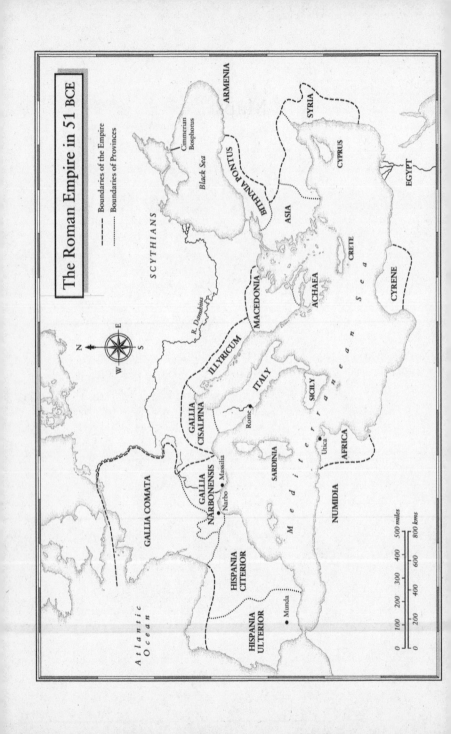

The Roman Empire in 51 BCE

- - - - Boundaries of the Empire
·········· Boundaries of Provinces

ARMENIA

Cimmerian
Bosphorus

Black Sea

SYRIA

BITHYNIA PONTUS

CYPRUS

EGYPT

ASIA

SCYTHIANS

CRETE

R. Danubius

ACHAEA

MACEDONIA

CYRENE

N
W—E
S

ILLYRICUM

Mediterranean Sea

GALLIA
CISALPINA

ITALY

SICILY

Rome

GALLIA
COMATA

SARDINIA

AFRICA

GALLIA
NARBONENSIS

Utica

Massilia

Narbo

NUMIDIA

*Atlantic
Ocean*

HISPANIA
CITERIOR

Munda

HISPANIA
ULTERIOR

0   100   200   300   400   500 miles
0   200   400   600   800 kms

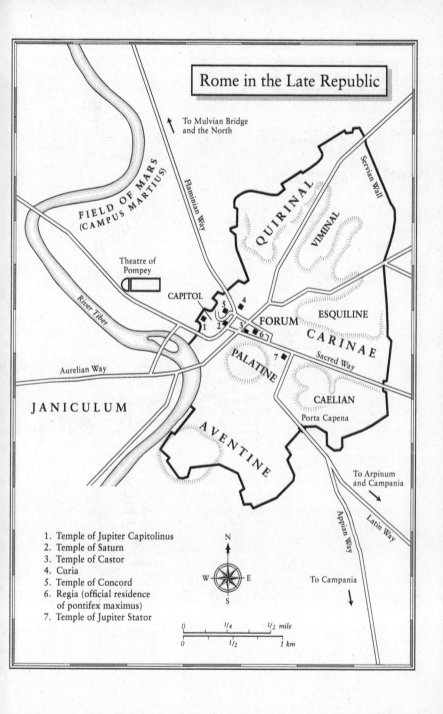

Rome in the Late Republic

To Mulvian Bridge
and the North

FIELD OF MARS
(CAMPUS MARTIUS)

Flaminian Way

QUIRINAL

VIMINAL

Servian Wall

Theatre of
Pompey

River Tiber

CAPITOL

5
4

1 2 3 6 FORUM
7

ESQUILINE

CARINAE

PALATINE

Sacred Way

Aurelian Way

JANICULUM

CAELIAN

Porta Capena

AVENTINE

To Arpinum
and Campania

Latin Way

Appian Way

To Campania

1. Temple of Jupiter Capitolinus
2. Temple of Saturn
3. Temple of Castor
4. Curia
5. Temple of Concord
6. Regia (official residence
   of pontifex maximus)
7. Temple of Jupiter Stator

N
W   E
S

0   1/4   1/2 mile
0   1/2   1 km

Italy and Sicily

PROVINCE OF
GALLIA CISALPINA

Mutina
Aemilian Way
Bononia

R. Rubicon

Luca
Pistoria
Ariminum
Pisae *R. Arno*
Faesulae
Pisaurum

ETRURIA
Volaterrae
Arretium

PICENUM
Ancona

ILLYRICUM

R. Tiber
Flaminian Way

Aurelian Way
Ameria

Adriatic Sea

Corfinium

Rome
Praeneste
Tusculum
Alba
Sora
Bovillae
Arpinum
Antium
Astura

SAMNIUM

Luceria

Formiae

Capua

CAMPANIA
Cumae
Misenum
Pompeii
Baiae
Puteoli
Neapolis

Appian Way

CALABRIA

LUCANIA

Tarentum

Brundisium

Tyrrhenian Sea

BRUTTIUM

Messana

Rhegium

△ *Mt Eryx*
Lilybaeum

PROVINCE OF
SICILY

Ionian Sea

Syracuse

N
W   E
S

0   50   100 miles
0   50   100   150 kms

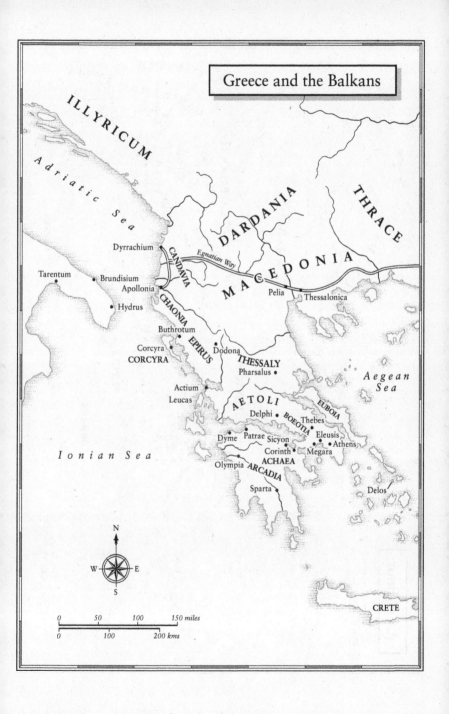

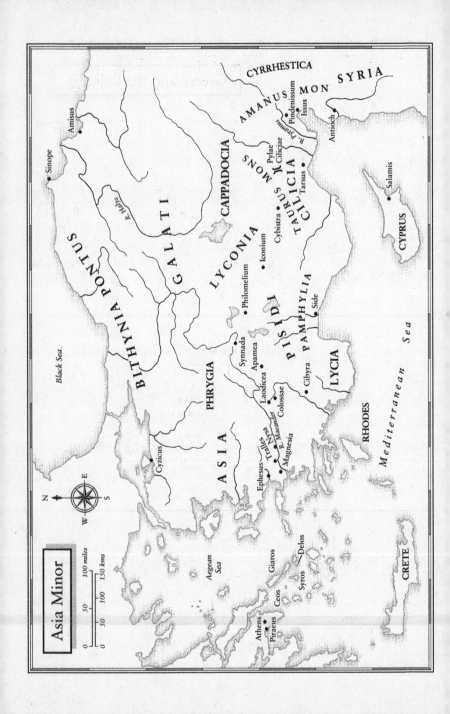

Asia Minor

Notes

NOTES TO *AGAINST VERRES I* (*IN VERREM I*)

1. *juries were drawn ... accused*: Equestrians had once provided the jurors for the extortion court but Sulla transferred control back to the senatorial class in 81. At the time of this speech, Lucius Aurelius Cotta proposed a law to give partial control back to the equestrians. Thus Cicero's opening gambit of representing this trial as a last chance for the Senate to prove itself worthy to hold onto sole authority in this court was very timely.

2. *case against Verres*: His speech, the *divinatio in Caecilium*, is still extant.

3. *consul*: The other consul would be Quintus Caecilius Metellus Creticus, another friend and ally of Verres.

4. *rarely ... cross-questioning*: A text of the speech he had planned to give was circulated later under Hortensius' name (Quintilian, *Institutes of Oratory* 10.1.22); it is hard to know if it was a forgery or actually written by Hortensius himself. In any case, the speech is no longer extant.

5. *class*: Although not a class in the modern sense, the order of the Senate was a distinct group with its own interests. To qualify for membership during this period one needed to run for office (the quaestorship) and to hold a certain amount of property (in the form of land in Italy) – worth at least 400,000 sesterces.

6. *a man ... cancer of Sicily*: The charges match up to Verres' elected positions: as quaestor to Gnaeus Papirius Carbo *c*. 84–82 in Cisalpine Gaul, Verres not only embezzled money but also deserted to the side of Sulla (see further, chapters 34–6); as lieutenant and then proquaestor for Gnaeus Cornelius Dolabella, praetor of Cilicia in 80–79, he tormented Asia; as city praetor in 74 he held responsibility for Rome's courts.

7. *Manius Glabrio*: As city praetor Manius presided over the extortion court.

8. *when I . . . formally indicted him*: The first stage in a Roman trial was for the prosecutor to make a formal accusation of the defendant before the praetor. If the defendant pleaded not guilty, the praetor then set a date for trial.

9. *Brundisium*: The primary departure point for Greece (modern Brindisi).

10. *a senator . . . his defence*: Referring to the Achaean investigation; one source tells us that the unfortunate senator selected was called Oppius, but beyond that we know nothing of him.

11. *original jury . . . challenged*: Juries for trials were selected by lot from a panel of jurors for that year. A certain proportion of those selected for a trial could be challenged by the prosecution and defence; while we do not know how many could be rejected, in the trial of Milo (*Defence of Milo*) eighty-one jurors were selected and the defence and the prosecution rejected fifteen each.

12. *his quaestorship . . . oath*: Like other magistrates, quaestors were normally assigned to their province by lot; each consul usually had one quaestor as his paymaster. As such, it was essential that there be some trust between them. Verres deserted the consul Carbo (a supporter of Marius) and went over to Sulla – with Carbo's paychest.

13. *lieutenant*: Verres was a lieutenant (*legatus*) to Gnaeus Dolabella in Cilicia in 80–79; this was not an elected position, though the Senate had to agree on a commander's selection of such lieutenants. After the death of Dolabella's allotted quaestor, Gaius Malleolus, Verres served as his quaestor and helped him plunder his province before turning evidence against him.

14. *public land*: Land that belonged to the Roman state was rented out to farmers. Verres apparently charged three times the actual rent, scooping off the extra for himself.

15. *our best . . . fleets*: A Roman fleet of seven ships under Cleomenes was destroyed by pirates; in one of his speeches against Verres, not delivered in court but published, Cicero blames this elsewhere on the condition of the crews, some of whom had bought their discharge from Verres, while others were weak from hunger (*Against Verres* V.160–62).

16. *restored to Sicilian communities*: Marcus Claudius Marcellus had erected statues of himself and his sons in Syracuse. After his conquest of Carthage in 146, Scipio Africanus returned some of the loot the Carthaginians had plundered from Sicily.

17. *smeared on a tablet*: To ensure jurors lived up to their side of the bargain, the briber or his agents watched to see if they made a mark signalling this.

18. *after the consular elections*: In July 70.

19. *arch of Fabius*: On the Sacred Way, along one route into the Forum.

20. *praetors-elect ... lot*: The various duties of the praetors were assigned by drawing lots; Marcus Metellus was the brother of the consul-elect and a friend of Verres.

21. *'by fate'*: Cicero echoes a famous line by the Roman poet Naevius, 'the Metelli become consuls at Rome by fate.' For this, one of the consuls of 206, Quintus Metellus, reportedly had him thrown into prison after saying (also in verse), 'the Metelli shall do harm to Naevius the poet.' Doubtless, this was a wittier retort in the third century.

22. *Gaius Junius' court*: As praetor for 74, Junius presided over the trial of Oppianicus for attempting to poison Aulus Cluentius. Oppianicus was convicted but not before both prosecution and defence had used such blatant bribery that the 'Junian' trial became proverbial for a crooked ruling. (Cicero later went on to defend Cluentius, one of the prosecutors in the trial of Oppianicus, for poisoning Oppianicus while he was in exile.)

23. *will be tribunes of the plebs*: Their term of office would begin in mid-December. Quintus Cornificius was later to run for the consulship in 63, the same year as Cicero.

24. *magistracy*: We are unsure what magistracy Publius Sulpicius was to hold.

25. *Lucius Cassius*: Although we are unclear of the precise identity of this man, he appears connected with Lucius Cassius Longinus, known for his impartiality and rigour when presiding over a trial. His phrase 'who benefited?' (*cui bono?*) is a favourite of Cicero, and a Cassian jury appears to have been a proverbially strict and impartial one. Cassius also introduced the secret ballot in Rome in 138, rather optimistically hoping to prevent bribery and corruption in the elections.

26. *at one o'clock*: Eight hours into the Roman day (which began at sunrise); the court would conclude its day in two hours.

27. *votive games*: Special games held to fulfil a specific vow as opposed to games that were held on a regularly scheduled basis; these were to celebrate Pompey's victory over Sertorius in Spain and would last from 16 August to 1 September. After that the Roman Games (*ludi Romani*) would take place (Cicero appears to be folding in with these the Great Games, the *ludi Magni*).

Including 2–4 September as holidays would mean the trial would be postponed for thirty-six days.

28.   *Victory Games*: Established by Sulla in 82 to commemorate his victory over the Samnites at the Colline Gate; these games were held annually on 27 October.

29.   *Plebeian Games*: Held from 4 to 17 November, these games celebrated the reconciliation between the plebs and the patricians after the first secession of the plebs to the Mons Sacer in 494.

30.   *Metellus as praetor . . . he is not*: As juror Metellus would be on his oath and would, besides, only have charge of one voting tablet – his own. As praetor his oath of office would be considered sufficient and he would not be sworn in for this particular case; for good measure Cicero suggests Metellus would interfere with the voting tablets.

31.   *time . . . lawfully entitled to*: A period of twenty days.

32.   *first stage*: Roman trials of this seriousness were divided into two parts. First the prosecutor and the defendant laid their cases before the court; then there was an adjournment of a day; the prosecutor could then respond to the defendant's case (his 'second action') and the defendant could answer once more. Cicero planned to cut short his speech and get the first stage of the trial over before the games; as it turned out, Verres' flight ensured he never had to take part in a second, although he later circulated the speeches that would have formed part of it.

33.   *my youth*: Cicero was thirty-six, Hortensius eight years older.

34.   *spectacle . . . aedile*: One of the jobs of the aedile was to provide public games, most of which he paid for out of his pocket.

35.   *ten years*: Actually eleven, since Sulla had transferred them into senatorial control in 81.

36.   *fifty years*: In fact forty-one, as the courts had been transferred to the equestrians by a law of Gaius Gracchus in 123.

37.   *Quintus Calidius*: City praetor in 79, he was convicted in 77 for extortion in Spain. He apparently thanked the jury for not selling him out for less than a decent price. Of the other individuals Cicero mentions here we know little, beyond that they were part of the jury that took prodigious bribes in the trial of Oppianicus.

38.   *a senator . . . defendant*: Gaius Aelius Staienus, who was both bribed by the prosecutor and the bribery agent for the defendant.

39.   *votes . . . colours*: The different colours were meant to ensure that bribe payers knew the deal had been honoured.

40.   *restore the . . . tribunes*: Sulla had removed the tribunes' powers of veto; in 78 Marcus Aemilius Lepidus unsuccessfully tried to

restore it but it was not until 70 that Pompey, as consul, finally did so.

41. *Pompey . . . outside the city*: Pompey was waiting outside the city until he was awarded his triumph for his victory over Sertorius.

42. *the law your father passed*: Glabrio's father was the author of a law on extortion which was passed in 101.

43. *grandfather*: The Mucius Scaevola Cicero next mentions; he was consul in 133 and pontifex maximus in 123.

44. *father-in-law Scaurus*: Glabrio had been married to Aemilia, daughter of Marcus Aemilius Scaurus, consul in 117 and 115; they later divorced and she married Pompey.

45. *summon them in a group . . . novel move*: Individuals were usually bribed one by one; Hortensius was planning on bribing the Sicilians in one fell swoop.

46. *it has been done before . . . leading citizens of our community*: In the 90s, by the brothers Lucius Licinius Lucullus (consul in 74; at this period he was fighting in Asia) and Marcus Terentius Varro Lucullus (consul) when they prosecuted either an augur Servilius or Lucius Cotta. The exact charge and the outcome of the trial are uncertain.

NOTES TO *FOR THE MANILIAN LAW* (*PRO LEGE MANILIA* OR *DE IMPERIO GNAEI POMPEI ORATIO*)

1. *Rostra*: The raised speaker's platform in the Forum; it took its name from the ships' beaks that decorated it, which had come from a victory over Antium in 338 BCE. It was in a slightly different location from the one that can now be seen in the Forum.

2. *this place*: The Rostra.

3. *when the postponement . . . candidates*: In 67; Cicero had received the votes of all the centuries and was thus the first to be declared elected. However, before the rest of the praetors could be announced, the elections were halted, perhaps because of street fighting. (Electoral violence was a constant problem in Rome of the Late Republic.)

4. *through provocation*: Tigranes' territory had been invaded by Lucullus while pursuing Mithridates.

5. *Roman equestrians . . . class*: Cicero had been born to the order

of equestrians and throughout his career he was at pains to maintain their support.

6. *Bithynia*: It had become a Roman province in 75 when Nicomedes III left it to Rome in his will.

7. *kingdom of Ariobarzanes*: I.e., Cappadocia, seized by Mithridates in the events which led up to the recall of Lucullus.

8. *successor*: Manius Acilius Glabrio, one of the consuls for 67; he was the praetor who had presided over the trial of Verres.

9. *first war with Mithridates*: Cicero here deliberately skips over the campaign of Murena (the Second Mithridatic War).

10. *his crime*: The massacre of Romans and Italians mentioned in the Introduction.

11. *situation . . . recalled Murena*: In 83. Cicero is being rather polite here: this was not an official recall as Sulla had been declared an enemy of the state at the time; rather, he returned to continue his struggle with Marius and his supporters. Sulla celebrated his triumph in 81 after the end of the civil war.

12. *war on two fronts*: Some Marian supporters, particularly Sertorius and Perpenna, kept up the struggle against Sulla in Spain even after the defeat of the Marian side in Italy. Sertorius was not defeated until 72, after ten years of war.

13. *addressed . . . disrespectfully*: In 146, four Roman ambassadors attending a meeting of the Achaean League which was taking place in Corinth were shouted down and driven from the meeting by a mob. Several sources say they were beaten or imprisoned, but for rhetorical purposes Cicero selects the mildest version of the story.

14. *an ambassador*: Manius Aquilius (co-consul with Marius in 101) was primarily responsible for the outbreak of the First Mithridatic War by urging Nicomedes of Bithynia to invade Pontus. He was defeated by Mithridates in 88 and was tied to a donkey and paraded through the streets. According to one version, he was finally killed by having molten gold poured down his throat.

15. *driven out of his kingdom*: Ariobarzanes, whom the Romans had established as king of Cappadocia, was particularly unfortunate in being driven out of his kingdom three times.

16. *a demand . . . someone else*: As Glabrio and Lucullus were still operating in the region, anyone who requested a change of generals would fear reprisals from them.

17. *one man . . . close to the action*: Pompey was currently in Cilicia, on the south coast of Asia Minor, having finished his war with the pirates.

18. *those who pay taxes ... armies are on their doorstep*: Rome's taxes were not collected by the state; rather, the right to collect was bid for by corporations of equestrians, who then dispatched staff (frequently slaves) to the provinces to do the collecting. The Latin term for those who collected (or 'farmed') taxes was *publicani*.

19. *Forum ... banking system*: The Forum was the centre of Rome's business community and the location of bankers' offices.

20. *Cyzicus*: An 'island' in the Propontis (now the Sea of Marmara, between the Aegean and Euxine seas) which was connected to the mainland by an isthmus. Lucullus raised the siege in 74 and Cyzicus was later made a 'free community' (one which did not have to pay taxes) for its loyalty during this war.

21. *By simply turning up ... Amisus*: In reality, Lucullus took almost two years to subdue Pontus; Sinope (modern Sinop, Turkey; Mithridates' birthplace) and Amisus (modern Samsun, Turkey) were particularly difficult to defeat.

22. *without ... drawing on our taxes*: In other words, Lucullus did not force the provincials to make contributions.

23. *Medea ... fled from Pontus*: Medea aided Jason in his quest for the Golden Fleece by betraying its owner and her father, King Aeetes of Colchis (this region was right beside Pontus and is sometimes seen as part of it). When she fled the kingdom with Jason, Aeetes followed in hot pursuit; she slowed his progress by dismembering her younger brother and scattering his body in the sea.

24. *Mithridates ... gold and silver*: According to one story, Mithridates scattered bags of gold behind him as he fled to delay the pursuit; according to another, he escaped when his pursuers stopped to plunder a mule laden with gold.

25. *revered shrine*: It remains uncertain what shrine is meant here, but given how often the Romans stripped shrines and temples and brought their various statues and ornaments back to Rome, it was not an unreasonable fear.

26. *I shall say no more ... here*: Cicero tactfully skips over the mutiny in Lucullus' army.

27. *defeat ... messenger from the battle*: The army of Triarius, one of Lucullus' lieutenants, was almost wiped out at Ziela (modern Zile, Turkey) in 67. Lucullus, who was advancing from the other direction, first heard the news of the defeat from natives of the region.

28. *He was tutored ... enemy*: Pompey (106–48) began his military career at the age of seventeen when he joined his father's army to

fight in the Social War; he served again under his father during the First Civil War of Marius and Sulla in 87. In 83 he became a commander when he raised three legions in his home region of Picenum (east of the Apennines on the Adriatic Sea) to fight against Marius the Younger.

29. *Sicily ... Africa*: Sulla sent Pompey to Sicily in 82, where he met with no opposition and personally superintended the execution of the consul Gnaeus Papirius Carbo, one of the Marian officers there. From here he went to Africa in 81 and defeated the Marian general Gnaeus Domitius Ahenobarbus at Utica (modern Utique, Tunisia).

30. *Spain ... enemies*: From 76 to 72 Pompey fought Marian forces under Sertorius and Perpenna in Spain.

31. *slave war ... when he arrived*: On his way back from Spain, Pompey encountered and slaughtered 5,000 slaves from the army of Spartacus fleeing from the battle in Lucania that had wiped out the rest of the slave army. Here, Cicero is extremely ungenerous with Marcus Licinius Crassus, who was responsible for that defeat; given the dislike between Crassus and Cicero, that is not surprising.

32. *In recent years ...* : Cicero now turns to Pompey's war with the pirates; from small beginnings in Cilicia, these had spread to control the Mediterranean with a fleet of 1,000 ships. Before their defeat they had captured 400 towns, various Roman officials and citizens (one of whom was Julius Caesar) and even sailed to Ostia (Rome's port) to destroy the fleet there (chapter 33) and plunder and burn the town.

33. *Brundisium*: The chief port of departure from Italy when going to Greece or further east (modern Brindisi).

34. *twelve lictors*: Praetors were accompanied by two lictors in Rome, six while in the provinces; Plutarch gives the names of the praetors they were attending as Sextilius and Vellinus (*Life of Pompey* 24).

35. *children ... abducted ... by pirates*: Cicero exaggerates slightly for rhetorical effect; the daughter of Marcus Antonius, who had defeated the pirates in 103, was captured while she was walking in the grounds of his villa in Misenum (modern Miseno, at the north of the Bay of Naples).

36. *banks of the Mediterranean*: The straits of Gibraltar.

37. *added ... Roman people*: An exaggeration: while the eastern portion of Cilicia had been a Roman province since 102, the western was a stronghold of the pirates.

38. *Cretans ... hostages*: Quintus Metellus Pius Creticus had been

waging war against the Cretans for two years and was on the verge of defeating them; they sent ambassadors to Pompey in Pamphylia, looking for better terms of surrender. Pompey appealed to a clause in the *lex Gabinia* which granted him authority of a distance of 50 miles inland from the sea, thus also covering Crete, hoping to steal the victory from Metellus. Metellus then appealed to the Senate, which granted him a triumph.

39. *towns of Roman citizens*: Roman citizenship had been widely granted to cities of Italy during 90 and 89 under the *lex Julia* and the *lex Plautia Papiria*; as Italy saw a great deal of fighting between Marian and Sullan factions during the 80s, many new-minted citizens were affected.

40. *Crete . . . surrender to him*: See chapter 35 above.

41. *an ambassador to Pompey*: All our other sources insist that it was Sertorius with whom Mithridates was negotiating (as Cicero admitted earlier: chapter 9). It is possible that Pompey caught a spy who saved himself by claiming that he had been sent by Mithridates to negotiate with him.

42. *Maximus . . . Scipio*: Quintus Fabius Maximus the Delayer (Cunctator) and Marcus Claudius Marcellus were generals in the Second Punic War. Scipio could either be Scipio the Elder (who defeated Hannibal in the final battle of the Punic War, in Zama, in 202) or Scipio the Younger (who destroyed Carthage in the Third Punic War, 149–146).

43. *Catulus . . . Hortensius*: Q. Lutatius Catulus, consul in 78, was now the most senior member of the Senate; Q. Hortensius was consul in 69 (and Cicero's opponent in the trial of Verres).

44. *against his law . . . platform*: Bills had to be posted up in a public space at least seventeen days before the meeting of the assembly which was to vote on a bill. During this time, any magistrate might call together a public meeting to address the people on the issue.

45. *Antiochus . . . Perseus*: Antiochus 'the Great' was king of Syria and was defeated by Scipio in the battle of Magnesia in 190; Perseus/Perses, king of Macedonia, was defeated by Aemilius Paulus in 168. In the latter case, the Roman fleet did not actually see much action and his fleet surrendered to the admiral Gnaeus Octavius at Samothrace without engaging him.

46. *Pompey's lieutenant . . . that position*: Lieutenants were chosen by the Senate but it normally voted for the commander's choice. Under the *lex Gabinia*, Pompey had the right to choose his own commander; however, Gabinius was still serving as tribune of

the plebs in 67, and the *lex Licinia* and the second *lex Aebutia* prohibited anyone who had proposed a special commission such as Pompey's from holding any office under that commission. All this meant that Gabinius' lieutenantship was illegal on several grounds.

47. *Falcidius . . . Lentulus*: We know nothing more of these tribunes; Gnaeus Lentulus is not the same as the Lentulus mentioned in chapter 68.

48. *appointment before the Senate*: As praetor, Cicero could bring a motion before the Senate. However, anyone who held the same or a higher office (such as the consuls) could veto the introduction of his motion. Additionally, the consuls had the right to issue a decree that declared any particular motion out of order and could block it not only for a particular meeting but for the entire year. Finally, even if the Senate approved something, the tribunes of the plebs had the right to veto anything they considered not in the interest of the people; this is the 'veto' that Cicero refers to next.

49. *Scipio . . . empire faced*: Scipio Aemilianus Africanus (also known as Scipio the Younger) was elected consul in 146 although he was below the legal age – he had, in fact, been standing for aedile; in that year he captured and destroyed Carthage. In 133 (in spite of a law of 150 which ruled that no one should be consul twice), he was again consul for the Spanish War which ended with his capture of Numantia.

50. *war with . . . Teutoni*: Marius' campaigns took place forty years before the date of this speech, despite Cicero's assertion that this was 'not long ago'.

51. *Sicily and Africa*: Pompey was sent to Sicily and Africa by Sulla when he was twenty-four; this was six years younger than the legal age to run for quaestor, the office that gave one admittance to the Senate.

52. *a Roman triumph*: Triumphs were awarded to those with *imperium*, the power to command legions (consuls, praetors, dictators, proconsuls and propraetors). Pompey had two triumphs, in 81 and 71, before he had held *any* magistracy.

53. *two consuls*: The consuls for 77 were Mamercus Aemilius Lepidus and Decimus Junius Brutus; both refused command of the war in Spain.

54. *consul . . . magistracy*: Pompey was thirty-five when he was first elected consul; the legal minimum age was forty-two. Consuls were also legally obliged to have first held the quaestorship and praetorship – neither of which Pompey had held. The lowest

curule magistracy was the curule aedileship; to run for that one had to be thirty-six.

55. *commander ... tribune*: Pompey had twenty-four lieutenants assigned to him; there were six military tribunes to each legion.

56. *Publius Servilius*: P. Servilius Vatia Isauricus, consul in 79, was given a command against the pirates in 77 and had some important victories against them. He held a triumph for his victories in 75.

57. *Gaius Curio*: C. Scribonius Curio, consul in 76, who as governor of Macedonia from 75 to 73 campaigned against the Thracians and Dardanians.

58. *Gnaeus Lentulus*: Cn. Cornelius Lentulus Clodianus, consul in 72, censor 70; as censor he struck sixty-four senators off the senatorial rolls. He was one of Pompey's lieutenants in the war with the pirates but had returned to lend his support to the passing of this law.

59. *Gaius Cassius*: C. Cassius Longinus Varus, consul in 73, was defeated by Spartacus in 72.

60. *once more ... in command*: A similarly huge crowd had gathered to vote on the *lex Gabinia* of the previous year which had given Pompey the command of the war with the pirates.

NOTES TO THE *SECOND SPEECH ON THE AGRARIAN LAW OF RULLUS* (*DE LEGE AGRARIA II CONTRA RULLUM*)

1. *models*: Cicero is referring to the *imagines*, the wax death-masks of ancestors who had achieved high public office; these were displayed in the house and also used in funerals to show the ancestry and achievements of the family. As the first person in his family to hold such office, Cicero had no death-masks on show.

2. *first ... within living memory*: The last new man before Cicero to hold the consulship was Gaius Caelius Calvus in 94; thus Cicero was the first man to achieve this in thirty years, an achievement for which he was justifiably proud.

3. *legal minimum age*: To hold the position of consul one had to be forty-two.

4. *we ... consuls*: Cicero's co-consul was Gaius Antonius Hybrida.

5. *annulments ... convicted*: Referring to calls for the restoration to full civic rights of the children of those proscribed by Sulla.

6. *two very distinguished ... Romans ... Republic*: Cicero's

positive attitude towards the Gracchi and their agrarian laws is extremely atypical of him; normally he praises those who brought them down.

7. *tribunes of the plebs*: Only the names of a few of these, besides Rullus, are known. One, Lucius Caecilius Rufus, opposed the bill. Two others (Titus Ampius Balbus and Titus Labienus) were Pompey's men; their attitude towards the bill is not known.

8. *hair ... full beard*: Romans of this period did not keep their hair or beards long (most were clean shaven) and to do so was considered slovenly. Rullus may have wanted to appear sterner and more like long past generations; his outfit and hair also resembles that of defendants in criminal trials, who dressed like suppliants to the jury to attract the maximum amount of pity.

9. *I ordered ... a copy of it*: Laws were posted publicly and copies were not necessarily distributed; frequently, interested persons had to have the law copied down or go and read it themselves.

10. *passed the law ... one of the ten*: There were thirty-five tribes in total; it is not clear why Rullus proposed that only seventeen of them should vote on the membership of the board; it is possible that Cicero is right and the intent was to ensure that bribery could be more effectively focused on a few tribes, as in this situation one could concentrate money on only nine of them.

11. *deprive the entire Roman people of their votes ... lots*: As the seventeen voting tribes would themselves be selected by lot.

12. *Domitius*: Gnaeus Domitius Ahenobarbus was tribune in 104; when he was not chosen for a priesthood his father had previously held, he passed a law transferring the election of members of the four major priestly colleges to seventeen tribes selected by lot. In 103 he was elected to the position of pontifex maximus.

13. *a noble*: If Rullus was a noble, he must have been descended from the plebeian Servilii Gemini and been distantly related to the eminent ex-consul Publius Servilius Vatia Isauricus.

14. *notorious men*: Presumably notorious for bribery.

15. *forbid the person ... commissions*: Cicero had previously called this unjust at *For the Manilian Law* 57–8, arguing that Gabinius should be allowed to be one of Pompey's lieutenants despite having proposed the law that gave Pompey command of the war against the pirates.

16. *one man alone ... every nation*: A reference to the decision to appoint Pompey to command the war against the pirates and the last stages of the Third Mithridatic War (see *For the Manilian Law* for more on this command).

17. *declare . . . in person*: A Roman citizen could declare their candidacy for any magistracy through friends, but had to be in Rome for the day of the elections; Rullus' law made it necessary to declare your intention to run in person. As Pompey was currently in Asia, this would be impossible for him.

18. *lex curiata*: Such a law could only be passed by the curial assembly, at which the plebs could not vote. These laws were normally passed to confirm a senatorial decree and confirmed or rejected what the Senate had already decided, rather than making policy or laws of their own. A *lex curiata* was necessary to confer on a dictator, the consuls and other magistracies the right to command (*imperium*).

19. *They made sure . . . same men*: Cicero's point here is rather obscure (it is possible this section is corrupt and was clearer once). The censors, for one, did not appear to face a second election. The *lex curiata* appears to have either granted *imperium* to certain magistrates or possibly granted them the right to take the auspices; at this assembly the lictors represented the tribes. We have no record of any lictor ever using this opportunity to reject these rights.

20. *people or the plebs*: While the people as a group included both plebeians and patricians, the plebs excluded patricians.

21. *commands the praetor*: A tribune of the plebs could not issue commands to a praetor or any other magistrate that had the right to take auspices. He could only use his veto to block them.

22. *assembly*: A reference to the curial assembly where the people were represented by lictors.

23. *sacred chickens*: The Romans consulted bird signs of all sorts; one way to see if the gods approved of something (such as the establishment of a colony) was to feed the sacred chickens a particular type of grain. Their reaction showed whether the gods approved or not. Besides the Gracchan land law and this law, the sacred chickens are only testified in the Republican period for commanders of the army; however, it is possible they were assigned to other magistrates. Perhaps, not unnaturally, commanders could grow impatient with their reluctance to eat in an auspicious manner. During the First Punic War, Publius Claudius Pulcher tossed the chickens over the side of his ship in frustration, with the words 'if they will not eat, let them drink'. He then suffered a horrible defeat at the battle of Drepana; on his return to Rome he was prosecuted for sacrilege and exiled. Thus it was that the sacred chickens got their vengeance.

24. *lex Sempronia*: The agrarian law of Tiberius Gracchus of 133.

25. *Ligurians*: The people of Liguria, a region in the northwest of Italy.

26. *a Capuan*: Capua was one of the major cities of Campania. During the Second Punic War, Capua defected to Hannibal after the battle of Cannae in 216; first, however, it seems to have promised to retain its alliance with Rome if a Capuan was made one of the consuls. A very prosperous city, it became proverbial in Rome for luxury.

27. *decurions*: Members of local senates.

28. *Vatican ... fertile plains*: The Vatican was a district on the west bank of the River Tiber; like the Pupinian region, also near Rome, it was unhealthy and infertile.

29. *Veii ... Nuceria*: Cicero here lists a number of Latin towns and compares them with a number of major cities in the Greek-speaking south of Italy.

30. *Brutus' crime*: The father of Marcus Brutus, the assassin of Caesar, Marcus Junius Brutus, was tribune in 83 and attempted to place a Roman colony at Capua.

31. *orders it*: The tribunes of the plebs could order any magistrate except a dictator to be imprisoned.

NOTES TO THE *FIRST AND SECOND CATILINARIANS (IN CATILINAM I–II)*

Catilinarian I

1. *Ahala killing ... with his own hand*: Ahala killed the plebeian Spurius Maelius in 440 after he was accused of selling grain cheaply in a time of shortage as a means to gain political power. For more on both see Glossary of Names.

2. *Opimius ... no harm*: Opimius was consul in 121, a time of great chaos in Rome caused by Gaius Gracchus' attempted reforms. The Senate passed its ultimate decree; this is the first record of its usage, though it was to be used more frequently thereafter. Opimius was later charged with killing Roman citizens without trial but was acquitted; Cicero was not so lucky.

3. *Marcus Fulvius*: A supporter of Gaius Gracchus, he was consul in 125 and then, unusually, tribune of the plebs in 122; his sons were killed with him.

4. *Saturninus*: An ally of Marius, who in 100 had arranged for his mob to beat to death Gaius Memmius, a candidate for consul.

5. *twentieth day*: A slight exaggeration; using the Roman inclusive

method of counting it was only nineteen days since the decree had been passed on 19 October.

6. *a private residence*: The house of Marcus Porcius Laeca; this setting and the meeting also crop up later in the speech (chapters 8 and 13). Laeca was a senator and one of those convicted for his role in the conspiracy.

7. *I said in the Senate*: This speech was never published.

8. *two equestrians*: Lucius Vargunteius and Gaius Cornelius.

9. *those you had sent . . . early in the morning*: A reference to the *salutatio*, the morning visit paid to great (and sometimes not so great) men by their clients or those seeking favours from them.

10. *Jupiter Stator*: 'Jupiter the Stayer', the aspect of Jupiter responsible for stopping soldiers from fleeing the battlefield; Romulus had vowed a temple to the god in return for his aid in helping his soldiers in a retreat from the Sabines in a critical battle in the region of the Forum. Cicero had convened the Senate in his temple and took advantage of the location to suggest a new identity for the god as a guardian of the city, and at this point of the speech to use his statue to good advantage.

11. *my own destruction . . . downfall*: If Cicero died his co-consul Antonius would be sole consul; it would be up to him to decide whether to hold elections for a replacement. Given Antonius' ties to Catiline, Cicero subtly suggests that he would hold elections at which Catiline would be chosen as his replacement.

12. *What personal disgrace . . . :* Cicero here begins on some of the standard invective charges: sexual misconduct, hatred of family, wasting one's patrimony, plundering private and public property. The entire speech, of course, makes use of another of these charges: aspiring to tyranny.

13. *crime on . . . crime*: Catiline was accused of having killed his son to please his new wife.

14. *15th of the month*: Debts had to be settled either at the start of a month (the Calends) or the middle (the Ides).

15. *consulship . . . armed*: In 66; a reference to the supposed first Catilinarian conspiracy. It was a criminal offence to carry any weapon in the Campus Martius during an assembly or within the *pomerium* (see Glossary of Terms).

16. *Lepidus . . . suspicion*: Manius Lepidus was consul in 66; it is unclear what connection he had with Catiline.

17. *Metellus*: Q. Metellus Celer, consul in 60.

18. *Marcus Metellus*: We know nothing of this person outside this passage.

19. *Publius Sestius*: At this time, the quaestor of the consul Anton-
     ius, later active in getting Cicero recalled from exile in 57; in 56
     Cicero defended him against a charge of assault (see *In Defence
     of Sestius*).
20. *Marcus Marcellus*: Consul in 51; afterwards he was a bitter
     opponent of Caesar's.
21. *Forum Aurelium*: A small town in Etruria on the Aurelian Way;
     its route was along the coast of Etruria to Pisae (modern Pisa).
22. *silver eagle*: Catiline had apparently set up a silver eagle (a
     legionary standard) as a talisman for future military success; it
     may have been the same as that which Marius kept with him on
     his campaigns.
23. *at such a young age*: Cicero ran for every office at the youngest
     possible age – and was elected in every instance.
24. *tribunal . . . city praetor*: Located in or near the Forum.
25. *Jupiter . . . established . . . as this city*: Traditionally, the temple
     of Jupiter Stator was thought to have been vowed by Romulus
     during the war with the Sabines; however, it was not actually
     built until 294.

Catilinarian II

1.   *the Curia*: The official Senate meeting-house, although the Sen-
     ate often met elsewhere.
2.   *boy's toga*: A toga with a purple border (*toga praetexta*; like that
     of the magistrates) which was worn until the age of sixteen.
3.   *Tongilius . . . Publicius . . . Minucius*: These men are otherwise
     unknown.
4.   *Picenum and Gaul*: Picenum was a region east of the Apennines
     on the Adriatic Sea; it was the birthplace and stronghold of Pom-
     pey the Great. By Gaul here Cicero means Cisalpine Gaul.
5.   *praetor's edict*: Used to collect the bail for debts that they had
     forfeited, hence Cicero's 'joke'.
6.   *purple*: A purple-bordered toga was restricted to magistrates and
     ex-magistrates.
7.   *the night before last*: 6 November, when the conspirators met at
     Laeca's house.
8.   *Aurelian Way*: It ran along the west coast of Italy.
9.   *slave's part . . . love*: In Roman sexual relations it was critical for
     free men to play the active part; this was particularly so in homo-
     sexual relations, where by becoming the passive partner a man
     was thought to play a slavish or effeminized, inferior role.

10. *one man*: I.e., Pompey.

11. *rods ... axes*: The *fasces* (rods) and *secures* (axes) were carried by lictors in attendance on senior magistrates, like the consul. By using these symbols Catiline was trying to claim the legitimacy of that position and the power associated with it.

12. *Massilia*: A Greek colony popular with exiles (modern Marseilles); both Verres and Milo spent their exiles there.

13. *cancellation of debts*: One of Catiline's rallying cries was *novae tabulae*, 'new account books' or 'the cancellation of debts'; it remained an appealing promise over the years.

14. *they must raise up Sulla from the dead*: I.e., they must have more proscriptions and civil war, as occurred under Sulla.

15. *prison cannot hold them all*: At this point, Rome only had one prison, on the Capitoline Hill; one section could be used for execution and the other for very temporary custody during a trial. It was later used for the execution of some of the Catilinarians.

16. *slick ... togas*: Any elaborate attention to one's appearance could mark one out as effeminate.

17. *on these nights*: I.e., cold January nights. This speech was delivered in November; however, because of issues in the Roman calendar which caused it to run far behind until the reforms of Julius Caesar, the true date was in early January.

18. *gladiators ... by my authority*: Another source, Sallust (*Catilinarian Conspiracy* 30.7), tells us that Catiline's supporters were dispersed to various towns.

NOTES TO *IN DEFENCE OF ARCHIAS, THE POET (PRO ARCHIA POETA)*

1. *Magna Graecia*: This Greek-speaking region of Greek colonies covered much of the southern half of Italy.

2. *my natural ability ... little time on*: See General Introduction, Cicero's Life.

3. *Aulus Licinius*: Cicero deliberately introduces the defendant using his Roman name and is careful to use it frequently throughout the trial.

4. *public court*: There was not a distinction between courts that the public could attend and those they could not; public courts dealt with offences which were thought to harm the community as a whole, while private ones dealt with those that only harmed individuals.

5. *praetor*: Cicero's brother, Quintus.

6. *Antioch*: The capital of Syria and for a long time the second most important city in the East after Alexandria; it suffered greatly during the Mithridatic Wars and from attacks by the Parthians.

7. *Tarentum ... Neapolis*: The principal cities of Magna Graecia, modern Taranto, Locri, Reggio di Calabria and Naples.

8. *came to Rome ... Catulus*: In 102; Gaius Marius was then holding his third consulship. That year would see his victory over the Teutones, 101 his victory over the Cimbri (both were northern tribes that threatened Rome). Quintus Lutatius Catulus aided in the victory over the Cimbri and was far more interested in the literary arts than Marius, something which Cicero later acknowledges.

9. *boy's toga*: As a non-Roman, Archias would not have been entitled to wear one so this is a deliberate attempt by Cicero to make Archias seem more Roman.

10. *Lucullan ... home*: The Luculli were an important plebeian family; at this time its most important members were Lucius Licinius Lucullus and his two sons. The father was city praetor in 104 and governed in Sicily during a slave revolt (which he failed to quash). On his return, he was convicted of extortion and exiled. The elder son, also called by the same name, had considerable military success, especially over Mithridates; this did not stop him losing his command in that war to Pompey at Cicero's urging. See *On the Manilian Law*.

11. *Numidicus Metellus*: Consul in 109; he lost his command of the war with the Numidian king Jugurtha to his subordinate Marius, who engineered his exile in 102. His son was called 'the Loyal' because of his work towards his father's recall and was the praetor before whom Archias registered as a Roman citizen.

12. *Marcus Aemilius*: Consul in 115, censor 109, he built the Aemilian Way, a road in northern Italy that led from Ariminum (modern Rimini) to Placentia (modern Piacenza).

13. *father ... son*: The father was consul in 102 with Marius; his son was an associate of Sulla's.

14. *Lucius Crassus*: Consul in 95 when he and his co-consul Quintus Mucius Scaevola passed a law dealing with illegal aliens in Rome; he was also a famous orator and one of Cicero's objects of fannish devotion.

15. *Heraclea*: The city (modern Policoro) had become allied with Rome in 278 and appears to have been granted very generous rights under that alliance; it was on the way from Sicily to Rome and thus was not an out-of-the-way location for either party.

16. *'Roman citizenship . . . sixty days'*: As a citizen of an allied city Archias had considerable rights under Roman law, but not full citizenship; this law (normally referred to as the *lex Plautia Papiria,* from Silvanus and Carbo's cognomina) gave him that right. It appears that one could declare oneself before any of the six praetors.

17. *Italian War*: Another term for the Social War.

18. *Appius . . . diligence*: Appius Claudius Pulcher and Publius Gabinius Capito were praetors for 89 along with Metellus; Grattius had clearly raised doubts about the honesty of their record-keeping and Cicero responds by insisting that Metellus' oversight kept them (or, at least, their records) honest. Very little is known of Appius but Gabinius was convicted of extortion for his actions as governor of Achaea.

19. *he came to Lucius Lentulus . . . one name*: Lentulus remains otherwise unknown beyond that he was also praetor for 89; nothing is known of the situation Cicero is referring to. Perhaps Metellus, believing that some records had been tampered with, went to him as a colleague or perhaps Lentulus was in charge of forgery cases.

20. *lex Papia*: Proposed by the tribune Gaius Papius in 65, this law was aimed at expelling foreigners from Rome; as it also provided the legal basis for the prosecution of Archias, it must have been used in other cases to prosecute those believed to have falsely claimed Roman status.

21. *with the army . . . Asia*: With the army, not *in* it. Archias was with Lucullus as a companion and not as one of his soldiers during the Third Mithridatic War; Lucullus was also quaestor in Asia during the First Mithridatic War. Grattius must have pointed out Archias' name was missing from the census reports from 89 to 62; Cicero responds by pointing out that as Roman citizens had to appear before the censors in person to be included on the register, Archias could not have appeared on the registers as he was away from Rome.

22. *one before that . . . population*: Lucius Julius Caesar and Publius Licinius Crassus, censors in 89, held the first census after the Social War – or at least they aimed to, because it is clear from Cicero's comments that no census was held.

23. *made several wills*: Romans had a particular fondness for making wills and it was normal for wills to name many individuals as heirs as a sign of respect; however, only Roman citizens were entitled to inherit from Roman citizens. It also appears that only

Roman citizens were entitled to be rewarded by the treasury for particular services on a command such as Lucullus recommended for Archias.

24. *exposed ... your behalf*: An allusion to his role in suppressing the Catilinarian conspiracy in the previous year.

25. *self-controlled*: The ability to control oneself was a primary Roman virtue; it was also a major goal of many philosophical schools, the systematic training that Cicero refers to next.

26. *Africanus*: Scipio Africanus the Younger (185–129); he was friendly with Greek and Roman authors, including the historian Polybius.

27. *Laelius ... Cato the Elder*: Laelius and Furius were both close friends of Scipio. Cato the Elder was, like Cicero, a 'new man'. He often argued against Greek influence on Roman culture, though he was himself clearly familiar with it (and had his son educated in Greek culture). He wrote several early Latin prose works, one on farming (still extant) and an annalistic history of Rome, and was a respected orator.

28. *Roscius*: One of Rome's most famed actors and a friend of several important Romans, including Sulla and Cicero himself. He was responsible for Cicero getting one of his first cases (that speech, *In Defence of Quinctius*, is our first extant Ciceronian speech). Cicero later trained with and defended him (*In Defence of Roscius the Actor*).

29. *Ennius*: Quintus Ennius (239–169) was born in Rudiae, a Greek city of southern Italy; he came to Rome under the patronage of Cato the Elder. He wrote the first Latin poem to use the Greek hexameter, the *Annals*. This poem told the history of the Roman people from the landing of Aeneas in Italy and was highly influential on Virgil's *Aeneid*.

30. *Stones ... singing*: According to myth, wild animals became tame at the sound of the poet Orpheus' voice, while even the stones rolled closer to hear him. The equally mythic poet Amphion was said to have created the walls of the Greek city of Thebes by summoning stones with his voice.

31. *Colophonians ... argue over him*: The Greek poet Homer, author of the *Iliad* and the *Odyssey*, was considered the greatest poet of antiquity; not surprisingly, many places claimed to be his birthplace.

32. *dealt with ... Cimbrian campaign*: Apparently this was Archias' first epic poem on Roman themes.

33. *Themistocles*: An Athenian statesman responsible for the build-

ing of and commanding the Athenian navy against the Persians at Salamis in 480.

34. *Marius . . . accomplishments*: Lucius Plotius Gallus was one of the first people to teach rhetoric in Latin at Rome; he must have also written epic poetry (or possibly just prose works praising Marius); none of his works survive.

35. *Mithridatic War . . . finish*: The Third Mithridatic War was waged between Rome and Mithridates IV, the king of Pontus. (See Introduction to *For the Manilian Law* – a law which placed Pompey in command.) Despite Cicero's words here, Archias probably only covered the war up to that point, rather than finishing by celebrating Lucullus' replacement.

36. *routed . . . Armenians*: In 69 at the battle of Tigranocerta. Lucullus had around 16,000 men; Tigranes, king of Armenia, considerably more (one source gives 200,000). When Tigranes saw Lucullus' force, he apparently said, 'If they are an embassy there are too many of them, if an army there are too few' (Plutarch, *Lucullus* 27).

37. *saved Cyzicus . . . war*: Lucullus raised Mithridates' siege of Cyzicus in 73.

38. *naval battle . . . generals*: In 72 the Roman fleet, under the command of Lucullus' lieutenant Gaius Valerius Triarius, met with Mithridates' fleet near Tenedos, an island near Troy.

39. *Scipio . . . the Elder*: The great general who defeated Hannibal in the Second Punic War. The tomb of the Scipios is still standing, just outside Rome on the Appian Way.

40. *Maximi . . . Fulvii*: All these families had members who appeared in Ennius' *Annals*. Quintus Fabius Maximus the Delayer (Cunctator) and M. Claudius Marcellus were generals in the Second Punic War. M. Fulvius Nobilior, consul in 189, was Ennius' patron and took him on campaign with him against the Aetolians. After his victory, he built a temple to Hercules and the Muses adorned with statues taken from Greece.

41. *chroniclers to record his achievements*: Although we know many of the names of those who accompanied Alexander (Aristobolus, Ptolemy Lagi, Callisthenes, Anaximenes, Onesicritus, Clitarchus and Choerilus), none of their works is extant.

42. *Theophanes*: A Greek historian from Mytilene on the island of Lesbos; he met Pompey during his campaign against Mithridates and came to Rome in 62.

43. *Sulla*: Lucius Cornelius Sulla, the dictator (see Glossary of Names).

44. *Corduba*: The city in Southern Spain (modern Cordoba) on the River Baetis was made a Roman colony (probably) in 152 when it was refounded by Marcus Claudius Marcellus. It was the birthplace of several famous Romans under the empire.

45. *Brutus . . . Accius*: Decimus Junius Brutus was consul in 138; he received the name of Gallaecus for his victory over the Gallaeci, a tribe of northern Spain. The loot from his campaigns funded his building projects. Accius (170?–*c.* 86) was a writer of tragedies and epic poetry.

46. *Fulvius*: See chapter 22 and note 40.

47. *this man . . . a work . . . Republic*: Archias never finished this poem on the Catilinarian conspiracy; Cicero himself had to write an epic poem on the subject. The poem only survives in fragments, not all of them a credit to Cicero's poetic talents.

NOTES TO *ON HIS HOUSE (DE DOMO SUA)*

1. *college of the pontiffs*: There were four religious colleges or organizations. These were, in descending order of importance: the college of pontiffs, the augurs, the quindecemviri and epulones. The pontifical college was presided over by the pontifex maximus, a position which Caesar had held from 63 until his death (the position was elected and for life); members were nearly always senators and were involved in politics like other members of the elite; this was not a sequestered priestly caste.

2. *within 400 miles*: The traditional formula of exile was to forbid one access to 'fire and water' for so many miles around Rome. Some sources for Cicero's exile have 500 miles; one suspects 100 miles either way would hardly have made a difference to his misery.

3. *a client*: Publius Sulla. Cicero was heavily criticized for doing this, particularly because Sulla was charged with having taken part in the Catilinarian conspiracy (*Letters to his Friends* 5.6.2; *Letters to Atticus* 1.13.6, 1.16.10).

4. *Drusus*: Tribune in 91; he was an associate of Lucius Licinius Crassus, the orator.

5. *that disgrace . . . of the Republic*: Clodius.

6. *ceremonial grandeur*: In their presence and their attire.

7. *an honour for . . . Pompey*: A reference to Cicero's proposal that Pompey should be given control over the corn-supply for five years (corn was then in short supply). As Pompey was extremely popular with the people, and this audience was more likely to

find this somewhat problematic, Clodius may have used Cicero's proposal to drive a wedge between Cicero and them.

8. *adoption . . . sacred rites*: Adoption meant the adoptee would no longer perform rites for his original family; the pontiffs had to ensure that this did not mean those rites could no longer be practised because the original family had died out.

9. *senator*: The age for entry into the Senate was thirty-one. Clodius was around forty when he was adopted. While it was usual for Romans to adopt adults rather than children, it was not usual for young men to adopt men roughly double their age.

10. *in the case of . . . Pupius*: Aufidius was praetor in 108 and adopted Gnaeus Aurelius Orestes. Pupius adopted Calpurnius Piso, later consul in 61.

11. *because of your ages . . . the two of you have*: It is unclear what the legal situation was at that time; however, later law required that a man could only adopt someone who was eighteen or more years younger. Cicero manages both to make a legal point and suggest that Clodius and Fonteius were involved in a sexual relationship, which obviously would have been highly improper between father and son.

12. *emancipated . . . adopted him*: The oldest male in a Roman family (the *paterfamilias* or father of the family) had total power of life and death over his children, a power that lasted until he died. However, a father could emancipate his son by selling him in a fictional sale to a third party three times over; after the third sale, the son passed into a quasi-slave relationship with the third party, who could then free him, something which must have happened immediately in Clodius' case.

13. *plebs . . . consul*: At least one of the two consuls had to be a plebeian; there was no requirement for one of them to be a patrician.

14. *priesthood . . . hold one*: In three of the four priestly colleges (note 1), patricians could not outnumber plebeians; it seems likely that as positions opened up, a patrician would follow a patrician, a plebeian a plebeian. However, certain priesthoods, such as the *salii*, were exclusively taken from patrician families.

15. *in a short time . . . priests*: The *rex sacrorum* (King of the Rites), performed certain religious duties that had once been the responsibility of the king. There were fifteen *flamines*, each of which was in charge of the cult of a particular deity; the most important of these was the *flamen dialis*, the priest of Jupiter. The *salii* were the dancing priests of Mars. All of these priesthoods had to be filled by patricians.

16. *Aequimaelium*: In Cicero's day this was a market-place where lambs were sold.

17. *temple of Tellus*: In the Carinae, an area on the Esquiline Hill; the Senate sometimes met there. Tellus was an earth goddess, associated with Ceres. Spurius Cassius was consul three times (502, 493, 486); in the year after his third consulship he was charged with trying to make himself a king and was executed.

18. *name of the place*: Marcus (he is called Vitruvius by Livy 8.19–20) Vaccus' house was on the Palatine Hill; a native of Fundi (modern Fondi), a Volscian town, he led a revolt against Rome in 330.

19. *drove the Gauls back … Capitoline Hill*: In 390. The house of Manlius (see Glossary of Names) was on the site of the temple of Juno Moneta.

20. *Flaccus … Gracchus*: Marcus Fulvius Flaccus, consul in 125, tribune 122, was lynched along with Gaius Gracchus in 121 (see Glossary of Names).

21. *Catulus … portico on the site*: See chapter 114 for more on Catulus' portico.

22. *Piso … Gabinius*: Consuls during 58, the year of Cicero's exile, and, according to Cicero, allies of Clodius. Whether they were completely under Clodius' thumb or not, they certainly did nothing to help Cicero (and made it harder for his allies) and gained considerably from Clodius' various bills.

23. *house of the pontifex maximus*: Caesar was pontifex maximus at the time of the Bona Dea affair and the rites were held in his house as he was then the senior consul.

24. *vilest abuse … topic*: In the Bona Dea affair when the Senate voted to try Clodius for sacrilege.

25. *the blind one*: Appius Claudius Caecus (censor in 312); he went blind in old age.

26. *who is that goddess … her shrine*: The joke here is that Clodius intruded on the rites of Bona Dea.

27. *temple of Castor*: In January 58, Clodius, with his supporters, occupied the temple of Castor and used it to organize his factions. The steps to the temple were demolished, making it a secure bastion from which they could sally forth to the Forum and disrupt public and private business and trials.

28. *this man here … person*: It is uncertain to whom Cicero is referring here; perhaps Marcus Terentius Varro Lucullus, consul in 73.

29. *tyrannical law … I had had no trial*: After passing his initial law on those who had executed Roman citizens without trial (the one which caused Cicero to flee, as it was obviously aimed at

him), Clodius passed a second law exiling Cicero specifically and confiscating his property.

30. *leader of the . . . world*: Pompey.

31. *A certain noble . . . aedile*: Clodius' older brother, Appius Claudius Pulcher, was in Greece in 61 collecting (without paying) statues to adorn Rome during the games he would hold as aedile. The normal sequence of offices was quaestor, aedile or tribune, praetor, consul, but one could skip over the second position. In the next sentence, Cicero imputes the worst possible motives to Appius – a desire to save money and defraud the Roman people by not bothering to have an aedileship (chapter 112), let alone games.

32. *rival . . . shared his initials*: In other words, after a voter had marked the initial on his ballot, the consul overseeing the elections (Piso) could then claim that all those marked with the same initial (or similar ones) belonged to one candidate.

33. *Catulus . . . father . . . son*: See Glossary of Names. The father died in 87, the son in 61.

34. *two consuls*: Piso and Aulus Gabinius, consuls for 58.

35. *a Senate . . . on my behalf*: Gabinius had used a consular edict to refuse the Senate permission to wear mourning in support of Cicero.

36. *Quintus Seius*: Nothing of this man is known.

37. *Marsian*: The Marsians were an Italian tribe of central Italy.

38. *allotted the lower part . . . hard life*: Clodius may have turned part of the site over to a place where the rights of his clan could be celebrated; according to Cicero, no one would come there to do so except those who needed a handout.

NOTES TO *IN DEFENCE OF SESTIUS* (*PRO SESTIO*)

1. *the consuls*: Piso and Gabinius.

2. *fearing the danger to you . . . loved it*: One of the accusations flung at Cicero was that he had shown great cowardice in fleeing Rome before he had been formally exiled; his standard response was that he was worried that remaining in Rome would cause riots and chaos and thus he had left to save the Republic harm.

3. *On the day itself*: The day that Clodius' law forbidding any man from giving fire and water to anyone who had put Roman citizens to death without a trial was the same day that the consuls gained their two provinces (Macedonia for Piso and Cilicia for Gabinius; the latter was later changed to Syria: see chapter 55).

4. *My wife ... threatened*: After Cicero's exile, his house on the Palatine was looted and demolished (see *On his House*) and Terentia took refuge in the house of the Vestal Virgins (her half-sister Fabia was a Vestal Virgin). She was summoned (and perhaps dragged) to the Valerian Exchange, where the tribunes of the plebs met. Presumably Clodius summoned her; for what reason it is not known, but it may have been with regard to Cicero's property, which had been confiscated as he was now an exile. Nothing is known of a threat on his children's lives.

5. *son-in-law*: Cicero's daughter, Tullia, married Gaius Piso Frugi, a distant relative of the consul, in 63 or 62. He worked hard for Cicero's return but died before it happened.

6. *censor's black mark*: One of the functions of the office of censor was to review the rolls of those belonging to the Senate; they could expel members because they no longer had the financial resources to be a senator or for moral reasons. Cicero is bending the truth here: this particular Clodian law only required censors to review each member of the Senate at the same time, rather than selecting members here and there; it stopped the censors from expelling anyone unless they both agreed, and they had to give him a chance to plead his case.

7. *reducing ... by six and one third asses*: This reduction in the cost of grain sold by the state to citizens meant it now cost nothing; not surprisingly, this was an extremely popular law. It was also a huge burden on the treasury, but it is unlikely that it cost the state as much as Cicero claims.

8. *that gladiator*: Clodius. These associations (called *collegia*), originally mutual aid societies organized by district or trade, had largely been suppressed by the Senate in 64. Clodius' laws of 4 January 58 revived them and allowed the creation of new ones.

9. *the law ... vote*: Clodius' law aimed at the ability of various magistrates to block legislation by announcing that they were watching the sky for auspices, by insisting they could not announce this suddenly while the assembly was in session (a popular tactic for blocking legislation).

10. *foreign nations ... that year*: Foreign affairs were traditionally under the Senate's governance; however, it appears that a decree of the Senate supported the annexation of Cyprus.

11. *the Magna Mater at Pessinus*: The site of the cult of the Great Mother was located in Phrygia; however, since 205/4 her cult had also been practised in Rome.

12. *gave the title of king ... community*: The Senate alone was

legally entitled to grant the title of king, so this represented a serious encroachment on its authority. Byzantium was a 'free state' and responsible for her own self-government; Rome demanding she restore men exiled after trial (and convicted of a capital charge as Cicero says later in the speech) was a breach of her autonomy. The exiles were restored by Marcus Cato; beyond that we know nothing more of their identities or their offences. The last reference is to Cicero's own exile.

13. *King Ptolemy*: From 80 this Ptolemy, the illegitimate son of Ptolemy IX Soter, the ruler of Egypt, was king of Cyprus, while his older brother, Ptolemy XII Auletes ('the Flute-player'), ruled Egypt.

14. *that honourable title*: In 59, Ptolemy XII Auletes was given the title of 'ally and friend' by the Senate (more or less installing him as legitimate ruler) after extremely generous bribes (144 million sesterces in total) to various senators, including Caesar and Pompey; soon after, his people expelled him from Egypt for having too close a connection with Rome. He was restored in 55 by Gabinius, then governor of Syria.

15. *Antiochus the Great ... Attalus*: The Romans under Manius Acilius Glabrio and Lucius Cornelius Scipio respectively defeated Antiochus III, king of Syria, at Thermopylae in 191 and Magnesia in 190. The terms of the peace were that he would give up all of his territory north and west of the Taurus Mountains. This territory was not in fact given to Attalus but to Eumenes II of Pergamum and brother of Attalus II. Attalus III later bequeathed this kingdom to Rome.

16. *Tigranes ... war against us*: Tigranes II (see Glossary of Names) undertook aggressive campaigns in Cappadocia, Syria and Cilicia. For more on his and Mithridates' war with the Romans, see *For the Manilian Law*.

17. *banish ... special commissions*: In a master stroke, knowing Cato's opposition to special commands being given to those not currently holding a magistracy, Clodius passed a law to send Cato off to annex Cyprus and sort out the internal affairs of Byzantium. Cato's commission was special because he had only held the position of quaestor and tribune of the plebs, neither of which held *imperium*, the power to command which praetors and consuls had, so he was sent with the rank of quaestor but with the *imperium* of a praetor.

18. *sworn ... passed*: Caesar's agrarian law of 59 had a clause requiring all senators to swear that they would uphold it.

19. *risked his life ... head on the block*: Cicero here refers to the debate over the fate of the Catilinarian conspirators who were in custody in December 63; this was five days before Cato's term of office as tribune of the plebs began. He argued for their execution.

20. *You all remember ... hero*: The colleague was Quintus Metellus Nepos, the temple that of Castor and Pollux; in January 62 Cato prevented Nepos from passing a law to transfer the command of the war against Catiline to Pompey (then on his way to Rome from his successful conclusion of the Third Mithridatic War).

21. *the previous year*: During Caesar's consulship; despite Cicero's claim here, it seems unlikely that Cato stayed away for an entire year (and indeed this is the only source that claims such a thing).

22. *Could he ... condemned?*: Presumably, as someone who had proposed that the Catilinarian conspirators be killed, Cato would have felt that in exiling Cicero for their execution his own argument was being attacked.

23. *'clique of the finest citizens'*: Cicero uses the term *optimates*. The Latin word translated as 'clique' is *natio*, a word which normally denotes foreigners, not Romans.

24. *'men of the people'*: *Populares*. This is the only place where Cicero defines what this faction is, but he is hardly an unbiased observer.

25. *Marcus Scaurus*: M. Aemilius Scaurus was the praetor presiding over the trial; he was the eldest son of M. Aemilius Scaurus, who had been consul in 115, censor 109 (when he refused to resign despite the death of his colleague). He wrote an autobiography (perhaps the first in Rome); it is now lost.

26. *stood his ground*: From 123 to 90 (when Varius was tribune of the plebs). Scaurus was prosecuted under Varius' law on treason for provoking Rome's allies to war (an action which led to the Social War). During the tribuneships of Gaius Gracchus, he would still have been a junior member of the Senate and we know nothing of any actions he took against Gracchus. Scaurus was also responsible for the final decree of the Senate voted against Saturninus in 100.

27. *Metellus ... Gracchus*: Q. Caecilius Metellus Numidicus, censor in 102, tried to expel Saturninus and Servilius Glaucia from the Senate. (Saturninus had led a riot against him when he was a candidate for censor.) Metellus' colleague, Metellus Caprarius, did not agree and so they remained members. The person he struck off the citizen rolls was a Lucius Equitius who claimed to be Tiberius Gracchus' son ('fake Gracchus'), even though he was

not acknowledged by Gracchus' sister. He was elected tribune of the plebs in 100 but was killed on 10 December – his first day in office. Q. Caecilius Metellus was the uncle of Caecilia Metella, who married the dictator Sulla after the elder Scaurus died. Fausta, her daughter by Sulla, went on to marry Milo.

28. *he . . . from his beliefs*: Metellus refused to swear allegiance to an agrarian law passed by Saturninus in 100 (it allotted land to Marius' soldiers and gave a grain dole). As a result, Metellus went into voluntary exile in 100; he was restored in 98.

29. *Catulus*: Consul in 78, the year of Sulla's death; he fought hard against the annulment of his reforms, coming into conflict with Marcus Aemilius Lepidus, his co-consul that year. He was defeated by Julius Caesar in the elections for pontifex maximus in 63 and died in 60, four years before this speech.

30. *'There are many traps for decent men'*: This and the following two quotations are from the tragedy *Atreus* by the poet Accius (170–c. 86).

31. *Lucius Cassius . . . citizens*: The *lex Gabinia* of 139 had introduced the secret ballot in elections; L. Cassius Longinus Ravilla, tribune of the plebs in 137, extended its use to juries in all criminal trials except for charges of *perduellio* (treason).

32. *Gracchus . . . long time*: Tiberius Gracchus' law (the *lex Sempronia agraria*) of 133 limited the public land that could be held by an individual tenant to 500 *iugera*, plus 250 *iugera* per son for up to two sons. Landless citizens would receive the public land this freed up by amounts of 30 *iugera* each; they and their descendants would have security of tenure over this land but could not sell it. As this measure would have taken away huge amounts of land that the wealthy currently farmed, it was extremely unpopular among the elite.

33. *Gracchus . . . treasury*: In 123, Gaius Gracchus first made grain available to citizens in Rome at a reduced price; this was later cancelled by Sulla but reintroduced in 78 by the consul Marcus Aemilius Lepidus.

34. *That . . . gladiator*: Clodius.

35. *an assembly on my fate*: The day after a meeting of the Senate, c. 9 July 57, which voted that Cicero alone had saved the country and should be restored from exile.

36. *prostrated himself*: For someone of Pompey's status to appeal to the people in this way implied a very close connection and considerable affection for Cicero. Given Pompey's popularity, it would have been a very effective move.

37. *assemblies . . . pass laws*: This type of assembly (a *comitia*) of the
     full people – patricians and plebs – was convened by the praetor
     or consul. It could vote yes or no to laws and it elected the mag-
     istrates.

NOTES TO *IN DEFENCE OF MILO*
(PRO MILONE)

1.   *7 or 8 April 52*: Legislation passed by Pompey specifically for
     this trial allowed for five days; an ancient commentary written
     by Asconius in the 60s CE states that it took four days and began
     on the 4th and that Cicero's speech was given on the last day of
     trial. However, our manuscripts sometimes give a date of 7 April,
     sometimes 8 April.

2.   *law . . . on public violence*: The *lex Pompeia de vi*. There were
     already laws in place to deal with public violence (something
     Cicero mentions in his speech: chapter 9) but presumably none
     of them were thought capable of dealing with a case of this par-
     ticular type.

3.   *for his defence*: The other speakers for the defence were Marcus
     Marcellus and Milo himself.

4.   *accompanied by . . . Birria*: Milo's escort was considerably larger
     than Clodius' – perhaps up to 300 men.

5.   *Quintus Metellus Scipio*: He was later (1 August) appointed by
     Pompey as his co-consul.

6.   *novel form of . . . court . . . brings terror to my eyes*: This trial,
     like others, took place in the Forum. Pompey was positioned in
     front of the temple of Saturn and was surrounded by soldiers.
     This was not just for his protection; as this was also the treasury
     it would be a magnet for rioters. Cicero appears to have been
     positioned in front of him, though at a slight distance, given the
     references in the speech to speaking up (e.g., in chapter 67) so
     that Pompey can hear him. Other soldiers may have been sta-
     tioned in front of other temples to prevent them being occupied
     by rioters or Cicero may be exaggerating the number of forces in
     the Forum. Clodius' supporters (which were many) formed part
     of the crowd.

7.   *jurors . . . distinguished classes*: Juries of this period were drawn
     from the Senate, the equestrians and a third order, the *tribuni
     aerarii*.

8.   *Horatius . . . own hand*: M. Horatius was a legendary hero of

ancient Rome; after killing three brothers in the enemy's army, he returned to Rome in triumph only to kill his own sister, who had met him in tears because one of his victims had been engaged to her.

9. *Publius Africanus*: Also known as Scipio Africanus the Younger (see Glossary of Names).

10. *Ahala . . . Opimius*: P. Scipio Nasica was involved in the death of Tiberius Gracchus in 133; L. Opimius in Gaius Gracchus' in 121 (see Glossary of Names for all four).

11. *legendary story . . . avenge his father*: Orestes killed his mother Clytemnestra because she had killed his father. Pursued by the Furies she had sent to avenge her, he arrived in Athens where he was put on trial for his crime. When the human jury was evenly divided on the subject of his guilt, Athena (the Roman Minerva), the goddess of wisdom, voted for acquittal.

12. *Twelve Tables*: Rome's oldest law code, drawn up in 451–50.

13. *violated a soldier*: The soldier was called Trebonius; the rapist was Gaius Lusius, Marius' nephew; the event took place in 101.

14. *The law*: This may be the law passed by Sulla on assassins (*lex Cornelia de sicariis*) in 81; if so, Cicero's basic point – that the law does not forbid the killing of a man in self-defence, but does forbid the carrying of a weapon with the intent to kill – is a problematic reading of the wording of the law. It may, however, be a reference to Pompey's law on violence (*lex Pompeia de vi*).

15. *tribune of the plebs*: Titus Munatius Plancus. Fired with enthusiasm in their speeches on the death of Clodius, he and another tribune (Quintus Pomponius Rufus) were nearly singed by the fires of the Curia on 19 January 52.

16. *Given that the Senate . . . his death*: When Clodius was charged with profaning the rites of Bona Dea, the Senate wanted the jurors to be chosen by the praetor who would preside over the trial, but instead they were chosen by lot (the usual manner). Cicero was very disparaging of those selected (*Letters to Atticus* 1.16.3).

17. *besieging . . . house*: Two days after the death of Clodius, the Senate appointed M. Aemilius Lepidus (the future triumvir) as *interrex* to oversee the elections. However, normally the first *interrex* did not hold the elections, but Milo's competitors for the position of consul were eager for elections to be held as Milo's unpopularity guaranteed he would be defeated. When Lepidus refused, they besieged his house, eventually breaking down his door and making their way in, smashing furniture and his wife's looms. Milo's own men intervened and further fighting ensued.

18. *Gracchus . . . his brother . . . Saturninus*: All three were tribunes of the plebs (see Glossary of Names).

19. *mad tribune of the plebs*: Munatius Plancus.

20. *split into two parts*: The two parts were a censure of the riots of 18 and 19 January and a recommendation to Pompey that Milo be immediately tried using the established laws and courts. Fufius Calenus was the 'someone' who requested it be split; the first part was carried and Munatius vetoed the second.

21. *notorious night . . . slept*: Scipio Africanus the Younger died suddenly in 129. Some suspected foul play but no one was ever charged with his death.

22. *ancestor's monument*: The Appian Way was built by Appius Claudius Caecus, an ancestor of Clodius.

23. *Papirius*: He was killed in a scuffle with Clodian supporters over Tigranes, an Armenian prince, in 58. Tigranes, son of Tigranes II, had been given by Pompey to a senator (Flavius) to keep under lock and key; after Flavius brought him to a dinner-party held by Clodius, he was never returned, despite a request from Pompey. When Tigranes managed to escape, both Clodius and Flavius tried to recover him and Papirius and several others were killed in the struggle.

24. *he . . . wished you . . . preside over this trial*: In actual fact, the assembly appointed Domitius, but presumably Pompey's influence was the deciding factor in their decision.

25. *elections . . . delayed . . . the next*: Clodius had been aedile in 56. One had to wait two years after holding office before running for another, so the first chance he could have run for praetor would have been in 54 (taking office in 53). That would have been 'his year'; however, the elections for that year were delayed and only took place in mid 53, causing Clodius to postpone running until the next year (to hold office in 52). Despite Cicero's words, Lucius Paulus was not a paragon of virtue and was eventually proscribed by his own brother, the triumvir Lepidus.

26. *not for some religious reason*: I.e., because the auspices had been unfavourable.

27. *Colline tribe*: There were four urban tribes of which the Colline was one (these four tribes voted last when the praetors and consuls were elected and thus had little electoral power). It is hard to see how adding to this tribe would help Clodius; Cicero may be suggesting that Clodius was planning on dividing this tribe into two, which would double its voting power.

28. *Lanuvium's dictator*: Lanuvium was Milo's home town and

about 18 miles from Rome; this dictatorship was a purely ceremonial position, restricted to religious duties.

29. *formal clothes*: While attending the Senate senators wore a specific type of shoe only worn by senators and the toga; Milo
changed out of these for less formal and more comfortable travel
attire.

30. *3 p.m. or so*: Asconius places the event an hour and a half earlier;
by moving the time later, Cicero puts it close to sundown, which
makes the danger seem more threatening.

31. *'Who benefited?'*: Lucius Cassius Longinus was a legendarily
strict jurist who liked to pose this question in trials. It was one of
Cicero's favourite sayings.

32. *consuls*: Quintus Metellus Scipio and Plautius Hypsaeus. Despite
Cicero's assertions here and despite the fact that these were asso-
ciates of Pompey, it is dubious that they would be entirely in
Clodius' pocket.

33. *Sextus Cloelius*: Clodius' secretary (his name is given as Sextus
Clodius in the manuscripts). He was later convicted for his role
in the burning of the Curia, hence Cicero's comment about him
being a 'burning light'.

34. *the Palladium*: An ancient statue of the goddess Minerva (the
Greek Athena) which was thought to have been brought from Troy
by Aeneas. It was kept in the temple of Vesta in the Forum; when
the temple caught fire in 241, the pontifex maximus Caecilius
Metellus entered the temple (which was forbidden to men) and
rescued it, along with other sacred objects. For this he lost his sight.

35. *You dragged out . . . in the night*: It was customary for the
corpses of members of distinguished Roman families to be carried out from their homes in a funeral procession; accompanying
this procession were people wearing the funeral masks (*imagines*) of famous ancestors and a train of mourners. At the final
site of burial or cremation, a member of the family would deliver
a eulogy over the body. Instead of this, Clodius was burned
along with the Curia, which can hardly be described as a traditional burial. The 'cursed wood' is a reference to the benches of
the Curia, used to fuel the pyre; it was only 'cursed' because it
had been used for such an inappropriate purpose.

36. *lex Plotia*: This law (also spelt *lex Plautia*) on public violence
was probably passed in the 80s or 70s, although it remains
somewhat obscure. The case suggested seems to have never come
to trial; Cicero refers to this in chapter 40, where he talks of
Milo taking Clodius to court twice.

37. *when I left Rome . . . trial*: Cicero left Rome before he was for-
     mally exiled and liked to assert that he left not because of his fear
     of Clodius but to save Rome turmoil.

38. *Hortensius*: He was among a group of senators sent to the consul
     Gabinius asking him to receive a deputation of equestrians who
     were speaking in support of Cicero; he was set upon by Clodius'
     supporters.

39. *Vibienus . . . lost his life*: Asconius says Vibienus died in the riot
     after Clodius' death, not during those in 58; it is curious that
     Cicero would err when discussing such a recent event, particu-
     larly when his audience would know the truth.

40. *palace of Numa*: On the Sacred Way, near the temple of Vesta. It
     is true that Cicero was attacked by Clodius near there, but that
     was five years earlier, in November 57, which seems to stretch
     the meaning of 'not long ago'.

41. *defending . . . from attack*: On 12 November 57 Clodius at-
     tempted to set Milo's house on fire; he was driven off and
     retreated to the house opposite Milo's, which belonged to Publius
     Sulla. For a full account, see *Letters to Atticus* 4.3.

42. *Sestius . . . Fabricius*: Sestius was a tribune of the plebs, in 57,
     along with Clodius, but supported Cicero loyally and worked
     hard for his recall (for more on Sestius' importance to Cicero, see
     Introduction to *In Defence of Sestius*). Fabricius was also a trib-
     une in 57 and helped bring in the bill for Cicero's recall.

43. *Lucius Caecilius*: Praetor in 57, also active in securing Cicero's
     recall.

44. *Lentulus . . . exile*: P. Lentulus Spinther, consul in 57, had been
     Cicero's quaestor in 63. Despite being the brother of the Lentu-
     lus executed for his involvement in the Catilinarian conspiracy,
     he worked hard for Cicero's recall and after that for the restor-
     ation of his confiscated property.

45. *seven praetors*: The one praetor who did not join in was Appius
     Claudius Pulcher, Clodius' older brother.

46. *private citizen . . . crushing Clodius*: After Milo's tribuneship
     ended, Clodius was aedile for 56; as Milo was no longer a magis-
     trate, he could be prosecuted for violence and for using gladiators;
     eventually the prosecution was dropped. In reality, Pompey had
     finished his speech before the riot started.

47. *Mark Antony*: He was at that time in Rome to stand for quaes-
     tor. He had been a friend of Clodius' during Clodius' tribuneship
     but was then supporting Milo. However, after the death of
     Clodius he turned against Milo and was one of the prosecutors

Cicero and Milo were now facing. For more on this incident with Clodius, see *Philippic II*, chapter 21.

48. *voting enclosures*: During elections for consul and praetor, voters were organized by century in temporary pens positioned in the Campus Martius.

49. *swords . . . stones thrown*: In 52, violence and rioting meant that several attempts had to be made to hold elections for the consuls; in this incident the consuls for 53 (Gaius Domitius Calvinus and Marcus Valerius Messala) were hit by stones.

50. *Petilius . . . Cato*: Petilius is otherwise unknown; for Cato, see Glossary of Names under Cato the Younger.

51. *at the same time*: This explanatory comment is deleted by some as coming from an interpolator. During Clodius' trial over the Bona Dea sacrilege, he called on Causinius to testify that he had been in Interamna (about 80 miles from Rome) at the time of the offence. Cicero testified that he had seen him in Rome that day.

52. *there have been those who . . . said*: According to Asconius, the rumour-mongers were Pompeius Rufus and Gaius Sallustius.

53. *an open will*: Cyrus not only wrote out a will but repeated its contents before witnesses.

54. *The place itself*: This site, the monument of Basilius on the Appian Way, was a notorious location for robbers to lie in wait.

55. *Aricia*: Modern Ariccia, 16 miles southeast of Rome, at the foot of the Alban Hills.

56. *Alsium*: Modern Palo; this was a resort town in Etruria, about 20 miles from Rome, and popular with wealthy Romans.

57. *rushing to . . . Etruria*: Either a reference to the rumour that Clodius had set out to join Catiline's camp or a reference to his estates in Etruria, which his slaves (according to Cicero) would use as strongholds from which to pillage the area.

58. *under torture . . . slaves*: The testimony of slaves was only admissible in court if it had been obtained by torture.

59. *the one about . . . ceremonies*: Another reference to the Bona Dea affair.

60. *Ocriculum*: A town in Umbria, north of Rome, near modern Otricoli.

61. *butcher Licinius*: The priest's assistant who killed the sacrificial animal.

62. *home of Gaius Caesar*: As pontifex maximus, Caesar had official quarters on the Sacred Way.

63. *in charge of the Republic*: As Pompey was sole consul, he alone was in charge of the entire state.

64. *meeting of the Senate . . . silence*: In the temple of Jupiter on the Capitol; the senator was called Publius Cornificius. Cicero is exaggerating somewhat, though the circumstances were embarrassing enough: Milo was accused of carrying a weapon and had to lift his tunic to prove otherwise. In any case, to strip in a temple was considered an offence to the gods.

65. *loudly . . . hear me*: Pompey was seated in front of the Treasury, before the temple of Saturn, and thus at some distance from Cicero.

66. *'see . . . no harm'*: A reference to the ultimate decree of the Senate, the *senatus consultum ultimum*, used in times of crisis.

67. *Lucullus*: Married to Clodius' younger sister, he used his rights as paterfamilias to torture his wife's slaves and this evidence formed part of Clodius' trial in 59 over the Bona Dea affair.

68. *a fellow-citizen . . . lives*: Cicero is referring to himself, a topic he never tired of.

69. *Scantia . . . Apinius*: We have no other knowledge of either.

70. *Appius . . . close friend to*: Here Cicero is not only getting out of character as Milo but is rather overstating the case. Appius had been the only praetor to support Clodius and not vote for Cicero's recall. He was consul in 54 and preceded Cicero as governor of Cilicia. Cicero forced himself to be on good terms with him rather than be considered a close friend.

71. *The Greeks treat heroes . . . like gods*: The greatest example of a Greek city giving honours to tyrant killers were those Athens gave to Harmodius and Aristogeiton, who killed the tyrant Hipparchus.

72. *Alban hills . . . Latium*: Alba Longa was the city founded by Ascanius, Aeneas' son, and the ancient capital of Latium. As such it had shrines of great antiquity and symbolic importance to the Romans. On Mount Alba there was a shrine to Jupiter Latiaris which was the religious centre of the Latin confederation.

73. *the man*: Pompey.

74. *a consul who had acted heroically*: Cicero.

75. *made our slaves his freedmen*: Perhaps a reference to Clodius' proposal to allow freedmen to be spread across all the tribes, instead of the four city ones; this would increase the value of their vote. See also note 26.

76. *was being silently listened to . . . unpopularity*: M. Caelius Rufus was also, not uncoincidentally, one of the other defending counsels.

77. *three inheritances*: The first was Milo's original fortune, the second from his adoptive father Titus Annius, the third from either his mother or his wife.

78. *The whole population ... voted him consul*: Although the vote had been going in Milo's favour, the interruption of the elections meant that he was never formally declared consul.

NOTES TO THE *FIRST AND SECOND PHILIPPICS (ORATIONES PHILIPPICAE)*

Philippic I

1. *at least fourteen Philippics*: There may have been three more, but these are no longer extant.
2. *Philip of Macedon (hence their name)*: Philip is better known as the father of Alexander the Great; Demosthenes (384–322) delivered a sequence of speeches against him in response to his interventions in Greece.
3. *assembled at the temple of Tellus*: On 17 March. This temple, which faced the Forum, was chosen because it was near Antony's house (which, as we learn in the course of these speeches, had previously belonged to Pompey). Despite Cicero's words here, he left Rome on 7 April and only returned on 1 September.
4. *as Athens once had*: In 404, after Sparta defeated her in the Peloponnesian War, Athens was ruled by the Thirty Tyrants, who lived up to their name. When they were ousted and the democracy restored, an 'amnesty' (probably the 'Greek word' Cicero refers to here) was declared for all past actions; it did not include the Thirty and a few others directly connected to them.
5. *peace ... through his child*: Even after the amnesty was proclaimed, the conspirators would not come down from the Capitoline Hill until Antony and Lepidus each promised to send a son to them to be held as a hostage. In actual fact only one child (Antony's son by Fulvia) was sent (see *Philippic II*, chapter 90); he was probably only around two years old.
6. *Were any exiles restored?*: Sextus Cloelius, a client of Publius Clodius, was the exception; he had been exiled for his role in the riots after the death of his patron. Antony consulted Cicero about the matter, and Cicero wrote a letter in which he fulsomely assented to his recall, although he also commented in a letter to Atticus that he thought this was not one of Caesar's wishes. Antony read this letter out in the Senate, an act which Cicero attacks in *Philippic II*.
7. *no decree ... posted*: In Rome laws were inscribed in bronze and posted on the Capitol or other public locations around Rome.

8. *dictator*: Caesar had been made 'dictator for life', which was certainly unconstitutional; it was also one of the primary reasons for his assassination.

9. *runaway slave ... Marius' name*: The man's real name was Herophilus or Amatius; he was an eye and horse doctor who had claimed to be the grandson of Marius and taken his name. Antony had him summarily executed; the hook referred to is that which was used to drag the body of dead criminals to the Tiber to be disposed of.

10. *absent*: Antony was away from Rome from around 25 April to 18 May.

11. *when evil ... Forum*: After Caesar's death, a frenzied crowd stirred up by Antony's funeral oration cremated Caesar's body on a makeshift pyre in contradiction to the laws of the Twelve Tables. According to Suetonius (*Life of Julius Caesar* 85), the people built on this spot a column made of Numidian marble almost 20 feet high, and inscribed on it 'For the Father of the Country' in an allusion to the title the Senate gave Caesar. Cicero avoids mentioning this explicitly.

12. *punished ... freemen*: The slaves were crucified, while the freemen were thrown from the Tarpeian Rock.

13. *everything changed on the first of June*: The Senate usually met on 1 June after a spring recess in April and May; according to Cicero, the Senate was too alarmed to turn up for this meeting (see the full account in *Philippic* II, chapters 108–9).

14. *consuls-elect*: Aulus Hirtius and Gaius Vibius Pansa, both Caesarians and nominated by Caesar himself for 43. Both were moderates and not fond of Antony and his policies.

15. *Liberators ... not in the city*: Marcus Brutus and Gaius Cassius had both been driven from Rome because of the unrest.

16. *honorary commission as a lieutenant*: Roman senators were restricted in their movements out of Italy except when they left for specific public reasons; these honorary commissions or embassies without duties allowed them not only to travel but to do so at public expense, and also to enjoy the status and benefits of regular embassies. Cicero was appointed a lieutenant by Dolabella on 2 June, which allowed him freedom of movement.

17. *that city, so closely connected to me*: Cicero was closely tied to Sicily since his time there as quaestor and his prosecution of Verres (see *Against Verres*).

18. *the next day*: 7 August.

19. *edict of Brutus and Cassius*: We are not sure what edict Cicero is

referring to here. This may have been their goodbye edict in which they said that they were willing to live in eternal exile if it was necessary for the good of the Republic; however, it may have been a stop-gap measure proposed before this (perhaps a request to be relieved of certain duties assigned to their office), which was unsuccessful.

20. *Gallic provinces*: Although Caesar had given these provinces to others (Lucius Munatius Plancus and Decimus Brutus), Antony persuaded the assembly to award him the provinces of Cisalpine and Transalpine Gaul instead of Macedonia; in November of this year, he headed north to take possession of them. He besieged Brutus at Mutina (modern Modena), which he could not take. In the end, he was beaten by an army led by the two consuls for 43, Hirtius and Pansa (both of whom died in the battle), and was driven across the Alps.

21. *Lucius Piso*: Caesar's father-in-law. Although he was a long-time political enemy of Cicero's, Cicero was willing to support him when he briefly led the opposition to Antony; that opposition did not last long.

22. *a service he did me*: Antony spared Cicero's life at Brundisium.

23. *Hannibal . . . carried in*: Hannibal was a Carthaginian general of the third century and Rome's greatest enemy, defeating (and almost entirely wiping out) several Roman armies before he was himself defeated by Scipio Africanus the Elder in 202. To say that 'Hannibal was at the gates' was a proverbial way of saying that some great crisis was at hand. Appius Claudius Caecus (the Blind) was said to have been carried into the Senate house in a litter to give a speech which led the Romans to reject a peace treaty with the Greek general Pyrrhus.

24. *Public thanksgivings*: A public thanksgiving was a period of (normally) five days in which thanks were given in various temples for the Republic's escape from some disaster; Antony had proposed that an extra day be allocated to all such thanksgivings in honour of Caesar.

25. *smash up . . . a home . . . public expense*: As the speech *On his House* makes clear (chapter 12), Cicero's house had been torn down during his exile in 58; when he returned the next year, it was rebuilt using public funds, despite the opposition of Clodius who had torn it down in the first place (and had turned the site into a temple).

26. *festival of the dead*: The Parentalia, a festival in honour of the dead which was held from 13 to 21 February; offerings were

given to the dead and meals were held at their tombs. Cicero argues that Antony is impiously mixing up two types of religious ceremonies: the Parentalia (for which one needs a tomb) and thanksgivings.

27. *more than one . . . worthy of the Republic*: There were sixteen ex-consuls, of whom only one (Piso) opposed Antony. Five others (like Cicero) were away from Rome; three supported Antony.

28. *speak . . . as I am doing*: The order of speaking in the Senate was according to rank. First the consuls spoke, then any consuls-elect and then the ex-consuls.

29. *'legal team'*: In court one used a legal team to provide legal, oratorical and moral support; Cicero here refers sarcastically to Antony's soldiers whom he had packed into the Senate house on several previous occasions.

30. *If only . . . Ops*: Caesar had lodged 700 million sesterces in the temple of the goddess Ops, an Italian goddess of wealth and plenty; Antony appears to have embezzled it over the course of several weeks. Cicero calls it 'bloodstained' because it was partially gathered through the sale of the property of those who had been on the Pompeian side in the Civil War.

31. *Sempronian . . . Cornelian laws*: Gaius Gracchus was from the Sempronian clan, Sulla from the Cornelian, hence the names of the laws. Cicero refers to them and Pompey here because all three had passed laws which affected the composition of juries.

32. *govern their provinces . . . more than two*: A province was normally held by an ex-consul or ex-praetor for one year only; however, in practice people held their provinces for much longer. Verres, for example, governed Sicily for three years as propraetor; Caesar himself held Gaul for even longer.

33. *the law . . . about the courts*: The *lex Aurelia* of 70 had established the three classes for jury service: senators, equestrians and the *tribuni aerarii*; the last of these was below the rank of equestrian (how far below it is hard to know for sure). In 55 Pompey passed a law requiring the city praetor to take his jurors from the richest members of all three classes. Caesar had abolished the third class in 46. Antony wanted to add again a third class from which jurors could be drawn. Cicero classified this group as coming from the dregs of society, though it is more likely to have been intended to expand the range of jurors in order to deal with a shortage.

34. *centurions*: Each centurion led a company of sixty soldiers; they were quite well paid and extremely important in the structure of the Roman army, but not, strictly speaking, considered officers.

35. *legion of Gauls*: This legion (the Fifth, nicknamed 'The Larks' from the plumes on their helmets) was a Gallic legion, formed by Caesar. They had only recently been granted citizenship and Cicero mentions them for shock value.

36. *made public another law ... people*: We cannot be sure if this law was actually passed. If it was, it would have been repealed, along with the rest of Antony's laws, in March 43.

37. *recalled from exile ... by a dead man*: The recalled exiles were called Charonitae, because, just as Charon ferried the dead into the underworld, the dead Caesar brought them back to Rome. (Antony granted citizenship to the people of the province of Sicily in April under a Julian law. He also made Crete immune from taxes.)

38. *invoking a religious prohibition*: Here Cicero refers to the frequent usage of the auspices to block the passage of legislation – a tactic Antony himself used to block the election of Dolabella as consul, one of Cicero's grounds of attack in *Philippic II*.

39. *previous actions ... offended them*: When Dolabella was tribune of the plebs, he opposed the cancellation of debts; as might be imagined, this made him *extremely* unpopular.

40. *you as an augur ... announced*: See *Philippic II*, chapters 79–84, for a description of how Antony tried to derail Dolabella's consulship by blatant misuse of his position as augur.

41. *those ... brave men*: Caesar's assassins.

42. *'Let them hate ... as they fear'*: From Accius' tragedy *Atreus*; the speaker is Atreus whose revenge on his brother (he fed him his two sons at a banquet) was repaid by death at the hands of his brother's remaining child.

43. *Cinna ... murdered him*: L. Cornelius Cinna (consul in 87) was the father of Julius Caesar's first wife. During the civil war between Marius and Sulla, he sided with Marius and was ejected from Rome. He retook the city late in 87; Mark Antony's grandfather was then killed as part of the proscriptions that followed.

44. *two tribunes of the plebs*: We know of three tribunes who were particularly hostile to Antony: Tiberius Cannutius, Lucius Cassius Longinus and Decimus Carfulenus. All three were forbidden to enter the meeting of the Senate on 28 November. We cannot be sure which two Cicero is referring to here.

45. *Games of Apollo*: An annual festival in honour of the god, held from 6 to 13 July, this time produced by Marcus Brutus as city praetor. As he was absent, Antony's brother Gaius took his place and replaced a play on Brutus' famous ancestor with Accius'

Tereus. Despite this, there were demonstrations in favour of Brutus at the performance.

46. *happy men*: The Liberators; though, presumably, Brutus particularly is being referred to.

47. *Aulus Hirtius*: One of the consuls-elect for 43 and a supporter of Caesar (he wrote Book 8 of Caesar's *Gallic War*); he fell out with Antony and Caesar's veterans and led the Senate's troops into the battle of Mutina where he fell (April 43). He seems to have fallen ill in 44, whereupon the Roman people made vows for his recovery.

Philippic II

1. *in court at some time*: We know very little about this case; it was apparently a civil case in which Cicero appeared for a person named Sicca who was from Vibo and against a friend or connection of Antony – possibly Quintus Fadius. It seems that Antony found a tribune of the plebs who would use his veto (which was possible in civil cases) to make the case go his way.

2. *influence gained ... attractions of youth*: This is Cicero's polite way of suggesting that sexual favours were exchanged to obtain influence with (presumably) Antony.

3. *Fadius, an ex-slave*: Antony's relationship to Quintus Fadius is controversial; elsewhere in the *Philippics* (III.17) Cicero only refers to Antony acknowledging his children by Fadia, so it may not have been a legal marriage.

4. *Curio*: Gaius Scribonius Curio was married to Fulvia (Antony's second wife), who was Clodius' widow; he was also Antony's lover. He first supported Pompey, but although elected as tribune of the plebs in 50 as an opponent of Caesar, he soon went over to his side and was killed in action in Africa in 49.

5. *the augurship*: A priesthood, one of the four great 'colleges' of priests and an elective position like many priesthoods in Rome. Cicero was elected in 53 to the place left vacant by the death of Marcus Licinius Crassus, the triumvir's son; Antony was elected in 50. We are not sure of the exact procedure but it seems as if two or three members nominated candidates and one of these was voted on by seventeen out of the thirty-five tribes.

6. *at Brundisium*: After the Pompeian side was defeated at the battle of Pharsalus in 48, Cicero threw himself on Caesar's mercy. Caesar sent him a letter telling him to return to Italy; however, Caesar later instructed Antony to expel all of Pompey's support-

ers from Italy. Cicero waited in Brundisium (modern Brindisi, the chief port by which one entered Italy from Greece) and showed him the letter from Caesar, whereupon Antony issued an edict exempting him from Caesar's order. (See further Cicero's comments at chapters 6 and 59–60 of this speech.)

7. *killed a man who had saved them*: Many of Caesar's assassins, such as Marcus Brutus, were originally supporters of Pompey and had been beneficiaries of Caesar's clemency after the Civil War; this did not stop them assassinating their benefactor.

8. *many great disagreements of this sort*: Cicero and the triumvir Marcus Crassus were frequently on bad terms; Crassus was one of Catiline's backers in 64, during his campaign for the consulship.

9. *letter ... deal with each other*: The letter in question, from 26 April 44 (which Cicero did write despite his equivocation here and later), is still extant (*Letters to Atticus* 14.13b) and is a rather embarrassingly ingratiating response to a request by Antony that Cicero agree to the recall of Sextus Cloelius.

10. *Mustela ... Tiro*: Two of Antony's henchmen; they were the leaders of his armed guard at meetings of the Senate.

11. *a profitable knowledge of that*: A reference to Antony's forging of documents that he claimed Caesar had written (see *Philippic I*).

12. *recalled by Caesar's law*: In his letter to Cicero (still extant), Antony claims that there was a note of Caesar's agreeing that Sextus Cloelius should be recalled from exile, rather than claiming there was a specific law dealing with the topic.

13. *my restraint ... decorum ... provoked me to*: Despite his comments here, Cicero was highly adept in the art of invective, as his speeches attacking Publius Vatinius and Piso can attest.

14. *the way he was elected*: See Cicero's comments (chapter 79) on Antony's election as consul.

15. *you have at home ... fatal to both of them*: A reference to Antony's wife Fulvia, who was the widow of Publius Clodius and Gaius Curio (both of whom died violently).

16. *Publius Servilius ... consul*: Cicero here drops the names of consuls who had held the consulship in the seventeen years before the Catilinarian conspiracy. The most important are Lucius Lucullus, M. Licinius Crassus the triumvir and the orator Q. Hortensius. Publius Servilius Vatia Isauricus had died earlier in 44 at the remarkable age of ninety. The only person mentioned who had not held the consulship is Marcus Cato.

17. *Pompey ... my service*: Pompey's thanks were less than Cicero

had hoped for, something he complained of in his letters (*Letters to his Friends* 5.7.2–3 and *Letters to Atticus* 1.13.4).

18. *stepfather*: Publius Cornelius Lentulus Sura ('Legs' Lentulus). Antony's mother Julia married him in 63, the year of the Catilinarian conspiracy. As an ex-consul (he was consul in 71) Lentulus was the most high-profile person to be executed.

19. *suburban residence*: This had belonged to Pompey and had been bought by Antony at auction.

20. *Phormio . . . Gnatho . . . Ballio*: All the names of famous characters in Roman comedy: the first two were parasites (hangers-on who flattered in return for handouts), the last was a pimp.

21. *temple*: The temple of Concord, at the foot of the Capitoline Hill; this was where Cicero had addressed the Senate on 3, 4 and 5 December 63, in the midst of the Catilinarian conspiracy. The *First Catilinarian* was delivered there.

22. *Ityraeans*: A people from Syria, who were known for their archery. Antony, who had served with Pompey when he conquered them in 63, apparently brought some of them to Rome as a bodyguard.

23. *mime-actress wife*: She called herself Cytheris, in honour of Venus, but as a freedwoman of Volumnius she was also called Volumnia (see chapters 57–8 below). She was a celebrated actress (and also, according to some stories, the mistress of Marcus Brutus). The level of her celebrity may be gauged from Cicero's excitement at once attending the same dinner-party as her.

24. *'Let weapons yield to the toga'*: This is half a line from Cicero's poem on his consulship, written around 60. It became infamous in antiquity because of its lack of literary quality and Cicero's incessant self-praise. The full line is 'Let arms yield to the toga, the laurel give way to praise'. As the toga was a garment of peace, it would appear Cicero was attempting to elevate his accomplishment as a civilian above that of military leaders (who wore the laurel in the triumph). Not unnaturally, this would have been highly controversial in a society where so many sought status through military achievements, which is presumably why Antony used the line.

25. *he had been killed . . . barricading them*: See *In Defence of Milo*, chapter 40, on Antony's attempted murder of Clodius in the Forum.

26. *Bibulus*: M. Calpurnius Bibulus was consul with Caesar in 59. For most of his consulship he sat closed up in his house declaring every day that because of bad auspices no state business could

occur. He also posted public screeds accusing Caesar of all manner of offences. Caesar simply ignored him and hence that year
was often referred to as the 'Consulship of Caesar and Julius'
instead of 'Caesar and Bibulus' as was normal; Cicero here
reverses that as a sneer against Caesar.

27. *candidate . . . while absent*: In 52 all ten tribunes of the plebs had
sponsored and passed a law granting Caesar the right to stand
for a second consulship *in absentia*. Pompey, however, passed a
law stating that all candidates had to announce their candidacy
in Rome, but later, after his law had been passed, he added a
rider exempting Caesar from this requirement. Caesar was anx-
ious to avoid returning to Rome from Gaul in 49 (when his
command ran out and with it his immunity from prosecution) to
run again for consul, fearing prosecution by his opponents.

28. *set up a fake prosecutor against myself*: It was not unheard of for
those facing prosecution, particularly in extortion courts, to col-
lude with a friend who would 'prosecute' them incompetently,
thus ensuring their acquittal. Cicero had to see off such a fake
prosecutor before Verres' trial (see Introduction to *Against Verres*).

29. *uninvolved people . . . concealed*: Some people did pretend to
have been part of the conspiracy; in fact, Publius Lentulus
Spinther and Gaius Octavius (see Plutarch, *Life of Caesar* 67)
were executed by Antony and Octavian for boasting of being part
of the plot, even though, according to Plutarch, no one believed
they had been.

30. *among so many men . . . concealed*: Of the more than sixty men
said to have been part of the plot to kill Caesar, Cicero only lists
here the most important eight.

31. *the Bruti*: Referring to the two leading conspirators: Marcus and
Decimus Brutus. Both were supposedly descendants of the
Brutus who had driven the kings from Rome in 509. Marcus was
said to have been urged by anonymous notes to live up to the
example of his ancestor. He could also claim descent from Gaius
Servilius Ahala who had killed Spurius Maelius in 439 for
allegedly aiming to become a tyrant. As their descendant, he
would have had *imagines* (death-masks) of both men on display
in his house.

32. *that deed . . . my guidance*: Cicero is the only authority for this
plan for murdering Caesar, and its veracity is doubtful.

33. *father . . . uncle*: Gaius Domitius' father was killed while fleeing
after the battle of Pharsalus in 48; his uncle was Cato the Younger,
who committed suicide in 46 after Caesar's victory at Thapsus.

34. *Gaius Trebonius*: Praetor in 48, consul-suffect 45; on the Ides of March he drew Antony away from Caesar. His career was extremely indebted to Caesar.

35. *Cimber*: On the day of Caesar's assassination, Cimber approached him and pretended to ask for pardon for his brother; he then signalled to the other conspirators to attack by pulling Caesar's toga and entangling his arms.

36. *two Servilii*: Publius Servilius Casca Longus was the first to stab Caesar; his brother was Gaius. Their family belonged to a clan, the Servilii, that also included the Ahalas.

37. *freed ... for more than ten days*: As city praetor, Brutus was not legally permitted to be outside the city for more than ten days because he was responsible for administering civil justice in the city. However, the Senate could vote to exempt an individual from such a restriction, as it did in this case on Antony's suggestion.

38. *hatched a plot ... killed*: This 'plot' seems to have been completely Cicero's invention and based entirely on Trebonius' and Antony's friendship and the fact that Trebonius was the person assigned to make certain that Antony did not enter the Senate with Caesar. Narbo is modern Narbonne.

39. *if someone should take you to court*: Lucius Cassius Longinus Ravilla (consul in 127) was known for his severity in court and for his proverbial question 'Who benefited?'.

40. *temple of Ops*: Antony either used money from this temple, which was also the treasury, or destroyed records of his debts there.

41. *sales office ... taxes*: Antony granted citizenship to Sicily (see chapter 92) and tax exemptions for Crete (chapter 97); Cicero may also be referring to Antony taking bribes from tax-farmers in return for granting them contracts to collect taxes.

42. *flung at me ... armies*: We cannot be sure what Antony said but Cicero seems to have spent most of his time in Pompey's camp being snide, critical and advising peace at any cost, without offering substantial suggestions. He also annoyed Pompey by refusing to follow him to Pharsalus (owing, he said, to poor health). After Pompey's defeat, Cicero turned down Cato's suggestion that as the most prominent ex-consul alive Cicero should take over resistance to Caesar, preferring to return to Italy and await Caesar's pardon.

43. *all those ex-consuls*: Nine ex-consuls and the two current consuls went over to Pompey's side during the war; of these, only two (Servius Sulpicius and Cicero) were still alive.

44. *'my speech estranged me from Pompey'*: Here, presumably, Cicero is quoting Antony's words in his attack on Cicero.

45. *received . . . in inheritances*: This seems a little strange to us, but it was customary for people to show their respect for individuals by leaving them inheritances. To receive none was a sign no one regarded you highly; however, to receive inheritances from people you had no relationship with was looked upon askance.

46. *would not accept . . . your own father*: Antony's father left an estate so encumbered with debt that Antony's guardians (Antony himself was only eleven or twelve at the time) refused to accept it.

47. *another man's villa*: As mentioned in the Introduction, this had previously belonged to Pompey's father-in-law, Metellus Scipio.

48. *Leontini*: A fertile region on the east coast of Sicily (modern Lentini).

49. *fourteen benches*: The *lex Roscia* of 67 allocated fourteen rows of seats for the equestrians right behind those of the senators; those who attempted to sit in these seats and were not equestrians could be fined.

50. *man's toga . . . woman's*: Boys put on the toga of manhood at the age of fifteen or sixteen; prostitutes also wore togas, whereas married women wore a *stola*, a long robe.

51. *six million sesterces*: It is difficult to come up with modern equivalents for ancient figures, but this was a *very* large debt and could have forced Antony to go into exile to avoid paying it.

52. *father's . . . authority*: Roman fathers had *patria potestas*, the complete right of life and death over their children.

53. *a little something . . . in his home*: Cicero is implying that Antony had something going on with Fulvia (then Clodius' and now Antony's wife).

54. *Gabinius . . . wanted*: Aulus Gabinius was then governor of Syria (Cicero hated him because, as consul in 58, he did nothing to stop Cicero getting exiled); in return for an enormous bribe, he helped Ptolemy XII Auletes to regain his throne in 55 – despite the fact that a Sybilline oracle supposedly forbade it. Antony actually spent some time in Greece before he joined Gabinius' staff, but he did play an important role in Ptolemy's restoration.

55. *own property . . . time-share*: Cicero here refers to Sisapo (in Spain) where there were mines owned by corporations, suggesting that Antony was only a part-owner of his property at Misenum (modern Miseno, at the north of the Bay of Naples).

56. *husband*: I.e., Curio.

57. *consulship of . . . Lentulus . . . Marcellus*: In 49. Curio handed

the Senate a letter from Caesar, in which he said he would give up his army if Pompey did the same. If the Senate rejected this offer, Caesar said he would have to act to protect his own safety. Antony and Quintus Cassius Longinus, who were both tribunes, forced the consul Lentulus to have the letter read out loud; Cicero called it harsh and threatening in tone. However, the letter's offer was not put to a vote; instead, the Senate voted to demand that Caesar give up his army on the threat of being considered an enemy of the state if he did not. Antony and Cassius vetoed that measure and the meeting was adjourned at nightfall with no final resolution on the validity of their vetoes; threatened by the Senate, Antony and Cassius fled Rome that night. The debate resumed on the 5th and the 7th and the Senate passed the *senatus consultum ultimum*, the 'Final Decree of the Senate'.

58. *deal that blow to you*: The Final Decree of the Senate, referred to in chapter 51.

59. *uncle*: Gaius Antonius Hybrida, Cicero's co-consul in 63, was exiled following a conviction (probably for his actions as governor of Macedonia) in 59, after an unsuccessful defence by Cicero. Despite Cicero's insinuations, it appears that Antony's law of 49 applied only to those convicted for electoral corruption and bribery and thus did not cover his situation.

60. *Denticulus*: Otherwise unknown. Gambling was illegal except at the Saturnalian festival and the fine was four times the amount wagered. Conviction meant the loss of certain citizen rights, but not exile – at least not in this case.

61. *A tribune . . . Volumnia*: As a tribune of the plebs Antony was not entitled to lictors; to make matters worse, these were wearing laurel wreaths to celebrate the defeat of Pompey and the consuls at Pharsalus (or by a more charitable interpretation, for Caesar's victories in Gaul). He was also not supposed to be riding around in a fancy and rather effeminate type of chariot, like the one Cicero is describing here, and should certainly not have been accompanied by his mistress while on official business.

62. *master of the horse*: It appears that Caesar was appointed dictator (probably at the end of October 48) at the same time Antony became his master of horse, rather than appointing him after the event.

63. *Studs*: The Latin says *Hippia*, a Greek name; *hipparchus* was the Greek for 'master of the horse' and Cicero puns with the name of Antony's newly acquired position.

64. *handed over . . . to . . . Sergius*: We are not quite sure of the

NOTES   311

details of this giveaway; Cicero may be accusing Antony of giving these horses to Sergius or possibly means he gave him the
contract to bid on them.

65. *Marcus Piso*: Either the consul of 61 or his son.

66. *decrees . . . heirs*: As Caesar's master of the horse, Antony probably ruled on inheritance cases.

67. *wine . . . next day*: We get more details of this later (chapter 84),
where Cicero tells us that it happened at the Portico of Minucius
in the Campus Martius. Plutarch (*Life of Antony* 9) adds the
revolting detail that one of Antony's friends held out his toga to
catch the vomit. Cicero's description of Antony's drinking and
vomiting was considered a masterpiece by later Roman authors
such as Quintilian, and it certainly leaves little to the imagination.

68. *Caesar left Alexandria*: June 47.

69. *sign for an auction*: Literally, a spear; a spear stuck in the ground
was the sign for a public auction, presumably because histori-
cally a great deal of loot from military campaigns was sold off at
such auctions.

70. *'Evil profits become evil losses'*: From a tragedy by the poet Naevius (third century BCE).

71. *luxury . . . a rich one*: Pompey was, in fact, immensely wealthy;
in 44 the Senate voted his son, Sextus Pompey, 200 million sesterces in compensation for the loss of his father's property. This
was probably only a fraction of its worth.

72. *Charybdis*: A mythical creature thought to live in the strait that
separates Sicily from Italy; she was imagined as a whirlpool
which sucked down the waters of the sea.

73. *naval trophies*: Cicero specifically refers to *rostra* here, prows
taken from captured ships and placed on the front of the home
to record its owner's triumphs. These ones probably commemo-
rated Pompey's victory over the Mediterranean pirates in 67.
Antony's father, however, was better known for a disastrous
naval defeat at the hands of the Cretans, for which he mockingly
received the epithet 'Creticus'.

74. *Twelve Tables*: Rome's oldest law code, drawn up in 451–50.

75. *'I am both a consul and an Antony!'*: Presumably to draw attention to his own noble heritage as compared with Cicero, who
was only a new man and had no consuls in his pedigree.

76. *an assassin . . . financial difficulties*: We know nothing about this
plot; it seems hardly credible that Caesar attacked Antony for
sending an assassin to his house one day and then shortly afterwards decided to give him an extension on his payment plan.

77. *Pompey's children ... country*: The Pompeian forces were now concentrated in Spain and led by Gnaeus and Sextus Pompey. Gnaeus was killed after the battle of Munda in 45; Sextus Pompey escaped and spent some time being a pirate king in Sicily. Cicero's point is that Antony should by rights have been fighting them, since he had both caused the war and was now living in their father's house.

78. *Red Rocks*: A small town about 9 miles north of Rome.

79. *the woman*: Fulvia. Cicero is very careful not to name her throughout this speech.

80. *you unsettled the city ... for many days*: Although Cicero is exaggerating for effect, Antony's unexpected arrival did cause alarm in Rome. Antony was asked to address a public meeting, giving his reasons for his return, as rumours had flown around that Caesar was dead or that Antony had come back early to start a purge of Caesar's enemies.

81. *Lucius Plancus*: Consul in 42; he was one of the six or eight city prefects (not to be confused with the city praetors, elections for which were not held until late in this year, 45) who were left in charge of regular business in Rome after Caesar left for Spain.

82. *went a very long way*: As far as Narbo.

83. *this good augur ... election results*: Antony had been an augur since 50. The upper magistracies (the consul, praetors and censors) took the auspices, while the augurs provided rules and could, if consulted, give an opinion about the interpretation of the auspices. If a magistrate took the auspices and announced they were unfavourable, nothing could be done on that day and whatever matter was under consideration had to be postponed. If the auspices had been taken incorrectly, then anything passed on that day could be annulled. It was assumed that if a magistrate said he was going to look for auspices, he would inevitably find a negative one, hence if he just said that he *planned* to look for them, business was still postponed. In 58, the tribune Publius Clodius (Cicero's inveterate enemy) had passed a law limiting this, forbidding a magistrate from using the auspices as a reason to interfere with polling after it had started.

84. *colleague's litter*: I.e., Caesar's.

85. *first voting century is selected*: The Romans voted in order of census classes in this assembly. There were five classes and 193 'centuries': the first class (those with the most property) had 89 centuries; as only 97 were needed to gain a majority, clearly the first class had considerable voting clout. Out of this first class,

one century (called the *centuria prerogativa*) from the men of military age was selected by lot to vote first; how this century voted had considerable influence on later voting, so its vote was closely regarded. Hence, the logical place for Antony to intervene would be either after its selection had been announced but before it voted (if he knew that it was likely to go for Dolabella), or just after it had voted as it would influence the rest of the centuries.

86. *suffragia*: This refers to six of the eighteen centuries of equestrians which were not part of the first class.

87. *Laelius the Wise*: This is rather intense sarcasm. Gaius Laelius, consul in 140, was a friend of the great statesman Scipio Africanus the Younger and was a well-known augur, noted for his wisdom.

88. *'Not today'*: The formula was *alio die*, 'another day' – meaning that business had to be postponed to another day because the auspices were bad.

89. *the Lupercalia*: The Festival of the Wolf was held on 15 February. The priests (Antony was one) sacrificed a goat and a dog in the cave where Romulus and Remus as babies were supposed to have been suckled by a she-wolf. They then smeared the blood on themselves and ran almost naked around the foot of the Palatine Hill. They carried strips of goat-skin with which they hit people along the way; this was thought to bring fertility to women.

90. *naked*: As a priest of the Lupercalia, Antony would have been almost naked; as Romans wore the toga on important occasions, such as when delivering orations, this was not appropriate attire (or rather lack of attire) for speaking publicly.

91. *I ... came to the temple of Tellus*: The meeting of 17 March, mentioned at the start of *Philippic I*.

92. *grandson of ... Bambalio*: Antony's son. Bambalio (the Stutterer) was Fulvia's father. By not mentioning the more noble ancestors on Antony's side, Cicero is being deliberately and subtly insulting.

93. *behaved so atrociously at the funeral*: The speech given by Antony at Caesar's funeral is no longer extant, though it seems that Antony whipped up the crowd by referring to the kindnesses Caesar (the tyrant Cicero refers to) had done to his assassins and showed the people the bloodstained toga; the result was, predictably, a riot. Perhaps the best-known 'version' of this speech is the one Shakespeare gives in *Julius Caesar*, which begins 'Friends, Romans, countrymen'.

94. *Bellienus*: We know nothing of this person; presumably he was a

supporter of the Liberators whose house was burned down by
the frenzied crowd at Caesar's funeral. Their other prominent
victim was the unfortunate tribune (and poet) Helvius Cinna,
who was mistaken by the crowd for the conspirator Cornelius
Cinna and lynched.

95. *citizenship ... to whole provinces*: An exaggeration: Antony
extended the citizenship to the province of Sicily only.

96. *700 million sesterces ... war taxes*: The temple of Ops was being
used as a bank vault for money Caesar had collected for his war
with Parthia (much of which was confiscated from those who
had been on Pompey's side). No Roman had paid direct taxes
since 167, when the money from the conquest of Macedonia had
removed the need for such taxation. In the following year the
Senate had to reintroduce these taxes to pay the expenses of their
campaign against Antony.

97. *your close connections*: Probably a reference to Fulvia, Antony's
wife, given what Cicero says in chapter 95.

98. *Deiotarus*: Originally only one of the tetrarchs of Galatia, he
went on to gain sole control of it; he offered help to Cicero when
he was governor of Cilicia in 51 and sided with Pompey in the
Civil War. Caesar deprived him of some of his territory and in 45
he was accused by Galatian rivals of having tried to assassinate
Caesar and of having raised troops for the revolt of Caecilius
Bassus. Cicero defended him in a trial that took place in Caesar's
house.

99. *Massilia*: This city (modern Marseilles) tried to remain neutral
during the Civil War; Caesar's army captured it in October 49.

100. *one of his Greek cronies*: Mithridates of Pergamum.

101. *lady's boudoir*: Cicero uses a Greek term for 'woman's quarters'
(in fact, Roman houses had no separate quarters where women
alone lived); it appears the deal was sealed through Fulvia.

102. *a lawyer in your eyes only*: We are unsure who this person is; it
may be Sextus Cloelius who also helped Clodius draft laws or
one of Servius Sulpicius' students, such as Publius Alfenus Varus.

103. *uncle ... censorship*: Antony's uncle, Gaius Antonius, had been
removed from the Senate in 70 by the censors, which would have
made him an unlikely candidate for the position – as would his
exile for almost a decade.

104. *Board of Seven*: This body of seven men (the septemvirate) was
given the responsibility to survey and distribute land in Italy and
Sicily to Caesar's veterans; this would hopefully win them over
for Antony.

105. *his daughter, your cousin*: Antonia, who, with Antony, had one daughter; she was married to Marcus Lepidus the triumvir in 36. The new match was Fulvia.

106. *offensive . . . against Dolabella*: This is a remarkable statement as Dolabella was a notorious womanizer; Cicero, who had the misfortune of being his father-in-law, knew this very well.

107. *Campania . . . tax stream*: Campania was given away in 59 under Caesar's agrarian law; he settled more soldiers there in 45.

108. *a colony . . . already founded one*: Casilinum (modern Capua, which is not the same as ancient Capua) was a town about 3 miles from Capua; the colony there had been founded in 59. In 44 it provided Octavian with many recruits in his struggle with Antony.

109. *Marcus Varro*: (117–27) A polymath, scholar and author of extant books on the Latin language and farming among many others that no longer survive; he had written as many as 470 by the time he was seventy-eight! He sided with Pompey in the Civil War, but Caesar pardoned him after he surrendered his province of Hispania Ulterior. However, Antony proscribed him in 43.

110. *'now labours . . . master'*: A quote from an unknown play.

111. *that tomb in the Forum*: Another reference to Caesar's informal 'tomb'.

112. *divine couch*: At thanksgivings, the Romans would lay the images of gods on sacred couches and feast them.

113. *Roman Games*: These games were held from 4 to 18 September; the last four days were devoted to chariot races in the Circus Maximus. Antony proposed adding a fifth day of racing in honour of Caesar, although this did not happen until Augustus' reign. Cicero objected to this because as Caesar was only dead and (not yet) a god, it would pollute the sacred character of the other days.

114. *grandfather*: Marcus Antonius, consul in 99, was a famous orator and appears as a character in Cicero's dialogue *On the Orator*.

115. *owes . . . her third 'instalment'*: The first two 'instalments' were the violent deaths of Fulvia's first and second husbands, Publius Clodius and Gaius Curio.

116. *men . . . reins of the Republic*: The assassins of Caesar.

THE STORY OF PENGUIN CLASSICS

Before 1946 ... 'Classics' are mainly the domain of academics and students; readable editions for everyone else are almost unheard of. This all changes when a little-known classicist, E. V. Rieu, presents Penguin founder Allen Lane with the translation of Homer's *Odyssey* that he has been working on in his spare time.

1946 Penguin Classics debuts with *The Odyssey*, which promptly sells three million copies. Suddenly, classics are no longer for the privileged few.

1950s Rieu, now series editor, turns to professional writers for the best modern, readable translations, including Dorothy L. Sayers's *Inferno* and Robert Graves's unexpurgated *Twelve Caesars*.

1960s The Classics are given the distinctive black covers that have remained a constant throughout the life of the series. Rieu retires in 1964, hailing the Penguin Classics list as 'the greatest educative force of the twentieth century.'

1970s A new generation of translators swells the Penguin Classics ranks, introducing readers of English to classics of world literature from more than twenty languages. The list grows to encompass more history, philosophy, science, religion and politics.

1980s The Penguin American Library launches with titles such as *Uncle Tom's Cabin*, and joins forces with Penguin Classics to provide the most comprehensive library of world literature available from any paperback publisher.

1990s The launch of Penguin Audiobooks brings the classics to a listening audience for the first time, and in 1999 the worldwide launch of the Penguin Classics website extends their reach to the global online community.

The 21st Century Penguin Classics are completely redesigned for the first time in nearly twenty years. This world-famous series now consists of more than 1300 titles, making the widest range of the best books ever written available to millions – and constantly redefining what makes a 'classic'.

The Odyssey continues ...

The best books ever written

PENGUIN (🐧) CLASSICS

SINCE 1946

Find out more at www.penguinclassics.com